"In a manner scarcely paralleled elsewhere in history, the Jewish pe[...] tained a constant identity [...] three millennia. Since the [...] of the sixth century more [...] outside their own land than [...] Nevertheless, Jews continued to be Jews, stubbornly resisting assimilation into environing races and cultures. Landless and stateless, the remnant of ancient Israel jealously guarded its distinctive existence among the nations.

"We regard the Jewish Tradition as the shared consciousness, passed along from generation to generation, of a transcendental origin, obligation, and destiny. Thus in the face of changes—ideological, social, economic, political—which the historical process inevitably forces upon all peoples who are not spatially isolated, and despite [...] have been able to function creatively in relation to a multitude of alien cultures."
—*from the Introduction*

The B. G. Rudolph Lectures in Judaic Studies at Syracuse University, begun in 1963 through the philanthropy of Bernard G. Rudolph in the hope that "questing spirits may learn to appreciate the legacy of their forbears," are annual essays by distinguished interpreters of Jewish thought and culture. The individual lectures combine scholarly research on and popular interpretations of wide-ranging topics. Published for the first time in its entirety, the series of fourteen lectures is an enlightening contribution to the continuing dialogue between the major religious and cultural traditions that are blended in the rich pluralism of our society.

TRADITION AND CHANGE IN JEWISH EXPERIENCE

The B. G. Rudolph Lectures in Judaic Studies

TRADITION AND CHANGE IN JEWISH EXPERIENCE

Editor

A. LELAND JAMISON

*The B. G. Rudolph Lectures in
Judaic Studies*

Department of Religion

SYRACUSE UNIVERSITY

SYRACUSE, NEW YORK

1978

Produced and Distributed by Syracuse University Press,
Syracuse, New York 13210

Library of Congress Cataloging in Publication Data
Main entry under title:

Tradition and change in Jewish experience.

   (B.G. Rudolph lectures in Judaic studies)
   CONTENTS: Jamison, A. L.   Introduction.—Davis,
M.   The Jewish people in metamorphosis.—Samuel, M.
Race, nation, and people in the Jewish Bible.—
Neusner, J.   Politics and theology in Talmudic
Babylonia.   [etc.]
   1. Judaism—History—Addresses, essays, lec-
tures.   2. Jews in the United States—Intellectual
life—Addresses, essays, lectures.   3. Judaism—
United States—Addresses, essays, lectures.
I. Jamison, Albert Leland, 1911–   II. Series.
BM42.T72   909′.04′924   77–26716
ISBN 0–8156–8096–1
ISBN 0–8156–8097–X pbk.

TRADITION AND CHANGE IN JEWISH EXPERIENCE

was composed in 10-point Linotype Times Roman, leaded two points,
with display type in Ludlow Eden Light, and
printed letterpress in black ink on 55-lb. P & S Vellum Offset
by York Composition Co., Inc.;
Smyth-sewn and bound over boards in Columbia Bayside Linen
by Maple-Vail Book Manufacturing Group;
and published by

Department of Religion
SYRACUSE UNIVERSITY
SYRACUSE, NEW YORK

THE B. G. RUDOLPH LECTURES IN JUDAIC STUDIES

THROUGH A GENEROUS GIFT by Mr. B. G. Rudolph in 1963, Syracuse University has been privileged to present a series of annual lectures by distinguished interpreters of Jewish thought and culture. The individual lectures have been widely distributed among scholars and academic libraries throughout the world. It now seems appropriate to issue the series in a more durable form, as a contribution to the continuing dialogue between the major religious and cultural traditions that are blended in the rich pluralism of our society.

Bernard G. Rudolph (1885–1970) admirably combined success as a merchant with leadership in religious, civic, and philanthropic affairs. His career may be fairly summarized by Harry Golden's phrase, "only in America," and he amply repaid the opportunities which were afforded him. In retirement he wrote and privately published two books which throw light on the encounter between immigrant Jews and this strange new land of freedom. *Tell Me More* (1966) drew upon recollections of his childhood in Lithuania and growth to maturity in upstate New York. A more ambitious work, *From a Minyan to a Community: A History of the Jews of Syracuse* (1970), is the only comprehensive account of the origins and development of the Jewish community in that city. The task of research and writing was a labor of love, indeed, performed under the stress of great physical pain. Happily, he lived to complete it, sustained by his hope that, in the words of Dr. Isidore S. Meyer, "questing spirits may learn to appreciate the legacy of their forebears and to transmit that heritage enhanced by act and thought, by word and deed, to those who will follow them in the years that lie ahead." That ideal also inspired B. G. Rudolph's support of the Lectures in Judiac Studies. To his memory we dedicate this volume.

ALJ

ACKNOWLEDGMENTS

ALL COPYRIGHTED MATERIALS in this book have been reprinted with the permission of the authors. The holders of copyright to whom thanks are due are Mrs. Edith Samuel, the literary executor of Maurice Samuel, Jacob R. Marcus, Jacob Neusner, Bertram W. Korn, Samuel Sandmel, W. Gunther Plaut, Arthur Hertzberg, Emil L. Fackenheim, and Abraham Karp.

The editor wishes to express his appreciation for advice and assistance in the planning of the lectures and this book given by the following; Dr. Irwin Hyman, Rabbi Emeritus, Temple Adath Yeshurun, Syracuse; Dr. Theodore S. Levy, Rabbi, Temple Society of Concord, Syracuse; Dr. Alan L. Berger, Department of Religion, Syracuse University; and Dr. Judah Shapiro, formerly Secretary of the National Foundation for Jewish Culture.

Summer 1977   ALJ
Syracuse, N.Y.

CONTENTS

Introduction
A. LELAND JAMISON   xi

1. The Jewish People in Metamorphosis
MOSHE DAVIS   1

2. Race, Nation, and People in the Jewish Bible
MAURICE SAMUEL   26

3. Politics and Theology in Talmudic Babylonia
JACOB NEUSNER   46

4. The American Colonial Jew: A Study in Acculturation
JACOB R. MARCUS   75

5. American Impact: Judaism in the United States
in the Early Nineteenth Century
LOU H. SILBERMAN   89

6. German-Jewish Intellectual Influences
on American Jewish Life, 1824–1972
BERTRAM WALLACE KORN   106

7. Jewish Tradition in the Modern World:
Conservation and Renewal
ROBERT GORDIS   141

8. The Sabbath as Protest:
Thoughts on Work and Leisure in the Automated Society
W. GUNTHER PLAUT   169

9.   Mutations of Jewish Values
in Contemporary American Fiction
LEO W. SCHWARZ   184

10.   After the Ghetto:
Jews in Western Culture, Art, and Intellect
SAMUEL SANDMEL   198

11.   Anti-Semitism and Jewish Uniqueness:
Ancient and Contemporary
ARTHUR HERTZBERG   211

12.   The Human Condition after Auschwitz:
A Jewish Testimony a Generation After
EMIL L. FACKENHEIM   226

13.   Jewish Perceptions of America:
From Melting Pot to Mosaic
ABRAHAM J. KARP   244

14.   At the Threshold of the Third Century
ABRAM L. SACHAR   257

CONTRIBUTORS

MOSHE DAVIS is Stephen S. Wise Professor in American Jewish History and Institutions and Director of the Institute of Contemporary Jewry, Hebrew University of Jerusalem; he is also Research Professor of the American Jewish Theological Seminary in Israel.

EMIL L. FACKENHEIM is Professor of Philosophy, University of Toronto.

ROBERT GORDIS is Seminary Professor of Bible and of Philosophies of Religion, Jewish Theological Seminary of America; he is also Editor of *Judaism*.

ARTHUR HERTZBERG is Rabbi, Temple Emanu-El, Englewood, New Jersey; he is also Adjunct Professor of History, Columbia University, and President, American Jewish Congress.

A. LELAND JAMISON is Professor Emeritus, Syracuse University, formerly Willard Ives Professor of the English Bible.

ABRAHAM J. KARP is Professor of History and Religious Studies, University of Rochester.

BERTRAM WALLACE KORN is Rabbi, Reform Congregation Keneseth Israel, Elkins Park, Pennsylvania; he is also Visiting Professor of

American Jewish History, New York School of Hebrew Union College—Jewish Institute of Religion, and Dropsie College.

JACOB R. MARCUS is Milton and Hattie Kutz Distinguished Service Professor, Hebrew Union College—Jewish Institute of Religion; he is also Director of the American Jewish Archives and the American Jewish Periodical Center.

JACOB NEUSNER is University Professor, Professor of Religious Studies, and the Ungerleider Distinguished Scholar of Judaic Studies, Brown University.

W. GUNTHER PLAUT is an author and editor; Rabbi, Holly Blossom Temple, Toronto, Canada.

ABRAM L. SACHAR is Chancellor, Brandeis University.

MAURICE SAMUEL (*obit* 1972) was a novelist, essayist, interpreter of Jewish culture, international lecturer, and co-host of the summer series of "The Eternal Light," a nationally broadcast program sponsored by the Jewish Theological Seminary of America.

SAMUEL SANDMEL is Professor of Bible and Hellenistic Literature and formerly Director of Graduate Studies, Hebrew Union College—Jewish Institute of Religion.

LEO W. SCHWARZ (*obit* 1967) was an author, editor, lecturer, and *quondam* visiting professor at the University of Iowa and Carleton College.

LOU H. SILBERMAN is Hillel Professor of Jewish Literature and Thought, Vanderbilt University.

INTRODUCTION

A. LELAND JAMISON

T HE ESSAYS IN THIS VOLUME were first delivered as lectures to university audiences, having been commissioned not solely as exercises in scholarly research, but also as appropriately popular interpretations of selected aspects of Jewish history, thought, and culture. Although there was no attempt to impose a unified pattern on the several contributions, certain common themes surfaced irrepressibly throughout the series. To the Editor those themes seem most aptly described by the rubric "tradition and change." In a manner scarcely paralleled elsewhere in history, the Jewish people have maintained a constant identity during the past three millennia. Since the Assyrian conquest in the eighth century before the common era, and particularly since the Babylonian Exile of the sixth century, more Jews have lived outside their own land than in it, dispersed through Western Asia, North Africa, Europe, and in modern times the American continents. After brief periods of semi-independence under the Hasmonean and Herodian regimes, and an abortive resurgence in the second century C.E., Jews remained without the protection of political sovereignty until 1948. Nevertheless, Jews continued to be Jews, stubbornly resisting assimilation into environing races and cultures. Landless and stateless, the remnant of ancient Israel jealously guarded its distinctive existence among the nations. To be sure, biological relatedness was the major factor in that remarkable survival, but genetic exclusiveness was fostered—rather, made imperative—by something greater than endogamy, namely, the cohesive power of a common tradition.

Tradition is a very elastic term. In its narrow theological sense it denotes a code of law, written and unwritten, presumably revealed to Moses on Sinai and during the wanderings of the Exodus. This body of divine law was transmitted and elaborated by successive generations of authoritative teachers. Beyond the Biblical canon, the theocratic tradition was codified in the Mishnah and Talmud, all subsumed under

xi

the category of "Torah." In the orthodox view, then, the study of Torah is the indispensable means of preserving tradition. For the purposes of the present volume, however, we understand "tradition" in a broader sense to refer to an inherited culture, including beliefs, customs, and a way of life rooted in a remembered and revered past. In brief, we regard the Jewish tradition as the shared consciousness, passed along from generation to generation, of a transcendental origin, obligation, and destiny. Thus, in the face of the changes—ideological, social, economic, political—which the historical process inevitably forces upon all peoples who are not spatially isolated, and despite the peculiar traumas of a disenfranchised minority, *K'lal Yisroel* has maintained an essential unity. By some remarkable chemistry of spirit and will, Israel has neutralized the acids of every new modernity, and Jews have been able to function creatively in relation to a multitude of alien cultures.

The specifics of the tradition have been variable, depending on place, time, and social milieu. As a religion, certainly, Judaism has had its share of schismatics, heretics, and conflicting modes of thought and practice. From one point of view, indeed, Christianity itself may be seen as the most successful Jewish heresy. The more extreme divergences aside, however, a remarkable degree of unity has prevailed over the pluralisms within the ongoing Jewish experience. Until roughly the European Enlightenment, any definition of the tradition would have focussed on the religious component, and that in a very conventional sense.

Faith and observance were the hallmarks of authentic Jewishness, along with the often confused factor of biological descent. The stubborn fidelity of Jews gave constancy to the religious element, even when public profession and observance were suppressed, as in the case of the Marranos. Moreover, Jewish communities had their own ways of dealing with radical dissidents and apostates. Spinoza offers the egregious example of the Jew who did not wish to convert to another faith, but who seemed to challenge the foundations of traditional Judaism from within—and was summarily expelled from the synagogue. Until the emergence of modern libertarianism, the Jew in Christian Europe had only two options: either he must remain, nominally if not by conviction, within the Jewish group, which was legally defined and regulated as a religious entity; or he might, by baptism and profession of faith, become absorbed into the Christian majority and acquire first-class citizenship. This intolerable alternative survived into the twentieth century in the anachronistic medievalisms of Russia, Spain, and their like. An Albert Einstein, who believed only vaguely and observed not at all, would have been a *tertium quid* in that pre-Emancipation world, without legal status.

The eighteenth century saw quite different developments in the relations between Jews and the general society. From being a *religio licita* (barely tolerated in most instances), Judaism began to move gradually into equality with Christianity as a *religio non accipienda*. That is, the religious test of full participation in social and political process was increasingly eliminated, although the old restrictions yielded reluctantly to purely secular criteria. The wave of the future was formulated most unequivocally in Article VI and the First Amendment to the American Constitution. These elementary "human rights" provisions did not, of course, immediately nullify all forms of social pressure and legal discrimination—for example, restrictive property "covenants" were not declared illegal until fairly recently in the United States. Nevertheless, American citizenship was divorced from religious affiliation, so that it became possible for even avowed atheists to vote and hold office. The American mode has prevailed in the Western democracies and ostensibly in the totalitarian nations, which perversely honor neither the letter nor the spirit of their written guarantees.

The secularization of personal status has brought about profound changes in the self-awareness of both Jews and Christians. The latter have been somewhat less affected, because the ethnic dimensions of religious affiliation have been less tenaciously maintained. The permissiveness of American religious freedom has accelerated the weakening of those ties of common national origin, language, and inherited customs which formerly kept Christian denominations in a significant degree of separation from each other. Accordingly, one can speak of the "Christian tradition" only in the most latitudinal terms, with connotations of disparately accepted theological beliefs and ethical values. The shattering of the medieval synthesis opened a religious can of worms, and modern democratic neutrality has compounded the confusion by making it possible for every person to seek heaven or hell in his own way or no way at all, so long as he pays taxes and refrains from such idiosyncrasies as child sacrifice and polygamy. The single instance of official religious differentiation which comes to mind is the inclusion of the letters *C, J,* and *P* on military identification tags, for hospitalization and burial purposes. The effective American religious tradition may well be what Robert Bellah and others have described as "civil religion," a sanctified patriotism drawing from classical Judaeo-Christian sources liberally diluted with Enlightenment rationalism and optimism.

Our present concern, however, is with the Jewish tradition as a viable option in a voluntaristic society. The problem is that in the modern

situation one can be a Jew without being also a Judaist, a member of
the "Eternal People" quite apart from any religious profession or affiliation. This circumstance beclouds the understanding of tradition as a
factor in Jewish experience. If the religious component is no longer a
sine qua non, what is left? Biological descent? (Hitler applied this test
in a horrifying manner.) Linguistic or dietary habits? (But you don't
have to be Jewish to enjoy bagels and lox, and some self-acknowledged
Jews are fond of shrimp!) Shared historical memories, as dramatized in
the religious feasts and fasts, and now in commemorations of Israeli
independence? (But sundered from their transcendental roots, such
memories may degenerate into chauvinism or simple ethnolatry, more
benign forms of the Nazi's *Blut, Boden, und Volk.*) Common cultural
expressions in literature, the arts, and life style? (At a popular level,
it is ironic that Irving Berlin, straight from the Lower East Side, has
written the perennial favorites relating to Christian celebrations—"White
Christmas" and "Easter Parade.") Adherence to the highest ethical
values and passionate striving for social justice, in the prophetic manner? (But a Southern Baptist President is no less committed, in his own
way, and Pius XII declared, rather ineffectually, that "We are all
Semites.") A sympathetic outsider is moved to inquire: Just what is
this tradition which runs as a golden thread through the totality of
Jewish experience? No doubt all of the foregoing, synthesized by some
mysterious extra-ingredient buried deeply within the Jewish psyche. It
may be that the concept of tradition has been metamorphosed into what
Ernest van den Haag calls "the Jewish mystique": a complex of variably
accepted beliefs, ethical values, tribal loyalties, historical memories
("roots" are more important to Jews than to most other people), and
nostalgia for the joys and even the sorrows of a social microcosm, the
shtetl in which Jewishness could be cultivated without apology. All of
this may be as much visceral as rational.

Recent history, however, has given fresh substance and vitality to
a very ancient element in Jewish tradition—Israel, the land which
Torah affirms that God Himself gave to His people. Especially since
the Holocaust and the subsequent establishment of the state, Jews everywhere echo with fervent conviction the Psalmist's cry: "If I forget you,
O Jerusalem, let my right hand wither . . . if I do not set Jerusalem
above my highest joy!" Devotion to Zion *redivivus* increasingly serves
as the measure of the authentic Jew, as the future of universal Jewry
is perceived to be inextricably bound to the fate of geographical and
political Israel. Jacob Neusner, for one, argues, in effect, that Zionism,
the concern for and sacrificial loyalty to Israel (apart from a renuncia-

tion of other citizenship or, for that matter, without acceptance of the Biblical claim to "divine right" of ownership) is a—perhaps *the*—indispensable mark of genuine Jewishness in our time. He grants that "the bulk of Western Jewry (exclusive of Orthodoxy) will not concur that to be Jewish is to be a Judaist." Nevertheless, he contends that neo-Zionism is actually religious in nature. The "thirst for salvation and quest for redemption," here and now in a predominantly secular, historical embodiment (Israel), is, in fact, a religious impulse: "To sacrifice and focus one's whole being upon the object of sacrifice is a salvic mode of life." Accordingly, the tradition has become incarnate in the Israeli experience, and the State of Israel serves as a kind of "Jewish Vatican," an authoritative paradigm of Jewish collective life. Neusner goes so far as to suggest that the United Jewish Appeal, the American source of massive financial support for Israel, functions as a "shrine" in the Diaspora. Does this mean, then, that the cohesive tradition of Jewish existence will be determined by whatever cultural patterns and life styles may be developed in the historical experience of modern Israel? Just what will be the reciprocal influences of inherited tradition and evolving historical change on the future shape of Jewish identity? Put boldly and simplistically, will that future be molded by Torah, or by technology and *Realpolitik?* Or, as in the past, by a dialectical interaction of the three components?

Questions such as these have arisen in the mind of the Editor and are submitted only as possible perspectives from which the essays of this volume may be considered. The latter do not retrace the fascinating course of Jewish history, nor do they systematically analyze the mystique of Jewish thought and experience. Rather, they offer selective probings in a vast terrain, tentative explorations of a few significant aspects of the Jewish continuum, with particular attention to the American scene. This emphasis may be justified on the ground that any conceivable normative tradition of Jewishness will be evolved in Israel *and* America, the sole remaining centers of substantial Jewish population and creativity. So far, certainly, American Jewry has been revitalized, and its self-consciousness intensified by the political and human vicissitudes of Israel. Conversely, it is difficult to imagine that Israel could have maintained its position as an autonomous state without the financial and moral assistance provided by the American Jewish community. In any case, the hopeful future of Jewry lies not in Soviet Russia, Western Europe, or South America, but in Israel and the United States (with important assistance from Canada). These represent the two extremes: Israel, a more or less homogeneous society, pioneering under the constant threat of external attack; and the American minority, as secure as any minority can ever be. In either case, the temptations to modify hallowed tradition beyond recognition operate powerfully. Such dilemmas are not unprecedented—the seductions of Canaanite paganism were a major issue in all pre-exilic prophecy, and it has never been comfortable to sing the Lord's song in any Babylonia, ancient, medieval, or modern. To these temptations and dilemmas—engendered by shifting opportunities and hostilities, even the nihilism of the Holocaust—the chapters of this book are addressed.

THE JEWISH PEOPLE IN METAMORPHOSIS

MOSHE DAVIS

IN A WORLD marked by rapid change, the Jewish People is experiencing a new ferment. The whole world is shaken by radical alterations, and the accelerated pace of events compounds the problems. Formerly, a man, his son, and grandchild lived in one age. Today each of us lives through several eras in a lifetime. Moreover, many of the peoples and faiths of the world are now in contact with diversified and often conflicting influences at the same time. The problems of our generation are universal. No one lives in isolation.

Change in itself is not new to the Jewish People. In their long history, the Jews and Judaism had to confront various civilizations. The unique factor in the contemporary Jewish situation is its global nature. Worldwide in scope, unprecedented in content, and characterized by a constant interplay of Jewish and general societal factors, the challenge of contemporary civilization confronts the Jewish tradition and the Jewish People in many parts of the world at the same time. In order to comprehend the problems which concern the Jews today, it is important briefly to formulate the historic ideas of the Jewish People, the ideas which guided the Jews in the past to meet the impact of their environment while maintaining their continuity; secondly, to assess some of the forces which continue to change the Jewish world.

In Judaism, the tradition and the People are inextricably bound together. As "a child of the Covenant," a Jew inherits both the Tradition and the historic experience of all the generations who lived by that tradition. There have been many formulations of the basic ideas of Judaism, each with its own emphasis. As I understand it, the continuing Jewish tradition of faith in, and service to, God may be expressed in the following aspects:

TORAT YISRAEL:	Torah as learning and the love of learning, the central pillar of Judaism, whereby the exemplary Jew is not merely the *learned* Jew but the *learning* one.
MIDOT YISRAEL:	The affirmation of the moral life as the purpose and unifying thread of all human existence and the practice of Judaism based on this conception.
AHAVAT YISRAEL:	Love of the Jewish people as individuals for one another, that which brings them to share a common destiny in living fellowship.
K'LAL YISRAEL:	The communities of Jews bound by a common tradition and mutual responsibility, united throughout the world and the generations.
MIKDASH YISRAEL:	The synagogue as historically understood, community sanctuary and meeting-house for prayer and instruction.
ERETZ YISRAEL:	The homeland of the Jewish People and the center of its tradition.

This is the Jewish heritage interpreted conceptually. Six points are interlaced into one pattern like the Star of David. One word weaves through all six aspects: *Yisrael*—the People of Israel. It is the living Jewish People which bears and interprets its tradition. In every generation, and in this moment, too, Jews, wherever they dwell, are the historical Community of Yisrael. Through them the ancient heritage is embodied, and only through them can the ancient heritage address mankind.

Fortified by their tradition and by their faith in it, the Jewish People learned to apply themselves creatively to historical change. Some of the most difficult confrontations of the Jews with new environmental forces were overcome by relating the tradition to developing world thought, even as the Jews guarded their solidarity and integrity as a People. From the earliest contact of the ancient Hebrews with Egyptian civilization, through the spiritual struggle during the First and Second Commonwealths with the cultures of the Near East and the Mediterranean, and after the dispersion, with the spreading dominion of Christianity and Islam, the Jews as a People, sooner or later, came to grips with the environing culture, contributing to it and accepting what they could from it.

In the perspective of world evolution the very survival of the Jews and Judaism seems remarkable. Yet at the same time the losses cannot be ignored. These losses were sustained not only because of physical persecution, but because of spiritual and intellectual inability to cope with the challenge of the new societal influences. However varying the factors which confronted the Jews in the respective civilizations with which they were in contact, from the ancient cultures of the Fertile Crescent to those of modern Europe, the Biblical idea of *She'erit,* Remnant, seemed to be the inexorable law of Jewish history. Whether understood as Divine Will or the destiny of Israel, out of the crucible of each epoch, in their own Land or in the countries of the Dispersion, always a remnant remained. And this remnant carried forward the Tradition of Judaism and its People.

All true history, Benedetto Croce said, is contemporary history. Yet each historical situation has its particular characteristics. In an era when change has become a constant, a new and radical adjustment is imperative. To achieve this adjustment, all the conceivable processes of initiated change or, to borrow a biological concept—metamorphosis—may have to be imaginatively brought into play. What I mean to emphasize, by the application of the concept of metamorphosis to the human condition, is the need for psychological readiness, wherever necessary, to transform both self and group. In the mutations of our time, as in some of the particularly complex periods in the Jewish past, anticipatory action and premeditated decision are indispensable for creative survival. There were periods in Jewish history—as the response to the Arabic world of the seventh century and to the nationalist movements in the nineteenth century—when delayed reaction to great world movements brought deleterious results to the Jewish People. On the other hand, an outstanding example of far-reaching and deliberate change in Jewish history was the new direction given the Jewish tradition by the Pharisees when faced with the onslaught of the Greco-Roman civilizations.

If this sense of readiness for change is to lead to wise and creative action, conscious knowledge of the present is indispensable. Such knowledge builds, in the first instance, on the recognition and interpretation of the salient elements shaping world Jewry. These elements fall into a wide range of categories. These include the creation of new settlements throughout the world; economic restratification; the movement from town to metropolitan communities; the environmental cultural impact

on Jews in the open societies; the increasing variety of Jewish identification; the continuing tension between the Jewish tradition and contemporary secular civilization; the developing acceptance of the religious
difference as the most legitimate distinction between citizens in the
western countries; the evolving influence of the sovereign State of Israel
on world Jewry; the changing relationships between the respective communities in world Jewry. Here the intention is to touch upon a few of
these elements only in order to present a general illustration of the
theme.

NEW SETTLEMENTS

The climactic events of twentieth century Jewish history—the Holocaust, the birth of the State of Israel, and the extension of the diaspora
into more than one hundred and twenty countries—changed the face
of the Jewish world. The very listing of the currently estimated population figures in the main centers of Jewish residence points up the
impact on the Jews of two world wars, the shattering of empires, and
the rise of new political orders.[1] According to Nehemiah Robinson's
survey based on 1962 figures, there are now 12,915,000 Jews in the
world.[2] Ten million Jews live in three countries: an estimated
5,500,000 in the United States; about 2,300,000 in the Soviet Union;
2,045,000 in Israel.

After these three great centers, the most dramatic demographic
movement is in France. As a result of the slow depletion of North
African Jewry, and primarily as a result of the inflow from Algeria,
French Jewry is today the fourth largest Jewish community, number-
ing some 500,000.[3] Following in order, according to the estimates, are
Argentina (450,000); Great Britain (450,000); Canada (250,000);
Rumania (150,000); Brazil (140,000); Morocco (125,000); The Re-
public of South Africa (110,000).

Thus, in these eleven communities 93 percent of the total Jewish
world population resides. Israel is, of course, in a special position—the
only country where Jews are in the majority. As soon as sovereignty
was established, Israel enacted the "Law of Return," granting the privilege of entry to any Jew who wishes to come, the indigent as well as the
self-sufficient. It soon became a "land of ingathering" of entire com-

munities. Some 80 percent of the Jewish population of Asia has been absorbed: the communities of Kurdistan, Yemen, and Iraq, virtually in their entirety; those of Persia and Turkey, to a considerable extent; and the intensive emigration from North Africa, particularly Libya, Tripolitania, Morocco, and Tunis.

Of the many lessons these figures teach us about Jewish migration and resettlement in the twentieth century, one striking fact emerges: almost the entire Jewish population in the world now lives in different countries than formerly, or under altered economic, political and cultural conditions. The majority of the diaspora communities are of recent growth. Beginning in the eighties of the past century, when "the storms in the South" (the pogroms in southern Czarist Russia) gathered and broke, and until the middle fifties in our century, some 5,250,000 Jews migrated from one country to another. This migration laid the foundations in the United States for what has become the largest Jewish community in history, and led to the transition of about one-half of the world Jewish population to the Western Hemisphere. In addition to the United States and Canada, Jews live in thirty-one countries in Central and South America, ranging in number from some eight families in British Honduras to the Argentinian Jewish community estimated at 450,000 strong. Most of these communities are of twentieth century growth.

The blessing of this new birth was mixed with the tragic dissolution and annihilation of many ancient communities—communities old in years and in spiritual and cultural tradition. While millions of Jews escaped to the freedom of North America, South America, England and France, the Jewish learning and traditions nurtured in Russia, Poland and North Africa, in the greatest measure, were destroyed. With the exception of those who came to Eretz Yisrael, the intensity of Jewish life was not transplanted with them, and fresh beginnings had to be made.

Again, comparative statistical data delineate the drastic demographic changes. In 1900, the world Jewish population was twelve million; in 1938–40, about seventeen million; in 1946, eleven million The last number is the most painful. Even as we write that number, we also intone *Kaddish*—a prayer of sanctification and remembrance—for six million men, women and children who were taken in those scorched years, which ended an age in Jewish history. And we will never know the uncounted, the unborn. Yet they too must be remembered and included. For when we remember the Holocaust, we think as Moses did at Sinai, not only of those gathered at the foot of the mountain to receive the Torah, but of those future generations waiting to be born and to live in the light of Torah.

The lasting result of all these happenings is that Europe is no longer the focus of world Jewry. In our times, the Jewish communities of Europe—the original source of the contemporary American and Israeli communities—are of only secondary importance. The Jews of today are principally a Western-hemispheric and Middle-eastern people.

ENLARGEMENT OF CULTURAL CONTACT

In most of the new countries to which they came, the Jews quickly acquired freedom. Moving from the category of tolerated non-citizens, or limited citizens, to full citizenship, they enjoyed expanding political and economic opportunities. Industrial urbanism and technological advances increased the size of the middle classes in the general population, and the Jews shared in this evolution in time. They have become a predominantly middle-class and urban group, engaged in business, clerical, administrative and professional occupations.[4] Living in countries with high and continually rising standards of civilization, and with educational and cultural institutions increasingly available to all citizens, the Jews also benefited greatly. In the United States, for example, some two-thirds of Jewish college-age youth are receiving a university education.[5]

Yet varying degrees of discrimination in many spheres of the economy and in the larger society exist. Nor has anti-Semitism disappeared from even the most advanced democratic societies. It assumes different shades and different forms—covert or organized, ideological, religious, racial, nationalistic, economic or social anti-Semitism. But it is ever present.[6] On the other hand, a remarkable intellectual receptivity to the values and ideas of Judaism has developed in recent decades in many centers of culture, particularly on the European continent and in the United States. Perhaps the reasons derive from the shame of western civilization for the Holocaust, but the general literary scene is marked by scholarly works, novels and essays on Jewish themes, which are read in ever-widening circles by a growing non-Jewish public. Moreover, the more sober elements of the various populations are beginning to recognize anti-Semitism as an affliction to the society-at-large.[7]

In the process of this socio-economic and cultural enlargement, Jewish group life has been profoundly affected. As the Jews participated in the cultures around them, they were no longer apart, but organic to the wider context in which they flourished. The Jews naturally began to draw from the national and human cultural roots of their respective environments. In their desire to become indigenous, to create in and for their new countries, most of them neglected their Jewish source.[8] The result is that the historic Jewish tradition no longer fills the basic experience of most of diasporic Jewry. Radical changes in Jewish education and language demonstrate this emphatic shift in twentieth century Jewish life.

While the Jewish passion for learning has remained undiminished in modern times, its center has moved from Jewish classic study to broader humanistic and scientific education. In most lands of their residence, the Jewish People, founders of universal education in the First Century, c.e., conduct Jewish educational systems which are regarded as inferior to, subordinate, or supplementary to the prevailing systems of general education.[9] A paradox reigns: of all generations, the present generation of Jews is probably the most educated in general studies; in Jewish learning it is perhaps the least literate.

This condition is reflected in the area of language. As recently as the beginning of the present century, many Jews within the framework of their own educational system possessed sufficient knowledge of Hebrew to study the classic literature, and the People as a whole, in their major components, used their self-created vernaculars of Yiddish and Ladino. Today, most Jews lack such knowledge, and the Jewish People has relinquished its vernacular.[10] There have been two major results. In the first place, English has in fact become the most common language of the Jews. It is the mother tongue for the majority of world Jewry and a secondary language for growing numbers in the other countries where Jews live. Secondly, in the process the entire complexion of Jewish cultural expression has changed, each community having found its expression in its native idiom. Without entering into a discussion of the remarkable role of Yiddish as a vernacular in the European and Western communities, and Ladino for Sephardic Jewry, or into an analysis of the common cultural body of experience these languages made possible in the diaspora, the meaning of the substitution must be emphasized. Culture in translation is a diminution of authenticity. Transmuted into a strange context, distortion, albeit well-meaning distortion, is introduced. Precisely because these changes have come in countries with widening cultural frontiers, the dilemma is correspondingly greater. Such modification of the variant Jewish cultural heritage is a loss to itself and to the other cultures with which it interacts, as well as to the whole society to which it could contribute its maximum potentialities.

These manifestations are, of course, specific to the Jewish People, but the causal factors are not unique to it; they are part of the entire problem facing traditional cultures in their meeting with the contemporary world. Indeed, the role of the historic tradition is not as powerful as it once was in the shaping of Jewish individual and group life. However, several Western scholars have recently concluded that the Jewish tradition, while secondary, has not at all become a recessive element. The associational bonds with Judaism, for the most part, have been attenuated, but the communal bonds with the Jewish group have remained strong, and within the religious association there has been a continuity.[11] Nevertheless, the challenge remains: to establish in the face of the increasing power of change a way for the Jewish collectivity in the open societies to remain the heirs of its Tradition and at the same time to be part of its various national societies.

THE INCREASING VARIETY OF JEWISH IDENTIFICATION

The dual development of enlarged general cultural experience and the weakening of the Jewish historical culture in the shaping of the Jewish self-image has brought many Jews into a state of constant confusion of self-identification. They feel caught between their contemporary environment in the dominant society and the Jewish heritage from which they do not wish to detach themselves. The experience of alienation has expressed itself in a variety of ways: the attenuation of ties with the Jewish group, so that an individual Jew born into Judaism can live his lifetime as a Jew without any relation to it, simply by not severing his bond; the growing phenomenon of mixed marriage without conversion, wherein the intermarried neither leaves his Faith nor formally accepts another, and where his children become members of a new element of "half-Jews"; the development of an amorphous cult of Jewish intellectuals who profess "Jewishness" but avoid the road to knowledge of Judaism or to its practice as a way of life.[12]

Here one must emphasize that the spectrum of Jewish identification is very large. In many Jewish circles the very same factors which brought confusion to some have generated in others emotional and intangible reactions which are reflected in increasing synagogue association, communal support and campaign contributions. And for the Jewish community as a whole these influences have intensified religious life, motivated Jewish education and increased commitment to the aspirations of the Jewish People in many sectors of Jewry where formerly such developments were hardly conceivable.

In one of the ongoing studies on Jewish identity (social scientists in the United States, Latin America, Europe and Israel are now exploring this problem), Mme. Roland in France is concentrating on this very question of the broad range of identification differences among Jews. It is her thought that an analysis of the behavior patterns of Jews in different places within a country and in different countries, and a comparison of these behaviors with the corresponding mean behavior of the respective non-Jewish national societies, can perhaps establish a broad principle of identification which extends beyond subjective, legal or existentialist definitions—an identification which is due to the persisting action of a *directing idea* (the Jewish religion), even though forgotten or rejected by the majority of contemporary Jews. Since strong directing ideas create strong cultures which are difficult for others to absorb and are particularly difficult to assimilate, Mme. Roland would then seek to determine the relation between the directing idea of the Jewish group and the specific nature of Jewish behavior in order to chart the channels of transmission through which this Jewish identity can be preserved.[13]

Whether or not the effort to discover a unifying theory of Jewish identity can be realized, the very basis of the search is compelling. Henceforth the conception of diversity, and not uniformity, as determining the content and form of contemporary Jewish life, will have to be part of any unifying theory of Jewish identification. Unity within diversity is a principle of all human life, and of Jewish life in particular. It is a myth to assume a monolithic Jewish community either in a country or on a worldwide basis. There is no one manifestation of Judaism which answers the needs of the different groups whether they live in separate countries or in one country. The divergences of Jewish identity extend from those Jews who are completely out of the focus of organized Jewish life—those who are neither members of any Jewish organization or are not Jews by religion but consider themselves as Jews[14]—to members of the *Neturei Karta,* who live in Jerusalem and cling to the Holy City even as they reject the idea of a non-theocratic Jewish State.

Significant evidence of the differentiation in contemporary Jewish life is to be found in the collection of responses to the popularly called "Who is a Jew?" question. This correspondence grew out of the letter addressed by the then Prime Minister of Israel, David Ben-Gurion, to Jewish scholars in Israel and the diaspora, in December, 1958, in connection with the proposed law on how to register the children of mixed marriages in Israel. This law was to be formulated "in keeping with the accepted tradition among all circles of Jewry, orthodox and non-orthodox of all trends, and with the special conditions of Israel, as a sovereign Jewish State in which freedom of conscience and religion is guaranteed, and as a centre for the ingathering of the exiles."[15]

For the purpose of our discussion, the formulation of the request transcends the particular issue insofar as it is based on the principle that "the people of Israel [the reference is to the Jews in the State of Israel] do not regard themselves as a separate people from diaspora Jewry." While the recognition of the political allegiances which Jewish citizens have to their respective countries is implicit in this document, the statement delineates the character of Israeli Jewry's special relationship to Diaspora Jewry:

> There is no Jewish community in the world that is inspired by such a profound consciousness of unity and identity with the Jews of the world as a whole as the Jewish community in Israel. It is by no accident that the Basic Principles of the Government lay it down that the Government shall take measures for "the intensification of Jewish consciousness among Israel youth, the deepening of their roots in the past of the Jewish people and its historic heritage, and the strengthening of their moral attachment to World Jewry, in the consciousness of the common destiny and the historic continuity that unites Jews the world over of all generations and countries."

Mindful of its "moral attachment" to world Jewry, the Government of Israel, when faced with an internal question which was interlaced with traditional religious law as well as with the diverse prevailing practices in Jewry throughout the world, felt impelled to consider "statements of opinion by Jewish scholars in Israel and abroad on this subject." This sensitivity to diaspora Jewry also derived from the understanding that, of all issues, mixed marriages were at the very heart of the Jewish problem in the diaspora, and represented "one of the decisive factors making for complete assimilation and the abandonment of Jewry."

An analysis of the correspondents and their responses indicate the peculiar nature of the contemporary problem of identification.[16] Of forty-five respondents, the division by countries is as follows: Israel, twenty; U.S.A., twelve; England, four; Italy, three; France, three; Belgium, one; Holland, one; Switzerland, one. Only about half of the group served in rabbinic functions, and among them reform, conservative and orthodox rabbis were scrupulously selected. As for the other half, the respondents included scholars of Judaism, literary figures, and representative learned laymen whose chief distinctions were in general humanistic and legal studies.

The responses bear no regional stamp and cut across ideological lines. Secularists disturbed by the complexities of the internal Jewish situation took positions grounded firmly in traditional Jewish law. Some looked forward to immigration from Eastern European countries "of thousands and perhaps tens of thousands," and anticipated many cases of mixed marriages among them; they favored nonreligious nationality regulations. Others suggested modifications in the existing Israeli law which would reckon with Jewish religious requirements and still not restrict individual choice. The great majority of the respondents in Israel and the diaspora felt that religious law, despite the difficulties imposed in individual cases, must prevail.

This documentation, precisely because it includes a highly select group of representative figures, impressively demonstrates the accepted divergences even among those elements devoted to the continuity of Jewish existence. The legitimate categories of Jewish identification and association have come to represent, in addition to religion in all its phases, the secular, ethnic, cultural, political, national, communal and individual aspects, as well as combinations of any of these. While in the past, too, there were varieties of Jewish identification among Jews, for the most part these differences rose within a common universe of discourse. In our time, all these elements, though ofttimes radically differing from one another, belong to the totality called the Jewish People, because Jews choose to identify themselves with it, and their choice is recognized and accepted by the community of Jews.

THE LEGITIMATION OF THE RELIGIOUS DIFFERENCE

In most Western countries the motive force of Jewish group life is socio-economic integration and preservation of religio-cultural identity. Under varying circumstances and within the respective contexts of national policy, Jewish religious separateness is legally defined and guaranteed as individual or group volition. Yet invariably the social and cultural milieu in the western countries is strongly influenced by Protestant or Catholic Christianity even where secularism is a powerful factor, and the tendency is to fall under the sway of the dominant, or established, religion.

However, an exceedingly important basic change is taking place in world attitude towards religious affiliation, a change which is being expressed in different ways within the religious groups. In the United States and elsewhere, for example, religious pluralism is taking root both as an idea and as a social reality. Formerly the dominant religion not only taught the exclusiveness of its truth but brought its weight to bear on the total national culture and polity. Now many religious groups are divesting themselves of the aura of exclusiveness in organization and policy, although not in theology. This has been felt in inter-religious group activities that have developed on local, national and world levels.[17] An emphatic expression of the ecumenical spirit was reflected in the establishment of the World Council of Churches in 1948. Initiated by the Protestant churches it achieved the later participation of Catholic observers. Another historic development is the present Ecumenical Council which has been called to reconsider Catholic attitudes in a mid-twentieth century world.[18]

In the course of the new development religion may become once again a unifying influence in the world. Within the western countries where most Jews live, religious difference is respected. In the past religious differences divided; in these lands the religious difference unites. Indeed, association with any Faith is encouraged by the society as a constructive form which builds up citizenship. The synagogue, like the church, has become a vital part of the civilization, organic to its social and civic life. As mother religion to Christianity, Judaism's past is cast in a light more glorious because of its present role.[19] In this regard, the individual but highly considered views of Reinhold Niebuhr within Protestant thought may be cited. Analyzing contemporary developments on the background of historical errors from a Christian viewpoint, he proposed that Christians should cease to attempt to convert Jews. The Christian majority, particularly in America, Dr. Niebuhr wrote, should "come to terms with the stubborn will to live of the Jews as a peculiar people, both religiously and ethnically."[20] Thus a new tone has been added to the growing inter-religious discussions, an approach which would recognize the opportunities for interaction between faiths on a non-converting basis. And this idea has been introduced in Europe too, in German and French Catholic quarters.[21]

In such conducive settings, the synagogue is becoming the strongest and most comprehensive local organizational unit of the various forms of Jewish group life. This is not to say that the synagogue has become the representative or controlling voice in these communities, but rather to emphasize its recognized relevance to the lives and needs of individual Jews and its re-emergence in the mid-twentieth century as the central institution in Jewish communal life. British Jewry affords a good example of this pattern. The most authoritative and representative Jewish body in England is "The Board of Deputies of British Jews." Founded in 1760 as "The London Committee of Deputies of British Jews," it now embraces virtually every facet of Jews and Judaism in England. From a structural point of view, it is the most comprehensively organized major countrywide Jewish body in the world, and its representative and authoritative character is recognized by the British Government. The board's work includes the review of parliamentary bills affecting the Jews, Jewish foreign affairs, internal defense of Jewish rights, education, and youth activities, relations with Israel, and other *ad hoc* concerns of the entire community. Overarching in structural conception, yet its keystone is essentially synagogal. Of 389 Deputies elected to the board (according to the figures at the end of 1961), 338 represented 228 synagogues.[22]

The phenomenal growth of the synagogue in recent decades has correspondingly broadened its base and functions. The pace is slower in Europe and Latin America than in North America, but there, too, the trend is to follow the forms of synagogue organization created in the United States and Canada. In addition to its ritual functions for the individual and the group, the synagogue institution embraces within its sphere education, culture, social activity, charity and Jewish interests at large. The changes in Jewish education indicate the general condition. As Alexander Dushkin pointed out, whereas in the United States in 1918 only 24 percent of Jewish pupils in the Jewish school system were taught in synagogue schools, in 1958 the proportion grew to over 88 percent. And many of the Hebrew schools which remained under secular auspices incorporated religious elements into their curricula, introducing prayers and religious practice. In Latin American countries where the secular Yiddish schools still dominate, Hebrew and religious studies are growing in importance, and there, too, as Orthodox, Conservative, and Reform congregations continue to be established, the pressure for congregational auspices is likely to develop. On the European continent and in England the curricula of almost all schools are religiously oriented.[23]

We have seen the emergent pattern of synagogal centrality in Jewish institutional life in the democratic countries. What of the other lands of Jewish residence? A glimpse at the most recent developments in two small communities, Spain and Czechoslovakia, is revealing, precisely because they are located in opposite social and economic orders.

In Spain, the two main Jewish communities in Madrid and Barcelona (numbering about 800 and 1700, respectively) are in fact religious community organizations.[24] For several centuries since the 1492 edict of expulsion, authorization to readmit into Spain members of "The Hebrew Nation" had been sought by various Spanish governments. But these were frustrated, one after another, by the Inquisition and the church. At the beginning of this century, a trickle of settlement found its way into Spain, and in 1909 the royal government abolished the law forbidding synagogues. However, restrictions are still imposed on the open exercise by Jews of their religion—a restriction also imposed on all other non-Catholic faiths. Yet the communities do conduct regular services, youth extension education, social and cultural activities. During both World Wars many refugees were helped along their passage to lands of freedom with the knowledge and support of the Spanish government, and some of them, Ashkenazim and Sephardim, remained to constitute the present communities.[25] More recently these synagogue communities joined in the *Amistad* (Friendship) *Judeo-Cristiana* movement, and its first publication carried the authorization of the Chancellery Secretary of Madrid-Alcala, duly sealed with his grant of *Nihil obstat*. Paradox of paradoxes in Jewish destiny: a memorial service for Pope John XXIII was held in the synagogue of Madrid, former land of Inquisition, Marranoism, and Exile. The fact that this service took place is its commentary.[26] Whether an indigenous Jewish community will rise again in Spain is still a moot question. But whatever its numbers, in the Catholic ambience, the character of the community will surely be distinctively religious.

An indication of what may develop in the Communist countries if some religious and cultural expression is granted to the Jews comes out of the scanty Jewish community records now being published in Czechoslovakia. The Jewish population is estimated at no more than 12,000. Between two thousand and four thousand live in Prague; the other centers are in Bratislava, Kosice, and Brno. More telling perhaps than the absolute figures of population decrease in recent Jewish Czechoslovak history (in 1948 some 45,000 Jews lived in the country)[27] is the present state of synagogal life—the only sanctioned form of Jewish group association. Of some 320 synagogues in Slovakia before World War II, about 40 are used for prayers today. The other synagogue buildings, which were not destroyed, are put to sundry uses, some as storage places.[28] Only one Jewish school exists, and five rabbis are left to serve the Jewish communities of Czechoslovakia.

Yet, out of this depression emerged a strange documentary, revealing at once the tragedy and the possible future direction of the remaining community. Bearing a Biblical verse as its title, "They who sow in tears will reap in joy" (Psalms 126:5), a profusely illustrated volume of the contemporary scene, "The Jewish Communities in the Czechoslovak Republic after World War II,"[29] was published officially in 1959. More a martyrology than the reflection of a creative Jewish community, nevertheless the slender and moving book speaks of the opportunities for future Jewish life, the continuity between past and present, the strengthening of Jewish religious life and the need for religious teachers.[30]

The *Informationsbulletin* published in Prague underlines similar themes and reports the evolving religious activities in the country.[31] These significant developments followed the convening conference on November 22, 1953, of the Union of Jewish Religious Communities, when it was declared that a revolutionary step forward was to be taken in Jewish religious life in Czechoslovakia: the government would grant the Jewish religion the same rights as all other faiths. Henceforth, it was stated, the Jews, in addition to their existing full rights as citizens, were granted equal religious rights as individuals and as a community, guarded by the Constitution of the People's Democracy.[32] As a result of this declaration a small group of consecrated men and women began a valiant effort to take every advantage of the new equal status privileges. From the vantage of the religious freedom in western countries, one must be careful not to confuse the refraction of light with light itself. On the other hand, as one compares these manifestations with the darkness in Russia in these very areas, hope does spring.[33] And in terms of our discussion, while the present rights are clearly restricted to the religious aspects of Jewish life (Zionist and other activities have been prohibited since 1949), the accepted line of religious distinction between citizens is again borne out.

The progressive formation of Jewish group life around the religious distinction, whether by choice, social force, or political imperative, poses new problems for Jewish communities everywhere. The one kind of tension evolves from the growing need for regrouping within Jewish communal life. The centrality of the synagogue in Jewish life is not a new phenomenon. Until the era of Emancipation about one hundred and fifty years ago, it was the primary institution around which, and through which, other Jewish associations drew strength. Moreover, the process of recognizing Jewish communities as religious collectivities has been an ongoing one into our own time.[34] But centrality is not totality. Confusing even the nucleus for the whole, as some Jewish religious leaders have pointed out, may lead to a weakening of the center itself. Coordinate roles in the Jewish scheme of things have to be worked out for all the other elements in Jewry, for example, for those who may or may not profess belief, but whose attachments are to the secular, cultural, ethical, ethnic or political expressions of Jewish life. If community is to become co-extensive with synagogue, will these Jews fall away and seek expression for these attachments outside the Jewish group? Or does this imply more profound changes in the synagogue outlook? Can there be a meeting between these two broad categories within a synagogal framework? And if not, can distinctive Jewish forms in the diaspora survive outside the religious tradition?

Obviously these questions are not academic. They represent a serious challenge to the character of Jewish life during the contemporary period of transformation. And they bear the seeds of even greater challenges if the Jewries of the West someday will meet and interact, as it is hoped, with the Jews of Russia. In this great segment—the second largest—of diaspora Jewry, two generations of the Communist regime and education have not stamped out the feeling of Jewish identification, although the majority of Jews in Russia have been divested of religious association.

From another vantage entirely, the pervasive influence of Israel needs also to be considered in this connection. Although Jewish religious life and institutions in Israel are flourishing and increasing in influence— indeed, antagonists of the religious groups contend that their influence is disproportionate—nevertheless the basic cohesive force in Israel is modern secular nationalism. Ultimately devoted to the welfare of the Jewish people everywhere, and granting authority to the rabbinate in matters of personal status and in other areas, yet its own commitment is to create on the basis of its sovereignty a modern civilization with all that this connotes in the contemporary world.

Another cluster of problems comes from the crisis in religion itself in the Western world. We need but allude to the summaries of a vast literature on this subject, which conclusively demonstrate that modern Western society has developed a religiousness without religion, church and synagogue associations which escape faith, religious orientations which are more socially directed than theologically rooted. The result is, to cite one American scholar, Carl Bridenbaugh, that this age marks "the decline of religion."[35] On the other hand, there are those who marshal the very same evidence to argue that sufficient quantity may produce a new quality of religious experience.[36] These very questions and counter-questions are part of an entirely new complex of factors in the religious equation to which the Jewish communities will have to face up, in the context of their environing cultures, and all the more in those lands where religious neutralism and apathy are the real antagonists of religious opportunity.

In more than one sense what has been discussed is but a preface to a subject which requires systematic and scientific research. The Jewish world is being transformed, and it stands at a new beginning, seeking the meaning of this transformation.

The understanding of the contemporary Jewish situation is very often hindered by the lack of basic knowledge. To select one of the categories listed earlier, that of economic restratification of the Jews, Professor Morris Ginsberg pointed out that there are very few comprehensive studies of the social structure of any large scale modern societies, and "the difficulties encountered in studying the distribution of occupation among Jews are in part due to the fact that the study of social structure in general has only recently come to be taken seriously."[37] Or, to take another suggested category—the tension between the Jewish tradition and contemporary secular civilization—what, in fact, is the reality of that secularism? Is it only an external characteristic of the modern age, or is it a permanent feature of the psychology of modern man? Social science has yet to develop the basic instruments to examine this problem in its fullness. Without such systematic probing, answers can best be based on personal, theological or ideological views.

The effects of the growing influence of the State of Israel on world Jewry and the changing relationships between the diasporic communities also raise questions which cannot be evaluated with adequate objectivity. Sixteen years after the establishment of the State, its real place as a creative force in world Judaism is far from being understood by either diasporic or Israeli Jewry. Israel, and all that brought it into being, have given an impetus to Jewish creativity in all its manifestations throughout the Diaspora. The fact, for example, that Hebrew—and all it implies—is spoken again as a living tongue, and that out of Zion have come forth scholars, scientists and artists, has evoked an attitude of renewed respect for Jewish culture in the broader intellectual circles. Great numbers of Jews have come to learn about their People and Tradition through the creative power of Israel. Yet, one of the dominant problems which grew out of the very fact of the new state's emergence is far from being resolved. Never before in their history were the Jews granted the combination of two simultaneous freedoms: on the one hand the freedom possessed by great concentrations of Jewry in various countries to maintain and deepen their own religio-cultural identity as Jews and, on the other, the freedom for Judaism to flourish as it will in its native Hebraic tradition in the sovereign home of the Jewish People. One of the most complicated issues facing world Jewry is avoiding the possibility that these simultaneous freedoms will lead to separated diasporic and Israeli cultures. A question permanently on the agenda of world Jewry is to determine how spiritual interdependence between Israel and the diaspora can be defined and effectuated.[38]

The evolving character of the relationship between the respective communities in the diaspora enters emphatically into this nexus. Perhaps a new vision of the Jewish People as a living and creative organism will emerge, with Eretz Yisrael as its nuclear center, embracing the totality of the Jewish tradition and historic experience of all Jewish communities in time and in space. This might well be the singular transcendent concept which will weave the variegated strands of worldwide Jewish thought and action into a unified whole. Certainly the astounding advances in technology and worldwide interaction offer a spectacular opportunity to examine this possibility in a way never before attempted or conceived. A new physical unity exists among the Jews, between Israel and the diaspora, and between the various Jewish communities. How the space revolution influences ideas is already manifest by the new forms of Jewish coordinated effort in the spheres of mutual aid, culture and religion. It has become possible for distant Jewish communities in different sectors of the world to think and plan together in a manner not hitherto anticipated.

To raise all these questions, and even doubts, is not to fear the future, but rather to confront the realities of the world we live in with faith in the future and in the power of our generation to meet its challenges. A people, like an individual, is measured not only by what it is, but by what it is becoming. While it is impossible to anticipate the outcome of this struggle with world elements in which the Jewish People is now engaged, the Jews can draw upon two major historical forces in this struggle: the Jewish tradition, the continuing Idea which has motivated Jewry throughout the generations, and the vast experience which has taught the Jews how to live, meet and learn from the civilizations of the world. By virtue of their long and tried history as a world people, the

Jews have developed a measure of sensitivity and alertness which can enable them not only to respond but perhaps even to anticipate the phenomena of this age. It is therefore not inconceivable that as the Jews pursue a solution to their own crises they may demonstrate to the world how to maintain cohesiveness and integrity in the midst of technological, social and spiritual evolution.

(1963)

NOTES

1. See Appendix. Also cf. Roberto Bachi, "World Jewish Population" in *The Illustrated History of the Jews,* edited by Benjamin Mazar, Moshe Davis, and Chaim H. Ben Sasson (Jerusalem, New York, 1963), pp. 401–408.

2. *The Jewish Communities of the World* (New York, 1963), Except for Israel and Canada it is not possible to give more than a close estimate of Jewish population figures. While many countries have included a question on religion in the official population censuses (e.g., in Europe: Switzerland, The Netherlands, Germany, Austria and Italy), less than half of world Jewry is covered in such censuses. In the majority of Western countries indication of religious affiliation either is not solicited, or it is optional in official censuses. Moreover, the information published most often is confined to the total number of Jews with perhaps a classification by sex and/or local geographical distribution. Hence we do not possess scientifically determined statistical data on the world Jewish population. For the most recent discussions of the problems of Jewish demographic research, see *Papers in Jewish Demography* (Part I), Second World Congress of Jewish Studies (Jerusalem, 1957). See also the section on demography in *Jewish Life in Modern Britain,* edited by Julius Gould and Shaul Esh (London, 1964) and in *La Vie Juive dans L'Europe Contemporaine* (Bruxelles, 1964).

3. For a map and chart portraying the spread of the new immigration in France, see *L'Arche* (Nov. 1962), p. 2, and (July 1963), p. 25. One-half of the Jewish population in France is settled in the Paris area and its many suburban communities. About 30,000 are scattered in the remotest villages of France. The meaning of these figures can be studied in the *JDC Statistic Abstract 1962* published by The American Joint Distribution Committee (July 1963).

4. In other parts of the Jewish world, economic upgrading is also taking place. According to the 1963 annual report of ORT (Organization for Rehabilitation Through Training) which conducts probably the largest non-governmental vocational training system in the world, "a historic transformation" has occurred in Jewish occupations. The former carpentry, tailoring, and other traditional courses" have been replaced, and the new courses introduced into the ORT

curriculum in the last decade include metallurgy, electronics, telecommunications, architectural drafting, and construction technology. Since ORT functions primarily in the lesser developed economic sectors of the Jewish group, chiefly in Israel, and in nineteen countries of North Africa, Iran, India, Western Europe, and Poland and other areas, this evaluation indicates the levelling factors in Jewish economic restratification on a world scale. For a statistical and summary statement of the changing role of the Jews in the Argentinian economy after World War II, see Abraham Scheps "Transformaciones y tendencias en las actividades economicas de los Israelitas a partir de la segunda guerra mundial." in *Primera Conferencia de Investigadores y Estudiosos Judeo-Argentinos en el Campo de las Ciencias Sociales y la Historia,* held in October 1961 in Buenos Aires under the joint auspices of the Institute of Contemporary Jewry of The Hebrew University and the Communidad Israelita de Buenos Aires. Following the conference the Buenos Aires Kehilla established a permanent Institute of Social Studies. Its first publication, *La Nupcialidad en la Kehila de Buenos Aires,* Estudio Estadistico (Buenos Aires, 1962), contains new data on the economic and social structure of the community.

5. See *Changing Patterns of Jewish Life on the Campus* (Washington, D.C., 1961), particularly the section "International Aspects of Hillel Service: A Report on Jewish Students Overseas," pp. 25–64. Also Alfred Jospe, *Judaism on the Campus* (Washington, D.C., 1963).

6. For an analysis of the philosophical roots of anti-Judaism in modern thought, see Nathan Rotenstreich, *The Recurring Pattern* (London, 1963). The penetration of Nazi ideology into the thought-concepts of the German language is treated by Shaul Esh, "Words and Their Meaning" (Twenty-five Examples of Nazi-Idiom), *Yad Vashem Studies V,* edited by Nathan Eck and Aryeh L. Kubowy (Jerusalem, 1962–3). For a comparative list of selected descriptions of Jews and Judaism in American, and English dictionaries, see Jacob Chintiz, "Jews and Judaism in the Dictionary," *The Reconstructionist* (Jan. 11, 1963), pp. 9–15. See also the survey of *Current Anti-Semitic Activities Abroad,* published by the American Jewish Committee (June, 1963).

7. In France, an entire school within Catholicism is dedicated to the eradication of anti-Semitic feeling through "self-examination and purification." Following the publication of Jules Isaac's study, *Jesus et Israel,* after World War II, a permanent organization called *L'Amitié judéo-chrétienne* has been established. For an example of intergroup organization to counter anti-Semitic activities in South America, see the publications of FUCA (Frente Unido Contra El Antisemitismo). In the United States several major studies are being conducted at the present time. Two recent publications which treat the problem from the aspects of schooling and cultural transmission of prejudice are Charles Herbert Stember, *Education and Attitude Change* (New York, 1961), and Bernard E. Olson, *Faith and Prejudice: Intergroup Problems in Protestant Curricula* (New Haven, 1963).

8. Cf. Isaiah Berlin's parable of the tale of the Jews in Europe and America, "Jewish Slavery and Emancipation," in *Forum,* edited by N. Rotenstreich and Z. Shazar, (Jerusalem, 1953), vol. 1, pp. 54–57.

9. Cf. Nathan Morris, *Jewish Education and Social Change* (London, 1959).

10. A research project to reconstruct the role of the Yiddish language in its past European cultural setting is the Yiddish Atlas described by Uriel Weinreich, "Mapping a Culture," *Columbia University Forum* (Summer 1963), pp. 17–21.

11. See Gerhard Lenski, *The Religious Factor* (New York, 1961); also, Charlotte Roland, "Sociologie Juive: Méthode d'une expérience en cours" in *La Vie Juive . . . ;* and Maurice Freedman, *The Structure of Jewish Minorities* (London, 1957).

12. The interest in the identification patterns of Jewish intellectuals as Americans and Jews extends beyond the Jewish community, as seen in a recent symposium in the United States, "The Jew in American Culture," in *Ramparts,* the Catholic Layman's Journal (Autumn 1963). See particularly Maxwell Geismar's statement on "The Jewish Heritage in Contemporary American Fiction," pp. 5–13.

13. Charlotte Roland, *op. cit.* (Mimeographed edition), p. 14.

14. In the diaspora this category raises a perplexing practical demographic question. Even in small communities the differences in computation can be enormous if one applies only the religious principle or communal participation lists. For example, see A. Vedder, "Reconstruction de la Vie Communautaire en Hollande, in *La Vie Juive. . . .*

15. The complete text was published in *The Jerusalem Post* (Dec. 5, 1958).

16. File in the Office of the Prime Minister.

17. See the report of the recent "Feast of Brotherly Love" (*Un'agape Fraterna*) in Rome (Jan. 13, 1963), arranged by the Universita Internazionale degli Studi Sociali "Pro Deo" in which there participated representatives of twenty-one religious groups, among them Christians, Buddhists, Taoists, Moslems, Jews, etc. *Israel* (Rome) (Jan. 24, 1963). Cf. *Study of Discrimination in the Matter of Religious Rights and Practices, by* Arcot Krishaswami, special rapporteur of the Sub-Commission on Prevention of Discrimination and Protection of Minorities of the Human Rights Commission, published by the United Nations (New York, 1960).

18. As regards the Jews, a draft document, "The Attitude of Catholics Toward Non-Christians, Particularly Toward the Jews," which re-evaluates the Church's position toward them is to be considered by the Council at a future meeting. See the official communiqué issued to the Vatican Council Fathers on Nov. 8, 1963.

19. See *The Jews,* by Friedrich Wilhelm Foerster (London, 1961). Also "The Jew in American Society," a series of essays in *The Commonweal* (Sept. 28, 1962), pp. 3–14.

20. "The Relations of Christians and Jews," in *Pious and Secular America* (New York, 1958), p. 88.

21. See, for example, Jean Toulat, *Juifs, Mes Frères* (Paris, 1962), p. 32; also pp. 261–63. A basic statement which calls for a revision of Jewish Christian attitudes is "The Ten Points of Seeligsberg" adopted at the International Congress

at Seeligsberg in 1947 by the assembly of Catholics and Protestants. The ten points are included in Father Toulat's book, pp. 266–68.

22. 122 London synagogues (192 deputies); 99 provincial synagogues (139 deputies); seven Commonwealth synagogues (seven deputies); and 46 institutions. See the paper by Adolph G. Brotman, "Jewish Communal Organization," in *Conference on Jewish Life in Modern Britain.* Also *Annual Report, 1962,* Board of Deputies of British Jews (London).

23. Alexander M. Dushkin, "Analysis of Some Recent Developments of Jewish Education in the Diaspora," *Scripta Hierosolymitana* (Jerusalem, 1963), Vol. XIII, pp. 56–74.

24. A sprinkling of Jewish families live in Valencia, Seville, Cordoba, San Sebastian, and Bilboa. The estimated total Jewish population of Spain is some 3,000.

25. One of the famous "guest-exiles" in Madrid during the first World War was Max Nordau. A description of the Jewish "war colony" in Spain can be found in the biography by Anna and Max Nordau (New York, 1943), chaps. 16 and 17. About the founding of the synagogue, the authors say: "One of the members of the war colony, M. Salzedo, together with the family of the banker Bauer, determined to found a synagogue. These gentlemen rented a dark apartment going out on a court-yard. The plan was tolerated, but not permitted. The sight of a Jewish house of worship was supposed to be shocking to fervent Catholics to a point of excitement and riot . . . There were marriages in the little synagogue and bar-mitzvahs and other celebrations." For some of the activities of the Joint Distribution Committee during World War II and its Pyrenean operation, see Herbert Agar, *The Saving Remnant* (New York, 1960), particularly pp. 134–42. A detailed study based on archival materials and oral documentation of this chapter in Jewish history—the rescue of Jews through Spain and Portugal (1940–44)—is now being completed by Haim Avni, graduate fellow at the Institute of Contemporary Jewry.

26. See *Amistad Judeo-Cristiana,* Boletín información, Num. 1 (Junio de 1963).

27. The pre-World War II Jewish population was estimated in 1937 at 260,000.

28. A commentary on the physical and spiritual decimation of the community is the transport, in February 1964, of 1562 Torahs from synagogues in Czechoslovakia to London, to form the nucleus of a museum. The Torahs had originally been collected by the Nazis, as part of their "final solution" of the Jews. Their intention in this collection, they declared, was a postwar study of an extinct race. Ninety-five percent of the adult population in the places from which the Torahs were collected and 98 percent of the children in these communities of Bohemia and Moravia were annihilated. Almost forgotten, except by the remnant Jewish community, the Torah collection will now become a memorial in London to the destroyed communities in Czechoslovakia. Most of the Torahs are less than one hundred years old, although the oldest is dated 1719.

29. *Die aussäen unter Tränen, mit Jubel werden sie ernten* (Psalm 126). Die jüdischen Gemeinden in der Tschechoslowakischen Republik Nach Dem Zweiten Weltkrieg. Herausgegeben vom Rate der jüdischen Gemeinden in den böhemischen Ländern und vom Zentralverband der jüdischen Gemeinden in der Slowakei im Zentral-Kirchenverlag zu Prag. Redaktion: Dr. Rudolf Iltis.

30. See, for example, the introduction of the section on Slovakia, pp. 119–21 by the Chief Rabbi Elias Katz.

31. *Informationsbulletin:* Rat Der Gemeinden Im Bohem Und Mahrn Zu Prag.

32. The convening meeting was attended by representatives of some thirteen districts in Bohemia, Moravia, and Silesia and was officially authorized. For reports of the development of the communities, see *Informationsbulletin* (July 26, 1962), pp. 9–10.

33. Another encouraging announcement from an East European country came during the visit to the United States of Professor Alexander Scheiber, director of the Hungarian Rabbinical Seminary in Budapest. He declared he would initiate action to affiliate Hungarian Jews with the World Council of Synagogues. Prof. Scheiber was the first official representative of the Jewish Community in Hungary to come to America since World War II. His brief statement also reflects the different attitudes to Jewish religious life and institutions in the European Communist sector: "The Jews of Hungary can derive immense religious and spiritual benefit from direct contact with organized synagogue communities elsewhere. At the same time, I believe we can make an important contribution to this worldwide network of religious mutual aid. I see no reason why we should not join our fellow Jews the world over in advancing the cause of Judaism. The Jews of Hungary lead an actively Jewish life, and the government helps us in our efforts to do so. Our synagogues are well attended and our Jewish institutions, particularly of scholarship, enjoy a wide reputation. In addition to the 86-year-old Rabbinical Seminary, we have a Jewish high school and many Hebrew schools. Our community has a flourishing museum and library, an excellent Jewish hospital and homes for the aged. We publish regularly many books of Jewish interest." *News from World Council of Synagogues* (July 18, 1963). Thus spoke a rabbi coming from the Hungarian community of some 75–80,000 Jews to the press in the United States. Cf. the statement issued by Chief Rabbi Yehuda-Leib Levin of Moscow, also speaking to the American public on "That's How We Live," in the official English language publication *USSR Soviet Life Today* (April 1963), p. 12. (in Moscow alone there are some 236,000 Jews out of a total Jewish population of 2,268,000 as registered in the last Russian census): "You ask me how we live. No one in my congregation, thank the Lord, complains that he does not have enough to live on. The services in our synagogue are attended mostly by old people. Some are on pension, some are supported by their children, and those who are younger work. Our Central Moscow Synagogue holds regular services weekdays and holidays. On weekdays about 500 people come to the synagogue, and on holidays there are twice and sometimes three times as many. We also have two Jewish prayer houses in Moscow, one in Maryina Roscha and others in Cherkizovo, and a synagogue in the suburban village of Malakhova. There are 96 synagogues all told in the

Soviet Union. My community published a prayer book, and we put out a religious calendar every year. Last fall our congregations were supplied with calendars long before *Rosh Hashana,* our New Year." The dim hope for any renewal of Jewish life in Russia is scarcely illuminated by this authorized statement, especially when it is placed beside the statements of the infinitesimally smaller Jewish communities of Czechoslovakia and Hungary.

34. Strangely even in Nazi racial legislation the criterion for the definition of a Jew was based on the ancestral religious affiliation, thus denying its own racial premises.

35. "The Great Mutation," *The American Historical Review* 68 (Jan. 1963): 320–21. See also "A Survey of Political and Religious Attitudes of American College Students," published by *The Educational Reviewer* (New York, 1963).

36. Important aspects of this general problem are discussed in "Religion in American Society," *The Annals* (November 1960). For statements on the Jewish religion in the United States, cf. the presentations submitted to the symposium "Major Issues Facing the Organized Jewish Communities" (Section IV) arranged by the Council of Federations and Welfare Funds. Contributors to this section were Samuel Belkin, Louis Finkelstein, Nelson Glueck, Mordecai Kaplan and Morris Liebermann. European Jewish religious problems are discussed in *Addresses given at the Conference of European Rabbis* (held at Amsterdam, 1957; Westcliff-on-Sea, 1959; Paris, 1961) and published by the Standing Committee (May 1963). See also the papers of André Néher "Crise Spirituelle" and Jean Halperin "Problèmes Culturels" in *La Vie Juive;* and Norman Cohen's paper "Trends in Anglo-Jewish Religious Life" in *Jewish Life in Modern Britain.*

37. *Jewish Life in Modern Britain;* see the discussion on "The Economic and Social Structure of Anglo-Jewry."

38. For a comparative analysis of this problem in its historical and contemporary settings, see Salo Baron, "The Jewish Commonwealths and the Dispersions," in *The Ethic of Power: The Interplay of Religion, Philosophy, and Politics,* edited by Harold D. Lasswell and Harlan Cleveland (New York, 1962), pp. 3–24.

APPENDIX

The following is a composite of the basic chart prepared by H. S. Halevi in *The Influence of World War II on the Demographic Characteristics of the Jewish People* (Jerusalem, 1963 [English Summary]), p. 11, and Nehemiah Robinson's compilation in *The Jewish Communities of the World* (New York, 1963).

THE MAIN COUNTRIES OF JEWISH POPULATION
(IN DESCENDING ORDER) IN THE TWENTIETH CENTURY

Ordinal Number	Beginning of Century	Between Wars (around 1925)	Eve of World War II	Around 1955	1962
1.	Russia	U.S.A.	U.S.A.	U.S.A.	U.S.A.
2.	Austria-Hungary	Poland	Poland	Russia	Russia
3.	U.S.A.	Russia	Russia	Israel	Israel
4.	Germany	Rumania	Rumania	Britain	France
5.	Turkey	Germany	Germany	Argentina	Britain
6.	Rumania	Hungary	Hungary	France	Argentina
7.	Britain	Czechoslovakia	Palestine	Canada	Canada
8.	Morocco	Austria	Czechoslovakia	Rumania	Rumania
9.	Holland	Britain	Britain	Morocco	Brazil
10.	France	Morocco	Argentina	Algiers	Morocco
11.	Algiers	Argentina	France	Hungary	South Africa
12.	Tunisia	Turkey	Austria	South Africa	Iran

The significance of Halevi's table is more pointed if one considers the percentage of the Jewish People residing in these principal countries in the periods listed. The cumulative percentages (the sum of individual percentages relating to the countries from the serial numbers 1 to 12) are arranged in descending order of the magnitude of the Jewish population in the respective countries.

CUMULATIVE PERCENTAGES OF THE JEWISH PEOPLE
RESIDING IN THE PRINCIPAL COUNTRIES
OF DISPERSION IN THE TWENTIETH CENTURY

Ordinal Number	Beginning of Century	Between Wars (around 1925)	Eve of World War II	Around 1955
1	47.5	24.6	29.8	43.6
2	66.5	44.1	49.0	60.3
3	78.0	63.0	67.7	73.9
4	83.4	69.1	73.3	77.7
5	87.7	73.3	76.4	80.7
6	90.1	76.5	79.1	83.4
7	91.8	78.9	81.6	85.3
8	93.2	81.3	83.8	87.1
9	94.1	83.3	85.6	88.8
10	94.9	84.7	87.2	90.0
11	95.4	86.1	88.7	91.9
12	95.9	87.4	89.9	92.0

For some variations in the statistical data for the period between the Wars, see *Statistical Tables* Submitted on Behalf of the Jewish Agency for Palestine to the Inter-Governmental Conference for Refugees at Evian-Les-Bains, July 1938.

2

RACE, NATION, AND PEOPLE
IN THE JEWISH BIBLE

MAURICE SAMUEL

THE PROBLEMS OF RACE AND NATIONALISM loom larger in the world today than they have ever done before. The shrinkage of space which is the result of rapid communication and transportation serves to bring into more intimate contact the groupings which have hitherto felt some degree of isolation or of comparative privacy. The effect is sharpened by the growing interdependence of economic interests, and within recent years it has been dramatically heightened by space exploration, which reduces our planet to a tiny island in a corner of the universe. A lively perception of the provincialism of the globe has hitherto been confined to persons of a philosophic turn of mind; today it is forcefully borne in on hundreds of millions who, not given to abstract speculation, see on television what has never been seen before: our world viewed from the outside.

This new perspective has come upon us with breath-taking suddenness. It has not given us the time to adjust to it our traditional views and prejudices on the subject of human relations. The result of this abrupt disparity between what is forced upon our attention and what we are accustomed to feeling has, in fact, been a heightening of the emotions, a reaction of reluctance to adapt the mind to the new image of the world and of mankind.

In America particular conditions have given a new and fateful urgency to the race problem. Local developments have been influenced by the overall world factors just mentioned, and also by the emergence into political identity of peoples hitherto vaguely perceived in the mass. Who would have dreamed a generation ago that the accredited representatives of a score of African Negro states would sit in the same assembly of world debate with the representatives of the great Western powers? But even without these external circumstances the race problem in America, and, to be exact, the problem of the relations between black and white, was developing toward a dénouement. Today it is impossible to ignore it or to permit it to drift along. And so there is a searching of hearts in what is perhaps a greater crisis than that of the Civil War. It is, fortunately, not so bloody in its confrontations, but it is as fateful in its implications. It is, acutally, the rising of that drama to its final act.

In the searching of hearts, some of it sincere, and some of it only a search for the rationalization of traditional attitudes, there is frequent recourse to the most influential document in the possession of man— the Bible, and particularly to that more voluminous section called by the Jews the Jewish Bible and by the Christians the Old Testament. It may be true that the Bible is more quoted by hearsay than read, that sentences here and there are detached and bandied about without reference to their context or to the Jewish Bible as a whole. But these sentences, these fragments of narrative, are presented as final and authoritative utterances of divine origin. It is therefore proper to attempt, even in the brief compass of a paper, to review what the Jewish Bible has to say on this burning issue.

It would be well to begin with a definition of what is generally understood by the term "race"; but it must be noted at once that "what is generally understood" need not, and in this case does not, correspond with the view held by informed students of the subject. A "race" is popularly held to be a group of common descent which is marked by hereditary physical characteristics and by equally hereditary mental and spiritual aptitudes or deficiencies bound up with or even determined by the physical characteristics. Now in this sense the term "race" is not recognized in the informed or scientific world. What the informed world—by which is meant the body of trained anthropologists—does recognize is the grouping of human beings under their hereditary physical characteristics alone, and the word race, if used at all, is applied with extreme caution. There is no concensus as to the number of "races" constituting the human species. Certain standard classifications are used: stature, pigmentation of the skin, skull shape, facial angle, hirsuteness or glabrousness, flatness or sharpness of the nose, round or oval cross section of the hair. But it is impossible to isolate a group on the basis of these characteristics. Tall groups may have either round or oval skulls, hirsute groups may be tall or short. Acute facial angles may be accompanied by tallness or shortness, by hairiness or glabrousness. In any case, these characteristics are chosen for their observability; others, less observable, may be equally important—whatever "important" may mean in this connection. Thus the attempt to define or isolate a race even in physical terms ends in complete confusion. The attempt to link any of these characteristics, or any combination of them, with inherited mental and spiritual aptitudes is not made by any serious scientist.

It must however be observed that large numbers of scientists credit the Jewish Bible with presenting or advocating the point of view which they repudiate, and a considerable body of public opinion concurs with them—which merely proves that scientists are as little prone to read the Bible carefully as are ordinary people. Here is a typical quotation from a popular scientific book by two reputable scientists. "How much the ancient Hebrews believed in the power of heredity must be plain to anyone who follows the Biblical leaders and prophets to the places assigned to them (i.e., to the ancient Hebrews) by the ways in which they differed from their fellows."[1]

Now the strange thing is that though the Jewish Bible speaks a great deal about hereditary privileges and duties, these are nowhere linked with physical characteristics. Moreover, these hereditary privileges were renewed from generation to generation only as they were deserved. The privileges could be, and were, withdrawn as a consequence of dereliction of duty, and nowhere is this more observable than in the destiny of "the chosen people" itself.

But the confirmation of this fact would necessitate, for the scientist and the layman, a reading of the whole Bible, which one cannot expect of most of them. It will, I believe, be more instructive to cite at first instances which establish beyond cavil that hereditary privileges could be, and were, withdrawn, and that they were not in any wise associated with hereditary physical characteristics, or, as it is sometimes popularly put, with the blood.

Let us begin with privileges and their withdrawal. The kings of the Bible, whether they reigned over the briefly united kingdom or over the separate kingdoms of Judah and Israel, were in principle hereditary monarchs. But it is nowhere stated that they were forbidden to, or did not, marry commoners. The majority of them come under the heading of the "bad" kings—they did "that which was evil in the sight of the Lord"—and they forfeited the right to see their progeny on the throne. This is true not only of kings denounced for outright misbehavior, like Jeroboam, Ahab, Manasseh and many others, but even of the very first king, Saul, and that for a form of disobedience which some of us would not find it in our hearts to condemn.

The priests of the Hebrews were—and for the orthodox still re-

1. L. C. Dumand and Th. Dobzhansky, *Heredity, Race and Society* (New York: Mentor, 1960), p. 9.

main—a hereditary caste. But they were not forbidden to marry the daughters of non-priestly Israelites. They were only forbidden to marry a divorcee. That their priestly privileges were conditional, depending on their performance of the duties, rather than on descent, was established almost at the moment when the priesthood itself was established. We are told that the two sons of the founder of the priesthood, Nadab the first-born, and Abihu his brother, "died before the Lord, in the wilderness of Sinai, when they offered strange fire before the Lord, and they had no children" (Num. 3:4). Many generations later, the priesthood was temporarily taken away from the Aaronic line, and even outside the Levitic tribe. The two sons of Eli the priest are represented as dissolute and corrupted men; they were cut off, slain before the Lord, the function passing to Samuel, an Ephrathite. And again we are not told of the privilege being continued in the sons of Samuel. The choosing of a branch of Israel for some particular duty or privilege was a matter of organization, and not of blood endowment which would ensure perpetual fitness or retention of status.

On his deathbed Jacob bestowed certain distinctions upon the fathers of the tribes to be, and later, when the exodus had taken place, the sons of Levi were assigned no territory in the Promised Land—they were "scattered in Israel." They remained the humble servants of the tabernacle and later of the temple, and they also served the local altars. But Moses, incomparably the greatest figure in the Jewish Bible, was exempt from such service.

Reuben, the eldest son of Jacob, was stripped of his rights of primogeniture for his misbehavior with his father's concubine, while Simeon and Levi were passed over because they had sacked the city of Shechem, and the position of primacy for the Messianic line was conferred on the tribe of Judah. The tribe of Zebulon was given a place on the sea-coast, and the tribe of Issachar was relegated to heavy labor. Nowhere in these utterances of Jacob do we find a hint that a peculiar quirk of constitution predestined certain sections of the people to certain positions and functions. It was arbitrary organization and not heritable faculties which was responsible for these assignments. It may be conceded that the founder of a line was invested with certain rights, duties, or functions, and that these were in principle transferable in perpetuity to his descendants in the hope that they would prove worthy of their progenitor, but this has as little to do with the idea of transmitted characteristics as the heritability of property.

The term "chosen people" has become a shibboleth which for no reason discoverable in the Bible is associated with the racist principle.

Whatever objections one may raise to the idea of a "chosen people," it is clear that the term has never implied, and has never been supposed to imply, a relationship to God inherent in the genes, or "the blood." This is as true of the Biblical "choice" as it is of the hereditary continuity in certain trades and professions in the guilds of the middle ages—and for that matter to some extent in hereditary occupations in our own times—which never implied that a man's inherited profession, as cooper, or wheelwright, or plumber, is supposed to be in the blood.

The choice of Abraham as the founder of the people so chosen was not altogether arbitrary, since it was based, according to the account, on Abraham's pioneering observance of "the laws, statutes and commandments" of God (Gen. 26:5). In the valedictory addresses of Moses to the Israelites before their passage over the Jordan into the Promised Land, he warned them: "Because He loved thy fathers, and chose their seed after them, and brought thee out with His presence . . . to drive out from before thee greater and mightier nations than thou . . . know this day and lay it to thy heart that He is God in heaven and upon the earth beneath; there is none else" (Deut. 4:37–39).

The word "seed" here is simply a synonym for descendants. There is no suggestion of genetic fixation of spiritual qualities—such a concept was in fact wholly alien to the Hebraic world and the ancient world generally. It is quite apparent that the relationship to God was being renewed, which would have been unnecessary if it was in the blood. We read, again: "God did not set his love upon you, nor choose you, because ye were more in number than any other people—for ye were the fewest of all peoples—but because the Lord loved you, and because He would keep the oath which he swore to your fathers" (Deut. 7:7–8). And, still more pointedly: "Not for thy righteousness, or for the uprightness of thy heart, dost thou go in to possess the land; but for the wickedness of these nations the Lord thy God hath driven them out before thee" (Deut. 9:6).

The Israelites in the wilderness did not show themselves deserving of God's favor; nor did He seem to place too much reliance on their conduct for the future. "When thou shalt beget children and children's children, and ye shall have been long in the land, and shall deal corruptly, and make a graven image . . . and shall do that which is evil in the sight of the Lord thy God to provoke Him, I call heaven and earth to witness against you this day, that ye shall soon utterly perish from off the land" (Deut. 4:25–26). The covenant between God and Israel was not mechanical and irrevocable, as it would have been as the accompaniment of mechanically transmitted spiritual characteristics first evident in the Patriarchs. Its continuance was contingent upon cease- less renewal in every generation, an effort of the will, a discipline ac- cepted and passed on from father to son—not like the instincts of animals, which are independent of tuition, but a tradition of the heart and mind. Hence the solemn admonition, foremost among the prayers of the Jews till this day: "And these words, which I command thee this day, shall be upon thy heart, and thou shalt teach them diligently to thy children, and thou shalt talk of them when thou sittest in thy house, and when thou walkest by the way, and when thou liest down, and when thou risest up."

God's covenant with the Hebrews meant a long and arduous and painful regimen which was never completely successful. Nor did the Israelites wait till they had been long in the land before demonstrating that their mission was not implanted in the seed, but had been entrusted to an unreliable memory and a reluctant will.

The beginning of the history of Israel was marked by defection and rebellion. At the foot of Sinai the people worshipped the golden calf, and God was prepared to destroy them, saying to Moses: "Let Me alone, that My wrath may wax hot against them, and that I may con- sume them, and I will make of *thee* a great nation" (Ex. 32:10). There is a touching anthropomorphism in this passage, as if God were saying: "Let Me work Myself into a rage." But He yielded to the supplications and arguments of Moses.

At the end of the long, tortured story of the people, before the collapse of the kingdom of Judah—the kingdom of Israel had already gone into exile, its warning example unheeded—God sent word through some unnamed prophets: "I will wipe out Jerusalem as a man wipeth out a dish, wiping it and turning it upside down . . . because they have done that which is evil in My sight, and have provoked Me, since the day their fathers came forth out of Egypt, even unto this day" (II Kings 21:13–15). The vicissitudes in the conduct of Israel had its parallel in the ambivalence of God's attitude toward it. In one of the most mov- ing—and again "human"—utterances of God, a forgiving and forgetting tenderness is poured out upon the people practically at the time when the dread sentence of destruction was issued through the mouths of the anonymous prophets. "I remember for thee the affection of thy youth, the love of thine espousals, how thou wentest after Me in the wilderness, in a land that was not sown" (Jer. 2:2). The contumacious behavior of the Israelites in the wilderness is obliterated in an outburst of sheer sentimentality.

The attitudes of the prophets toward the Hebrew people was, if
deeply loving, utterly unflattering, and the proneness of the people to
repudiation of the task imposed on it stares out from almost every book
of the Jewish Bible. Its tendency to "go whoring" after false gods, its
susceptibility to alien and corrupting influences, made its early contact
with the surrounding peoples a continuous danger. It was this susceptibility, this weakness, especially during the formative period, that
drove the teachers to warn them against intermarriage. The prohibition
had nothing to do with the notion of racial corruption, or adulteration
of the stock, or miscegenation. Everywhere the prohibition is linked
with the conservation of the faith. One of the favorite passages quoted—
out of context and in truncated form—to prove a racial viewpoint in the
Bible, relates to the period of the return of the exiles after the destruction. Forty-two thousand pioneers left the Persian Empire under Zerub-
babel and Joshua to rebuild the homeland. Within less than a century
this infant state–in–the–making seemed to be going the way of the old
kingdoms; and when Ezra and Nehemiah came out of Persia to take
charge, they were told by the local leaders: "The people of Israel, and
the priests and Levites, have not separated themselves from the people
of the land, doing according to their abominations, even of the Canaanites, the Hittites, the Perizzites, the Jebusites, the Ammonites, the
Moabites, the Egyptians, and the Amorites. For they have taken of their
daughters for themselves and their sons, so that the holy seed have
mingled themselves with the peoples of the land" (Ezra 9:1–2). A can-
did reading of the text discloses that "seed" is here again used as a
synonym for "people," and it is not the physical mingling which is condemned, but the watering down and the ultimate wasting away of the
mission and the faith: that mission and that faith which were to be,
incidentally, the seed–bed of Christianity. Hence we read: "In those
days I saw that the Jews had married women of Ashdod, of Ammon, of
Moab, and their children spoke half in the language of Ashdod, and
could not speak in the Jews' language, but according to the language of
each people" (Neh. 13:23–24).

Wherever there seemed to be no danger of assimilation and of the
disappearance of the tradition, intermarriage was not only permitted, it
was actually provided for. So we read: "When thou goest forth to battle
against thine enemies, and the Lord thy God delivereth them into thy
hands, and thou carriest them away captive, and thou seest among the
captives a woman of goodly form, and wouldst take her unto thee for
wife; then thou shalt bring her to thy house, and she shall shave her
head, and pare her nails, and she shall put the raiment of her captivity

from off her, and shall remain in thy house, and bewail her father and mother a full month; and after that thou mayest go unto her, and be her husband and she shall be thy wife. And it shall be, if thou have no delight in her, then thou shalt let her go wherever she will; but thou shalt not sell her at all for money, thou shalt not deal with her as a slave, because thou hast humbled her" (Deut. 21:10–14).

How is it possible for anyone to speak of a blood-purity obsession among the ancient Hebrews in the face of this enactment?

It is perhaps this passage which explains the exclamation of the prophet, addressing the inhabitants of Jerusalem: "Thine origin and thy nativity is of the land of the Canaanite; the Amorite was thy father and thy mother was a Hittite" (Ezek. 16:3).

After the battle with the Midianites in the desert, Moses issued this command to the Israelites: "Kill every male among the little ones, and kill every woman that hath known man by lying with him, but all the women children that have not known man by lying with him, keep alive for yourselves" (Num. 31:17–18). We have here an instance of mass commingling of "races." Individual instances of intermarriage are frequent. Moses himself, a Levite, married out of the people. His first wife, Zipporah, was not only a non-Israelite but the daughter of the priest of a foreign cult. In his old age Moses married an Ethiopian woman, that is, a negress (Num. 12:1), at which Aaron and Miriam "murmured," and were rebuked for it by God. Abraham begot Ishmael on his Egyptian concubine, Hagar, and when Sarah forced him to send away mother and son, Abraham did so with obvious reluctance. In the desert, when they were at the point of death, an angel came to succor them, and made promises of future greatness to the son. In his old age Abraham married one Keturah, and had several sons by her. The line of faith came down only through Isaac, but there is never a word about "blood pollution" in this or any other of the exogamous marriages just listed.

It has been argued that when Abraham sent Eliezer to Mesopotamia to find a wife for Isaac it was out of concern for the purity of the race. But it is perfectly natural for immigrant parents to send to the old country for brides and bridegrooms for their sons and daughters, without any reference to hereditary principles. It would have been strange if Abraham, the founder of a religion, had not wanted to extend its benefits to members of his own family in spite of his disastrous experience with his nephew Lot.

The marriage of Bathsheba to Uriah the Hittite is mentioned without comment. Uriah is a Hebrew name, so is Bathsheba—whence it might be argued that she too was a Hittite. If so, David committed murder for the sake of an alien woman, and from this union with her was to spring the wisest of the kings, Solomon. But if Bathsheba was Israelite, *she* was the transgressor in marrying a Hittite. Because of the murder of Uriah the Hittite David's life work in unifying the kingdom was undone. And finally we must remember that David was himself the descendant of a mixed marriage, being the great-grandson of Ruth the Moabitess, and from him the Messiah was to spring in the fullness of time.

The Bible gives a careful and detailed account of the creation of man. It is silent on the creation of the varieties of man, of the "races," as they are loosely called. Evolution is of course a purely modern concept, and what the writers of the Bible thought about the origins of races, if they thought about it at all, we do not know. Since they did not believe in the multiple origins of the human species but ascribed to them a common descent, it would seem that the question of the racial unity of man was settled once and for all. The interpretative legends of the Jews, the *Midrashim,* some of which are as old as the Bible but were transmitted as oral tradition, have much to say regarding this one–time creation of man. God is represented as having taken dust from all over the earth to fashion the body of Adam, red soil and black soil and yellow sand, so that no people, of whatever color, might be looked upon as excluded. But the word Adam itself means, simply, "Man," and *ben Adam,* "the son of man," though it came to be used sometimes in a special sense, is synonymous with "human being" at large.

That physical characteristics, however and whenever they appeared, were regarded as hereditarily fixed and ineradicable, is attested by the famous verse, "Can the Ethiopian change his skin or the leopard his spots" (Jer. 13:23). That the color of the Ethiopian's skin did not imply any kind of spiritual inferiority is implied just as clearly by the verse, "Are you not to Me as the children of the Ethiopians, O children of Israel?" (Amos 9:7).

Silent on the origins of the physical varieties of man, the Bible has something to say on the origins of cultures and linguistically separated peoples. One of the sons of Adam was a herdsman, another a settled tiller of the soil. Jubal, the son of Lamech, invented the harp and pipe, and his half-brother Tubal-Cain brass and iron knives. The variety of languages was a visitation designed to frustrate the arrogance of the generation which built the tower of Babel.

Hereditary status, like hereditary occupations, occurs frequently in the Bible; but we have seen that, besides having no racial basis, hereditary status was not by any means an inviolable principle. Much has been made in popular argument of a famous incident in the life of Noah.

Ham, Noah's son, seeing his father lying naked and drunk, told his brothers. Against him Noah pronounced a curse, repeated three times, dooming his descendants to inferior status: "Cursed be Canaan [the son of Ham]; a servant of servants [or a slave of slaves] shall he be to his brethren. Blessed be the Lord, the God of Shem; and let Canaan be their servant. God enlargeth Japheth, and he shall dwell in the tents of Shem, and let Canaan be their servant" (Gen. 9:25–27). For some reason this explosion of anger on the part of Noah is supposed to have had divine sanction, ensuring fulfillment of the curse. It does not, of course, imply some racial characteristic, but in any case the numerous peoples descended from Canaan according to the tenth chapter of Genesis are not described as having been condemned to any kind of servitude, and such of them as were later the inhabitants of the Promised Land were in fact prosperous and powerful.

Another episode is frequently cited as evidence that the Bible countenances the perpetual subordination of one people to another. The Gibeonites were a branch of the Hivites, one of the peoples the Israelites were presumably bidden to exterminate (I shall justify the word "presumably" in its proper place). Foreseeing the conquest of their country, the Gibeonites resorted to a ruse. They put on shabby clothing and appeared before the Israelites pretending they had only just arrived from a distant territory and were therefore exempt from the fate of the other peoples. The ruse was successful, and their lives were spared; but as soon as the deception was discovered they were condemned to be "hewers of wood and drawers of water for the congregation of the Lord," which they remained "unto this day" (Josh. 9:27). "Hewers of wood and drawers of water," like many another Biblical phrase, has become a shibboleth. What is the complete record? We do not know when the words "unto this day" were set down, but by the time of King David the status of the Gibeonites was certainly not that of hewers of wood and drawers of water. They were under God's protection because of the promise they had obtained by a ruse, and when Saul put a number of them to death Israel was smitten with a three year famine (II Sam. 21).

I return to the conquest of Canaan and what is generally described as the unequivocal divine command regarding the extermination of the seven peoples who were its original inhabitants: the Hittites, the Girgashites, the Amorites, the Canaanites, the Perrizites, the Hivites, and the Jebusites. "When the Lord thy God shall deliver them before thee, then thou shalt smite them and utterly destroy them; thou shalt make no covenant with them; thy daughter shalt thou not give unto his son, nor his daughter shalt thou take unto thy son" (Deut. 7:2–3). We have seen that the Gibeonites were not only spared, but were regarded as God's wards. Among David's thirty outstanding warriors Ishmaiah the Gibeonite was the foremost—"a mighty man among the thirty and over the thirty" (I Chron. 12:4). We have already mentioned Uriah the Hittite, a captain in David's armies, and the husband of an Israelite woman. The Jebusites were one of the seven "doomed" peoples, but it was from Araunah the Jebusite that David purchased the land for an altar, just as in the ancient time Abraham had purchased a grave for Sarah from Ephron the Hittite. The Jebusites were never driven from the land, let alone exterminated. With the conquest of Jerusalem, Jebusite territory, it might have been assumed that David would correct this "lapse." Instead, he even refused to confiscate Araunah's land, even refused to accept it as a gift.

In one striking passage, little noted, there is an overall modification of the seeming decree of extermination. "The Lord thy God will cast out these nations from before thee little by little; thou mayest not consume them quickly, lest the beasts of the field increase before thee" (Deut. 7:22).

No attempt is being made here to deflect attention from the savagery of the conquest. According to the record, cities were razed, their inhabitants—men, women and children—indiscriminately slaughtered. We look back with horror on these cruelties, and draw no consolation from their everlasting repetition throughout the ages, or their eclipse by the genocide of our own times. But in making comparisons, we must observe again that apart from the life and death need for a territory, without which it seems neither Judaism nor Christianity could have developed, the overriding principle was not racial in character. It was political and cultural. The safeguarding of the spiritual heritage would be endangered by the presence of a multitude of the original, idol-worshipping peoples. The failure to safeguard the heritage would bring down upon the chosen people the calamities *it* had visited upon the earlier peoples. There was, however, one difference, but that a fateful one. A remnant of the chosen people would always remain to renew the covenant, so that while the peoples Israel had conquered and displaced would be almost forgotten were it not for the Bible, the descendants of the Patriarchs broke through the barriers of history to continue "unto this day." It might be said that the "seven peoples" could have had no place in the human record—certainly not the Girgashites and the Hivites —had they not disappeared to make room for the creators of Judaism and Christianity.

The Jewish Bible has been widely misread—and not only by non-Jews—on the question of monotheism, and on the human capacity to recognize the One and True God. It is generally asserted that only Abraham and his descendants knew the One and True God. Such a view is flatly contradicted in several passages, which show that God-knowledge was not an exclusive, inherited or racial privilege. Very early in the history of the human species, long before Abraham, we are told that "men began to call upon the name of the Lord" (Gen. 4:26). Long before Abraham, again, "Enoch walked with God" (Gen. 5:22). The contemporary of Abraham, Melchizedek, came to meet him with bread and wine, and "he was a priest of God the Most High. And he blessed Abram [as he was still called] and said, 'Blessed be Abram of the God Most High, maker of heaven and earth" (Gen. 14:18–19). The deep impression left on the future ages by this "alien" knower of God is indicated in the words long afterwards applied to the anointed and triumphant king (David in the tradition): "Thou art a priest for ever after the manner of Melchizedek" (Ps. 110:4). But even without this confirmation it is inconceivable that Abraham should be represented as receiving a blessing in the name of any other than the True God from Whom he had already received the promise and to Whom he had already built an altar (Gen. 2).

Knowledge of God, and of the true and enduring life, was according to the Jewish Bible, open to all peoples before and after Abraham; and if they chose not to know Him, and became corrupted, so, for that matter, did the descendants of Abraham. Of Noah we read that he was "in his generations a man righteous and whole-hearted" (Gen. 6:9). "In his generations" has been hermeneutically thrown up to Noah as a sort of damning with faint praise, but that is not the plain meaning of the text, which should be read: "throughout that period."

In a way more curious than the references to Noah are those to his father Lamech, who said, when Noah was born: "This same shall comfort us [the Hebrew Noah means "comfortable"] in our work and in the toil of our hands, which cometh from the ground which the Lord hath cursed." The text therefore credits Lamech both with the knowledge of God and with belief in His mercy. Lamech, however, perished along with all others excepting Noah and his sons and daughters-in-law.

Two of the books of the Hebrew Bible stand out for their revelation of what, considering the ages in which they were written, must be called an amazing regard for the high qualities inherent in all human beings, regardless of their affiliations with any people.

It is not often remembered, or sufficiently emphasized, that one of the noblest books of the Bible, Job, is placed outside a framework of time, place or people. The land of Uz, the home of Job, is, to be sure, identified with Edom in a single extraneous reference (Lam. 4:21). It is therefore definitely not Israelite territory, and it might as well have been Ethiopia, or Babylonia, or Elam. Of Job is it written that he was "whole-hearted and upright, one that feared God and shunned evil" (Job 1:1), and no other figure in the Bible seems to have meditated so intently on the nature of God, or to have entered into such intimate argument with Him. Yet nowhere in the book of Job is there any mention of the chosen people, or of Jerusalem, or of any circumstance that might identify Job with the rest of the Biblical record. If it is something of a puzzle that the book of Esther, which contains no mention of God, and the equally secular book of Ecclesiastes, should have been admitted to the canon, it is even more puzzling that the copyists of the book of Job should have resisted the temptation to link this magnificent drama with the Jewish people. One of the most highly regarded books of the Jewish Bible, the influence of which radiates far beyond religious circles, is tacitly credited to a non-Jewish source. If the one hint is to be taken seriously, it was an Edomite, that is, a member of the people classically at war with Israel, and that since the days when Jacob and Esau struggled in their mother's womb, who made this superb contribution to Israel's sacred literature, or at least provided the material for it.

In some ways on a lower level than the book of Job, with its sublimity of discourse, and in some ways higher, in its simplicity and poignancy, is the book of Jonah. The vignette of the non–Jewish sailors brings out a humaneness, a piety, and a decency which stands in sharp contrast to the gloomy recalcitrance of the Prophet himself. One might say that Jonah is the villain of the story, the sailors are its heroes. They are not portrayed as thinkers, as meditators on God and His ways. They are simple people. That they are neither Hebrews nor converts is clearly indicated in their manner of addressing Job: " 'Call upon thy God . . . Whence comest thou? What is thy country? Of what people art thou?' And he said to them: 'I am a Hebrew, and I fear the God of heaven, Who hath made the sea and the dry land' " (Jon. 1:6–9). Jonah, who was prepared to drown rather than execute the commission God had laid on him, asked the sailors to throw him into the raging sea when the lot pointed to him as the cause of the storm; but the sailors could not bring themselves to do it. "The men rowed hard to bring it [the ship] to the land; but they could not, for the sea grew more and more tempestuous against them. Wherefore they cried unto the Lord, and said: 'We beseech Thee, O Lord, we beseech thee, let us not perish for this man's life, and lay not upon us innocent blood, for Thou, O Lord, has done it as pleaseth Thee" (Jon. 1:13–14).

After the sailors had overcome their compunctions and thrown Jonah overboard, the storm died down suddenly, and "the men feared the Lord exceedingly; and they offered a sacrifice unto the Lord and made vows" (Jon. 1:16). The legends of the Jews have it that on landing, the sailors made their way to Jerusalem and were converted; but it is difficult to see wherein their conversion could have brought them nearer to God.

Of larger significance than the exquisitely delineated episode of the sailors is the central theme of the story, dealing with the fate of Nineveh, that mighty city whose hundred and twenty thousand inhabitants were remote from the Hebrew people and its faith, but who were, within less than a generation, to destroy the northern Kingdom of Israel. The text says "six score thousand that cannot discern between their right hand and their left hand," which has led to the surmise that the number refers only to the children. But the obvious meaning is figurative: six score thousand persons sunk in ignorance, but for them God took thought, and held them capable of redemption, and commanded His Prophet to go to them and "proclaim against them, for their wickedness is come up before Me" (Jon. 1:2). As we know, Jonah rebelled against the command, refusing to fulfil his function as a prophet; and when he was compelled to apply himself to the task, he did not preach as a prophet should, he offered no alternative, he played the seer. He did not cry: "Repent and be saved"; he only proclaimed: "Yet forty days and Nineveh shall be overthrown" (Jon. 3:4). To his utter dismay the Ninevites repented and the city was spared. It does not say anywhere that the Ninevites were converted to the faith of Abraham. We only read that the king and the nobles and the people put on sackcloth and ashes and cried mightily unto God and repented and turned from their evil ways and from violence, and "God saw their works" and He "repented of the evil which He said he would do unto them, and He did it not" (Jon. 3:10).

Perhaps the most curious feature of the episode is Jonah's reason for rebelling against the mission. He did not say that as a Hebrew prophet his business was only with the Hebrews and that he would not waste his time on pagans. He may, as a seer, have pleaded that he could not be a party to the terrible role Nineveh would play in the destruction of his people. Instead he rebelled against God's inveterate habit of forgiveness, and when Nineveh was saved he all but died of chagrin. He sat outside the city and reproached God for His leniency, and explained why he had preferred to drown rather than take up his mission. "Was not this my saying when I was yet in my own country? . . . I know that Thou art a gracious God and compassionate, long-suffering and abundant in mercy, and repentest Thee of the evil" (Jon. 4:2).

Jonah was unique among the prophets in what we might call his

professional pride. When he preached doom he wanted to see it fulfilled. But he was by no means unique in having been entrusted with
a mission to other peoples than the Hebrews. The Jewish Bible holds all
peoples responsible for their actions, and therefore capable of repentance
and salvation: it applies to all peoples the same standards as to Israel,
except that it makes fidelity to the Jewish faith a condition of survival
only with Israel. In later times the distinction was more explicity formulated. Salvation was open to all peoples without their acceptance of
Judaism, and their place in Paradise was assured if they observed "the
seven laws of Noah," which consisted of prohibition of idol-worship,
adultery and incest, murder, blasphemy, robbery, injustice to one's fellow man, eating flesh cut from the living animal—no Sabbath observance, no sacrifices, no Day of Atonement, no tithes, none of the onerous
disciplines of the Jewish faith.

But the unity of humanity, the equality of potential for good and
evil among all peoples is affirmed in the equality of treatment meted
out to Israel and all other peoples. Nowhere is this more brilliantly expressed than in the book of Amos, in which we see the circle of doom
being drawn around Israel, falling first upon the surrounding peoples and
closing in upon Israel like a bracketing artillery fire: "For three transgressions of Damascus, yea for four, I will not reverse it . . . because
they have threshed Gilead with sledges of iron . . . For three transgressions of Gaza, yea for four, I will not reverse it; because they have
carried away captive a whole captivity, to deliver them to Edom" (Amos
1:3–10), and so on, for Tyre and Ammon and Moab. And finally, as
the central targets: "For three transgressions of Judah, yea for four, I
will not reverse it, because they have rejected the word of the Lord, and
have not kept His statutes" (Amos 2:4), and then Israel, "because they
sell the poor for silver and the needy for a pair of shoes" (Amos 2:6).

The word "nation" as it appears in various translations of the
Bible is only an approximation to the word 'am in the original. Nationalism as we understand the term is a modern concept. Yet it may be said
that the Jewish Bible already contains the seeds of international law,
that is, of inherent rights of peoples inhabiting a certain territory under
unified rule, and this in itself bespeaks the acceptance of the principle
of equality.

Before they advanced to the conquest of the Promised Land, the
Israelites were enjoined regarding the Edomites: "Ye are to pass through
the borders of your brethren the children of Esau, that dwell in Seir; and
they will be afraid of you; contend not with them, for I will not give
you of their land, no, not so much as for the sole of your foot to tread
on; because I have given mount Seir unto Esau for a possession" (Deut.

2:4–5). "Be not at enmity with Moab, neither contend with them in battle; for I will not give thee of his land for a possession; because I have given Ar unto the children of Lot for a possession" (Deut. 2:9). In regard to Moab the injunction continues: "Ye shall purchase food of them for money, that ye may eat, and ye shall also buy water of them, that ye may drink" (Deut. 2:6).

This carefulness, like the use of the word brethren, or brothers (*ahikhem*), is all the more remarkable in view of the traditional enmity, already referred to, between Esau and Jacob. There is, indeed, only one instance of enmity to the death between Israel and another people—the Amalekites. Of them it is written: "Remember what Amalek did unto thee by the way as ye came from Egypt; how he met thee by the way and smote the hindmost of thee, all that were enfeebled in thy rear, when thou wast faint and weary" (Deut. 25:17–18). This experience with the Amalekites seems to have left an ineradicable rancor in the folk memory, bitterer than the centuries of slavery in Egypt. We have seen how Saul was rebuked and punished for not having killed out of hand Agag the Amalekite, and it was Samuel who "hewed Agag in pieces before the Lord" (I Sam. 15:33). It was perhaps in justification of this irreconcilable spirit that later history made of Haman, who sought the total destruction of the Jews of the Persian Empire, and who has remained until this day the personification of anti-semitism, an Amalekite. But the Egyptians were to be forgiven and taken into brotherhood with the children of Israel, as we shall see.

The acid test of a people's attitude toward other peoples is its treatment of alien minorities in its midst. In the case of Biblical Israel the test was all the sharper because of the continuous temptation—to which it so frequently succumbed—to abandon the faith in favor of the less disciplined modes of life, and because of the punishment which awaited it for such abandonment. Nevertheless, side by side with the furious admonitions against letting itself be infected by foreign ways of life, a series of laws not only protected the stranger, but made him an object of solicitude, to be treated with affection.

"One law shall be to him that is homeborn and to the stranger that sojourneth among you" (Exod. 12:49). "There shall be one statute both for you and for the stranger that sojourneth with you, a statute for ever throughout your generations; as ye are, so shall the stranger be before the Lord" (Num. 15:15). "If a stranger sojourn with thee in your land, ye shall do him no wrong. The stranger that sojourneth with you shall be to you as the homeborn among you, and thou shalt love him as thyself; for ye were strangers in the land of Egypt" (Lev. 19:33–34).

Thus in three separate books of the Torah, or Pentateuch, which is so to speak the Holy of Holies within the Jewish Bible, the stranger who has settled in Israelite territory is, by unchangeable law—"throughout your generations"—placed on a footing of equality with what we should call today the citizen. Let it be noted that the stranger did not even have to become naturalized, as we should call it today. He did not accept the religion of the Hebrews, and he did not merge his identity with them. The Gibeonites and Hittites and Jebusites remained identifiable as such for centuries.

The command, "Thou shalt love him as thyself" calls for remark. It illustrates the spirit which informed social law in the Bible, distinguishing it from the social laws of other peoples of antiquity in so far as these are known. Social regulations were not, in the Hebrew view, simply mechanical adjustments. The basis of legal relations is not the efficiency of society, as in Plato's Republic. Love is the foundation of law. The stranger is not simply to be tolerated, treated with cold fairness. He is to be loved. And in one place the memory of wrongs suffered by the Israelites is turned into a lesson of compassion rather than into an occasion for resentment.

This demand made by the law on our emotions is quite incongruous with our modern ideas of jurisprudence. One cannot enact for the emotions. Such a concept was possible only when the source of the enactment was a personal God who dictated the rules of human behavior. The last court of appeal was not some human institution, but God Himself. One passage illustrates this notion with peculiar clarity: "If thou lend money to any of my people, even to the poor with thee, thou shalt not be to him as a creditor, neither shall ye lay upon him interest. If thou at all take thy neighbor's garment to pledge, thou shalt restore it to him by that the sun goeth down; for it is his only covering, it is his garment for his skin; wherein shall he sleep? And it shall come to pass, when he crieth unto me, that I will hear, for I am gracious" (Exod. 22:25–27).

The expostulation is utterly human. One might almost say that it is a man–to–man cry. The taking of interest on a loan is frowned on in all primitive non-mercantile societies—for instance Europe in the Middle Ages—where money does not beget money, and such a prohibition is not infrequent. But the emotional appeal, the call upon fellow-feeling *as part of the law,* is peculiarly Biblical. It is present in the intramural enactments for the Israelites, and in those which concern the stranger.

One quite extraordinary statute, which for some reason has not attracted the attention it merits, gave the member of an alien minority in the land the right to own Israelite slaves. "If a stranger who is a settler with thee be waxen rich, and thy brother be waxen poor beside him, and sell himself unto the stranger who is a settler with thee, after that he is sold, he may be redeemed" (Lev. 25:47–48). To get the full force of this statute, let us try to imagine a law in the former slave states permitting negroes to own white slaves.

Another statute places the homeborn Israelite who has lost all means of support on a footing with the stranger. "If thy brother be waxen poor, and fallen in decay with thee, thou shalt relieve him; as a stranger and a settler shall he live with thee" (Lev. 25:35). That is to say, he shall have all the privileges and rights of the stranger and settler. What were these? Among others, the enjoyment of what may be called the social security system of ancient Israel. "Thou shalt not glean thy vineyard, neither shall thou gather the fallen fruit of the vineyard, thou shalt leave them for the poor and for the stranger" (Lev. 19:10); and again: "When ye reap the harvest of your land, thou shalt not wholly reap the corner of thy harvest; thou shalt leave them for the poor and the stranger" (Lev. 19:9).

Participation in the religious life of the Israelites was of course forbidden to a stranger who had not entered the faith. But the moment he did so he became a full-fledged member of the chosen people, irrespective of "race" or origin. "This is the ordinance of the Passover: there shall no alien eat thereof . . . When a stranger shall sojourn with thee, and will keep the Passover, let all his males be circumcised, and then let him come near and keep it, and he shall be as one that is born in the land; but no uncircumcised person shall eat thereof" (Exod. 12:43–48). The last provision is directed at all who are uncircumcised, of whatever descent, and therefore applies to the Israelite or Hebrew, who, in a family that has strayed from the faith, has not been circumcised.

Not a legal enactment or a commandment, the prayer offered up by Solomon at the dedication of the Temple condenses into a single brief statement the overall view of the Jewish Bible on the inborn, inalienable equality of peoples and races, and the unity of the human species. "Concerning the stranger that is not of Thy people Israel, when he shall come out of a far country for Thy Name's sake . . . when he shall come and pray toward this house; hear Thou in heaven in Thy dwelling place, and do according to all that the stranger calleth to Thee for" (I Kings 8:41f.) There is no mention of conversion to the faith or acceptance of the laws and ritual, any more than in the case of the Ninevites in the story of Jonah.

Thus far we have explored the Biblical philosophy of race and peoples as expressed in contemporaneous enactments, utterances and incidents. In its vision of the far-off future, of the ultimate fulfillment of man's role on earth, the brotherhood of man is depicted without a hint of the elimination of folk identities. A world without conflicts, a world united in harmony, does not imply a world reduced to a faceless uniformity. The Bible sees all peoples as containing the same supreme potential, even in their peoplehoods, and that supreme potential is to become an unfolded reality in the recognition of God. In the time to come there will be reconciliation in equality without the destruction of identity—every identity being equally precious in the sight of God. "In that day there shall be a highway out of Egypt to Assyria, and the Assyrian shall come into Egypt, and the Egyptian into Assyria; and the Egyptians shall worship with the Assyrians. In that day shall Israel be the third with Egypt and Assyria, a blessing in the midst of the earth; for the Lord of Hosts has blessed them, saying: 'Blessed be Egypt My people, and Assyria the work of My hands, and Israel Mine inheritance' " (Isa. 19:23–24). The extraordinary relevance of this vision to our own times points up the slowness of humanity to learn and the durability of human hope. Assyria and Egypt are still enemies of Israel. The only thing that has changed is the name of Assyria, which is now called Iraq.

We come to the greatest and most famous eschatological utterance of the prophets. It occurs twice, in Isaiah and Micah. It was possibly a folk saying, a sort of anonymous prediction. In both passages (Isa. 2:2–4, Mic. 4:1–3) the nations are seen as flowing to the mountain of the Lord's house, to the house of the God of Jacob, in order to learn of His ways. God will then adjudicate the disputes of the nations. Thereafter "they shall beat their swords into ploughshares and their spears into pruning hooks; nation shall not lift up sword against nation, neither shall they learn any more war."

Several aspects of this celebrated pronouncement have a bearing on our subject. The nations shall flow to the mountain of the Lord's house. They are seen as accepting the rule of God without relinquishment of their ethnic personalities. Their submission is not to the Jewish people, but to God.

There were dreams of a universal state among the Greeks and Romans. Alexander the Great tried to create one; Virgil in the sixth book of the Aeneid foresees Rome as imposing her rule upon the world, to protect the weak and humble the strong. In both instances it was by force and conquest that the ideal was to be achieved. In the Jewish dream the word goes forth from Jerusalem, not the sword.

But the operative sentence is the last: "Neither shall they learn any more war." The belief that war is an innate necessity of man, with the implication that powerful warrior states are born to rule other states, falls away. War is something that is learned. It is not in the genes, in the blood. It is a vice that man has picked up, learned, acquired, rationalising it with the belief that rivalry is more creative than cooperation, that only the stimulus of war brings out the highest capacities of man. This belief is in essence racial, since it subordinates man to an unchangeable psychological make-up; and it is therefore natural that the most warlike peoples should be the most prone to racist illusions. Such illusions find no countenance in the Jewish Bible, or in any religion which has been organically influenced by it.

(1967)

3

POLITICS AND THEOLOGY
IN TALMUDIC BABYLONIA

JACOB NEUSNER

I

COMMON TO BOTH politics and religion is the question, 'Why should I . . . ?" The predicate contains diverse conclusions: Why should I pay taxes? Why should I obey the law? Why should I believe in God? Why should I keep the Sabbath? Why should I serve in the army? Why should I wait for the Messiah? But in both realms of human society, the claim is made that normative, not merely descriptive, statements may be made *and* enforced. That is to say, one *must* love one's neighbor, one *must* uphold the Constitution.

It is, therefore, quite natural that politicians have made use of religious emotions, myths, and institutions to provide either normative, prescriptive legitimacy for their enterprise, as in the case of societies in which church and state are united, or to gain for political institutions and symbols the charisma forthcoming from religious associations or sentiments, as in the case of societies which separate church and state. "I pledge allegiance," a political action, depends upon "under God," a religious assertion which lends a sanctity the flag otherwise cannot claim.

If this is obvious, it is equally clear that religious institutions and elites have rarely enjoyed sufficient security to eschew the support of political institutions, including the coercive, this-worldly power to be derived from them. So far as religious institutions have wanted something from people—obedience to a moral code, submission to a set of ritual taboos, confession of a theological creed—those institutions have seldom failed to make use of political means to achieve the works of the spirit.

The analysis of Babylonian Jewish politics and theology that follows is based upon my *History of the Jews in Babylonia* (Leiden: E. J. Brill, Studia Post-biblica), I. *The Parthian Period* (1965, 1969); II. *The Early Sasanian Period* (1966); III. *From Shapur I to Shapur II* (1968); IV. *The Age of Shapur II* (1969); V. *Later Sasanian Times* (1970).

46

It is, therefore, a reciprocally useful relationship. Both parties need, as I said, to move men, better yet, to provoke men to move themselves through patriotism or through conscience, to conform to the needs of the state or society, on the one hand, or to the imperatives of the divinity and his agencies on the other. Each party contributes—the one worldly force, the other legitimacy "under God" to that force. Both rely upon myth, upon a statement of ultimate reality in highly symbolic form. Whether it is the myth of the state or the myth of the holy nation, the myth of the God, or of the true meaning of meaningless, shapeless events, hardly matters. Since both politics and theology speak of ultimate concerns and make normative demands, they share common convictions of meaning or truth based upon all-embracing myth. This is, I think, why they seem so similar not only in function, but also in structure.

These observations of self-evident facts may lend perspective to the detailed examination of a specific historical example of the complex relationships between church and state—the conflict between two claims of legitimacy in Jewish Babylonia in late antiquity. The specific example has special interest, for in Babylonian Jewry in the first five centuries A.D. it was by no means clear which was church and which was state. All parties expressed their politics in theological terms, and none was divorced from political life. Within Jewry two claims of legitimacy, two justifications of authority, two definitions of the meaning of Israel's history and the way to its salvation competed, on unequal terms to be sure. If in the West church was church and state was state, and people generally knew which was which, in the ancient community of Babylonia such distinctions were hardly so clear.

II

Modern Judaism contains within itself two major theories of authority and legitimacy—Orthodox and Reform. If we approach the past without careful recognition of how we imagine it on the basis of contemporary ideas, we shall distort it more than need be. We begin, therefore, with a brief review of regnant theories of authority in contemporary Judaism.

Legitimacy in Orthodoxy now derives from the latest decisions of the Torah-sages. Such sages are men not only pious and learned but also widely accepted as pious and learned, a status partly achieved, but even more conferred by others. The Torah-sages are presumed both to know and to embody the will of God as revealed in the Oral and Written Revelation of Sinai. The oral Torah is believed to have been handed down from Moses to the prophets, then through various media to the rabbis of the Talmud who put it into writing in Talmudic and cognate literature. Afterward others came along to study and apply the law, an endless chain from Sinai to today. For Orthodoxy, therefore, the authority of the law derives from revelation at Sinai. Its practical operation is in the hands not of merely anybody who knows the law, but of the sage who qualifies himself through discipleship in the rabbinical schools and circles, through piety, through the approval of those who have gone before.

When reformers of Judaism sought to achieve changes in the traditional modes of life and thought, they could hardly hope to work within the established patterns of legitimacy, for these were so structured as to prevent articulated, recognized change. Innovation was absolutely prohibited, unless justifiable in terms of tradition. Those in charge of the tradition were selected by a process guaranteeing that innovators would gain entry with difficulty, if at all. New principles of authority and of legitimacy therefore had to be found, or change would connote disintegration. Properly justified, change could be shown to signify the will of God, not merely the outcome of expediency, convenience, or other base motives. Whether in fact the things reformers sought to excise and introduce "really" represented matters of convenience—conformity to a world Jewish men badly wanted to enter—is of no interest here. We must take it for granted that while ordinary folk may have had slight concern for the theological bases for change, they greatly wanted another way. But the elite, the intellectual virtuosi, needed justification; they had to satisfy themselves that they were serving not merely their ordinary human needs or their social aspirations, but the one true God.

Three sorts of theories presented themselves, explored within Reform and Conservative Judaism in Europe and America. The first was the appeal to reason, which meant "common sense." The second was the appeal to the will, to the social reality, of "Catholic Israel," in Schechter's infelicitous term; that is to say, the way the people, universal Israel, do things must be regarded as legitimate, for the "Tradition," often hypostatized, is borne by the community, and the community's way and the traditional *halakhah*—law, or way—cannot be thought to diverge. Social mores were thus raised to the level of normative truth; customs became commandments; ordinary, routine habits not merely achieved, but conferred legitimacy. Change proved acceptable because it had happened.

The third was to appeal to the "golden age" of the faith, to return to the true moment when revelation came forth whole, to measure all things by the heavenly model revealed "in that perfect time." Historians of religion will, of course, recognize what lies before us, namely, a peculiarly modern, post-archaic, and therefore all the more ironic, exemplum of the myth of the eternal return. Reformers in Judaism followed the excellent precedent of reforms in Christianity, based upon the way Jesus had really wanted things or upon the life of the early church. If only we can conform to the reality of that time, we shall achieve not merely "reform," but rather the true state of the tradition. What has happened since, the accretions of time, the conglomerations of profane, often regrettable history—these can be wiped away, cut off in a clean stroke. We can once more achieve true faith, and when we do, final redemption cannot be long postponed. The new messianism produced legitimacy for reform, but only incidentally, for its profound direction was clear: the New Jerusalem. If change was now justified and seemed not merely proper according to social requirement, but called for the will of God properly understood, that was a happy by-product. In 1875 Isaac Mayer Wise, founder of American Reform Judaism, predicted that by 1900 Reform Judaism would be the religion of the greater part of mankind. So grand a vision of the world, so keen a sense of introducing the eschaton, lent remarkable consequence to changes of trivialities.

The golden age was, of course, the age of the prophets, and the part of the prophetic message found truly godly was the part Jews found both reasonable and personally germane: the ethical teachings. Prophetic apocalypse was regarded as inauthentic, unless, as we saw, the prophets were still alive. The demand for justice and lovingkindness, the return to the ethically-centered faith of old, a faith without ritualism and with little ritual, without legalism and with only the law of love (which meant, more or less, to do pretty much as you liked, within the limits of the moral apothegms whose ambiguity no one then articulated) this demand, this proposed return constituted a new theory of legitimacy, a new norm for authenticity, thus a new basis for authority in Judaism. The demand for justice and mercy, moreover, conformed to the needs of European Jewry. Jews were Europe's Negroes, and Germany was their Mississippi or New York. It was only natural to suppose God's primacy requirement was to do justice, love mercy, and walk humbly with God, for these were both the very opposite of the traits of profane society, and the most necessary requirements for decent life for Jews themselves. God wanted what they required, and had so stated to the prophets; now, by conforming to that imperative, Jews might work not only for themselves, but for the Lord.[1]

III

The competing claims of normative authority, of legitimacy in modern Judaism, serve to set into perspective the religious politics of Talmudic Babylonia, for as in the recent past, so in remote times, two fundamentally different theories of authority and legitimacy presented themselves to Jewry. Like those of modern Judaism, both were based upon myth, but the myths were different, if interrelated.

Our frame of reference is Babylonian Jewry in Iranian times, that is, under the Parthian (ca. 240 B.C. to A.D. 226), and Sasanian (A.D. 226–640) dynasties. The community, perhaps half a million people, consisted of the descendants of the Judeans exiled in the early sixth century B.C. Of its culture before the first century A.D. we know practically nothing. We may take it for granted that the Jews revered Yahweh, the Temple in Jerusalem, and the Mosaic Law. The community must have possessed its own authoritative traditions on what God expected of them, and those traditions would have consisted of the Law and *ad hoc* interpretations, presumably by local priests and other sages, of its laws and theology. For the rest, we have no evidence other than the Talmud's anachronistic attribution of a fully articulated rabbinic tradition to Babylonian Jewry from earliest days. Such an attribution presupposes that Moses did indeed receive both an oral and a written Torah at Sinai, and that the oral tradition was brought, along with the written one, by the exiles. But we can hardly presuppose the historical part of the Torah-myth of rabbinic Judaism and then describe Babylonian Jewry as the rabbis later on would like it to have been from the beginning. In fact, our primary evidence, the Babylonian Talmud, was edited in the sixth century A.D., and its useful data on Babylonian Jewry pertain to the second century A.D., and afterward.

The Babylonian Talmud was, moreover, produced by the rabbis in their academies. Their viewpoint, their records, their interpretation of events predominate to the exclusion of all else. Men in antiquity did not preserve literature they believed to be false. They either allowed it to fall into oblivion, or they revised it to conform to their own ideas of what was right and wrong, of what was worth preserving. The only knowledge independent of a tendentious historical tradition reaching us from antiquity derives from archaeology. But if the texts are equivocal, the stones are silent. (In any case, apart from the Dura synagogue and the magical bowls, we have no pertinent archaeological materials.[2])

It is important to stress the Talmud's limitations as a historical source at the outset, for, as we shall quickly see, its viewpoint on the state of Jewish politics in Babylonia is one-sided indeed. As a historical record, it is approximately comparable to the faculty minutes of Harvard and Yale Universities, the record of some Supreme Court decisions, and the pious "lives" by Parson Weems. On such a basis, our knowledge of American history would not be abundant. What, moreover, should we know of American politics if we had only the platforms of the Democratic National Conventions? And how should we conceive the politics of the Republican Party on the basis of what the Democrats say in their campaign literature?

Two known competing political viewpoints were those of the Babylonian rabbis, represented in the Babylonian Talmud, on the one hand, and of the exilarch, *resh galuta,* recognized by the Iranian government as ruler of the Jewish community, on the other. Of the latter, we know, as I said, only what the rabbis reported. We have no exilarchic account of Babylonian Jewish history. We have no court records compiled and preserved by the exilarch. We do not know, except by indirection, how he explained his politics, how he justified his rule, how he won assent from Jewry.

IV

My notion of the rabbis' political theory derives at the outset from a strange story in the Babylonian Talmud (b. Gittin 62a). The story concerns a rabbinical master of the second half of the third century, Geniva, a trouble-maker who was finally put to death by the exilarch of the day, Mar 'Uqba:

> R. Huna and R. Hisda were sitting, when Geniva happened by. One said to the other, "Let us arise before him, for he is a master of Torah."
>
> The other said, "Shall we arise before a man of division?"
>
> Meanwhile he came, and said to them, "Peace be unto you, Kings, peace be unto you, Kings."
>
> They said to him, "How do you know that rabbis are called *kings?*"
>
> He said to them, "As it is said, *By me, kings rule*" [Prov. 8:15, referring to wisdom].
>
> "And how do you know that a double greeting is given to kings?"

"As Rav Judah said in the name of Rav, 'How do you know that a double greeting is given to the king?' As it is said, *Then the spirit came upon Amasai who was chief of the thirty* [I Chron. 12:18, continuing 'Peace, peace be upon you']."

They said to him, "Would you care for a bite with us?" He replied, . . .

The story of his trial and execution is as follows (b. Gittin 7a):

Mar ᶜUqba sent to R. Eleazar [ben Pedat], "Men are opposing me, and it is in my power to hand them over to the government. What is to be done?"

He drew a line and wrote to him, *"I said, I will take heed to my ways, that I sin not with my tongue, I will keep a curb upon my mouth while the wicked is before me* [Ps. 39:2], that is, even though the wicked is against me, I shall guard my mouth with a muzzle."

Again he said to him, "They are greatly troubling me, and I cannot overcome them."

He replied, *"Resign thyself unto the Lord and wait patiently for him* [Ps. 37:7], that is, wait for the Lord and he will bring them down prostrate before you. Arise early and stay late in the academy, and they will perish of themselves." The matter had scarcely left the mouth of R. Eleazar when they placed Geniva in a collar.[3]

The difficulty Geniva gave the exilarch Mar ᶜUqba had something to do with the relationship between the rabbi and the exilarch. Geniva and his party had said or done something the exilarch found extremely irritating, which led the latter, who had no capital jurisdiction over the Jews, to hand him over to the Iranian government. To support its functionary's authority, the Persian regime would properly see to matters.

Since the bulk of Geniva's reported sayings are quite standard rabbinical traditions, it is only the passage on the "double-greeting" which provides a hint of what it was he might have done, so to irritate Mar ᶜUqba. We may suppose that he had publicly declared something the academic rabbis kept to themselves, namely, that the exilarch, who judged cases according to Persian law, who derived his authority not from knowledge of the rabbinical traditions, but from the support of a heathen government, who collaborated in the affairs of that government —that such a one was not really qualified to administer Jewry's affairs, but that the *rabbis,* who were kings, ought to rule. Such a threat to the exilarchic position could have elicited one response only—to put the trouble-maker out of the way. Before that time, the exilarch would have encouraged rabbis to keep their distance from Geniva, despite his obvious mastery of Rav's traditions. Indeed, R. Huna, who was Rav's chief student apart from Rav Judah, and R. Hisda, who was Mar ᶜUqba's teacher, were well aware of the dangers of associating with the "man of division." Their respect for his learning was tempered by their hesitation to have anything at all to do with him. Geniva for his part responded by quoting traditions deriving from Rav, which they quite obviously did not know. By stressing their being "kings" he meant to point out the egregious quality of the relationship: they should not serve one lesser than themselves. They were rabbis, therefore kings, and Scripture had said so.

V

The viewpoint of the exilarch appears from a saying of one of his rabbinical adherents, Nahman b. Jacob, who lived at the same time as Geniva. He stated (in b. Sanhedrin 98b): "If [the messiah] is among the living, he is such a one as I, as it is said, *And their nobles shall be of themselves and their governors shall proceed from the midst of them* [Jer. 30:21]."

As part of the exilarchate, R. Nahman saw himself in an extraordinary light. Jeremiah refers to the time of the Messiah when the fortunes of Jacob will be restored. The restoration would be signified by the Jews' once again governing themselves. So R. Nahman implied that the rule of the exilarchate certified, and might in time mark the fulfillment of that particular messianic promise. Such a saying reflects the political theology of the exilarch. Being both scion of David and recognized governor of the Jews, the exilarch represented the fulfillment of prophetic hopes for the restoration of a Jewish monarch of the Davidic line. Hence his rule was legitimate and should be obeyed. R. Nahman's citation of Jeremiah provides one of our few glimpses into the way the exilarch explained his rule to the Jews. It shows that not merely Persian approval and support, but a wholly proper basis in Jewish genealogy and history provided the theoretical foundation of his power. By contrast, not Davidic overlordship, but obedience to the Torah, the rabbis held, would signify the advent of Messianic rule.

The Davidic origins of the exilarch were first referred to in the time of Judah the Prince, patriarch of Palestinian Jewry at the end of

the second century A.D. Judah asked R. Hiyya, a Babylonian who was
probably related to the exilarch (in b. Horayot 11b):

> Rabbi [Judah the Prince] inquired of R. Hiyya, "Is one like
> myself to bring a hegoat [as a sin-offering of a ruler, according to Lev.
> 4:23]?"
> "You have your rival in Babylonia," he replied.
> "The kings of Israel and the kings of the house of David," he
> objected, "bring sacrifices independently of one another."
> "There," Hiyya replied, "they were not subordinate to one
> another. Here [in Palestine] we are subordinate to them [in Babylonia]."
> R. Safra taught thus: Rabbi inquired of R. Hiyya, "Is one like
> me to bring a hegoat?"
> "There is the sceptre, here is only the law giver, as it was taught,
> *The sceptre shall not depart from Judah,* refers to the Exilarch in
> Babylonia who rules Israel with the sceptre, *nor the ruler's staff be-
> tween his feet* [Gen. 49.10] refers to the grandchildren of Hillel who
> teach the Torah to Israel in public."

The reference to Gen. 49:10, *The sceptre shall not depart from Judah,* is
striking, for it shows that the Davidic claim was tied to the exercise of
political authority. So far as the Palestinians were concerned, the exilarch's claim was taken as fact.

VI

The rabbis believed that, along with the written Torah, God had revealed
to Moses at Mount Sinai an oral, unwritten Torah, which had been preserved and handed on from prophets to sages, and finally to rabbis.
Israel's life was to be shaped by divine revelation. The rabbis alone knew
the full configuration of the will of God. Their claim to rule rested upon
that conviction. It thus clashed with the consequence, phrased in equally
theological terms, drawn by the exilarch from the belief that he was
qualified to rule because he was descended from the seed of David.
Moreover, rabbinic political theology ran counter to the widespread conviction of Jews that anyone holding political power over them had better be able to claim Davidic ancestry. The rabbis, by contrast, authenti-
cated *their* claim not only by their teaching of Torah, but also by their
knowledge of the secrets of creation, including the names of God by

which miracles may be produced, the mysteries of astrology, medicine, and practical magic, as well as by their day-to-day conduct as a class of religious virtuosi and illuminati. They eagerly recruited students for their schools who would join with them in the task of studying the "whole Torah," and go forth afterward to exemplify, and, where feasible, enforce its teaching among the ordinary people. They were seeking totally to reform the life of Israel to conform to the Torah as they taught it. They believed that when Israel would live according to the will of "their father in heaven," then no nation or race could rule over them, but the Anointed of God would do so. History as a succession of pagan empires would come to an end. Israel would live in peace in its own land. An endless age of prosperity on account of Israel's reconciliation with God would follow. So the issues were not inconsiderable.

"How do you know that rabbis are called kings?" The reply is, "Scripture says, 'By me kings rule'." Such was not the view of the exilarch, who wanted it to be believed that he ruled because he was an heir of David, and indeed exercised more direct control of the Jewish community than the Palestinian patriarch. It is worth quoting the entire passage to which Geniva made reference:

> By me kings rule,
> > and rulers decree what is just;
> By me princes rule,
> > and nobles govern the earth.

This passage was part of a key proof-text for the rabbinical schools, for in it, "Torah," which they believed they alone properly expounded, is described as the beginning of the works of creation, as the foundation for right politics and the sole source of righteousness, justice, knowledge. Torah came before creation, and provided the design for the world. The chapter (Prov. 8:34–6) closes,

> Happy is the man who listens to me
> > watching daily at my gates,
> > waiting beside my doors.
> For he who finds me finds life,
> and obtains favor from the Lord;
> But he who misses me injures himself;
> all who hate me love death.

It was far more than a matter of power politics. When the rabbis read a reference to the gates and doors of Torah, they knew what it meant, namely, the gates of *their* academies, and none other.

The crux of the matter was, as has been stated, how was redemption to be gained? The rabbis believed it was through a legal reformation of Israel. The exilarch and his relatives thought differently, for R. Nahman supposed that their Davidic connection ought to prove sufficient in time to produce a messiah, even in their own day, if God willed it. Redemption would proceed from the academies, or it would come from the Davidides, but the two were mutually exclusive: "All who hate me love death." The exilarchs were seen by their enemies to "hate me," namely, "Torah." Beyond the concrete issues of the day, the question of redemption smouldered in the shadows, lending eschatological significance to a politics which was, from our perspective, concerned with trivialities. "Torah" was central in the redemptive process; a legal reformation would effect "Torah" and so bring about the Messiah's coming. Had the exilarch subordinated himself to the academies and accepted their direction—as the academicians later said he did—the potential conflict between the conflicting legacies might never have been realized.

But the exilarch had a powerful claim too. He was of David's seed, and from him, or one of his relatives, would come the Messiah. That claim was probably far older and better established in the mind of Babylonian Jewry than the rabbis', and for far better reasons. The exilarch had no reason to subordinate himself to the academy, and he had very good reason not to.

VII

Which was church, and which was state? From the rabbis' perspective, it is clear that the exilarch was a merely political figure, but they were endowed with the sanctity deriving from Torah, revelation. So they would, in modern terms, have called themselves "the church," and the exilarch was "the state." And—"by me, kings rule." But the exilarch's viewpoint could not have conformed to theirs. So far as he was concerned, his rule was as the surrogate of the Messiah, indeed the best assurance that the Messiah would one day come—and would come from his own household. Israel was not rejected of God so long as she governed herself, and the exilarch's present rule was therefore proof of the continued validity of the covenant, of the enduring Messianic hope. The sceptre had *not* departed from Judah. The exilarch was *not* a secular authority. He claimed to descend from David, to be the link between the rule of David in the ideal past and the rule of David in the ideal future. The Torah-myth thus came into conflict with the Messiah-myth as the exilarch expounded it.

Nor can we say that the exilarch, a "merely political figure," was alone in making use of a religious myth for political purposes. The rabbis too sought to control political institutions—the courts and administrative agencies of Babylonian Jewry. They wanted to make use of those political institutions for religious purposes, that is, to coerce ordinary Jews to conform to the Torah as they taught it. Theirs was, therefore, a partially political aspiration.

In truth, both parties claimed to be "the church" *and therefore to be the state also.* No distinction was recognized between politics and religion. If one ruled, it was because God wanted him to do so. If another obeyed, he obeyed heaven, revelation, not merely the arbitrary fiat of a temporarily powerful individual. Society should be governed by God's law; on this, everyone agreed. The only issue was, who knows that law? And who is the one to interpret and apply it? Political argument was phrased in theological language, and only by accepting the claim of one party and rejecting that of the other are we able to describe one as "the church," the other as "the state."

Political theory obviously was subsumed under the eschatological, messianic issue: how is Israel to be saved? The rabbis' answer was phrased by R. Papa toward the end of the fourth century. He said, "When the high-handed disappear from Israel, then the Magi will cease [among the Iranians]. When the judges cease to exist in Israel, the *gezirpati* [gendarmes] will cease to exist [among the Iranians]."[4] R. Papa's saying was based upon Zephaniah 3:15, *The Lord has taken away the judgments against you, he has cast out your enemies. The King of Israel, the Lord, is in your midst, you shall fear evil no more.* Zephaniah's statement is in the prophetic present: these things come about, the Messiah is here. R. Papa transformed an unconditional promise into a conditional one: only when the one happens will the other come about.

We do not, by contrast, know the exilarch's answer. He certainly expected that some day the Lord would send the Messiah, raising him up out of the house of the exilarch, related as it was to the Davidic family. I suspect that theory, a commonplace one, represented the older political view of Babylonian, as of Palestinian, Jewry. Redemption would come in God's own time, through David's descendant. Anyone who presumed to exercise political authority over Jews had best begin with a claim to derive from the Davidic household. We know that Davidic ancestry was alleged in fact by practically every important Jewish figure in the political life of the late antiquity, including the Hasmoneans, Jesus, the Hillelite family in Palestine, the exilarch—and even Herod!

In Iranian culture, it was similarly conventional to claim to be an heir of the Achemenids. The Parthians did so, not at the outset of their rule, but only when they found that military superiority no longer could sustain the Arsacid throne. Then, in the first century, they announced they were descended from the Achemenids.[5] The Sasanians likewise stated from the very outset they were heirs of the Achemenids. They held the Parthians were illegitimate. The Sasanians were the restorers of the ancient, rightful dynasty of Iran. In fact, therefore, the claim to be descended from a remote, glorious emperor was a widespread political convention in this time. What was strikingly unconventional was the rabbis' Torah-myth and its political expression.

It apparently was not enough for anyone to claim to rule because he had power, because he was wise, because custom dictated it. Jewish politics revolved around the messianic issue. Others could obey because it was expedient or merely necessary, but Jews would listen only to the Messiah's surrogate, obey only the word of God. In the humblest details of daily conduct they sought significance of grand, metahistorical dimension. Ruling no state like other states, Jewry entered a fantasy world in which what they did control was believed to possess far greater significance, despite its worldly triviality, than even the deeds of great and impressive empires held by others: "Others are ruled by the court of Ctesiphon, by the king of kings. We obey the king of the kings of kings, the Holy One." The debate centered, therefore, on what obedience to God entailed, as I said, whether God's will was contained in the Torah of the rabbis or whether it was expressed through the rule of the exilarch, the scion of David. Theology imposed itself on politics because, I imagine, theology was all the Jews had left to render their politics worthwhile.

VIII

The two parties were not originally in conflict with one another. On the contrary, the exilarch probably fostered the growth of the rabbinical movement in Babylonia, and did so with good reason.

The exilarchate began to function effectively in the second half of the first century. Whether it was older than that—dating back to the time of Jehoiachin at the beginning of the sixth century B.C., as was commonly believed—we cannot say. But the only concrete information we have about the politics of first-century A.D. Babylonian Jewry omits all reference to an exilarch, even while discussing important matters in which an exilarch, if there was one, would have been involved. During the time of troubles of the first half of the first century, when one Parthian pretender after another seized the throne, Babylonia, like the rest of the Parthian empire, enjoyed no secure government at all. Josephus tells the story of two Jewish brothers, Anilai and Asinai, who in the chaotic times seized power in central Babylonia, ruling not only the Jewish communities but the whole area.[6] They set up their own government which lasted for nearly two decades.

The time of troubles began to abate with the rise of Vologases I. While the indecisive struggle between Parthia and Rome, ending in about 65 A.D., may have weakened his government, it appears that a number of constructive efforts must have curbed the power of the nobles and established a secure frontier with both Rome and Armenia (Roman preoccupation in Palestine from 66–73 was a factor), for Vologases I achieved something unknown in Parthia for more than half a century: he held power through several decades and avoided both foreign disasters and internal strife. His foundation of Vologasia, near Seleucia-Ctesiphon, doubtless greatly assisted the expansion of the silk trade with the east, on the one hand, and Palymra on the other, and the increasingly profitable trade probably provided new financial resources for the throne.

If the story of the Jewish "barony" in and around Nehardea is historical (and there is no reason to doubt it), then the central government must have had to give considerable attention to the government of this numerous ethnic minority. The very position of the great areas of Jewish settlement required it, for the Jews formed a large segment of the settled population around the winter capital of Ctesiphon, the Greek city of Seleucia, and the new emporium at Vologasia. The Jewish population surrounding the heart of the empire must be suitably governed. From the events of ca. A.D. 20–36, it must have been clear to the re-forming administration that Jews in Babylonia were not adequately governed.

What choices were open to the Arsacid authorities? They could, of course, ignore the problem, and allow events to take their course in the Jewish territories and settlements. This was manifestly unsatisfactory. They could, second, attempt to include the government of the Jewish ethnic groups within the territorial sovereignties of other places. The

Jews about Seleucia could have been under the Greek authorities of that
city (as doubtless those *in* the city itself were). But this course of action
would have been unsatisfactory for three reasons. First, the Greek cities
were not the regime's most loyal adherents. Second, the Jews and Greeks
got on no better, according to Josephus's narrative, than they did in
Alexandria. Third, the Jewish settlements were too extensive for incorporation into surrounding political units, while at the same time they
were not sufficiently compact or concentrated to form a separate unit
(this appears from the Greek massacre of Jews after the fall of the
Asinai-Anilai barony). An ideal solution would have been the establishment among the Jews in Babylonia of an *ethnic* authority of their own,
like that which probably existed after the destruction of the first temple
in Babylonian and in Achemenid times.

If such an authority could develop and win the loyalty of the
Jewish population to the Arsacid regime, then the Parthian government
would accomplish three useful purposes. First, it would assure an effective government in the Jewish villages and towns and over Jewish
minorities in the Greek and Iranian settlements. Second, it would secure
the peace of strategically vital territories near the capital. Third, in time
it might make use of the authority so constituted for its foreign policy,
by exploiting the Jewish authority's connections with Jews in Roman
Palestine. There is every evidence that some Jews in Palestine and
throughout the upper Mesopotamian valley did act in a manner favorable
to Parthian interests at a number of crucial points in the second century,
particularly in the time of Trajan's invasion in 116–17, the war against
Antoninus Pius and Marcus Aurelius in 161–65, and against Severus
Alexander in 193–200. It would have been very much in the interest of
the Parthian government, in its period of reorganization under Vologases
I and afterward, to found, or to encourage and support the foundation
of, a Jewish ethnarch, or exilarch, in Babylonia.

A further factor likely played a part in Parthian consideration of
the Jews' administration. The destruction of the Temple in Jerusalem in
70 posed a serious problem to the Parthian government. In former times,
Babylonian Jewry, like that in other parts of the diaspora, was loyal to
the Temple. Pilgrims went up to Jerusalem, and Temple collections of a
half-*sheqel* were gathered regularly in Nehardea, in the south, and in
Nisibis, in the north, and forwarded in armed caravans to the Temple.
The Temple authorities, for their part, sent letters to Babylonia, as did
the Pharisaic party, to advise the Jews on matters of calendric regula-
tion and other religious issues. After the destruction, the authority of

the Temple was assumed by the remnants of the Pharisaic party at Yavneh, where, with Roman approval, the powers formerly exercised by the Temple administration became vested in R. Yohanan ben Zakkai and R. Gamaliel II after him. The Parthians enjoyed the services of an excellent intelligence bureau, and must have known that the Palestinian Jewish authority would no longer be exercised by quasi-independent officials, but would be very closely supervised by the Romans.

If the Parthians had been willing to allow a limited, and on the whole politically neutral, authority to be exerted from the Jerusalem Temple over their subjects, they would never permit such authority to be exerted by a Roman functionary. Quite to the contrary, just as the Romans sought to mobilize Jewish support and to use Jewish officials for their own purposes, so the Parthians exploited the fact that within their hereditary enemy's territories flourished a large religious-ethnic group with strong ties across the Euphrates and a deep sense of grievance against Rome. They always tried to foment unrest among minority groups within the Roman Empire. The Romans, for their part, were keenly aware of the danger of leaving substantial ethnic groups to straddle their borders; for this reason they invaded Britain and attempted to retain Armenia in the preceding century and a half. They were, moreover, deeply concerned about Jewish public opinion in Parthia, and therefore hired Josephus to convey their view of war guilt to the Jews across the Euphrates.

Though the evidence that the exilarchate was actually created at this time is slight, it ought not to be ignored. First, Josephus's narrative contains no hint of an indigenous Jewish authority in Jewish areas of Babylonia before A.D. 40. On the contrary, the silence of Josephus on this point is made very striking indeed by his testimony about how the Jews actually *were* governed at this time, namely, by Asinai and Anilai. If there *was* an exilarch between A.D. 20 and 40, there is no evidence that that fact mattered in the slightest. He certainly did not exert any authority or affect events in any way.

There is, however, some evidence that after 70 A.D. an exilarchic line was founded. This evidence appears in the list of exilarchs of the *Seder ᶜOlam Zuta*. Among those from the time of the first destruction of Jerusalem to 70 A.D., the *Seder ᶜOlam Zuta* preserves no names or traditions worth taking seriously, and one may conclude that its eighth-century author had no reliable information on the subject. But its list after 70 includes names that are attested in other sources. The text gives the names as follows:

And at this time Shemaiah died. And there arose after him Shek-
henaiah his son, who is the tenth generation of Jehoiachin the King
at the time of the destruction of the Second Temple. . . . Shekheniah
died and Hezekiah his son arose. Hezekiah died and was buried in the
land of Israel in the valley of Arabella in the east of the city. 'Aqov
his son arose. 'Aqov died and Nahum his son arose after him. There
were sages with him, their names being Rav Huna and Rav Hinena,
Rav Matennah and Rav Hananel. Nahum died. After him arose Yohanan his brother, son of 'Aqov. His sage was Rav Hananel. Yohanan
died. After him arose Shefet his son. Shefet died. 'Anan his son arose.
When 'Anan died Nathan remained in his mother's womb. He is
Nathan of Zuzita, *Rosh Golah* [exilarch]. Nathan died. After him
arose Rav Huna his son. Rav and Samuel were his sages.[7]

Since Rav and Samuel date from the end of the Arsacid period, we may
conclude that the above list covers the period from ca. 70 A.D. to ca. 226.
Without examining the list in detail, we may suggest that at least some of
the names on it, particularly Nahum and Huna, find support in earlier
sources, and that the tradition recorded in *Seder ᶜOlam Zuta* may well
imply the beginning of sound information on an actual institution sometime in the latter half of the first century.

The exilarchate in Parthian Babylonia, like the patriarchate in
Roman Palestine, was the most convenient means to manage a potentially useful ethnic group's affairs at home and to exploit its connections
abroad. It was, as I said, most certainly a way of annulling whatever influence Jewish functionaries of Rome might exert over Babylonian
Jewry, by providing an alternate, home-born authority, supported and
closely supervised by the government. Both the exilarch and patriarch
were backed up by imperial troops, R. Judah having a detachment of
Goths at his command, the exilarch an armed retinue, and both eventually achieved great spiritual influence over their respective Jewish communities. Both were created in part because of the destruction of Jerusalem: the patriarchate as a means of governing internal Jewish affairs in
which the Romans had no special interest and at the same time of keeping the peace in Palestine; the exilarchate to do the same in Babylonia.
At the same time both were intended to prevent aliens from influencing
Jews under their control, and themselves to exert malevolent influence
across the frontier where possible.

In the second century, the exilarchate developed into a powerful
instrument of government with its agents enjoying the perquisites of the
Iranian nobility. It inflicted the death penalty and governed the Jews by

its own lights, enforcing its judgment with military force when it chose. If the several Jewish revolts against Rome, at times highly propitious from the Parthian viewpoint, were in fact instigated by its agents, and if the support given to the Arsacid throne in the crisis of Trajan's invasion was, in a measure, the result of exilarchic influence, then the Parthians must have judged the exilarch to be a great success indeed. By the end of the second century, the exilarch R. Huna was regarded with a mixture of respect and apprehension in Palestine, where his claim to Davidic ancestry in the male line, superior to R. Judah's allegedly in the female line, was recognized. Among the Jews and Parthians alike, the exilarchate played a major political and administrative role.

IX

The Babylonian Jews' first contact with the Pharisaic-rabbinic movement *may* have antedated the Bar Kokhba War by a century. But the movement first established its characteristic institution, the rabbinical academy, during that war. Refugee sages, fleeing the terrible struggle and its aftermath, settled in Babylonia. The school of R. Ishmael probably remained. What is of interest to us is the exilarch's relationship to the rabbis. It is clear that Nathan, son of the exilarch, was sent to school under rabbinical auspices, and later continued his studies in the Palestinian schools as well. Several other Babylonians in the Palestinian schools, including R. Hiyya and his sons and his nephew Rav, were probably related to the exilarch. The evidence thus points to the existence of a few Tannaim *from* Babylonia, and a few others *in* Babylonia, in the second century. Generally those who lived *in* Babylonia were colleagues or disciples of R. cAqiba and R. Ishmael before the Bar Kokhba War. Those who came *from* Babylonia were normally exilarchic relatives. When law-teachers came to Babylonia, the exilarch must have provided the means for conducting law schools, just as he had sent his son, and was to send his relatives later, to study in the Palestinian schools of the same sort.

The development of Tannaitic Judaism in Babylonia, therefore, was probably encouraged by the exilarch in his effort to secure well-trained officials. How shall we account for the pro-rabbinical sentiment of the exilarch? I suggest that the exilarch must have had to contend with other Jewish authorities, such as powerful local figures like Anilai and Asinai. These potentially dangerous competitors for the rule of Jewry were seen to be "assimilated" to Parthian culture. Babylonian Jewish officials such as Arda, Arta, and Pyl-i Barish[8] were "Parthian" in many ways, though very good lawyers. They were upper-class Jews who possessed wealth and influence, much as did the exilarch himself. One good way of circumventing their influence over the ordinary Jews, who could have had much less contact with Parthian politics, court life, and, therefore, general culture, would have been to present the exilarch himself as the protagonist of the ancient tradition of Moses, against the Iranized Jewish elite competing with him for power.

The ancient tradition of Moses was pretty much what one wanted it to be. But how to establish such a public "image"? How better than to associate oneself with the Palestinian rabbis, whose prestige had been rising ever since the destruction of the Temple, and who could send disciplined, learned, and charismatic rabbis to serve the exilarch, build his administration, and bolster his claim? Those rabbis, alleging themselves knowledgeable in the Mosaic law and accredited with wonderful powers over nature, were believed to be holy men. They thus could lend prestige to the peculiar political claim of the exilarch.[9] Against such holy men, what could local strong-men, powerful upper-class leaders offer? If, as I have suggested, the exilarchate was a relatively new institution, and if the Parthian government, which created it, was unable because of the terrible invasions and unsettled domestic conditions of the second century to provide necessary support, then the exilarch would have had his hands full simply establishing his preeminence over other, older kinds of local Jewish authorities. The Palestinian rabbis, as well as those Babylonians who might be trained by them, provided a ready and inviting means of setting up an effective and "legitimate" administration.

The rabbis thus served to enhance the legitimacy of the exilarchate, by providing stronger theological foundations for the exilarch's political power and by attesting to the validity of his claim to be descended from David. Their learning, holiness, and magical powers won the assent of ordinary people to their legal and exegetical doctrines. They were useful to the exilarch, for they could give him what he lacked, both a means of influencing the ordinary people, and a source of administrative talent and local leadership. For their part, the rabbis were prepared to collaborate with any political leader who would give them power over Jewry to achieve their religious program. Together the rabbis and exilarch might outweigh the competing, centrifugal forces constituted by older, local grandees of various sorts and in various places.

By the turn of the third century, the Tannaitic movement in Babylonia included a few local authorities, such as the father of Samuel in Nehardea, and a larger number of trained and authorized representatives. It hardly dominated Babylonian Jewish life and posed no threat whatever to the exilarch, who made use of Tannaim for his purposes and was probably glad to have more of them. The exilarch must have provided the chief source of financial support for the schools and of employment for their graduates. He was equally eager to accept the credentials of Palestine-trained rabbis, and to authorize newcomers to serve in his system of courts as lawyers, judges, and communal administrators.

The exilarch, moreover, was particularly anxious to employ men who could apply in Babylonia the newly-promulgated Mishnah just now issued in Palestine by the patriarch, Judah the Prince. Whatever old traditions and *ad hoc* decisions existed in Babylonia, the new Mishnah, based upon a viable and supple exegetical method, organized according to logical categories, and, most important, advertised as the very will of God revealed along with the written Torah by God to Moses at Mount Sinai and transmitted from that time to the present by faithful prophets, sages, and rabbis, had an irresistible appeal. Still a relatively new institution, the exilarchate must have been glad to associate with itself and its administration so grand a prestige as accrued to the Mishnah in the minds of those who accepted the Pharisaic-rabbinical claim.

Among these were the exilarch's own son, his relatives, and others close to him. He, too, was therefore probably a believer. The exilarch claimed to be of the seed of David. How better to win the loyalty and conformity of ordinary people than to couple that claim with the equally impressive one: "In the Jewish courts we at last apply not merely the scattered, though hoary, traditions of our forefathers of the *golah,* but the whole revelation of Sinai itself." In the decades after the revelation and promulgation of the Mishnah by the patriarch in Palestine, the exilarch gladly accepted its authority, and therefore hired men who would apply it—under *exilarchic* auspices to be sure. The Tannaitic movement, small and possessing little influence and authority in Babylonia to begin with, received the enthusiastic backing of the exilarch, who had earlier sent representatives to the Palestinian schools. Whatever other schools there were must have either ceased to exist or have begun to teach the Mishnah and its accompanying traditions, exegetical methods, and rules.

The Tannaim responded in kind by ruling that it was only with the authorization of the exilarch that one might judge cases in Jewish Babylonia. "Authorization" in rabbinic discourse meant actual bureaucratic appointment by the exilarch, and so an alliance was forged between the rabbinate, needing political support, and the exilarch, requiring prestigious and qualified functionaries.

One recalls the parallel policy of the Safavids of the sixteenth and seventeenth centuries. Coming to power as sectarian enthusiasts, the Safavids assembled doctors of the Shi'ite law from their places of refuge in the Moslem world in the time of Ismail Safavi (ca. A.D. 1500). As W. H. McNeill describes it:

> Not surprisingly, it proved easier for the court and the Shi'a doctors to agree upon what should be suppressed than upon details of positive doctrine. The shahs were reluctant to surrender any of their prerogative, even to men of religion; and Shi'a purists found it hard to forgive the remaining imperfections of even the most sympathetic regime. . . . Acquiring a reputation for miraculous powers and familiarity with God's will, these Shi'a doctors attained great influence over the people at large, until their opinions came to constitute a fairly effective check upon the actions of the shah himself.[10]

It would be difficult to find a better analogy to what was about to happen in Jewish Babylonia. The exilarch assembled, encouraged, and gave great powers to the doctors of Pharisaic-rabbinic law, which was, according to the rabbis, to be the only law of Judaism. The learning, charisma, and magical powers of the rabbis rendered them ever more influential over ordinary people, so that by the beginning of the fourth century, the exilarch found himself with a diminishing range of powers and options, ever more narrowly hemmed in by rabbinical influence, which was, by nature, inimical to his.

X

The practical conflict between the exilarch and rabbis may best be described in terms of an issue debated in the early fourth century: Do rabbis pay taxes?

The exilarch imposed taxes, divided them among Jews of various towns and groups, collected, and transmitted them to the state on specified occasions. It would hardly enhance his authority if he could not impose his will upon everyone, including the rabbis. Choosing to make the payment of the poll tax the decisive issue, the rabbis asserted that they were not like other Jews, but formed a special class, which should not be subjected either to the authority of the exilarch or to the control of the state. It was the rabbis who raised the issue for reasons of their own. For his part, the exilarch saw no reason to change the status quo of two centuries' standing.

Why did rabbis choose just this time to claim they did not have to pay taxes? In part, the reason was that they were convinced they had no other correct course, and in part the time seemed promising. From Shapur I's death in 273, to the end of the minority of Shapur II, in about 325, the central government was distracted by, among other things, disastrous foreign wars, the suppression of the Manichaeans, dynastic struggles every few years, and finally the centrifugal effects of the weak regency. When Shapur II came to power, his attention was drawn to international and military issues. The Sasanian government in his time never paid the Jews much attention, so long as the revenues were forthcoming, and nothing subversive happened. Both conditions were met. The rabbis' subversion was not directed at the Sasanian government. So long as the full quota of head taxes was paid, it hardly mattered to the state who actually paid them or who did not. Greater affairs of state must have occupied not only Shapur, who certainly was not consulted on trivialities such as these, but also the ministers of Ctesiphon. The Jewish question was a local matter without much consequence. Had they seen otherwise, the ministers of Shapur would have been perfectly well prepared to investigate anti-government activity and punish those they thought guilty. The same satraps and Mobads who tortured the Christian monks and nuns, priests, bishops, and laity of Babylonia and Adiabene for not paying taxes were quite capable of persecuting the rabbis, if not the Jews as a group, had they thought it useful to the security of the state. They did nothing of the sort and I suppose they saw no reason to. Once the great persecution against the Christians began, moreover, the exilarch could hardly have called to his aid those whose capacities for bloody mischief now stood fully revealed. Had he asked for state aid in suppressing the rabbinate as a class, he would have embittered the ordinary Jews against himself, and the record of rabbinical martyrdoms, accompanied by the conventional miracles done by both heavenly messengers and earthly saints, would have rendered him totally distasteful to common folk. Under normal circumstances ordinary people might have supported him, but not in a time of the martyrdom of a few particularly holy men. It seems to me, therefore, that the exilarch at first was unwilling, and then quite unable to enlist the powers of the state. And the state, unknowing and uninterested, paid attention to quite different matters. Still, in such a circumstance it was a chancy thing. The rabbis took that chance.[11]

The exilarch was perfectly well prepared to grant unusual favors to the rabbis as an estate. They had special privileges at court; they were given advantages in marketing their produce. The exilarch was quoted as instructing Rava to see whether a certain man, claiming rabbinical status and therefore privilege, was really a scholar. If so, Rava was to reserve a market-privilege for him, so that he might sell his produce before others.[12] Since the rabbis staffed exilarchic courts, it was certainly advantageous to protect them.

The rabbis' claim to be exempt from the poll tax, or *karga*,[13] was quite another matter. The exilarch could not exempt rabbis from the poll tax, for he would have had to make up the deficit himself. One of the principal guarantees of continued peace for the Jewish community was the efficient collection of taxes, which was the responsibility of the exilarch. All he could do was to shift the burden of taxes to others, so that the rabbis' share would devolve upon ordinary Jews. He naturally was not ready to do so, and I do not think ordinary people would have wanted him to. The tax rates were so high that poor people struggled to find the money to pay them. References abound to people's selling their property, or themselves into slavery, to raise the necessary money. The state was not prepared to compromise, for on its part it simply could not afford to do so. War was necessary to protect its territory, including first and foremost Babylonia itself. Armies cost money. Everyone must help pay, particularly those who lived in so rich and fertile a region. Moreover, those living closest to the capital were least able to evade the taxes. So the exilarch could hardly accede to the rabbis' demand. The Persians would not allow it; the ordinary Jews could not afford it.

The rabbis' claim of tax-exemption was phrased in comments upon Scripture. They were certain that from most ancient times, rabbis were not supposed to pay taxes, and it would be a transgression of Scriptural precedent if they now did so. Rava held that King Asa was punished simply because he imposed forced labor (ᵓ*ngry*ᵓ) on the sages of his day, citing the following Scripture, "Then King Asa made a proclamation to all Judah; *none* was exempted" (I Kings 15:22).[14]

Rava's comment was merely a warning. A more positive claim was made by R. Nahman b. Isaac (b. Bava Batra 8a):

> R. Nahman b. R. Hisda applied the head-tax to the sages.
>
> R. Nahman b. Isaac said to him, "You have transgressed against the teachings of the Torah, the Prophets, and the Writings. Against the Torah, as it is written, *Although he loves the people, all his saints are in your hand . . .* [Deut. 33:3].
>
> "Against the Prophets, as it is written, *Even when they study* [lit.: Give] *among the nations, now I shall gather them, and a few of them shall be free from the burden of king and princes* [Hosea 8:10].
>
> ['Ulla said, this verse is said in the Aramaic language, 'If they

all study, now I shall gather them, and if a few of them study, they shall be free from the burden of king and princes.']

"Against the Writings, as it is written, *It shall not be lawful to impose upon them* [*priests and Levites*] *minda, belo, and halakh* [Ezra 7:24], and Rav Judah explained, '*Minda* means the portion of the king, *belo* is the poll-tax, and *halakh* is the ^c*annona*'."

The several Scriptures are not of equal weight. The passage in Deuteronomy suggests that "his saints," who, the rabbis thought, were rabbis, were in God's hand. Therefore, they do not require the protection of walls or armies and should not have to pay for them. Likewise Rav Judah had said that everyone must contribute to the building of doors for the town gates except rabbis, who do not require protection.[15]

The meaning of the passage in Hosea is quite clear: when the Jews study the Torah among the gentiles (i.e., in Babylonia), a few should not have to pay taxes, and these, quite obviously, are the rabbis. 'Ulla's comment changes the eschatological sense of the verse, but the prooftext is clear as it stands. The citation from Ezra explicitly states that priests do not have to pay the "portion of the king" or the poll-tax. What was not made explicit, because everyone in the schools knew it, is that the rabbis believed they had inherited the rights and privileges of the priesthood, since study of Torah was now equivalent to the priestly offerings in Temple times. Therefore, according to Artaxerxes' order reported by Ezra, rabbis do not have to pay the head tax. This was quite explicit in Scripture, and beyond question. Even the Iranian government should not impose the poll-tax on them, they supposed. The following saying of Rava is extraordinary (b. Nedarim 62b):

> Rava said, "It is permitted for a rabbinical disciple to say, 'I will not pay the toll-tax,' as it is written, *It shall not be lawful to impose minda, belo, or halakh* [Ezra 7:24], and Rav Judah said, '*Minda* is the king's portion, *belo* is the poll-tax, and *halakh* is the corvée'."
> Rava moreover stated, "A rabbinical disciple is permitted to say, 'I am a servant of fire and do not pay the poll tax'." What is the reason? It is only said in order to drive away a lion.

Rava's remarkable saying that a rabbinical disciple may lie to evade the poll-tax, and even deny that he is a Jew, tells us nothing about what would have happened had he done so. The tax collectors in the Jewish community were Jews, not Iranians. What Rava has in mind is a Jew's telling the Jewish collector that he is an apostate. There may be an implied threat, that "if you do not leave me alone, I shall become a servant of fire." I doubt that Rava imagined a rabbinical disciple would so assert before a Mobad, who knew full well how to assess such a claim. His thought was that it is so wrong to collect the poll-tax from rabbis, that the disciples may perjure themselves and even pretend to commit overt apostasy. It is a very strong assertion, so extreme that I can hardly imagine anyone's attributing it to Rava had he not actually said it.

XI

We do not know what the exilarch said or did, for rabbinical sources, which are the only sources we have, do not tell us. If Torah, Prophecy, and Writings are brought to testify, and public apostasy theoretically was permitted to a rabbinical disciple, one can hardly suppose that rabbis were not under pressure. The greater likelihood is that they paid their tax but resisted as powerfully as they could through their most effective weapons, namely, ascription of their tax exemption to Moses, Hosea, and Artaxerxes, and publicly announcing permission to evade the taxes even by committing the worst sin they could think of.[16] I can only conclude that the exilarch exerted such pressure, because he both had and wanted to. The vehemence of the rabbis' traditions on the subject must be interpreted as evidence of his success.

We do not know whether R. Nahman b. Isaac actually managed to intimidate R. Nahman b. R. Hisda, or, as I said, whether *any* young rabbinical disciples in fact lied to the tax-collectors. We do know Shapur's police executed Christian tax-resisters. Since we have absolutely no evidence of "martyrdom" among the rabbinate on account of non-payment of taxes, I feel sure there was none. The rabbis protested, but they must have paid. To the exilarch, that would have been all that really mattered. But the rabbis would have been embittered because they not only lost money, which would have bothered the poorer ones, but also were forced to transgress their religious convictions about their own rights and privileges. Their view of the sanctity of the rabbinate is clear. They were the "saints" in God's hand. It was a sin for them to pay the poll-tax, and it was a greater sin still for the exilarch—heir of David and Asa—to force them to do so. Asa had been punished for imposing the corvée upon the rabbis. What they hoped would happen to the exilarch in the time to come, one may only imagine.

The exilarch had publicly to respond to the criticism and disloyalty of hostile elements in the rabbinate. I should suppose his response would have taken the form of propaganda no less venomous than the rabbis'. He would have stressed, to begin with, the fact that he was descended from the house of David, for that was the foundation of his politics. He would, moreover, have alluded to the cost to others of the rabbinical tax exemptions. Not only would the rabbis not pay their fair share of the rising imposts, but some of them even solicited funds, quite separate from those accruing to the Jewish government, for the support of schools which the exilarch in any case paid for. The rabbis wanted to establish a second Jewish government, which the Persians would never allow. "In these troubled times, when Christians are giving evidence of what happens to minority-communities that fall afoul of the state, it will not pay to solicit Persian hostility!" The condition of the Jews themselves provides the best testimony to the soundness of exilarchic rule. "Consider the fact that others are persecuted. Jews are secure. Chaos reigns everywhere, but at home, order, or, as much order as responsible government can bring when faced with such dissident, provocative elements." Hostility must have been directed against the rabbis on account of their indifference to the condition of Jewish slaves.[17] The exilarch could therefore have concluded his message by asking, "How many wish to enslave themselves to pay heavier taxes so that rabbis may now enjoy the full benefit of their private, fantastic, and self-serving Scriptural exegesis? Not all rabbis, to be sure, but only a minority of them are guilty of such intended subversion. Most of them," the exilarch would have concluded, "remain loyal to the house of David and its living representative." So the exilarch.

Three centuries earlier, Yohanan ben Zakkai, a Pharisaic leader, excluded from the bastions of power and displeased with the Temple's administration of its holy office, had found a suitable polemic in the words of Qohelet 4:18, *Guard your foot when you go to the house of God and be ready to hearken.* . . . He said that it was better to listen to the words of the wise than to offer the sacrifices of fools,[18] meaning the ancient priesthood. Now his words found an echo in the saying attributed to Rava (b. Berakhot 23a):

> *And be ready to listen.* Rava said, "Be ready to listen to the words of the sages, for if they sin, they bring an offering and carry out penance. *It is better than when fools give.* Do not be like fools who sin and bring an offering, but do not do penance."

Rava stressed that even sages may sin, but if they do, they repent and seek reconciliation with God. We do not know, of course, of any polemic, such as I have imagined, directed by the exilarch against rabbis. Rava's exegesis is quite outside of a historical context. Yet it would have been an evocative and appropriate response to such an indictment as the exilarch might have lodged against his opposition.

XII

The history of the conflict between the exilarch and the rabbi did not end in the middle of the fourth century. During the next fifty years, the exilarch was able to reassert complete control over the rabbinical schools. At the same time, however, he made certain that his functionaries and heirs received an excellent rabbinical education. So he capitulated, in effect, by becoming a rabbi himself—as in the case of Huna b. Nathan. But he also made certain that the schools where Jews became rabbis remained under his very close supervision. We can therefore designate no true victor. The rabbis rabbinized the exilarchate. The exilarch in the end exercised substantial control over the rabbinate. And all suffered in the common disaster during the reign of Peroz, when both leading rabbis and the exilarch believed the Messiah would come in 468—four hundred years after the destruction of Jerusalem—and foolishly acted upon the consequences of that belief. Jewish government was wiped out. But that is another story.[19] It was an ironic denouement. The rabbis followed the exilarch's messianism and endorsed it. If, therefore, the exilarch was "rabbinized," the rabbis were "messianized." The two theories were united; the two parties perished together.

Jewish theories of legitimacy, authority, and politics took one form after another over the next sixteen centuries. Yet whatever the guise, the Messiah-myth and the Torah-myth recurred again and again as if the presence of the one imposed upon the opposition the necessity of espousing the alternative. So the eschatological emphasis of Reform Judaism a century ago came into conflict with the stress of Orthodoxy on the tradition and its authority deriving from Sinai. What are the equivalent theories today? Where shall we find the contemporary Torah-myth, the living Messiah-myth? These questions, too, require study, perhaps a few centuries from now when the dust has settled.

(1969)

NOTES

1. See my "From Theology to Ideology: The Transmutations of Judaism in Modern Times" in *Churches and States. The Religious Institution and Modernization,* ed. K. H. Silvert (N.Y., 1967), pp. 13–51).

2. See my "Archaeology and the Jews of Babylonia," in *Near Eastern Archaeology in the Twentieth Century,* edited by J. A. Sanders (New York, 1970), pp. 331–47.

3. That is, he was imprisoned and was being brought out for execution.

4. Babylonian Talmud, Sanhedrin 98a.

5. See my "Parthian Political Ideology," *Iranica Antiqua* III, i: 40–59; Józef Wolski, "The Decay of the Iranian Empire of the Seleucids and the Chronology of Parthian Beginnings," *Berytus* XII, i (1956–57); 35–52; his critique of Elias J. Bickerman's "Notes on Seleucid and Parthian Chronology," *Berytus* VIII, ii (1944): 79–83. On the Sasanians, Richard N. Frye, *Heritage of Persia* (N.Y., 1963), pp. 198ff. The *Kar Namak* of Ardashir, among other sources, relates that Sasan was a shepherd, descendant of the Achemenids. On the Davidic claim in general, Y. Liver, *Toledot Bet David* (Jerusalem, 1959).

6. Antiquities XVIII, 310–79.

7. See W. Bacher, "Exilarch," *Jewish Encyclopedia* V: 288–93; Felix Lazarus, *Die Häupter der Vertriebenen,* in *Jahrbücher für jüdische Geschichte,* 1890; S. W. Baron, *The Jewish Community* (Philadelphia, 1942), I, 68–69, 145–50, 173–86, 192–93, III, 12, n. 12. The list of exilarchs before 70 is obvious a *midrash* of some kind on I Chronicles 3. But the names afterward begin to make sense. Jacob Liver, *Toledot Bet David,* pp. vi, viii, 141–47, and 28–46, discusses the uselessness of the earlier traditions, but he does not reject those relating to the period after A.D. 70. On the contrary, he holds (p. 44) that the data on the two or three generations before Rav Huna are of some value. He notes (p. 147) that the Davidic claim was a post-factum effort to legitimize authority held already, parallel to the Achemenid claim of the Arsacids. If so, the claim would have been advanced ca. 50–150 A.D., for by the time of R. Judah the Prince and R. Hiyya it is spoken of with great respect. This was approximately the same time that the Arsacids themselves were publicizing their Achemenid genealogy. Baron holds that the failure of Josephus to mention this office is not conclusive, as it affords at best an *argumentum e silentio.* But Josephus is not silent at all about the inner life of the Jewish community in Babylonia at this period. See also S. Funk, *Die Juden in Babylonien* (Vienna, 1910), I: 31–41; Y. I. Halevy, *Dorot Ha Rishonim,* II: 246–52. Lazarus discusses the phrase about the scholars at the side of the exilarch, pp. 16–17. It is likely to be an echo of a later polemic.

8. These are "Parthianized" Jewish officials who made trouble for Palestinian rabbis in mid-second century Babylonia, see b. Gittin 14a-b; Neusner, *History,* Vol. I, 2nd ed., pp. 94–97.

9. On the rabbis as holy men, see my "The Phenomenon of the Rabbi in

Late Antiquity," *Numen* XVI, i (1969): 1–20; and "The Ritual of 'Being a Rabbi' in Later Sasanian Times," *Numen* XVII (1970): 1–18.

10. *The Rise of the West* (N.Y., 1965), p. 679.

11. On the control of the schools, Neusner, *History,* Vol. IV, pp. 91–100, 119–24.

12. b. Bava Batra 22a.

13. See Geo. Widengren, "The Status of the Jews in the Sasanian Empire," *Iranica Antiqua* I (1961): 149–53.

14. b. Sotah 10a.

15. b. Bava Batra 8a.

16. Confessing "fire-worship" would have been seen by ordinary people as public apostasy. Since the rabbis had long insisted a Jew should die rather than commit murder, sexual crimes, or public apostasy, this must have been the worst sin the rabbis could imagine for such a situation.

17. Neusner, *History,* Vol. III, pp. 24–29.

18. See my *Life of Rabban Yohanan ben Zakkai* (Leiden, 1962), pp. 44–45.

19. See Neusner, *History,* Vol. V, 95–105. See Markham J. Geller, "Jesus' Theurgic Powers: Parallels in the Talmud and Incantation Bowls," *Journal of Jewish Studies* XXVIII, 2 (1977): 141–55. Geller contributes nothing new and seems to think he is the first to discover these altogether familiar materials, an unfortunate example of slovenly perusal of the available scholarly literature.

4

THE AMERICAN COLONIAL JEW
A Study in Acculturation

JACOB R. MARCUS

M ID-TWENTIETH-CENTURY AMERICAN JEWRY is the largest Jewish
community in the world. Ancient Israel in her palmiest days
sheltered but a fraction of the millions that are now to be found
in America's largest cities. Where did these people come from?

The first American Jews originated in Europe. By the sixteenth
century, most Jews in Western Europe had been forcibly deprived of
their ancestral faith and identity; an indeterminate number had been
driven underground as crypto-Jews. In Central Europe many had been
killed or expelled from their homes, and some had migrated eastward,
beyond the Oder River, into the towns, villages, and hamlets of sprawling
Poland. The Thirty Years' War, which wracked the Germanies during
the 1600s, brought the East Europeans additional emigres, but in 1648,
when that tragic struggle came to an end, new conflicts—beginning with
the revolt of the Cossacks—broke out in the Slavic lands. For the first
time in centuries, then, the tide of immigration began to move not eastward, but westward.

There was no choice for the Jews; they had to turn west, for
Russia was closed to them, and Western Europe had begun to take on a
new lease of life. Modernism was dawning there politically, economically,
and culturally, and the states between the Pyrenees and the Oder River,
seeking to rebuild themselves along national mercantilist lines, were now
more sympathetic to immigrants with skills. Men and wealth were
needed to speed the Commercial Revolution and to people the new
colonies in the Atlantic basin. Venturesome Jews from East European
lands moved into Germany, Holland, and England, and Iberians of
Jewish ancestry crossed the Pyrenees into France or sailed for Amsterdam, Hamburg, and London. Most Jews who wandered into this new
and rehabilitated Western Europe were happy to remain. They could
anticipate a promising future. A few, however, spilled over into the
American colonies.

Actually, "Jews"—people of Jewish origin—had been settling in the Western Hemisphere since at least the early 1500s. The very first Marranos came with Columbus, and in less than a century they had spread throughout the Caribbean and found their way into Mexico (New Spain) and South America, but the Inquisition made it impossible for them to establish viable communities. It was not until the mid-1600s that the first overt Jewish settlements sprang up in the New World—in Dutch Brazil and Surinam, on Curaçao, and on English Barbados and Jamaica. These were soon to become large and cultured metropolitan communities, for the Caribbean basin was at the time far more attractive and more populous than the mainland provinces to the north. The most important American Jewries of the eighteenth century were to develop in Surinam and in the Islands.

When the Portuguese recaptured Brazil, a handful of Dutch Jews, fleeing north, found refuge in the Dutch trading colony of New Amsterdam, soon to become English New York. Their arrival on the Hudson in 1654 represents the beginning of North American Jewish life. These twenty-three Jewish "Pilgrim Fathers" were followed during the next hundred years by immigrants from the Islands and from Spain, Portugal, France, Holland, Germany, and England. By 1730, Jews of Central European origin outnumbered their Iberian coreligionists in North America. The first settlers in the 1600s were characteristically traders who had little desire to remain, but a permanent community had been established by the turn of the century. The Jewish businessmen married, settled down, and began to raise families. Throughout the colonial period, however, American Jewry would remain an essentially immigrant group. Up to the Revolution, some 70 percent of the presidents of the New York synagogue were foreign-born, and the men who assumed leadership of colonial American Jewish life were, with one notable exception, all immigrants. Many of the emigres were competent merchandisers. Some of them had distinguished rabbinical ancestors; a few were unassorted misfits. The community's growth is reflected in the fact that there were about 250 Jews on the continent by the year 1700, whereas, by 1776, there were about 2,500. Jews never formed more than one-tenth of 1 percent of the colonial population.

What prompted Jewish newcomers to set sail across the Atlantic? Was it a quest for religious freedom? The fact is that even the Dutch exiles from Brazil and the Spanish—Portuguese emigres of converso ancestry who fled the Iberian Peninsula were not drawn to North American shores primarily for the sake of conscience; all of them could have found a haven in other lands, and if they came here, it was more often than not to better themselves economically. Nearly all of them sought, in addition, a measure of anonymity, an avoidance of public notice, for without exception they came from lands which still imposed disabilities on Jews and still enforced anti-Jewish laws of a medieval character. It is understood, of course, that these men would not have come to these shores if they had not been allowed to practice their faith. The immigrants took it for granted that they would be permitted to establish a community of their own.

Where did they settle? Some, to be sure, were found in the hinterland, but even they had trickled into the backcountry through the seacoast towns. Most Jews stayed well below the piedmont, in the tidewater areas. New Amsterdam–New York was the first and chief Jewish center, but only a short generation after the Brazilians arrived, a small settlement took shape at Newport, in the 1680s at the latest. That Rhode Island community did not last even a decade, however, and it was not until the 1740s that the New Yorkers, fanning out once again, reestablished Jewish life in Newport. Jewish newcomers, moving north, rarely bypassed the Rhode Island city; they tended to ignore Boston; apparently one center in New England sufficed them. That same decade of the 1740s saw the New Yorkers, in their southward trek, lay the foundations for a community at Philadelphia. Independently of New York, Charleston Jewry also established itself in the 1740s. Savannah, which had sheltered a substantial number of Jewish colonists in the 1730s, had already lost her first Jewish group by 1740, but, like Newport, would ultimately rebuild a durable Jewish settlement on the dead hopes of earlier emigres. After the French and Indian War, New Yorkers moved up the Hudson and Lake Champlain to found a new congregation in Montreal.

It is obvious that nowhere in the fourteen provinces were Jews qua Jews ever openly denied the right to strike roots. By 1740, they were allowed the exercise of virtually every economic immunity and privilege. Not that such rights were obtained without a struggle! The Dutch in New Amsterdam, under the medieval-minded Stuyvesant, sought to deny them nearly all rights; yet it took no more than three years for them to wrest from the governor and his superiors in the Dutch West India Company the right to remain, to trade, to own land, and to hold worship services in private. These rights were extended under English rule, so that, even before the coming of the new century, England had, however reluctantly, accorded her American Jewish subjects full civil equality. In

1740, an imperial naturalization law confirmed the status of the Jew and
offered him almost unlimited economic opportunity in the Empire as a
whole as well as in the American provinces themselves.

Civil equality was not, of course, political equality. Jews in some
colonies were certainly allowed the vote on a provincial and a local level,
but they were nowhere permitted to hold honorific office. Such office was
limited to Protestant Christians, especially those associated with the
dominant or established church in each colony. On the whole, prior to
the 1760s, the American Jew eschewed politics. Fourteen hundred years
of Christian-imposed disabilities had taught him that political plums like
lucrative offices were not within his reach, but this disability does not
appear to have disturbed him before 1765. After all, the constant wars,
the country's expanding economy, and the penetration of the West enabled the Jewish businessman to make a good living; he was simply too
busy building an estate for himself and his family to concern himself
with the fact that political appointments were denied him.

Still, when he was offered important communal committee assignments, he would seem to have gladly accepted them. Almost every town
had some Jewish merchants of substance and wealth, and in the English
world of mercantilism, the Jewish businessman, even if he could not sit
in the Assembly, on the bench, or in the provincial council, was undeni-
ably a part of the power structure. In Continental Europe, he could not
have aspired to authority in the general community, for Jewry as an
ethnic corporation was segregated by tradition and by the terms of
separatist and divisive *privilegia*. The colonial Jew, however, followed
the developing pattern of English Jewry; he aspired to enter the general
society within the ambit of a common unitary political system. He was
not averse to office, to its opportunities, and its responsibilities, nor was
he indifferent to the improvement of his status. Ultimately the Jew here
hoped to become one, politically at least, with the emerging American
people and to be accepted as a full fellow-citizen, but he was willing to
bide his time. And his hopes achieved fulfillment, if as yet mainly on the
federal level, in 1789.

The Jew of eighteenth-century America found his greatest opportunity in the world of commerce. Here, much more so than on the
Continent, or even in England, he was almost exclusively a shopkeeper.
To be sure, there were occasional dirt farmers in the northern provinces,
and even an aristocratic planter on the South Carolina frontier, but
farming was not the metier of these immigrants. Georgia Jewish merchants might hold good-sized ranches in the backcountry, and craftsmen,
especially silversmiths, might be found in nearly every province, but the

typical Jew was a businessman who owned a small shop. There he doled out credit to the customers who came to him for hardware, hard liquor, and dry goods. The successful shopkeeper became a merchant, and large-scale Jewish storekeepers were established even in the villages of Canada and as far west as Lancaster, Pennsylvania. The Montreal businessmen were primarily fur entrepreneurs, and Lancaster's outstanding merchant was well known as a supplier for the traders on the Ohio.

The important Jews in commerce were the tidewater merchant-shippers of Newport, New York, and Philadelphia. They exchanged American foods and forest products in Europe and the West Indies for consumer goods and for Caribbean staples like molasses, rum, sugar, and dyewoods. Sometimes, like the Jew who was Newport's commercial tycoon, they would participate in the African slave trade. Jewish merchant-shippers of that day were also industrialists, arranging through the put-out system for the manufacture of ships and barrels, the distillation of rum, the catching and processing of fish and whales, and the production of kosher and unkosher victuals for export. Above all, they were in the candle business. Indeed, it is no exaggeration to say that they constituted an important national factor in the manufacture of candles. Jews, however, were notably absent from the iron and tobacco industries, and though they included in their ranks substantial merchant-shippers, the total volume of their business, while it far exceeded their proportion to the population, was hardly determining in any field. The one exception, it might be said, was army supply: The most powerful Jewish commercial clan of the third quarter of the century was an Anglo-American family of army purveyors which reached its zenith during the French and Indian War. Like its Jewish counterparts in Europe, this clan carried on business operations reaching, at the very least, into the hundreds of thousands, if not millions, of pounds.

It may be fairly maintained that all but an infinitesimal number of North American Jews were to be included in a broadly-conceived middle class. Some Jewish merchants were even wealthy by contemporary standards; practically none of the Jews were paupers, very few were proletarians, and a substantial number were lower-middle-class petit bourgeois shopkeepers and middle-middle-class storekeepers and merchants. There were very few Jews who did not enjoy a degree of comfort; most of them made a "good living" and survived economically, though severe business reverses were by no means uncommon among them at some time or other.

The colonial American Jewish community could be accurately described as a socioreligious group—or even a religiosocial group—whose members had grown up, for the most part, in the small towns of pre-industrial Europe. Though they stopped to make no sharp distinctions between the religious and the secular, their orientation was definitely religious, and they were typically synagoguegoers. On their arrival here, they had immediately undertaken to set up de facto communities whose hub was, in every case, the house of worship. It was in a literal sense a meetinghouse. All newcomers were expected to join, to become paying members, or at least to attend the important services. Local Jewry was granted no state authority to compel membership, but social pressure generally saw to it that affiliation would be practically compulsory.

Even though religious devotions were undoubtedly held in every Jewish settlement as soon as the requisite quorum of ten adult males thirteen years of age or older could be mustered, the synagogue was not actually the first institution to be established. The first formal act was usually the acquisition of a plot of ground for a cemetery. Then came the synagogue. First the worshippers would rent a room, then a house; then they would purchase a building, and, finally, they would erect a synagogue of their own. The synagogue-communal organization was of the simplest type, featuring a president, a small board, and at times a treasurer. Frequently, the overburdened chief executive served also as secretary and treasurer; the major administrative duties were his. No rabbis—that is, no ordained, learned, professional officiants—were employed in North America prior to the second quarter of the nineteenth century. Colonial Jewry had no need for the services of experts to teach rabbinic lore to advanced students, or to sit as judges to adjudicate complex commercial disputes and matters touching on marriage, divorce, and estates. The chief salaried—or volunteer—officiant in every house of worship was the cantor who chanted the liturgy. His ministrations were complemented by those of the shohet, who slaughtered food animals ritually, and the beadle, who served as the omnibus factotum for the board. These functionaries were certainly not overpaid, and all of them engaged in some form of gainful enterprise, on the side, to augment their incomes.

The liturgy employed by all the colonial conventicles was the Sephardic or Spanish-Portuguese. Despite the fact that prerevolutionary American Jewry was overwhelmingly Ashkenazic (German–Polish) in ethnic origin, the Sephardic style had become the traditional American rite. Services were almost always held on the Sabbath and on all the holidays, though the difficulty of assembling ten busy adults often made it impossible to organize daily services. Ceremonial and ritual observance was expected of all Jews, even of those who lived in the backcountry,

and the communal leaders attempted to exact conformity by threatening
ecclesiastical punishments. The board was—or at least attempted to
be—an authoritative body exercising discipline in religious matters over
every confessing Jew in the region, but, unlike some of the Protestant
sects, there was no effort to exercise surveillance in business concerns or
even in the area of personal morals.

In the extant budgets of the country's chief synagogue, the largest
items were salaries, pensions, and relief for the poor. It is true that
congregants squabbled among themselves, often bitterly and vindictively,
but generous provision was nearly always made for the needy and the
impoverished. The Jews took care of their own. Itinerants from the
distant Islands were "dispatched" back home at communal expense;
Palestinian visitors were generously entertained and given gifts; and
aspiring petitioners were granted modest loans to set them up in business.
The sick received medical care, nursing, and hospitalization; the old
were pensioned, and all the dead were buried at the expense of the community or for a purely nominal fee. Most Protestant groups also attempted to take care of their poor. Whether the Jews did more for their
people than, for instance, Protestant sectarians like the Quakers, is difficult to determine, though a comparative study of budgets might answer
this question.

Only to a limited degree was education associated with charity.
Since the local community always included members who lacked the
means to educate their children, the synagogal authorities never failed to
provide a subsidized teacher for the children of the poor. Actually, however, the responsibility for providing instruction was the obligation of
the head of the household; it was not a communal responsibility. Beyond
question there had been private Hebrew instructors in New York City
ever since the seventeenth century, and a communal Hebrew school was
organized during the 1730s, at the latest, with all who had means paying
tuition. Not all the children in the community had resort to the congregational school. Even in New York City—and this was certainly true of
all the other Jewish communities as well—secular education was also
acquired in private schools or through tutors.

The curriculum of the congregational school probably included the
reading and translation of the prayer book and the Pentateuch, and at
most some familiarity with the classical biblical commentaries. By the
1750s, this Hebrew school had become an all-day "publick school"
teaching Spanish and the three "Rs"—what we might call a "parochial"
school. The language of instruction was English. The quality of the
teaching in Hebrew was probably not too bad, for the first American-

trained cantor is known to have had the capacity to consult the more
elementary Hebrew codes. We have no way to gauge the quality of the
instruction in "English reading, writing, and cyphering," but, since all
Jewish children, even the humblest among them, were prepared for some
form of business life, it may be assumed that the training the young
natives acquired was adequate. Male immigrants with very few exceptions were literate. They could read English, write it phonetically at
least, and keep a set of books. All were bilingual, for they knew English
and Yiddish or German, or English and Spanish or Portuguese. A few
had a third language at their command—Dutch, for instance—and some,
if not many, were multilingual.

Exceedingly few young people were tempted to attend the country's
colleges, although secondary schools were open to them in Rhode Island,
New York, and Pennsylvania. Most colonial Jews were not interested in
the liberal arts as such, and professional training in law and medicine
was not sought. The practice of medicine was not particularly lucrative,
while lawyers were in bad repute throughout much of this period, and,
if English precedent was determining, Jews would not have been permitted to practice in the courts. Prior to 1776, the American Jew wrote
nothing in English worth preserving as a literary monument. The typical
colonial synagoguegoer, an immigrant, was too busy learning the language and making a living to achieve any facility or distinction in
English letters; he could make no contribution even to the Jewish, let
alone American, literary arts.

What did their neighbors think of the Jews? Every Christian who
came to these shores brought with him "invisible baggage": his European and pagan traditions going back for millennia. The West India
Company in New Amsterdam never hid its distaste for Jews; the New
York rabble, headed by a "gentleman," attacked a Jewish funeral cortege
on one occasion, and the desecration of cemeteries was not uncommon.
"Jew" was still a dirty word, and it was hardly rare to see the Jews
denigrated as such in the press. A distinguished lawyer speaking in the
New York General Assembly did not find it too difficult to rouse his
fellow-members against the Jews as a people guilty of the great crime of
the Crucifixion.

Rejection does not tell the whole story, however, and one always
does well to bear it in mind that, if the Jewish businessman prospered in
this land, it was because the Gentiles patronized him. Jews did not make
a living by taking in each other's washing. There can be no question that
the Jews here found more acceptance than in any other land in the
world. Old-World traditions of Judeophobia were attenuated here. The

Christian drama of salvation—a drama in which the Jew played the villain—was not dominant in moulding public opinion in the colonies, for America offered everyone opportunity enough; there was no need to envy the Jew. In a society of Dunkers, Congregationalists, Moravian Brethren, Baptists, Christian Sabbatarians, Catholics, Methodists, Anglicans, Presbyterians (Old Side and New Side), Lutherans, Dutch Reformed, German Reformed, Mennonites, Schwenkfelders, a society of English, Scottish, Irish, German, Dutch, Welsh, Swiss, and Swedish settlers—not to mention Negroes and Indians—the Jew did not stand out too conspicuously. Christians in the villages and towns of the country discovered, sometimes to their dismay, that the Jews did not wear horns and that, if they had devil's tails and cloven feet, these were certainly not visible. The Christian who learned to know Mr. Judah, or Mr. Josephson, or Mr. Hays, or Mr. Gratz found that, after all, he was not so different, and the Jew was accepted. If he became a son-in-law, he was welcomed; he was a fine fellow.

The Jew was accepted, but did he accept America? What was this man like? What was happening to him on this side of the Atlantic? Was he different here? What had he gained for himself? What did he do for others, for this country which generously gave him a haven and a new home?

Apparently he was still the same "eternal" Jew, still the European traditionalist, equally untouched by deism and by Protestant religiosity, whether of the decorous Anglican kind or of the less conventional emotionalism of the Great Awakening. Yet he *was* different, if only because he found himself in a different milieu, and this was bound to influence and change him. It was not simply that, instead of speaking Yiddish or a bad German, he now spoke fractured English and dressed like any middle-class Englishman. This young American Jewish community of which he was a loyal and exuberant member shaped itself on a "frontier" far removed from the European *Judengasse* and its age-old classical traditions. The New World challenged his Old World. In order to survive here, the Jew found it expedient to extemporize, to compromise, and all this, in the final analysis, spelt a form of emancipation. Europe had never offered him more than a second-class citizenship; here in America, however, he encountered less paternalism and a more sympathetic government. Here, after 1700, he had full civil liberties and even a degree of civic recognition. By 1775, he had come very close to achieving first-class citizenship.

America connoted economic opportunity, and this was of paramount importance: "Bread to eat and a garment to wear." He was no

longer a peddler, a petty trader, a cattle dealer; he was now a shopkeeper, even a merchant. If only because of the "wealth" he was often
enough enabled to accumulate in America, he became something of a
community figure. Here he could rise on the social ladder; he could
improve his status and even enter into the world of Anglo-Saxon education and culture. Here the Jewish heritage reached out to absorb a new
language and new ideals: "democracy," "natural freedom," "dictates of
humanity," "constitutional trial by jury," "to live free or not at all,"
"rights, liberties and immunities." He had acquired a new vocabulary.

When the Jew left Europe, he left behind him there—physically at
least—the all-pervasive authority of the Jewish community. Ultimately,
his departure from the European home was to effect a measure of
spiritual distance as well. If Jewish orthodoxy in its most classical form
was to be found then in Poland, the Jews of these colonies were as remote from it physically as a sailing vessel could carry them. America
signified the ultimate frontier of Jewish life. Religious controls were inevitably relaxed here. There was much less concern about observance
and ritual. The individual was far freer to do as he pleased. He could if
he wished—and most commonly he did wish—pay much less attention
to the rabbinic learning which, for a thousand years, had been the leit-
motif of European Jewish life. The new American Jew, who was beginning to emerge on the colonial scene, much preferred to be a successful
merchant than a talmudic scholar. Yet this very Jew was not estranged
from his faith, and the communities which studded the North American
coast from Montreal to Savannah are eloquent testimony to his determination not to abandon his heritage.

The typical colonial Jew was true to his heritage because he was
not pressed to be untrue to it. There was no overwhelming, monochro-
matic culture here to force itself upon him. There was no national ethos
to exact conformity of him. If he acculturated, it was by his own choice.
Free here to express his religious loyalties, since the outside world imposed no religious limitations upon him and extorted no price of emancipation, he assimilated almost unwittingly and without hesitation. Slowly
but surely he sloughed off Europe. He felt completely at home here. The
Jewish immigrant—and this was very probably not characteristic of him
alone—manifested an aptitude for acculturation and even for total integration. Bear in mind that he had come originally from a Portuguese
city, a German *Dorf,* or a Polish hamlet; yet, when he appeared as an
urban businessman, he was already an urbane American. He had speedily
become acquainted with English amenities and often had even acquired
an Anglo-Saxon name. If he finally settled in a colonial village, it was

usually only a matter of time before he married a Christian and permitted his wife to rear his children as she thought fit. But conversion to Judaism, formal or informal on the part of the woman, might also occur, though with much less frequency. In a way, it is astounding how easy it was for many an observant European Jew to foreswear in a few years nearly twenty-seven centuries of hallowed tradition—seemingly without a struggle.

The Jew *was* different here. He had left the "ghetto" to become a pioneer on the American "frontier," a frontier which according to Frederick Jackson Turner gave its people

> coarseness and strength combined with acuteness and inquisitiveness; that practical, inventive turn of mind, quick to find expedients; that masterful grasp of material things, lacking in the artistic but powerful to effect great ends; that restless, nervous energy; that dominant individualism, working for good and for evil, and withal that bouyancy and exuberance which comes with freedom.

For Turner, the frontier which effected these changes in the American psyche was the "Great West." Yet a moment's reflection will remind the student that these enumerated characteristics bespeak the successful American businessman, Jew or Christian. Think of Thomas Hancock! Certainly for the professing Jew—who was never to become a backwoods hunter or an Indian fighter—all of America was a frontier. If to be a frontiersman is to be a man who dares to hazard, then the Jews as a whole are America's urban frontiersmen par excellence. As a group, they are, more than others, a "nation of shopkeepers," gambling with their future. (Actually, of course, the Diaspora Jew had always lived as a marginal man on the "cutting edge," where he had to struggle for survival juridically, commercially, and spiritually.) The Western frontier is in no sense important for the development of the American Jew; the Atlantic frontier is all important. It was determinative in changing him. It gave him his greatest opportunity in centuries to give free play to those traits which he had already brought with him and which had long been characteristic of him.

For the Jew, the style of life was different here. He learned to dispense with Slavic obsequiousness and Germanic servility. There was no need for him here to be submissive. Here he could be assertive—if that was his nature. If he possessed physical courage, America offered him ample opportunity to manifest it. He learned not to be easily cowed. Is there any doubt that it required moral courage to cross the broad ocean and to traverse the lofty mountains and the dark forests to distant Michilimackinac or the Forks of the Ohio? For the first time in centuries, the Jew felt free. He was no longer faced with the problem of treading softly in the presence of a virulent Judeophobia. It may have been hard for him, but he began to trust his Christian neighbors; he became less suspicious of them. They were his customers; often enough they were his partners in business ventures, and he learned to believe in them, for there is no intimacy greater than that of two men who are prepared to share profits and losses.

The Jew of the European village who could only dream of a great future had the chance here to prove his mettle. He could be venturesome, daring, and enterprising. Here there was an open road for the man of ambition. It was not ludicrous here to project gargantuan schemes. No one looked askance at the Christian-Jewish consortium which proposed to establish a western colony of millions upon millions of acres. America was one land where, more than any other, the Jew could fulfill his inmost self by attempting whatever career he wished. Here he could be an individual. With opportunity and achievement and the regard of others came self-respect and dignity. The Jewish merchant was conscious of his own works; he knew what he was doing for the land and the people—and it was good in his eyes. He was giving and getting. He had the pride of a merchant, and he expected recognition, not only socially, but in rights and in privileges.

It is undeniable: The American Jewish businessman *was* more than a European who dressed and spoke like an Anglo-Saxon. His children, too, were different. The father may have been a Spaniard or a Pole or a native Briton, but the children through intramarriage with Jews of other backgrounds were something new. This was a Jewish melting pot which fused together the Jews of half of Europe's lands to produce a new ethnic type—an "American" Jew. This American Jew "in becoming" struck a balance between his European religiocultural loyalties and his emotional identification with the spirit of this land. In Europe, he had been an outsider; in this land, he blended with the others. Here there were a dozen different breeds and stocks pouring into one another to become one in a common environment with common interests. This man was among that dozen, and though he would never have admitted it, he was becoming less of a Jew and more of an American.

In 1711, a number of New York's Jewish businessmen generously contributed to the building of an Anglican church; some fifty years later, the Jews of Savannah were active in a nondenominational charitable society. Such participation by Jews in American philanthropy can take on meaning only if we remember that in most European lands at that time the Jew was still held in disdain and that in some countries he was even outlawed and in danger of massacre. But here in the colonies, he believed, he knew, that he was part of the body politic. It is true that he had his own way of life, but, unlike others, particularly some of the Germans, he never locked himself behind the walls of a cultural enclave. Of course, he was fully conscious of the fact that he was not yet a first-class citizen. He realized it only too well, but his resentment never impelled him to withdraw into himself. He was very much moved by the political unrest of his neighbors and shared their hopes. Like all dissenters and all who labored under legal disabilities, he was not satisfied with the status quo; he sought more rights and more opportunities. A large measure of freedom had already been accorded him, but the Revolutionary spirit of the 1760s unleashed in him the desire for an even larger measure. It was this hope that prompted Jews to throw in their lot with the Whigs. By 1775, even many of the most recent newcomers thought of themselves as Americans, and "as a man thinketh in his heart, so is he."

By 1776, the typical Jew in this land was an urban shopkeeper of German provenance in the process of blotting out his German ethnic past. Yet he was firmly, proudly, and nostalgically rooted in his European religious traditions. He spoke English by preference, had regard for Anglo-Saxon culture, and enjoyed the same civil rights as did his Christian neighbors. Socially, he was a cut above the masses, the farmers and the mechanics, for he was a shopkeeper or merchant. As such, he expected—and he received—a measure of deference.

What did this man achieve for himself? He moved Europe across the Atlantic, no mean achievement. Synagogues, schools, charities, a "community" were transferred here, nailed down and fastened, firm and viable and visible enough to attract hundreds and thousands of others who never would have come to a "waste howling wilderness" where there were no Jewish institutions. A dozen families in seventeenth-century New York laid the foundations for a twentieth-century community of nearly six million Jews. Colonial Jewry wrote the pattern of acculturation which made it possible for the Jew to remain a Jew and to become an American. The pioneers of the eighteenth century succeeded in making an exemplary transition from a still medieval European Jewish life to the new American world of modernism and personal freedom.

What did this man achieve for the land? Not that this Jew was conscious of it, but together with all dissenters—and every American

denomination suffered disabilities in one or another of the provinces—
he helped teach his neighbor religious tolerance. The fruit of this tolerance was respect for the personality of the individual. The prerevolutionary Jew made no contribution to the literature of the colonies; he
cleared no forests and ploughed no furrow—yet he, too, built the land.
He, as much as any other, made American life more comfortable through
the necessities and luxuries which he provided. It is true that the trader
needed his customers, but it is equally true that neither city craftsmen
nor toiling rustics could exist without him. It is true, too, that in a literal
numerical sense the Jew was one man in a thousand, but, in an economy
where an overwhelming majority of all who labored made their living on
the soil, it is difficult to overstress the importance of the shopkeeper and
the merchant.

(1967)

5

AMERICAN IMPACT
Judaism in the United States
in the Early Nineteenth Century

LOU H. SILBERMAN

ON NOVEMBER 21, 1824, a group of members of *Kaal Kadosh Beth Elohim* (The Holy Congregation, The House of God) in Charleston, South Carolina, met together "for the purpose of petitioning the Vestry of the Hebrew Synagogue for such alterations and improvements in the present mode of Worship as would tend to perpetuate pure Judaism, and enlighten the rising generation on the subject of their Holy Religion." The petition in the form of a Memorial to be presented to the Public Adjunta—the self-perpetuating governing body of the Congregation— was sent to the President of the Congregation on December 23, 1824. On January 10, 1825, the Memorial was returned to the "Chairman of Convention and Committee" by the Secretary of the Congregation with a covering letter in which he reported that the President had submitted it to the Private Adjunta—an executive body elected from the Public Adjunta or the general membership—and had declared that the Memorial was contrary to the Constitution of the Congregation, hence undebatable. If the memorialists complied with the constitutional regulations, their memorial would receive "due and proper attention." On January 16, 1825, the members of this "respectable convention," faced by their inability to fulfill the constitutional requirements for petition, *viz.*, signature of two-thirds of the subscribing members exclusive of the members of the Public or Private Adjunta, decided to found a Society that would devise means for carrying out the intentions stated in the Memorial. A month later, on February 15, a Constitution for such a Society was adopted and signed by forty-three members.

This Society bore the resounding name, *The Reformed Society of Israelites for promoting true principles of Judaism according to its purity and spirit.* It was not, in the beginning, contrary to a widespread opinion, a new congregation. The formation of another congregation in

Charleston was prohibited by the Constitution of K.K. Beth Elohim, and there is no evidence that the members of the new Society contemplated withdrawal from Beth Elohim. In about 1826, however, having failed to accomplish its purpose, the Reformed Society decided to establish a new synagogue and solicited funds for the erection of a building. This latter project was never carried through. However, by 1830 the Society had prepared and published a new prayerbook in accordance with its principles. Three years later, in 1833, the Society was dissolved. Seven years following this, in 1840, when the issue of reform was raised again, K.K. Beth Elohim, which had rejected the Society's proposals, now began to move in the direction of the new ideas, and the tendency espoused by the Reformed Society, although not its exact position, now triumphed.[1]

This bare recital of facts describes, so far as we know, the first public corporate response on the part of a Jewish community, or at least a sizable fraction of one, to what we must speak of at present, for want of a more detailed description, as the American situation. This point, that the response was public and corporate, deserves our initial attention, if we are in any way to understand the facts before us. A demographic account of the growth and development of the Jewish community from the establishment of the first congregation in 1654 to the founding of the Republic discloses that at the latter date there were no more than three thousand Jews (at the very upper limit) in the nascent United States, out of a total population of some four million, *i.e.,* the Jewish population was less than one-tenth of one percent, a dilution of less than one in a thousand. These individuals were gathered for the most part in a few cities: New York; Newport, Rhode Island; Savannah, Georgia; Philadelphia, and Charleston, South Carolina. The basic problem of the communities was continuity—the preservation of inherited forms and structures, if not ideas—in the face of the all but engulfing environment. Single individuals and families, of course, responded to their situations in various ways, creating their own private patterns of adaptation, but there is no evidence that the institutions of Jewish life found it necessary formally and officially to undertake programs of adjustment and change. They remained committed unquestioningly to the institutional structures brought over from the Old World, however their members may have privately varied from them.

In the fifty years following the founding of the United States, the Jewish population increased four hundred percent, so that by 1840 there were some fifteen thousand persons, but again in a population of about seventeen million, so that the ratio remained approximately unchanged. During these fifty years, however, the frontier had moved westward. Jewish communities were now to be found in Louisville, Cincinnati, Cleveland, and New Orleans among other areas, and in circumstances and situations even more remote from the European pattern than those prevalent on the eastern seaboard. Once again it is evident that the adjustments, the adaptations and the changes that took place during this half-century remained private and individual. The communities had no other paradigm than that remembered from Europe. This it was they sought to follow. Yet it was easier said than done. The institutions, organizations, patterns, procedures, the very expectations in the political, economic and social order that had existed on the European scene, and had thus more or less guaranteed continuity and stability, were non-existent on the American scene. Little was fixed and immutable in the rapidly shifting American social order that might support and buttress fixity and immutability within Jewish life. The Revolution had challenged basic presuppositions in major areas of human living; the fluidity of the frontier kept forms and conventions from crystalizing quickly.

In religious life this was as true as elsewhere. The Federal Constitution had rejected religious tests for office-holders. The Bill of Rights had prohibited an establishment and had guaranteed religious freedom. Traditional theological formulations were under attack; older structures of church government were either decaying or being discarded, or at least being refashioned to meet the new and unexpected conditions of an expanding nation breaking new ground, figuratively as well as literally.

The Calvinism of New England was reeling under the onslaught of Unitarianism, as yet more a theological mood than an institution. Presbyterian and Congregational forms of church government were mingling and seeking modes of mutual adjustment. Restorationism, the demand for a return to the primitive New Testament church and the end of denominationalism, creedalism, sectarianism, found expression and support in several quarters. Independency and ecumenicity were somehow bedfellows in the great camp-meetings of the period.[2]

It is important thus to recognize what Timothy Smith has pointed to, the interrelatedness and interpenetration of the waves of religious interest and the "tensions resulting from rapid social change, the determination of large numbers of religious leaders to do something about them and the persistence among the mass of ordinary men of the simple ideas of evangelical religion."[3] All of this leads us back to our point of departure and a consideration of what were the dynamics of the situation out of which the Reformed Society of Israelites emerged in Charleston in 1824. In 1800, Charleston had the largest Jewish community in the United States. At the time of the events under consideration, there were approximately six hundred persons in the congregation, but it had been overtaken and was soon to be outstripped by New York City. Size is not to be overlooked in our discussion for it means that the impact of the environment was directed not toward more or less isolated individuals making their own private adjustments but toward a significant body within which there could emerge a group of like-minded men. Such a group could then, in terms of a shared response, attempt a formulation of Jewish religious life that was not limited to private solutions but looked toward and even demanded public, that is, institutional adjustments. In addition, it should be noted that this community had been stable in size for approximately twenty years, so that its social structures were not required to assimilate any considerable number of newcomers, in contrast to the more fluid situation in New York. Under these circumstances one might expect a greater degree of reflectiveness and self-scrutiny on the part of some elements within the community. In other words, transposing terms from nuclear physics into a sociological situation, a critical mass had been arrived at. This, however, important though it be, does not explain the explosion. For that to have occurred, the materials involved must have been, to carry our metaphor a step further before discarding it, fissionable. Which leads us further into the matter.

Is it at all possible to isolate more specific factors than the generalizations indulged in above? Or must we be satisfied with an impressionistic understanding? The former certainly recommends itself to us as of greater value if it can be carried through, and thus deserves our attention. Charles Reznikoff, in his book *The Jews of Charleston,* written in collaboration with Uriah Z. Engelman, has argued that "the movement in Charleston was native to the place." It had, according to Engelman, its "beginnings in the examination of the beliefs and traditions of the synagogue in the light of democratic thought and practice." Continuing this line of argument, the authors stated: "In Charleston, the Reform movement was inaugurated by a group of American Jewish intellectuals, cultured and wordly-wise, who were under the influence of the age (of which the American Declaration of Independence was another example)." That this had happened in Charleston was occasioned, according to these authors, by the fact that "the city itself had a long tradition, preceding the Revolution, of religious liberalism and pluralism." It was the freedom of the American scene, the equality they possessed, that engendered "the desire to become in their worship more like their friendly non-Jewish neighbors—particularly the Protestants who were in the great majority.[4]

The position here argued represented a revision of an earlier interpretation offered by the first historian of the Charleston movement, Barnett A. Elzas who, shortly after the turn of this century when he was serving as rabbi of Beth Elohim, republished the essential materials, the *Memorial*, the *Constitution*, and the *Prayerbook* of the Reformed Society. Elzas had argued on the basis of a quotation in the *Memorial* itself from the *Frankfort Journal*, a German newspaper, that the men of Charleston were "directly dependent upon the earlier movement that had taken place in Germany."[5] What was meant by "the earlier movement" here referred to is not entirely clear. The Memorial mentioned "the reformation which has been recently adopted by our brethren in Holland, Germany and Prussia." These apparently refer to the founding of the congregation *Adath Jeshurun* in Amsterdam in 1796, the Seesen Temple in Westphalia in 1810, the Beer Temple in Berlin in 1815, and the Hamburg Temple in 1818. In each of these instances the reforms were predominantly liturgical and, in several, of a very minor nature. But it is too much to infer from these references and even from the quotation describing the nature of the liturgical reforms that there was a direct dependence. Rather does it seem that this material was quoted to support the argument but was by no means the inspiration for the development.

I am rather in accord with the position quoted above that "the movement in Charleston was native to the place." However, here I am bothered by the ease with which the whole development is referred to the *Zeitgeist*, the spirit of "American thought and practice." This generalization, it seems to me, conceals as much as it reveals. The spirit of the times expresses itself in particular and concrete instances, and it is just this expression or these expressions that must be uncovered if we are more exactly to understand how a tradition is influenced and molded by its environment. The authors were well aware of this and, for example, attempted to explain the rather harsh phrase at the end of the Memorial, "wish to worship God, not as *slaves of bigotry and priestcraft,*" a phrase much out of keeping with the general tenor of the Memorial, by a general reference to Dr. Thomas Cooper of South Carolina College. The opinions of this gentleman, an English Jacobin and friend of Joseph Priestly, went, however, far beyond anything the Reformed Society ventured in its initial statement. That Cooper's controversies with the Presbyterians in 1821–1822 may indeed have influenced the thinking of some of the signers of the Memorial is altogether possible. Yet his theological or antitheological positions had little or nothing to do with the kind of practical reforms suggested in the original resolutions of the

Society. Possibly his renewed struggles in the early thirties may have influenced the theologically more radical turn which the thinking of the Society took at that time, but this is a matter of speculation.[6]

What we need to do at this point is to attempt to relate these valid generalizations more clearly to the actual texture of American life and most specifically to developments within American religion as they were to be found in Charleston at that time. What I am arguing here is quite simply that the relation of "religious innovations to issues of class, status and power," to use Timothy Smith's phrase, was mediated to the Jewish community through events and institutions in American Protestantism. What happened in Charleston was derivative and its proximate source is to be found within the context of Protestantism in Charleston in the years immediately preceeding the founding of the Reformed Society.

A clue to a background more revealing than merely pointing to a "long tradition, preceeding the Revolution, of religious liberalism and pluralism," or "the desire to become in their worship more like their friendly non-Jewish neighbors" is to be found in an article that appeared in the *North American Review* of July 1826. This was a review and discussion of *The Constitution of the Reformed Society of Israelites for Promoting True Principles of Judaism According to Its Purity and Spirit* and *Discourse before the Reformed Society of Israelites* by Isaac Harby, delivered on the first anniversary of the founding of the Society, November 21, 1825. Although the review was unsigned, a later index indicates that it was written by Samuel Gilman, minister of the Second Independent Church of Charleston.[7] The clue, however, is not to be found so much in Gilman's outright statement that the movement was indigenous to the American, indeed to the Charleston scene, but in the reviewer himself and the local history of the congregation he served as minister.

The Second Independent Church of Charleston was itself the result of internal dissension and struggle that had occurred no more than seven years previous to the events we are considering. At that time certain tensions that had been present in the old and distinguished First Independent Church for several years finally broke into the open. The congregation, possessing two houses of worship, had for a number of years been served by a series of co-pastors, who did not always see eye to eye. In 1815, during the illness of one, Mr. Anthony Forster had been engaged as a temporary pastor, and when the incumbent died in February 1817, it was assumed that Forster would be called to the post of co-pastor. There were, however, those in the church who had doubts, and rightly so, as to whether Forster was "in accord with the long-accepted doctrines of the church." Actually that young man, a native of Brunswick County, North Carolina, had been converted to "liberalism" by his father-in-law, Joseph Gales, a distinguished newspaper editor of Raleigh, North Carolina, who was, like Thomas Cooper, a friend of the English Unitarian Joseph Priestly and was himself a Unitarian. Forster had, after his marriage, set out to refute his father-in-law's position but, upon reading the literature for the controversy supplied to him, was himself convinced of its truth. He never, however, adopted the name Unitarian but merely shifted his doctrines from the Orthodox Calvinist position. Thus, from early in 1817 and on during the year, the congregation of the First Independent Church argued first Forster's appointment, which was rejected, and then the division into two separate congregations, which was accepted. Forster had, during the period when his appointment was under consideration, refused to commit himself to support the "stated doctrines" of the church. Following his rejection, he wrote an open letter to the church, publishing it under the title *The Blasphemy of Creeds.* He and his supporters took over one of the church edifices and established the Second Independent Church. Serious illness forced Forster's retirement in 1819, and he was succeeded by Gilman who came as a Unitarian, although the church did not assume that name for another fifteen years.[8]

Here, more immediately than the "religious liberalism and pluralism in the period before the Revolution" would seem to be a pattern for the attitudes of the Reformed Society. Gilman, in his review, made it evident that he had cordial relations with members of the Jewish community. He must have been an attractive and engaging man for, although Unitarianism was shunned by many people, he himself was not. "He was one of the most popular men in the city and with his wife the very center of its literary activities." It was undoubtedly through these activities that he had come to know the author of the *Discourse,* Isaac Harby, for the latter was the editor of *The Southern Patriot,* then of the *City Gazette.* He was as well an editoral writer for the *Mercury* and was the author of several plays. He was born in Charleston on November 9, 1788, the son of Solomon Harby who had arrived in the city in 1781 from London via Jamaica.[9] There is little doubt but that he was one of the moving spirits of the Society and that his views went far beyond the very modest proposals made in the *Memorial.*

Before, however, examining Harby's views, which were not apparent in the original document but most certainly effected drastic changes in the direction and development of the Society, it is necessary to look at the proposals set forth in the *Memorial* of November, 1824.

The petition began by noting "the apathy and neglect which have been manifest toward our holy religion" and then suggested that "certain defects which are apparent in the present system of worship, are the sole cause of the evils complained of." It is to the repair of these defects that the petitions were directed. The first suggestion was that certain parts of the Hebrew prayers be repeated by the reader (*Hasan*) in English. "The instruction in morals and the improvement of the minds accomplished by thus making the principles and precepts of Judaism accessible to those who knew no Hebrew would," says the Memorial, "be sufficient of themselves to induce the alterations requested." Further, the change would improve the discipline of the service. Gilman, in his review, described the worship service at Beth Elohim and wrote of the assembly as "seated or standing with their hats on, and generally wearing an air of much greater indifference, than is witnessed even among Christians, during the seasons of public devotion." It is important to recognize that Gilman here wrote of indifference in Christian worship, even if of a lesser degree. He recounted as well how a member of the congregation came over during the service to discuss "a curious point of Hebrew phraseology" [after all Gilman was a Harvard graduate and was expected to know Hebrew] and then "entered upon a much more general conversation." This it was, among other things, that disturbed the petitioners.

After this modest beginning, the petition moved on to more fundamental proposals. If there was to be a repetition in English of the Hebrew, perhaps of all the Hebrew, then there was "the absolute necessity of abridging the service." As it stood, the service took three hours to read. Were it to be read without change "with due solemnity, and in a slow, distinct and impressive tone," it would undoubtedly take five hours. As to the abridgments themselves, the *Memorial* "strenuously recommended that the most solemn portions be retained, and everything superfluous excluded."

Turning to the custom of making public offerings at certain times during the service, the petition pointed to the absurdity of reciting the announcement of these in Spanish. More than that, it condemned the entire procedure as unworthy and of no use financially to the Congregation since such offerings were deducted from the regular annual subscriptions required of each member.

The mode of reading the weekly lesson from Scriptures, the petition continued, "affords neither instruction nor entertainment, unless the hearer be competent to read as well as comprehend the Hebrew language." To overcome this difficulty it was suggested that "an English discourse" dealing with the lesson be delivered each week so that "at the expiration of the year the people would . . . know something of that religion which at present they so little regard." Gilman was less critical than the memorialists at this point, for he wrote, "that part of the liturgy, which consists in reading the portion of the laws, called the *Parasah* (the particular portion of the Pentateuch read each Sabbath), is generally well read, devoutly, and emphatically."

These changes would, argued the petition, bring back those "now wandering gradually from the true God, and daily losing these strong ties which binds every pious man to the faith of his fathers!" There is, the document continues, no desire "to abolish such ceremonies as are considered land-marks to distinguish the *Jew* from *Gentile*." The sole intent of the petitioners was "to preserve and perpetuate the principles of Judaism in their utmost purity and vigour, and to see the present and the future generations of Israelites enlightened on the subject of their holy religion." This was followed by the reference to European reforms together with the extract from the *Frankfort Journal* and the whole concluded with a peroration that contained the somewhat incendiary words *"slaves of bigotry and priestcraft."*[10]

The rejection, on constitutional grounds, of this petition, brought into existence the Reformed Society of Israelites. It was not, in the beginning, as I have already indicated and as an examination of its constitution makes clear, a congregation. That document made no provision for holding services of worship, although it declared its intention to educate young men "so as to render . . . them fully competent to perform Divine Services" and in the meantime to "adopt and support, as soon as practicable, any person so qualified for the sacred office." Certainly Gilman's review published a year and a half after the founding of the Society makes no mention of such services in contrast to those at Beth Elohim. The primary object of the Society, as stated in Article IV, was "to devise ways and means . . . of revising and altering such parts of the prevailing system of worship, as are inconsistent with the present enlightened state of society, and not in accordance with the Five Books of Moses and the Prophets." The rest of the Constitution dealt, for the most part, with organization details and was in many ways no less preemptory and non-democratic than the Constitution of the Congregation Beth Elohim adopted in 1820.[11]

There are, however, two phrases, the one from Article IV, quoted above and the other from Article II, that suggest the presence of ideas that were by no means expressed in the original *Memorial*. Article II spoke of "a blind observance of ceremonial law, to the neglect of the essential spirit of revealed religion contained in the Law and Prophets."

Article IV, as quoted above, set as the standard the "Five Books of Moses and the Prophets." This is something quite different from the simple suggestions for liturgical reforms made in the *Memorial*. This is a hint of a sharp theological distinction between Scripture and the Oral Law. Indeed, in Harby's *Discourse* this distinction is set forth in unmistakable terms. In it he wrote an exceedingly severe attack upon the Rabbis whom he called "fabulists and sophists, who, caught in the net of platonic subtlety, mingled Grecian metaphysics with Phariseean materialism; ceremonial and verbal refiners, who tortured the plainest precepts of the Law into monstrous and unexpected inferences." In a long note to this passage, he enlarged upon his theme, writing of "the whole tribe of Rabbis, who refined upon refinement; and who in the Portuguese form of prayer appointed to be read in Synagogues, have had the influence . . . to *interpolate* their own remarks, to the interruption of many sublime and pathetic passages." The source of these infirmities, wrote Harby, was the Talmud, which was the *Tradition,* or unwritten law of the Jews. It is not their Law. The only Law is the written one, found in the books of Moses. Even those Jews who have come to America, he wrote "bow beneath the sway of bigotry, and regard every attempt to shake off a *rabbinical* doctrine or ceremony, as rebellion against the *divine* word." Only a few understand that word and recognize "the necessity of adapting many of the institutions of the great legislator, to the circumstances of the times in which we enjoy our liberties."[12]

This anti-rabbinic position, so sharply stated by Harby, was echoed in the second anniversary address delivered by Abraham Moïse in 1826, who spoke of "the erroneous doctrine of the Rabbins" and proclaimed the "Law and the Prophets" as the Society's immortal guide. Isaac N. Cardozo, who delivered the third anniversary discourse, also joins his voice, although more moderately, to the condemnation.[13]

What the sources of this anti-rabbinism were is obscure indeed. The struggles that were taking place in Germany at the time had not yet polarized to the degree found in Charleston. Was it, then, the American situation that made such a position possible? Certainly there is language to be found in the writings of the Restorationist movement in Protestantism that paralleled the rejection of man-made institutions and insisted upon the primacy of the New Testament as the rule and standard of Christianity. Perhaps Anthony Forster's open letter *The Blasphemy of Creed* emphasized just such a point of view. Yet what we have here seems too well-formed, too crystalized to be attributed to these sources, although such influences may have provided a background for the development or expression of such ideas within the Jewish community.

The answer to our question must be sought elsewhere. It seems certain that Harby's knowledge of the Talmud was not first hand but entirely derivative. The sources of his knowledge may then have been the very sources of his violent criticism as well. Here, at least two possibilities offer themselves. In considering them it should be noted at the outset that this is highly speculative and very tentative and that the two possibilities are not necessarily mutually exclusive but may be supplementary or complementary, and may indeed not exhaust the field.

Jakob Petuchowski in his book *The Theology of Haham David Nieto,* has discussed the situation of English Judaism in the 18th century and collected the evidence pointing toward the existence in that country of "friends and sympathizers of the Karaite sect," *i.e.,* a group that opposed the Oral Law. In addition he has suggested that the views of Spinoza had circulated in England early in the 18th century and had continued to agitate the community during the whole of the century. He has indicated as well the presence of remnants of the Sabbatian heresy, the pseudo-messianic movement that broke out in 1665. There was, of course, the influence of English Deism, too. His discussion of the opposition to the Oral Law and its source in the Judaism of the Marranos, the crypto-Jews of Spain and Portugal, is of considerable interest and may point in the direction toward which the investigation of our problem must move.

While these clandestine Jews in the second, third and fourth generations were devoted to their faith, their knowledge of it had grown increasingly weaker as they were cut off from the literature of their community. In place of the Tradition, all that they had was the Latin version of the Bible. When after many vicissitudes they finally came out of Spain, the Judaism they possessed was basically the Bible: the Law and the Prophets. All the rest had been lost. As Petuchowski wrote: "Those Marranos who . . . were willing to foresake all their possessions and risk life itself, because they felt compelled to obey the Law of Moses which was given by God, expected Jewish life in Holland or Italy to conform to the pattern of the Law of Moses which, in its strictly literal sense, had meant so much to them." "Imagine," he continued, "their surprise when, in place of the 'Mosaism' they had expected to find, they were confronted by a Rabbinism which read the Bible through the spectacles not only of Judah the Prince, of Rab and Samuel, but also of Maimonides, Jacob ben Asher and Joseph Caro!" Their reaction to all of this was tragic and the results equally so. Thus Uriel da Costa, who died a suicide in 1647, wrote that "the manners and ordinances of the Jews do not correspond at all to those which Moses has prescribed. If, however, the Law was to be observed exactly, as it itself demands, then the so-called Sages of the Law have wrongly invented so many things which completely depart from the Law." And again: "The present-day Sages of the Law still retained their manners as well as their malignant character; stiff-neckedly they fight for the sect and the institutions of the *detestable Pharisees*." In another place he challenged certain traditional benedictions and suggested that there were passages in the prayerbook that should be erased.[14]

Of course, one may immediately ask what have the writings of a tragically embittered man who took his own life in Amsterdam in 1647 to do with Charleston in 1824. While no direct answer may be given, it must be noted that Isaiah Sonne, a close scholar of the subject, was quoted by Petuchowski to the following effect: "The heretical trend of da Costa was born with the coming into existence of the Sephardi community, and undoubtedly lasted for more than 150 years." Petuchowski has argued that what began in Amsterdam during the 17th century continued in London of the 18th, as evidenced by the polemic of David Nieto (died in 1728), Haham of the Spanish-Portuguese Synagogue of that city, against the opponents of the Oral Law. Now as to the relationship between these facts and our problems, we can only speculate. In the sketchy account of his family line, Isaac Harby reports that his grandfather fled to England from Fez in Morocco sometime around the middle of the 18th century and that his father, the youngest of six children, was born in London in 1762. All this has done, of course, is to set the Harby family at the locale of the controversy over the Oral Law. That the controversy or its echoes may have continued on through the 18th century seems to be supported by the fact that in 1758 "Dr. Jacob de Castro Sarmento severed his connection with the Jewish community . . . claiming that 'the different opinion and sentiments I have entertained long ago, entirely dissenting from those of the synagogue, do not permit me any longer to keep the appearance of a member of your body.' " Beyond such vague conjectures we cannot go. Yet it is possible that members of the Harby family were influenced by such dissenting opinions either, as is often the case, by an oral family tradition or by such correspondence as may have taken place between Charleston and London. Beth Elohim considered itself to be a daughter congregation of London's Bevis Marks and early in the 19th century had applied for and received a Reader from the London congregation.[15] Harby undoubtedly had family ties with London, and some of the demands made in the *Memorial* reflect matters agitating the mother synagogue.[16] Whether the more deeply-seated antipathies expressed in Harby's *Discourse* had their origins in London is a possibility at the moment beyond proof.

Far less speculative than this first possibility, although still only tentative, is the following suggestion that may be thought of standing on its own although it could well have been considered a complementary or supplementary source, should the previous conjecture ever be proved correct. Harby, in his *Discourse,* quoted as his sources for his understanding of rabbinic Judaism, Jacob Christian Basnage and Pierre Bayle.[17] The former was the author of *L'Histoire et la Réligion des Juifs Depuis Jésus Christ Jusqu'à Présent.*[18] Of him, Moïse Schwab, writing in the *Jewish Encyclopedia,* noted: "Whatever knowledge he could under these circumstances possess, he derived from the Latin version of the Mishnah . . . from a translation of the Pirke Abot . . . and from the Latin version of the two Talmudic treatises Sanhedrin and Makkot . . . he was well acquainted with all the works of Maimonides that had been translated into Latin with the exception of 'Yad ha-Hazakah.' " He continued: "Basnage's conception of Jewish theology and his interpretation of the religious controversies bear the marks of the same lack of direct knowledge." After indicating Basnage's sources, Schwab concluded: "Through such reading the most impartial mind must become biased."[19] Here then, it may be suggested, was a source of Harby's prejudice that a careful survey of Basnage may confirm.

The other author, Pierre Bayle, who wrote *Dictionaire Historique et Critique,*[20] seemed to have had a point of view that would have given Harby his particular attitudes toward rabbinic Judaism. In volume one of this work, he presented a biography of Uriel Acosta (da Costa) with voluminous quotations from his writings in the notes. He noted Acosta's observation that *"les moeurs et les observances des Juifs n'étoient pas conformés aux lois de Moise"* and reported that he had written a work justifying his position that *"les observances, et les traditions des Pharisiens, sont contraires aux Escrits de Moise."* While only a careful examination of Bayle's work can put firmer ground under the hypothesis that it is a source of Harby's anti-rabbinic position, a hasty survey suggests that this is more than plausible. At any rate, it does seem entirely correct to suggest that, while Harby's severe judgment of rabbinic Judaism had its source or sources outside of the immediate situation in Charleston or in American Church life at the time, nonetheless that situation may have made possible a freer expression of such radical opinions than was possible in the Old World.

There was, however, in addition to the influences discussed thus far, the tentative reforms in Europe, the prejudices of Christian or rationalist scholars transmitted to a writer unable to judge their tendentiousness, the generally shifting state of religion in the United States and the local upheavals in the churches of Charleston, all of which had given the members of the Reformed Society courage to present their own demands, an all-pervasive attitude, to which Reznikoff referred, that broke forth in passionate hymns of praise toward the end of Harby's *Discourse,* the joy of being an American. "With what pride and pleasure," he wrote, "must the happy few who composed our immediate forefathers . . . with what indescribable sensations must these pilgrims of the world have hailed the dawn of freedom as it illumined the western horizon." "Where is he," he asked, "that does not feel a glow of honest exultation, when he hears himself called an American!" "America," he cried, "truly is the land of promise spoken of in our ancient Scripture."[21] He had begun the *Discourse* with the reminder that "in this happy land . . . equality of laws and freedom of conscience" had given the Society leave to act. He concluded by calling upon his hearers "to share the blessings of Liberty; to partake of and to add to . . . political happiness . . . to educate our children liberally; to make them useful and enlightened and honest citizens; to look upon our countrymen as brethren of the same happy family worshipping the same God of the universe, though perhaps differing in forms and opinions," all this in the spirit of Psalm 133: "Behold how good and how pleasant it is for brethren to dwell together in unity."[22]

It was this overwhelming and passionate belief in the curative and restorative powers of the new nation, this unbounded optimism in the spirit, the genius of America, that seized hold of yet another leader who was to make his mark on the American Jewish community. Of all the things that are important to know about Isaac Meyer Wise who emigrated to the United States from Bohemia in 1846 and who, after a stormy career in Albany, N.Y., went west to Cincinnati in 1854, the most important is his unyielding and enduring belief in the transforming power of America. Facing the South and West in Cincinnati, near enough to the cutting edge of the frontier constantly to be aware of the excitement of the new and unexpected, dwelling in a part of the country whose religious ideas had been formed not by the New England but by the Southern wave of western migration, close to the center of the mid-century revival, Wise was in his own eyes not the purveyor of a Reform imported from abroad, but the protagonist of an American Judaism indigenous to the land, growing, as it were, out of its very soil, responsive to its challenges, its hopes, its forward thrust.

There is no continuity between what the Reformed Society of

Israelites in Charleston attempted and the path Wise followed. There is even less of a similarity in outlook. What does relate them is their conscious responsiveness to the new and ever renewing American situation, their passion for the United States. Wise rejected Europe *in toto,* unlike the reformers of the eastern seaboard who fought him so bitterly. He had no patience with denominationalism; he could envisage only one all-encompassing, all-inclusive American Judaism, American because it had been formed and fostered in a land and on the soil he was convinced renewed and revitalized all that touched it. Toward the end of his life (he lived until 1900) this vision diminished; the passion was spent. But essentially what he saw was true. There was, there is, for good or evil, for weal or woe, an American impact, a shattering, forming force that makes its demands upon, sets its mark on the ancient traditions from afar; bends, molds, shatters and rebuilds!

It is only when this is understood, only when the events, the institutions, the struggles, the personalities we have examined are seen within the context of the American scene, are set within the frame of the whole society, are viewed not as exotic occurrences unrelated to the larger movements but are recognized for what they are, the responses of the Jewish community to the unprecedented, often bewildering, always dynamic unfolding of a new nation on a vast continent; it is only then, when we have risen above parochialism, provincialism, sectarianism, claiming and embracing all, that the history of the Jews in the United States will come into its own. Thus viewed and understood, the conflicts and tensions, triumphs and failures, innovations and traditions will belong not to interested parties alone, nor to institutions with axes to grind, no, not even to the Jews alone, but will assume their places, find their perspective on the vast stage of American life, on which the manifold nations, tongues, hues, creeds of all mankind have come to play their roles.

(1964)

NOTES

1. Barnett A. Elzas, *The Reformed Society of Israelites of Charleston, S.C.* (New York: Bloch, 1916); *The Sabbath Service and Miscellaneous Prayers adopted by the Reformed Society of Israelites,* reprinted with an Introduction by

B. A. Elzas (New York: Bloch, 1916); *Constitution of the Hebrew Congregation of Kaal Kadosh Beth Elohim or House of God,* Charleston (S.C.), MDCCCXX, reprinted by B. A. Elzas, 1904; Charles Reznikoff and Uriah Z. Engelman, *The Jews of Charleston* (Philadelphia: Jewish Publication Society, 1950).

2. See Franklin H. Littell, *From State Church to Pluralism: A Protestant Interpretation of Religion in American History* (Garden City: Doubleday and Co., 1962), chs. 1 and 2.

3. Timothy Smith, "Historic Waves of Religious Interest in America," *The Annals of the American Academy of Political and Social Science* 332 (Nov. 1960): 9–19.

4. Reznikoff, *The Jews of Charleston,* pp. 113–36.

5. Elzas, *Constitution,* p. 20; see also his article in *The American Hebrew,* Literary Supplement (Dec. 7, 1906): iv–v.

6. For a discussion of Cooper's controversies see Dumas Malone, *The Public Life of Thomas Cooper* (New Haven: Yale University Press, 1926), Part Three.

7. See L. C. Moise, *Biography of Isaac Harby* (Macon, Ga., 1931).

8. *The Old and the New: or, Discourses and Proceedings at the Dedication of the Re-Modelled Unitarian Church in Charleston, S.C.* (Charleston: 1854), pp. 3–32; George N. Edwards, *A History of the Independent or Congregational Church of Charleston, South Carolina* (Boston: Pilgrim Press, 1942), pp. 59–65. Clarence Gohde, "Some Notes on the Unitarian Church in the Ante-Bellum South . . . ," *American Studies in Honor of William Kenneth Boyd* (Durham: Duke University Press, 1940).

9. Moise, *Biography,* pp. 46–47.

10. The petition is to be found in *A Selection from the Miscellaneous Writings of the late Isaac Harby, Esq.* (Charleston: 1829); Elzas, *The Reformed Society;* Moise, *Biography.*

11. See Elzas, *Prayerbook* "Introduction" where he makes much of the undemocratic nature of the Constitution of Beth Elohim. Light on the whole subject, particularly the prohibition against the establishment of another synagogue, is shed by Isadore Epstein, "Ascama I of the Spanish and Portuguese Jewish Congregation of London . . . ," *Studies and Essays in honor of Abraham A. Neuman* (Leiden: 1962).

12. The *Discourse* is found in the volume cited above in note 10, pp. 57–87.

13. Moise's and Cardozo's lectures are found in the work cited in note 7, pp. 122–40.

14. Jakob J. Petuchowski, *The Theology of Haham David Nieto* (New York: Bloch, 1954).

15. Reznikoff, *The Jews of Charleston,* p. 113.

16. A. M. Hyamson, *The Sephardim of England* (London: Methuen, 1951), pp. 240–95.

17. Harby, *A Selection,* p. 73, note.

18. 1st edition, Rotterdam, 1706–11; 2nd enlarged ed., The Hague, 1716–26; English ed., London, 1706; condensed English version, London, 1708.

19. *J. E.* II: 579b–582b.

20. 1st edition, 1696; 4th ed., Amsterdam, Leyden, 1730; English edition, 1734–41.

21. Harby, *A Selection* (4th ed), pp. 67–69.

22. Harby, *A Selection,* pp. 57–59; 82 et seq.

6

GERMAN – JEWISH INTELLECTUAL INFLUENCES ON AMERICAN JEWISH LIFE 1824 – 1972

BERTRAM WALLACE KORN

NLY A FEW THOUSAND JEWS live in Germany today.[1] Most of them are older people; very few are children. They are atomized fragments of yesterday, the remnant of one of the most creative communities of all of Jewish history, a stark reminder of a ghastly era of our story, equal in ferocity and poignancy to the devastations of Jewish life in the year 586 B.C.E. when the Babylonians brought the Temple of Solomon to a blazing end, and in 70 C.E., when the Romans reduced Jerusalem to rubble. The European Jewish holocaust, of which the Jews of Germany were the first victims, has already assumed a position of major significance as a landmark in Jewish religious historical consciousness equal to the destructions of 586 and 70.

Two other major developments in contemporary Jewish history resonate with the holocaust and the disappearance of European Jewry as a center of world Jewish life and thought. One cluster of events reached its climax in the rebirth of the Jewish Commonwealth of Israel— the direct heir to the national entity whose independence was ended in the year 70 C.E. but whose continuity was maintained through an unbroken chain of Jewish settlements in Palestine in the years and centuries in between. Israel today is a physical, cultural and religious reality which, in the Jewish mind, refutes the holocaust. The second notable change is the rise to a commanding position in world Jewry of the American Jewish community—a frontier as recently as seventy-five years ago, today the largest, freest, most secure and most affluent community of Jews in all of Jewish history. Indeed, the economic and political influence of American Jewry was probably the greatest single factor in the combination of circumstances which resulted in the creation of the state of Israel. Simultaneously, therefore, the era which has been marked by the extinction of European Jewry has also heralded the shift of leadership in

106

Jewish life from Europe (where it had been centered for almost a thousand years) to Israel and America.

A totally new amalgam of Jewish life is being compounded in the crucible of experience in Israel. Its contours are not yet clear. It will be unlike anything that has ever before existed. It will somehow evolve from the disparate ingredients of traditional religion, modern secular nationalism, ethnic pluralism and voluntaristic socialism which today still compete in various combinations for the advantage in Israeli society. If the Arabs and the Russians are restrained from perpetrating another holocaust, students of the social sciences will have a fascinating opportunity to observe the development in Israel, virtually under laboratory conditions, of a possibly unique society.

American Jewish life, on the other hand, represents a direct continuation of the effort of post-Emancipation European (primarily German) Jewry to create a new intellectual and spiritual rationale for Jewish identity. The American Jewish community is the primary heir of the intellectual achievements of German Jewry—the movements and trends in German Jewish life which resulted from the struggle to rationalize life in the two worlds of the Jewish tradition and modern society.[2] The outlines of American Jewish cultural and intellectual life were in large measure engendered by German Jewish thinkers.

RELIGIOUS ADJUSTMENT

The first way in which some of the leaders of German Jewry sought to solve the dilemma of living in two worlds was religious adaptation. What we call Reform Judaism today was the product of the effort (which began about the year 1800) to adjust the conceptual foundations and ceremonial forms of the Jewish religion to the secular and religious environment, to give to the Jewish individual a Jewishly approved opportunity to mingle freely with his neighbors (politically, economically, culturally and socially), to develop for the Jew an identity differentiated no longer by an alien nationality but simply by the house of worship he attended, the holy days he celebrated and the theological tenets to which he adhered. Reform broke sharply with tradition by rejecting the total authority of Jewish law and custom and by adding two further criteria as guides to Jewish practice and belief: first, the mores and standards of the non-Jewish environment, and, second, the perceptions and principles of contemporary (in most cases secular) philosophy. It is true that some of the lay leaders of religious Reform hoped to change the opinions of non-Jews about Jews and Judaism, and desired to prove that Jews could adapt themselves to the habits and customs of their neighbors. Reform of religious practice was one part of the multi-faceted campaign to gain full and equal rights as citizens for all Jews. But the primary objective of religious Reform was to convince Jews that they were not compelled to make a choice between Judaism and modern European culture, that there was no inherent contradiction between Judaism and the environment.

Reform Judaism, therefore, was a conscious effort to adjust Judaism to the nineteenth century temperament. Although the movement was originated by laymen, it reached its culmination in a series of German rabbinical conferences during the 1840s.[3] Many of the discussions and resolutions of these gatherings were so radical and revolutionary that they immediately stimulated the formulation of reactive philosophies. One of these, called the "Historical" or "Historical-Positivist" school of thought, was led by Rabbi Zacharias Frankel (1801–75); this movement recognized the need for change and adjustment, but insisted on the maintenance of continuity with the past and the avoidance of radical dislocation.[4] The second significant response to Reform was Neo-Orthodoxy, an attempt to preserve the integrity of *halacha* (the Jewish legal tradition) in personal and religious life, combined with an affirmative receptivity to scientific and cultural progress. Rabbi Samson Raphael Hirsch (1808–88) was the preeminent spokesman for this viewpoint.[5]

American Jewish religious life, except for the efforts of Isaac Leeser (1806–68),[6] was a pale, declining copy of European patterns until Reform was transplanted here under the leadership of German-trained rabbis, some of whom had participated in the fateful conferences and debates. While the Charleston modernization experiment of 1824 had demonstrated a strong desire and need for change, its collapse within nine years revealed its lack of coherent, affirmative ideological direction. Evidence that the Charleston group had some points of contact with German Reform in this early period is not wanting. The very name "Reformed Society of Israelites" offers conclusive proof that there was some awareness of a Reform movement. This is also substantiated by reference to Reform developments in Europe in the writings and addresses of some of the leaders.[7] But it is instructive that the victory of the Charleston community's liberal wing was delayed until the arrival in 1836 of Gustav Poznanski (1804–79), a rabbinical teacher who is reported to have been imbued with the ideas of German Reform in Hamburg.[8] In

New York City, Baltimore and Philadelphia, the founders of the new Reform societies and congregations during the 1840s were laymen, as in Charleston, but they were German immigrants, not native-born Americans—and because they were German they were probably more aware of the potentiality of the Reform movement and more eager for the leadership of German-trained Reform rabbis.[9]

The two major rabbinic spokesmen and propagandists of the first generation of American Reform—the moderate Isaac Mayer Wise (1819–1900) of Albany and Cincinnati, and the radical David Einhorn (1809–79) of Baltimore, Philadelphia and New York City—were in contact with the leaders of Reform in Germany, followed developments in Germany very closely and reprinted material from German publications in their own periodicals.[10] Both consciously traced their authority to the rabbinical conferences of Germany, Einhorn as an energetic participant at the meetings in Frankfurt (1845) and Breslau (1846), and Wise as an observer at Frankfurt.

The first American Reform rabbinical convention (Philadelphia, 1869) was conducted precisely as a continuation of the German meetings; its members made frequent reference to the discussions and experiences of the prior conferences, including that which had been held in Leipzig just four months before—indeed Kaufmann Kohler (1843–1926) immigrated to the United States immediately after attending the meetings in Leipzig and just in time to be invited to Philadelphia.[11] The famous Pittsburgh conference was also considered to be a successor to the previous sessions in Germany and in the United States. And when the first national American rabbinical association, the Central Conference of American Rabbis, was organized in 1889, the preamble to its constitution provided that: "the proceedings of all the modern Rabbinical Conferences, from that held in Braunschweig in 1844, and including all like assemblages held since, shall be taken as a basis for the work of this Conference, in an endeavor to maintain, in unbroken historic succession, the formulated expression of Jewish thought and life of each era."[12]

Older leaders of the second generation of American Reform, such as Gustav Gottheil (1827–1903) of Emanu-El of New York City and Kaufmann Kohler, second president of the Hebrew Union College, continued the dissemination of the attitudes of German religious Reform in America—a process which was fostered by the young men who were sent from the United States to study for the rabbinate in Abraham Geiger's Hochschule für die Wissenschaft des Judentums of Berlin, including Emil G. Hirsch (1851–1923) of Sinai Congregation of Chicago

—son of the philosopher Samuel Hirsch (1815–89) of Luxemburg and Philadelphia; Samuel Sale (1854–1937) of Baltimore, Chicago and St. Louis; and Samuel Schulman (1864–1955), successor to Kohler in New York City.[13]

The Reform movement achieved greater success in the United States than in Germany, but this was due to differences in the historic setting and the secular environment rather than to any fundamental changes in the Reform ideology which were introduced in the United States. The only significant contribution which American Reform leaders made to the principles of Reform Judaism was the concept of social justice/social action which was virtually unknown in Germany. Einhorn first voiced this concern in his abolitionist sermons and editorials during the period leading up to the Civil War. The theme was developed more generally by his son-in-law Emil G. Hirsch, who succeeded in securing majority support for the inclusion of a pronouncement on the subject in the platform adopted at Pittsburgh in 1885: "Eighth. In full accordance with the spirit of Mosaic legislation, which strives to regulate the relation between rich and poor, we deem it our duty to participate in the great task of modern times, to solve, on the basis of justice and righteousness, the problems presented by the contrasts and evils of the present organization of society."[14]

While the origins of American Reform Judaism in German thought-patterns are well-known, the identical background of Conservative Judaism is less familiar, primarily because the families of most of its adherents stemmed from Eastern Europe, and the descendants have assumed that the same geographical area was the source of their religious proclivities. The failure of the pioneering activist Isaac Leeser to establish a permanent movement in American Jewish life can be explained largely by three factors: he allied himself with the acculturated, Americanized "Sephardic" congregations, rather than the mass of German-speaking immigrants whom he preceded to the United States; he did not support a specific ideology, merely a general "traditional" viewpoint which was too vague; the opposition, the Reform group, had not yet hardened into an identifiable organization and had not yet codified its convictions.[15] Isaac Leeser had already died when conditions ripened for the creation of a counter-Reformation in American Jewish life. Conservative Judaism was organized as a formal movement (under the name of the Jewish Theological Seminary Association) in 1886 as a direct response to the famous "trefah" banquet in Cincinnati in 1883 which celebrated the first graduation/ordination of a Hebrew Union College class, and to the program of radical Reform which was adopted by the rabbis at Pittsburgh.[16] These events were the occasion for the separation of a number of traditionally-minded rabbis from the institutions which Isaac Mayer Wise headed (the Union of American Hebrew Congregations and the Hebrew Union College) but they were not the cause. The cause was a strong ideological difference. The rabbis who supported the organization of the Jewish Theological Seminary viewed the American Jewish process of adaptation from the "Historical-Positivist" position of Frankel and his Breslau Jüdisch-Theologisches Seminar (founded 1854). Perhaps no one described Frankel and his viewpoint better than Kaufmann Kohler: "the leader of Conservative Reform and the exponent of positive historical Judaism, in opposition alike to destructive Radicalism and to the blind worship of authority."[17]

Among the principal founders of the New York Seminary were graduates of Frankel's Breslau Seminary: Alexander Kohut (1842–94), perhaps the most dynamic of the group and a peerless rabbinic scholar; Frederick DeSola Mendes (1850–1927); Benjamin Szold (1829–1902); and Bernard Drachman (1861–1945). Sabato Morais (1823–97), the first president of the Jewish Theological Seminary, and Marcus Jastrow (1829–1903), the greatest Hebrew-Aramaic lexicographer of the time, both shared the Frankel philosophical position, although they were not products of the school in Breslau. (But Jastrow did send his son Morris [1861–1922] to study at the Breslau Seminary in 1881–84, rather than to the Hebrew Union College.[18]) Frankel's term "historical Judaism" was used time after time by the organizers of the Jewish Theological Seminary in their pronouncements and addresses—testimony to the fact that Frankel had expressed the essence of the commitment which divided the Conservatives from the Reformers on the left and from the Traditionalist/Orthodox on the right. The mass immigration of Eastern European Jews drove many of the Seminary's supporters of German background into the Reform camp—this was an unpredictable development which left the Seminary with a very limited constituency for a time—but the ideological position remained. When Solomon Schechter (1847–1915) was brought from Cambridge in 1902 to revive the Seminary, the trustees knew his ideological viewpoint. Although his background was complex and varied, it is clear that one of the most significant periods of his intellectual growth were the years in Vienna and Berlin when he mastered German-Jewish methodology under the tutelage of scholars who were spiritually committed to the Breslau viewpoint. In his inaugural address, Schechter proclaimed his convictions: "There is no other Jewish religion but that taught by the Torah and confirmed by history and tradition, and sunk into the conscience of Catholic Israel . . . We must either remain faithful to history or go the way of all flesh, and join the great majority. The teaching in the Seminary will be in keeping with this spirit, and thus largely confined to the exposition and elucidation of historical Judaism in its various manifestations."[19]

The distinguished faculty which Schechter brought to the Seminary were adherents to the concept of historical continuity in Judaism and— in the words of Schechter's successor, Cyrus Adler (1863–1940)—held the view "that Judaism was an historical growth and not a mushroom sect whose character was to be changed from time to time by platforms or resolutions."[20] Only Mordecai Kaplan (1881–   ), among all of the Seminary's faculty people over the years, moved sufficiently to the left to lead his colleagues to believe that he no longer adhered to the concept of the "Historical School." The fact that Kaplan's followers ultimately felt obliged to establish a Federation of Reconstructionist Congregations and Fellowships and a Reconstructionist Rabbinical College was evidence that Kaplan agreed with his former colleagues at the Seminary. Kaplan's Reconstructionist Movement is still the only native American interpretation of the Jewish religion; its sources and foundations are varied, ranging from Ahad Ha-Am to John Dewey—but it was not founded on any European progenitor or counterpart.[21]

Samson Raphael Hirsch's Neo-Orthodox movement was the only German Jewish religious philosophy which was not transplanted to the United States during the nineteenth century. Some of the immigrant rabbis knew Hirsch personally—Kaufmann Kohler, for instance, said that Hirsch was "the man who exerted the greatest influence upon my young life and imbued me with the divine ardor of true idealism."[22] But the Neo-Orthodox philosophy did not influence their thinking to any great degree, nor did they attempt to build an American equivalent of Hirsch's Frankfurt community—that would have been a practical impossibility. Bernard Drachman, a graduate of Breslau and a founder of the Jewish Theological Seminary of New York, ultimately repudiated the non-traditionalism which he deplored in the Conservative position and allied himself with the immigrant Eastern European Orthodox community of the United States. He resigned from the Seminary faculty in 1908, but in 1899 he had already published a translation of Hirsch's *Letters of Ben Uziel,* the first appearance of its author in book form in America.[23] But it was not until Hitler drove large numbers of German Jews across the ocean that an American branch of the Hirsch movement was established. Under the leadership of Hirsch's grandson, Rabbi Joseph Breuer (1882–   ), refugees primarily from Frankfurt created K'hal Adath Jeshurun in the Washington Heights area of New York City.

In contradistinction to another European Jewish refugee movement—the Lubavitch wing of Hasidism—Frankfurt Neo-Orthodoxy has failed to attract the mass following which alone could assure it a significant place in American Jewish life. It remains a small, transplanted—and therefore embattled—community. One of its achievements, however, has been the organization of the Samson Raphael Hirsch Publications Society which has sponsored the distribution of English translations of Hirsch's *Siddur* and a number of his penetrating commentaries on Biblical books.[24]

Many other rabbis (and rabbinical students as well) came to the United States from Germany in the years 1933–39, but almost all of them preferred to seek their own place in American Jewish life rather than to establish separate refugee communities or congregations. Some experienced great difficulty before they found a fulfilling place in the United States because most American Reform and Conservative congregations just at this time were determined to avoid the association of foreignness which rubbed off on a congregation whose rabbi spoke with an accent. On the other hand, two German rabbis—Max Nussbaum (1910–   ) and Joachim Prinz (1902–   )—rose to positions of commanding importance in American Zionist circles. Over a period of time, more than a dozen rabbinical students were fortunate enough to escape from Berlin to Cincinnati, where they exerted a significant influence on the religious thinking and practice of the student body of the Hebrew Union College. As rabbis, several of these German immigrants—W. Gunther Plaut and Herman Schaalman among them—have achieved positions of leadership in the American Reform rabbinate. But more impressive and dramatic is the latest development in the story of German Jewish influence on American Jewish life: the election of two German refugees—mere boys when they were brought from Germany by their families before the holocaust—to the highest professional offices in Reform Judaism: Alfred Gottschalk as President of the Hebrew Union College-Jewish Institute of Religion; Alexander Schindler as President-Elect of the Union of American Hebrew Congregations.

THE "WISSENSCHAFT" CONCEPT OF JEWISH LEARNING

The academic response to the dilemma of Jewish existence in the modern world was not a reform or modification but an utter transformation. The goal of traditional Jewish learning had been, for many centuries, the transmission of the knowledge and understanding of rabbinic literature, especially its legal portions (the *halacha*) from teacher to student, in order that the authentic application of the Jewish tradition to real life might be perpetuated in one generation after another. The *Wissenschaft* concept, which began to develop in the 1820's, applied secular/scientific/scholarly standards of evolutionary development and documentary methodology to the various aspects of Jewish experience: history, literature, law, philosophy and philology.[25] It constituted a totally different approach to the Jewish past, a true revolution, which Louis Ginzberg (1873–1953), one of its most distinguished practitioners in the field of rabbinic literature, has called "the most striking gift of the nineteenth century to Jews and Judaism."[26] *Wissenschaft*—the "science" of Judaism, or the "scientific study" of Judaism—was more than a Westernized, nineteenth century version of traditional *Torah lishmah* (Torah for its own sake); it was part of the effort to give intellectual validation to Judaism and Jewish history, hence also to the decision of individual Jews to remain loyal to the Jewish heritage. The method with which the research was pursued, and the form in which the results were couched, were as important as the contents themselves. As Nahum N. Glatzer (1903–   ) has reported so suggestively, the works of *Wissenschaft* were expected to achieve high levels of "scholarly objectivity, broad scope, meaningful context, proper form and style and—respectability."[27] The creators of the *Wissenschaft* literature believed that their research and writing would demonstrate to the intellectuals of Europe the contribution which Judaism and the Jewish people had made to civilization, the literary and spiritual treasures of Judaism which lay hidden in an unfamiliar language, and the moral idealism which infused the Jewish tradition. The truth about Judaism and Jewish history would free the Jews from the infamy with which ignorance and malice had assailed them. The ultimate objective of the exponents of *Wissenschaft* was the incorporation of Jewish learning into the vast record of human intellectual achievement, especially through the creation of a department of Jewish studies in a prominent German university.[28] This naturalization of Jewish culture by European civilization was never achieved in Germany, but the great *Wissenschaft* scholars, beginning with the pioneers—Leopold Zunz (1794–1886); Zacharias Frankel; Abraham Geiger (1810–74); Ludwig Philippson (1811–89); Moritz Steinschneider (1816–1909); Heinrich Graetz (1817–91)—and continuing in our own day with such masters as Saul Lieberman and Gershom Scholem, made possible the application of Western categories of scholarship to knowledge of the Jewish past.

Wissenschaft influenced American Judaism in a two-fold manner: through translation and transmission on the one hand, and through adoption on the other. From Isaac Leeser's day until almost our own, every American rabbi who sought to achieve some measure of academic mastery of Jewish life and literature needed to have almost as many German volumes on his shelves as Hebrew.[29] The works of Zunz, Geiger and all of their colleagues were fundamental sources of knowledge to any Jew who aspired to comprehend his people's past.[30] For the benefit of those who were unable to read German, translations of *Wissenschaft* works were made available in the United States. The pioneer American Jewish periodicals—*The Occident and American Jewish Advocate* (1843). *The Asmonean* (1849) and *The Israelite* (1854) turned frequently to material originally written in the German language for essays and articles which would give their readers authentic knowledge of the history and literature of the Jews. The two most productive Jewish publicists of the nineteenth century—Leeser and Wise—both encouraged the preparation of translations of scholarly materials from German into English.[31] A scholarly "forty-eighter" named Maurice (Moritz) Mayer (1821–67) was especially active in this field; between 1850 and his death seventeen years later, he translated works by Geiger, Zunz and Philippson, a textbook, a work of Biblical exposition, a devotional volume for women, and his own German version of Ben Sira.[32] Translations of essays by Graetz were published in the *Occident* in 1864 and in the *Israelite* in 1868.[33] All three books published by the American Jewish Publication Society of 1872–75, (the second of three efforts to establish such a cultural enterprise) were translations from the German: Wilhelm Herzberg's *Jewish Family Papers* (1875); *Hebrew Characteristics* (1875)—a compilation of two studies by Joseph Perles (1835–94), a graduate of the Breslau Seminary, which had originally been published in Frankel's *Monatsschrift für Geschichte und Wissenschaft des Judenthums,* and a section from Zunz' *Zur Geschichte und Literatur;* and Graetz's first appearance in book form in America, the translation by Rabbi James K. Gutheim (1817–86) of the fourth volume of Graetz's incomparable *History* (1873).[34] As late as 1880–83, a German Jewish journal published in Milwaukee, named the *Zeitgeist* (edited by two former Breslau students—Rabbis Isaac (1847–1926) and Adolph (1840–1902) Moses, and a Hochschule graduate—Emil G. Hirsch) featured serious academic studies, including a new paper by Graetz on

"Shylock in der Sage und in Geschichte," which appeared simultaneously in Breslau in the *Monatsschrift*.[35] The first major undertaking of the present Jewish Publication Society (organized in Philadelphia in 1888) was the entire six-volume Graetz *History* (1891–98), still a fundamental corner-stone of a Judaica library, although serious students cannot easily forgive the trustees' decision to omit the indispensible footnotes. So dependent upon German-Jewish research and literary activity was the new Jewish Publication Society that one exasperated rabbi asked, "Are we so wretchedly poor that we could not produce some fair specimen of our own make to open the list of our Publication Society?" American Jewry was to continue to rely upon the work of German scholars for many years to come.[36]

The first exponent of *Wissenschaft* to arrive in the United States was probably Isaac Nordheimer (1809–42) a graduate of the Pressburg (Hungary) Yeshiva and a Ph.D. from the University of Munich. Nordheimer was a brilliant, creative Hebrew and Semitics philologist who taught at the University of the City of New York and also at the Union Theological Seminary—the first known case of a practicing Jew's service on the faculty of a Christian theological institution. His death of tuberculosis at the age of thirty-three deprived the New York Jewish community of an intelligent leader, and American Jewry of a scholar who might so early have been able to inspire young American Jews to pursue careers in Jewish studies. Nordheimer's two-volume *Critical Grammar of the Hebrew Language* (1838, 1841) and other works marked him as a scholar of unusual promise to whom the Jewish present was as important as the Jewish past.[37]

Isaac Leeser was not a research scholar, nor a creative student, but his translation of the Bible was a trail-blazing venture for which American Jewry had reason to be grateful from 1853 to 1917. Leeser followed the example of Moses Mendelssohn (1729–86), Ludwig Philippson and Leopold Zunz, and indeed relied on their work in great measure. Mendelssohn's aim had been to teach German to Yiddish-speaking Jews with the Bible as a textbook; Philippson and Zunz were primarily concerned with scholarly precision. Leeser sought to combine accuracy of translation with commitment to Jewish tradition—one of his purposes was to make it unnecessary for English-speaking Jews to turn to the King James Protestant translation or other Bibles with a Christian orientation. In assessing the worth of Leeser's Bible, Professor Harry Orlinsky concludes that "the scholarship in general was on a consistently high level," although "too much Hebrew and German protruded in the translation."[38] But without Leeser's remarkable ability to perceive the basic needs of

American Jewry and his willingness to sacrifice his own comfort and security in order to supply the tools for American Jewish survival, American Jewry would have had to wait sixty-four years for its own translation of the Bible.

In 1892 the Jewish Publication Society undertook to provide a new Bible translation under the leadership of a team of German-educated *Wissenschaft* editors including Kohler and Frederick de Sola Mendes, with Jastrow as the chief editor.[39] The plan was to assign responsibility for each book to an individual scholar whose work would then be revised by the editors. This program was so unworkable that its only product was a translation of the Psalms by Kohler which was published by the Society in 1903. Jastrow passed from the scene, his place being taken by Schechter, but a new approach was devised in 1908: a special editorial board was appointed which would itself undertake the task of translation. The members of this committee were Schechter, Kohler, Schulman, Cyrus Adler, Joseph Jacobs (1854–1916), David Philipson (1862–1949) and Max Margolis (1866–1932). Schechter, Kohler and Schulman were certainly products of German *Wissenschaft;* Jacobs, an Australian with a degree from Cambridge, had studied Jewish sources in Berlin with Steinschneider, Moritz Lazarus and other scholars;[40] Margolis had been a student in Berlin for three years before he became the first man to earn a Ph.D. in Semitics at Columbia—under Richard J. H. Gottheil, himself a product of the German universities and the Hochschule;[41] Philipson never matriculated in Germany, but he was a member of the first graduating class of Hebrew Union, where he was thoroughly indoctrinated in *Wissenschaft* methodology; only Cyrus Adler was trained in a non-Jewish German academic tradition through his Ph.D. work at Johns Hopkins with Paul Haupt (1858–1926), under whose tutelage he became the first student to gain the degree in Semitics at an American university—but Adler had already been imbued with respect for *Wissenschaft* through his private studies in Philadelphia with Morais, Jastrow and Samuel Hirsch. The Bible translation which these men produced, in 1917, was, therefore, a genuine result of nineteenth century German-Jewish scholarship.[42]

The great *Jewish Encyclopedia* of 1901–05, the most distinguished work of Jewish scholarship ever produced in any place, in any language, was sure evidence that the torch of *Wissenschaft* had passed from Germany to America.[43] It was a harbinger of the transmission of practical leadership in the world of Jewish affairs from Europe to America. But most of the members of the editorial board and most of the highly productive contributors were trained in *Wissenschaft* techniques either in

German institutions or by graduates of German schools. Isidore Singer (1859–1939), the publicist/entrepreneur who directed the project from dream to fruition, was a Berlin Ph.D.[44] Of the original ten Jewish scholars who formed the editorial board, only Cyrus Adler was American-trained. Louis Ginzberg[45] and Jacob Z. Lauterbach (1873–1942) were two young *Wissenschaft* Talmudists whose work on the *Encyclopedia* gave them an unparalleled opportunity to gain recognition in American Jewish academic circles. The *Encyclopedia* represents a high peak of achievement in the categories of learning which were most greatly prized in *Wissenschaft:* philology, literary history, biography, rabbinic concepts, halachic origins, liturgical developments, political events and the like—but not social or economic history, psychological motivations or matters of popular culture: these were ultimately introduced to American Jewry by Simon Dubnow (1860–1941)—whose first appearances in America were in translation from the German[46]—and under the twin influences of the Vilna Yiddish Scientific Institute (the name is no accident)[47] and the development of new concepts of social history in the United States.[48]

Each of the pioneer American Jewish institutions of higher education was established for pragmatic reasons—Maimonides College, Hebrew Union College, and the Jewish Theological Seminary to provide rabbis for American synagogues; Gratz College as a teachers' college; Dropsie College for non-theological post-graduate studies which would lead to academic careers. Intellectual distinction did not have the same social/national signification and symbolism in the United States in the nineteenth century and first half of the twentieth century as in Germany. The creators of the theological and normal schools of American Jewry were more concerned with Jews than with Gentiles, with Judaism than the general culture. Although they were not indifferent to what the Gentiles would say, they never thought that the non-Jews would be impressed with the high quality of Jewish scholarship! Their goal was primarily to develop leaders who would give intelligent guidance to a new generation of American Jews, to help Judaism to take root in America. This was not the same kind of objective which had motivated the founders of *Wissenschaft*. But the methodology which was utilized by these colleges and seminaries was the "scientific" approach to Jewish learning. All of them, to a greater or lesser degree, were based on the model of Breslau.[49] Only in the area of Biblical studies did some of the scholars and leaders (including Isaac Mayer Wise) express reservations about the use of the historical method;[50] otherwise *Wissenschaft* was the foundation both of the classroom and of the research and writing of the professors. In the Orthodox movement a struggle ensued, and still persists, between those who pursue the traditional approach to Talmudic studies and those who seek to apply the categories of classical and historical investigation to the textual foundations of the *halacha*. While most students at Yeshiva University pursue rabbinic studies in the manner of the great Eastern European *yeshivot,* its Graduate School for talmudic research is very appropriately named for its former president, Rabbi Bernard Revel (1885–1940), the first recipient of a Dropsie Ph.D.[51] The difference between these two methods—the one influenced as much by German *Wissenschaft* as by the Vilna Gaon—is dramatized in Chaim Potok's exquisitely fashioned novel *The Chosen* (1967).

Notable among the scholars who introduced the traditions of *Wissenschaft* scholarship into the very fabric of the Jewish Theological Seminary was the historian Alexander Marx (1878–1954) whose biographical sketches of his teachers kept alive the memory of the human beings who edited the texts and wrote the books and synthesized the data.[52] Even before he came to the United States, Schechter paid extensive homage to Zunz in a lengthy essay on the man and his work which he submitted as an entry for a prize offered in 1886 by the Jewish Ministers' Association of America.[53] In Cincinnati, such men as the Talmudist Moses Mielziner (1828–1903) and Gotthard Deutsch (1858–1921) and Jacob Mann (1888–1940), both historians, carried on the direct traditions of *Wissenschaft*. When Stephen S. Wise (1874–1949) founded the Jewish Institute of Religion in New York City in 1922, among his many motivations was the conviction that "one of the offices of a rabbinical institution is to help men to pursue the richly rewarding career of learning and research in *Juedische Wissenschaft*."[54]

Well into the twentieth century, just as Eastern Europe was the source of traditional rabbinic learning, Germany continued to be the fountain-head of scientific Jewish scholarship. At the turn of the century, Judah Leon Magnes (1877–1948), who was to become the first head of the Hebrew University of Jerusalem, and Julian Morgenstern (1881–   ), who succeeded Wise, Mielziner and Kohler in the presidency of the Hebrew Union College, journeyed from Cincinnati to Germany to pursue doctoral studies.[55] After the First World War, the historian Jacob Rader Marcus, the archaeologist Nelson Glueck (1900–71), the Biblical scholar Sheldon Blank and Walter Rothman (1898–1966), for many years the librarian at Hebrew Union College, followed the same path. It was not until the 1930s (with the exception of Solomon B. Freehof who did not remain in the academic field) that Cincinnati undertook the training of its own graduates for academic careers. But the Theological Seminary anticipated Hebrew Union in this regard,

Rabbi Louis Finkelstein being the most notable example of an early American-trained Seminary scholar. JTS also began another new tradition by directing aspiring scholars to Jerusalem or seeking new faculty members in Jerusalem. But one of the greatest American Jewish historians of our day, Salo Baron (1895–   ), author of a distinguished multi-volume *Social and Religious History of the Jews,* published jointly by Columbia University and the Jewish Publication Society, is himself the result of a *Wissenschaft* education in the academies of Europe.[56]

In the midst of the religious disagreements and strife which sharply divide the faculties of the American Jewish institutions of higher learning, and their graduates, respect for creative, knowledgeable scholarship, largely in the *Wissenschaft* tradition, has been a uniting factor. In 1901, for instance, David Philipson offered a resolution at the convention of the Central Conference of American Rabbis in honor of the centenary of the birth of Zacharias Frankel, including a cash award for an essay on his works "in order to bring his productions nearer to the minds of American Judaism"—his academic "productions," of course, not his theological precepts.[57] The Jewish Theological Seminary in 1903 presented Kohler in a series of lectures on "The Apocryphal and Apocalyptic Literature of the Jews."[58] When Schechter spoke at the dedication of the new buildings of the Hebrew Union College in 1913, he said, "the fact remains that we are unfortunately divided both in questions of doctrine—at least certain doctrines—and even more in practice. But, thank God, there are still a great many things and aims for which both parties can work in perfect harmony and peace, and unite us. . . . There is, first, the question of Jewish learning, which concerns us all. This . . . can only be accomplished by the Jews and for the Jews. . . . To this, any student keeping pace with the productions of theology, philosophy and history will bear evidence."[59]

The team of scholars which cooperated on the translation of the JPS Bible demonstrated that their fidelity to scholarship transcended their theological commitments; Kohler assented to the selection as editor of Max Margolis whom he had dismissed years before from the Cincinnati faculty primarily for ideological (but also for personal) reasons![60] A similar respect for scientific pursuits led some of the savants of Dropsie, Hebrew Union, and JTS to organize the American Academy for Jewish Research in 1919 "to stimulate Jewish learning by helpful cooperation and mutual encouragement as well as to formulate standards of Jewish scholarship."[61]

While *Wissenschaft* may have been a sure guide to professors, it has not necessarily been acclaimed by rabbinical students. According to

Charles S. Liebman's painstaking investigations of contemporary rabbinical education, Yeshiva University students "do not take the Bernard Revel Graduate School program seriously . . . [they] are more at home with the traditional method of study." At JTS, "the textual orientation of the courses is the primary source of dissatisfaction among . . . students. Many found their courses uninspiring, and their preparation for the rabbinate inadequate, because problems raised by Jewish philosophy, theology, or the place of Judaism in the modern world are ignored." At HUC, "some students (and alumni) are unhappy with the general scholarly approach in the courses . . . most students prefer instructors with an integrative-theological position, rather than a scholarly-textual one." *Wissenschaft* has been more or less consciously rejected by students at HUC-JIR and JTS—they seek a training which is more thoroughly related to their responsibilities as rabbis; the majority of Yeshiva University rabbinical students are content to study the Talmud in the traditional manner and have little interest in a scientific, objective method. All this seems to be an expression of the rabbinical students' search for religious identity—the nature of their commitment to piety and calling—rather than a dependable index to their considered opinion of an abstract "scientific" body of knowledge: a significant difference![62]

But this same identity search has led increasing thousands of young American Jewish college students to enroll in courses on Jewish life, history, literature and thought, and thereby to dramatize the American fulfillment of Zunz' dream of the emancipation of Jewish learning from the ghetto. Germany never did assimilate Jewish studies into the university curriculum. That remained for American pluralism to effectuate —but not overnight. When William Rosenau published his survey of the Semitics Departments of American colleges and universities in 1897, he apparently discovered not one course in Judaism beyond the Biblical period, although "rabbinical Hebrew" was listed at several. In addition to Rabbi Emil G. Hirsch at the University of Chicago, Morris Jastrow was teaching at the University of Pennsylvania and Richard J. H. Gottheil at Columbia. Both Jastrow and Gottheil (as well as Abram S. Isaacs who taught Hebrew at New York University 1885–94 and 1906–20) were sons of rabbis, interested in a wide range of Jewish research, but perhaps it did not even occur to them that they might secure a foothold for Judaic studies in their institutions—they undoubtedly had very few Jewish students other than rabbis, and may have believed the subject was well covered in the rabbinical seminaries.[63] Beginning in 1919, the Intercollegiate Menorah Association sponsored an annual Zunz lecture, each year at a different university, in tribute to the pioneering scholar of

Wissenschaft, and in an effort to give recognition to distinguished Jewish research in America. Only four lectures were delivered (and in turn printed in the *Menorah Journal*). Significantly, the two Jewish lecturers were from Jewish institutions (Ginzberg from JTS and Margolis from Dropsie) while the two Gentiles represented non-sectarian institutions— Harvard and the University of Nebraska.[64] In 1925 Hyman G. Enelow of Temple Emanu-El of New York City, concluded a lecture on Zunz with an appeal: "Then let us agitate for academic chairs on the subject [of Judaism] in our universities."[65] It was the same year that probably the first chair in Jewish studies was established in an American college— Lucius Littauer's gift to Harvard. The chair's first occupant was the incomparable Harry Austryn Wolfson (1887–74). Five years later Baron was called to Columbia on the Miller foundation.[66] Courses were also taught at other institutions, but the field itself did not expand until the period following World War II when interest suddenly burgeoned. One notable example of this growth was Abraham I. Katsh's department at New York University. In 1969, an Association for Jewish Studies was organized, somewhat along the lines of similar academic societies. The now newly elected president of the Jewish Theological Seminary, Professor Gerson D. Cohen still then at Columbia, exclaimed: "Would Zunz, Steinschneider, or even Graetz have believed that in 1969 some fifty professors of Judaica, to a considerable degree American-born and trained, representing but a moiety of the universities sponsoring programs in Jewish studies and reflecting but a portion of the fields studied and taught, would gather at a major American university established by Jews [Brandeis University] to consider the status of their profession!"[67]

While it is true that most of the professors were American-trained, the majority are disciples or disciples of German-trained scholars—still probably almost without exception functioning within the *Wissenschaft* tradition. But, as Professor Irving Greenberg cogently points out, many students have turned to Jewish studies for emotional reasons—for "self-discovery and even psychic liberation." *Wissenschaft* may need to provide a warm truth as well as an objective one, if it is to serve the needs of these students.[68]

PHILOSOPHIES OF JUDAISM

A third response of German Jews to modernity was the development of systematic philosophies of Judaism. Moses Mendelssohn was the pioneer in this effort to define Judaism in terms philosophically acceptable to the most perceptive of his contemporaries—as indeed, to an incredible degree, Mendelssohn may in every respect be regarded as the pioneering modern Jew in the sense that he was the first fully to enter the modern world. But it was Mendelssohn's personal experience and example which made a memorable impact upon the thinking of American Jews, rather than his philosophical work. His major theological treatise, *Jerusalem,* did not appear in an American edition until 1852 when it was published by its translator, Isaac Leeser—but its thesis of "revealed law" and "natural religion" had no more enduring influence here than in Germany.[69] This is equally true of the theological and philosophical writing of Salomo Ludwig Steinheim (1789–1866), Solomon Formstecher (1808–89) and Samuel Hirsch (1815–89), each of whom fought to establish a secure position for the Jewish faith over against (but also in reference to) the dominant secular and Christian intellectual positions of the day. Even though Hirsch himself moved to the United States in 1866 and preached and worked here, his Hegelian approach gained no significant following in American Jewish circles.[70] By far the first influential Jewish work of a theological character was Kohler's descriptive and academic volume *Jewish Theology,* which was originally commissioned not by an American publisher but by the Gesellschaft zur Foerderung der Wissenschaft des Judentums of Berlin which issued it, in German of course, in 1910. Not until 1918 did it appear in the United States in an English translation which had been prepared by one of Kohler's students at Hebrew Union.

The German-Jewish philosophical enterprise reached its highest point in the period 1900 to 1930. The insights and perceptions of four men in particular have been of enduring, increasing significance: Hermann Cohen (1842–1918); Leo Baeck (1873–1956); Martin Buber (1878–1965); and Franz Rosenzweig (1886–1929).[71] Cohen articulated an interpretation of Judaism which centered primarily upon its prophetic idealism and exalted its ethical thrust; Baeck perceived Judaism as being in a constant state of tension, between reason and revelation, between mystery and commandment; Buber plumbed the depths of the Biblical text and Hasidic lore and emphasized the constant confrontation of God and man, the "meeting" despite the "eclipse"; Rosenzweig proclaimed the existential imperative of accepting the responsibility of revelation and of living within the *mitzvot.*

These teachers of Judaism—sages of the German-Jewish symbiosis —are today among the leaders of American Jewish thought. Only Abraham Joshua Heschel, scion of Hasidism and fighter for human rights;

Elie Wiesel, the passionate spokesman for those lost in the holocaust; the brilliant, creative *halachist,* Joseph B. Soloveitchik; and the penetrating Mordecai Kaplan can stand in the same rank as these German Jews whose thought continues to live and convey inspiration, though the world that brought them into being is dead.[72] Cohen's appeal for the primacy of the prophetic ethic is so strong that Kaplan has devoted an entire book to a summary of the neo-Kantian's views in an effort to refute them.[73] But only in 1971 did a new selection of Cohen's writings appear in English translation, prefaced with the philosopher's dramatic words "only the idea of God gives me the confidence that morality will become reality on earth. And because I cannot live without this confidence, I cannot live without God."[74] Baeck's *Essence of Judaism* continues to maintain its status as probably the most brilliant one-volume exposition of Jewish ideas in any language, and translations of his other writings (together with the exquisite biography by Albert H. Friedlander) bring increasing numbers of students under the spell of his unique "polarity" concept of Jewish thought.[75] Although Buber is under constant attack by traditionalists and *Wissenschaft* scholars for his failure to give serious weight to the claims of *halacha* in his "I and Thou" philosophy, his work exerts a continuing influence upon the minds and hearts of non-Jews—greater than any since Mendelssohn—while young American Jews continue to discover with amazement that he speaks to them too. More of Buber's writings have been translated into English than those of any other Jew who ever wrote on Jewish themes in a language other than Hebrew.[76] Rosenzweig's germinal ideas have appealed to a growing number of American rabbis even though his largest work, *The Star of Redemption,* was not published in English translation until 1971.[77] When the journal *Commentary* undertook a theological/philosophical survey in 1966, the editor in charge of the project defined 15 to 17 of the 27 non-Orthodox respondents as followers of Rosenzweig. Milton Himmelfarb commented that thirty-seven years after his death, Rosenzweig was "the single greatest influence on the religious thought of North American Jewry . . . a German Jew—a layman, not a rabbi—who died before Hitler came to power."[78] The twenty-year index of the distinguished quarterly *Judaism* lists nine articles about Buber and three excerpts from his writings; three articles about Baeck and an equivalent number by him; four articles about Rosenzweig; Cohen is the subject of only one article. Only Rav A. I. Kook of Jerusalem ranks high among non-German theologians: three articles about him and two by him.[79] These are mere indications of the influence of the four German Jewish spokesmen who have become major figures in American Jewish life.

In each case, however, as in that of Moses Mendelssohn himself, the man in living response to the actual conditions of life proved to be as inspirational as his writing: Cohen because he did not abandon Judaism in exchange for the gratifications of high academic status, and, in the crisis of the First World War, spoke out fearlessly in favor of the Jews of Eastern Europe; Buber because he was a charismatic *guru* of the Hasidic style who struggled both to uphold the originality of Judaism among the thinkers and leaders of the nations and also to turn his own people away from the dangers of idolatrous nationalism; Baeck because he spurned offers of personal safety, walked through the valley of tragedy in Theresienstadt and came forth from the prison-house with his personal faith undiminished; Rosenzweig because he rejected Christianity despite all its intellectual and theological allure and resolutely fought his own "way" back into the heart of his own faith—a "way" which stood the true test when he was required to bear the burden of dread paralysis. Cohen, Baeck, Buber and Rosenzweig have brought profound stimulation, creativity, and nobility to the student of Judaism, but they have also demonstrated the meaning of the faith in their courageous confrontation of challenge, their dignity in the face of personal dilemma and their staunch commitment to the Jewish people in every dire circumstance. They are worthy representatives of one of the greatest Jewries of all history.

REPRISE

If we combine the religious, academic and philosophical/theological aspects of Jewish life whose genesis we have traced in this paper with the practical and theoretical facets of Zionism—which in large measure represents an advance beyond Emancipation, in that it entails equality for the Jewish People as well as for the individual Jew—then we have rather completely subsumed the conceptual contours of American Jewish life. There is a good deal else, of course: among many other trends, the whining negativism of *Portnoy's Complaint* which makes a virtue out of the alienated misfortune of being a Jew, and the cowboy heroics of a Leon Uris novel which are as dreadful as the anti-heroics of a Saul Bellows volume. Much of American Jewish intellectual life is synthetic, vulgar, and nostalgic. What it possesses of vigor—again with the innovative exception of Kaplan—still derives primarily from Germany, and somewhat less from Eastern Europe. There are only glimmering suggestions of a distinctive Israeli talent for thought which give us the hope that—until American Jewry is mature enough to develop its own multivoiced spokesmen—"from Zion may indeed go forth Instruction, and an Eternal Word from Jerusalem."

(1972)

NOTES

1. Abbreviations utilized throughout the reference notes are: *AJA, American Jewish Archives* (1948–); *AJHQ, American Jewish Historical Quarterly* (1961–); *AJYB, American Jewish Year Book* (1899–); *CCARYB, Year Book of the Central Conference of American Rabbis* (1890–); *HJ, Historia Judaica* (1938–1961); and *PAJHS, Publication(s) of the American Jewish Historical Society* (1893–1961).

2. The beginnings of the struggle are portrayed in Michael A. Meyer, *The Origins of the Modern Jew: Jewish Identity and European Culture in Germany, 1794–1824* (Detroit, 1967).

3. European Reform is still best described in David Philipson, *The Reform Movement in Judaism,* originally written in 1907, reprinted with an updating chapter but without substantial changes in 1931 (N.Y.). W. Gunther Plaut, *The Rise of Reform Judaism, A Sourcebook of its European Origins* (N.Y., 1963), is a documentary study of Reform Judaism along thematic rather than strictly chronological lines.

4. The best essay on Frankel is still Louis Ginzberg's, in his *Students, Scholars and Saints* (Phila., 1928), pp. 195–216. Among the few English translations of pertinent statements by Frankel are several passages in Plaut, *Rise of Reform Judaism,* 22–6, 85–9, 162–2, and the condensation of an essay in Mordecai Waxman, ed., *Tradition and Change, The Development of Conservative Judaism* (N.Y., 1958), pp. 43–50. An interesting paper on Frankel is David Rudavsky's "The Historical School of Zacharia Frankel," *Jewish Journal of Sociology* V (1963): 224–44.

5. A good essay on the life and thought of Samson Raphael Hirsch by Edward W. Jelenko appears in Simon Noveck, ed., *Great Jewish Personalities in Modern Times* (Washington, 1960), pp. 61–96. Selections from his writings are to be found in Jacob Breuer, ed., *Fundamentals of Judaism* (N.Y., 1949), and L. Grunfeld, ed., *Judaism Eternal,* 2 vols. (London, 1956).

6. Korn, "Isaac Leeser: Centennial Reflections," *AJA* XIX (1967): 127–41.

7. A survey of possible intellectual origins of the Charleston Society (in Judaism and Christianity and in contemporary intellectual currents in Charleston itself) outside of German Reform developments was undertaken by Lou H. Silberman in the second of these Rudolph lectures, *American Impact, Judaism in the United States in the Early Nineteenth Century,* Chapter 5 in this volume. Many of Silberman's hunches and theories are suggestive, but none is so conclusive as to demonstrate that the Charleston movement was independent of German influence. Silberman is quite accurate in noting that the paragraph from a Frankfurt newspaper referring to Jewish religious Reform in Holland, Germany, and Prussia which is quoted in the Charleston "Memorial" of 1824 [the text of which may be consulted conveniently in Joseph L. Blau and Salo W. Baron, *The Jews in the United States 1790–1840, A Documentary History,* 3 vols. (N.Y., 1963), II, 553–60] was intended "to support the argument but was by no means the inspiration for the development." An additional point in Silberman's favor is that Harby, the major spokesman of the Charleston Society, probably knew no German. Nor did Jacob Clavius Levy (1788–1875), whose 48-page article on "The Reformed Israelites" in the *Southern Quarterly Review* (April 1844), contains many learned citations from Latin and other sources, seem to be able to read German or to have derived any of his liberal concepts directly from German works, since all of his references to Reform developments in Germany derive from the British periodical *The Voice of Jacob* and other publications in English. But Isaac N. Cardozo apparently did, and he and possibly other members of the Corresponding Committee were in touch with Reform circles in Germany, according to Cardozo's "Discourse" to the Society in 1827, reprinted in L. C. Moise, *Biography of Isaac Harby* (Columbia, S.C., 1930), p. 138. No student seems to have searched the Charleston daily press during the years preceding the organization of the "Reformed Society" for news reports of German Jewish Reform which may have influenced the Charlestonians. This would appear to be a necessary prerequisite for any definitive evaluation of the entire question. But whether the long-distance relationship between Germany and Charleston was vigorous or tenuous, it is clear that no individual directed the course of Reform in Charleston on the basis of prior personal experience with German religious Reform. This factor undoubtedly contributed to the failure of the early effort in Charleston.

8. The Poznanski case is a puzzling one: he served Shearith Israel of New York City for five years beginning in 1832 as *shochet, shofar-blower,* and, occasionaly, *hazan;* he came to Charleston certified to be an observant religionist; upon his departure from Charleston and his return to New York City after the Civil War he applied for membership privileges in Shearith Israel again—apparently satisfying the leaders of the Spanish-Portuguese congregation that he had abandoned his Reform ideas. A good deal more needs to be learned about Poznanski. What little is known of him is to be found in Barnett A. Elzas, *The Jews of South Carolina* (Phila., 1905), pp. 208–19; David and Tamar de Sola Pool, *An Old Faith in the New World* (N.Y., 1955), pp. 178, 247, 400, 430; Allan Tarshish, "The Charleston Organ Case," *AJHQ* LIV (1965): 411–49. Elzas is the authority for the statement that Poznanski was influenced by the Hamburg Temple. There seems to be no way of identifying the person in

Charleston who was responsible for the reprinting there of the 1839 London translation of Gotthold Salomon's *Twelve Sermons Delivered in the New Temple of the Israelites at Hamburgh* . . . (1841). The preface, signed with the initial "L." (for Levin, the Jewish partner of the publisher Levin and Tavel?) makes no reference to the liberal inclinations of Salomon: the first leaves of the book also advertise some of Isaac Leeser's works—perhaps an indication that the book was intended to represent Jewish theology, not *Reform* Jewish theology. At any rate, this was the first book published in the United States as a product of German Reform and it seems altogether appropriate that it appeared in Charleston. Leeser, incidentally, translated another of Salomon's Hamburg sermons, entitled "Moses and Jethro," and published it in *Occident* II (1844): 9–19, as the first of three "Specimens of German Preachers," the other two being Ludwig Philippson and Samuel Hirsch.

    9. Rabbi Bernhard N. Cohn makes the suggestion in his brief biographical sketch of Leo Merzbacher (1809–56), in *AJA* VI (1954): 21–4, that Merzbacher's dismissal from his rabbinical post with two New York City congregations on account of his liberal ideas in 1844 was the signal for Reform-minded laymen to create the Reform Cultus Verein which swiftly developed into Temple Emanu-El. It was Isaac Leeser's understanding that a "Mendelssohnian Society of New York" was being organized to foster "reform *à la mode de Hamburg*," and that its supporters "must be for the most part persons but lately arrived in this country, who have brought with them the spirit of 'young Germany,' alias 'experiment in religion and politics'" (*Occident* II [1844]: 515). One of the first actions of the Har Sinai Verein of Baltimore in 1842 was to order copies of the Reform prayerbook of Hamburg. Har Sinai's activity was weak and fitful until David Einhorn was brought to its pulpit from Europe, according to Isaac M. Fein, *The Making of an American Jewish Community, The History of Baltimore Jewry from 1773 to 1920* (Phila., 1971), pp. 63, 83. Einhorn was a leader not only to Har Sinai but also to Keneseth Israel of Philadelphia which became Reform in 1856 after it merged with a small radical Temple-Verein; Keneseth Israel adopted the Einhorn prayerbook after several years of experimentation with both the Hamburg and Merzbacher liturgies, as noted in *Sinai* I (1856): 254, 290; III (1858): 1075; V (1860): 124. *Die Deborah* II (1856): 98, reports that the great Rabbi Abraham Geiger was invited to come to New York City by Temple Emanu-El as Merzbacher's successor. Fein, *Baltimore*, 90, informs us that Oheb Shalom also sought Geiger as its rabbi in 1858, probably in response to Har Sinai's coup in securing Einhorn for its pulpit. In 1848 Charleston had elected a German rabbi sight unseen because he was highly recommended by Geiger, as reported in Elzas, *South Carolina*, p. 216. Even Zunz was considering the possibility of coming to New York City to occupy a pulpit in 1833, referred to in Guido Kisch, "Israels Herold: The First Jewish Weekly in New York," *HJ* II (1940): 75.

    10. James G. Heller's voluminous biography, *Isaac M. Wise, His Life, Work and Thought* (N.Y., 1964), pp. 85, 97, reports that he was in correspondence over a long period of time with Leopold Stein of Frankfurt and other Reform leaders in Germany. According to the digest of the Augsburg Synod of 1871 proceedings which was published in the first *CCARYB* (Cincinnati, 1891), p. 112, Wise had intended to go to Europe for the meetings, but wrote to Abraham

Geiger that he was prevented from so doing because of his overloaded schedule. It has not been possible for the writer to follow up the curious fact that there was an American layman at the Leipzig Synod of 1869—Simon Herman of N.Y., so listed in Philipson, *Reform Movement*, 291. He is not known to have amounted to very much in the United States. Wise published such important pieces as Immanuel Heinrich Ritter's summing-up of Holdheim's life-work in *Die Deborah* XI (1866): 6–7, 150–151, 156, 158. Einhorn reprinted some of the great German Reform writings in his *Sinai*, as, for instance, Holdheim's essays on "Old and New in Judaism of our Time" and "The Historic Basis of Reform."

11. The proceedings of the Philadelphia conference, as reported in *Protokolle der Rabbiner-Conferenz abgehalten zu Philadelphia, von 3. bis zum 6. November 1869* (N.Y., 1870), pp. 13, 21, 28–30, 44, were punctuated by references by Einhorn to Frankfurt, by Kohler, Mielziner, Einhorn and Felsenthal to Leipzig, by Mielziner and Felsenthal to Geiger, and by Chronik to Holdheim. The German Reformers were in attendance in thought, if not in body, as teachers and colleagues.

12. *CCARYB* I (1891): 23. A section of that volume, pp. 80–125, is devoted to compilations of the resolutions adopted at the prior meetings, beginning, strangely enough, not with Braunschweig, but with the French "Sanhedrin" of 1807.

13. Emil G. Hirsch was probably a member of the entering class of the Hochschule when it opened its doors in 1872; Sale began his studies in 1873. Hirsch received a grant from the Temple Emanu-El Theological Seminary of New York in 1873; Sale in 1874: Korn, "The Temple Emanu-El Theological Seminary of New York City," *Essays in American Jewish History (= Marcus Festschrift)* (Cincinnati, 1958), 367; *CCARYB* XLVII (1937): 233–5. Hirsch returned to the United States in 1876 fully prepared to enter the rabbinate; it was unlikely that he should even have considered matriculating at Hebrew Union after its opening in 1875—he was far too advanced for its curriculum, and his father's congregation, Keneseth Israel, had not yet joined the Union of American Hebrew Congregations in support of HUC. Sale (a native of Louisville) might have transferred to HUC but obviously prefered to continue his studies in Berlin. Even if Sale had expressed an interest in the Cincinnati institution. Geiger would probably have attempted to discourage him. Geiger was eager to have students from America in his school. In 1874 he wrote to Bernhard Felsenthal (1822–1908) of Chicago, who probably was busier corresponding with rabbis and scholars throughout the United States and Germany than any ten other men, "Will you send us new pupils from America? We could use them and they us." (Guido Kisch, "The Founders of 'Wissenschaft des Judentums' and America," *Marcus Festschrift*, p. 158). Felsenthal was in incessant contact with Reform leaders and scholars, as witness the references and excerpts from his correspondence thus far published in Adolf Kober, "Jewish Religious and Cultural Life in America as Reflected in the Felsenthal Collection," *PAJHS* XLV (1955): 93–127; Ezra Spicehandler and Theodore Wiener "Bernard Felsenthal's Letters to Ozias Schorr," *Marcus Festschrift* pp. 379–406. A classmate of Hirsch's at the Hochschule was Felix Adler, who returned to New York in 1873 to preach his only sermon at Emanu-El and then ultimately leave the synagogue to create the Ethical

Culture Movement. Rabbi Gottheil's son Richard (1862–1936) was later sent to the Hochschule for studies in Semitics, although he had no intention of entering the rabbinate. At least two other students were given scholarships to the Berlin institution by Temple Emanu-El in 1885, Julius Rosenthal, of whom nothing more is known, and Samuel Schulman. There was criticism that these men went to the Hochschule rather than to HUC, and Rabbi Gottheil felt compelled to publish an explanation in the *America Hebrew*, July 10, 1885, as quoted in Richard J. H. Gottheil, *The Life of Gustav Gottheil, Memoir of a Priest in Israel* (Williamsport, 1936), pp. 58–59, in which he protested that he hoped "to be known as a friend and not as an opponent of the Hebrew Union College," but the fact was that: "the two young men have arrived in their theological studies, nearly at the point where Cincinnati sends her students to fields of practical labor . . . What would have been the use of sending them to the Hebrew Union College? Indeed, if they had gone there they would have only proved an embarrassment to the governors, as no provision is as yet made for students of that advanced state." Among other young men sent to the Hochschule by Emanu-El was Abraham Ilich (1858–85) who was in Germany from 1880 to 1884, Jacob Voorsanger, *The Chronicles of Emanu-El* (San Francisco, 1900), 168–9. No other names of students from America can be culled from the *Annual Reports* of the Hochschule/Lehranstalt, but the officers exhibited great pleasure over the appointments of Henry Malter (1864–1925) to the faculties of Hebrew Union and Dropsie (1900, 1910 *Reports*), A. Gunsz to JTS (1894 *Report*, but no JTS source refers to the man!), Max Schloessinger (1877–1944) to Cincinnatti as instructor and librarian (1905 *Report*) and David Neumark (1866–1924) to the Cincinnati faculty (1908 *Report*).

14. W. Gunther Plaut, *The Growth of Reform Judaism, American and European Sources until 1948* (N.Y., 1965) pp. xx-xxiv, offers some interesting observations on the differences in background which account for the progress of Reform in America, Plaut, *Growth*, 113–14, gives the text of "Principles of Social Ethics" which were adopted by German-Jewish liberals in 1872; the "Principles" speak with none of the directness of the eighth point of the Pittsburgh Platform, which is reprinted in full in *CCARYB* I (1891): 121–1. Einhorn's position on slavery and the Civil War is reviewed in Korn, *American Jewry and the Civil War*, 3rd. ed. (N.Y., 1970), pp. 20–31. Hirsch's social justice views are evaluated in Plaut, *Growth*, 117; Roland B. Gittelsohn, "The Conference Stance on Social Justice and Civil Rights," in Korn, ed., *Retrospect and Prospect* (N.Y., 1965), 85–6; Bernard Martin, "The Social Philosophy of Emil G. Hirsch" *AJA* II (1954); Leonard J. Mervis, "The Social Justice Movement and the American Reform Rabbi," *AJA* VII (1955).

15. Some of the reasons for the failure of Maimonides College, Leeser's rabbinical academy, are weighed in Korn, "The First American Jewish Theological Seminary: Maimonides College, 1867–1873," *Eventful Years and Experiences* (Cincinnati, 1954), pp. 151–213.

16. Moshe Davis, *The Emergence of Conservative Judaism, The Historical School in 19th Century America* (Phila., 1963), traces the coalescence of many factors, moods, forces and reactions into the formation of the Jewish Theological

Seminary. Davis offers incisive biographical sketches of the many rabbinical leaders of the Historical School. As his title reveals, he believes that the Historical School and Conservative Judaism are identical. An interesting interpretation of "The *Trefa* Banquet" as a deliberate affront to the traditionalists by radical Reform leaders in Cincinnati is offered by John J. Appel in *Commentary*, February 1966, pp. 75–8.

17. Kohler, *A Living Faith* (Cincinnati, 1948), pp. 225–6, reprints his tribute to Frankel from *Menorah* XXXI (1902): 364–6. Davis is less concerned with the flow of ideas from Germany to the United States than with sociological growth within the American Jewish community. Marshall Sklare, *Conservative Judaism, An American Religious Movement* (Glencoe, 1955), pp. 229–38, concentrates on the inner contradictions of the Conservative movement in the post-World War II era and barely mentions its intellectual origins in the nineteenth century. Herbert Parzen, *Architects of Conservative Judaism* (N.Y., 1964), offers only the briefest reference to the movement's ideological origins in Germany. Waxman, *Tradition and Change*, 42–3, most clearly voices the conclusion that "Zacharias Frankel . . . is generally regarded as the intellectual progenitor of Conservative Judaism and he is clearly the source of many of the ideas and some of the phrases which played a significant role in the birth of the Conservative idea and movement . . . [He was] the ideological founder of the Conservative movement in Judaism."

18. Adolf Kober, "Aspects of the Influence of Jews from Germany on American Jewish Spiritual Life of the Nineteenth Century," in Eric E. Hirshler (ed.), *Jews from Germany in the United States* (N.Y., 1955), 134–7, 143–4, refers to some of the Breslau graduates who came to the United States. Fascinating details of the life and work of teachers, students and graduates of Breslau in America are scattered throughout Guido Kisch (ed.), *The Breslau Seminary, The Jewish Theological Seminary (Fraenckel Foundation) of Breslau 1854–1938 Memorial Book* (Tübingen, 1963), especially Alfred Jospe's section of "Short Biographies and Bibliographies," 381–442. Unfortunately no similar volume assembles in one place all of the records and achievements of the Hochschule/ Lehranstalt or the Hildesheimer Seminary. The Drachman case is unique: he was sent to Breslau (a Conservative institution) to study during the years 1882–1885 at the expense of the radical Reform Congregation Emanu-El who, he said, gave him total intellectual freedom: "No influence was exerted upon me to shape my vows . . . to influence my theological opinions or rabbinical policy . . ." The story is traced in his autobiography *The Unfailing Light: Memoirs of an American Rabbi* (N.Y., 1948), esp. 164–5. Graetz' intimate relations with Jastrow and Szold are reported in Davis, *Emergence*, 343, and Fein, *Baltimore*, 183. The first American student to go to Europe to undertake rabbinical studies, Simon Tuska, spent two years at Breslau, 1858–1860, but left without securing ordination; he was particularly fond of Frankel and Graetz: Abraham J. Karp, "Simon Tuska Becomes a Rabbi," *PAJHS* L (1960), 79–97. Henry W. Schneeberger (1848– 1916) was apparently the "first American-born, university-trained, ordained Rabbi in the United States"—after studies with Bondi and Lehmann in Mainz, he joined Hildesheimer in Hungary, then followed him to Berlin, where he received *smicha* in 1871. (Israel M. Goldman, "Henry W. Schneeberger: His Role in

American Judaism," *AJHQ* LVII [1967], 153–90.) The use of the term "Historical Judaism" is illustrated on page after page of Davis and Parzen; the term was rarely used by Reformers.

19. Kisch, in *Marcus Festschrift,* 159, offers some interesting information on Schechter's relations with Breslau. The quotation is from Schechter, *Seminary Addresses and Other Papers* (Cincinnati, 1915), 23, 25. It is unclear to this writer whether Schechter meant Reform Judaism or Christianity when he referred to "the great majority."

20. An address which Adler delivered to the Rabbinical Assembly in 1923, printed in his *Lectures, Selected Papers, Addresses* (Phila., 1933), 256.

21. The most thorough analysis of Reconstructionism is by Charles S. Liebman in *AJYB*, 71 (1970), 3–99. Liebman's introduction states the case very succinctly: "Kaplan probably is the most creative American Jewish thinker to concern himself with a program for American Judaism. He is one of the few intellectuals in American Jewish life who have given serious consideration to Jewish tradition, American philosophical thought, and the experiences of the American Jew, and confronted each with the other. Reconstructionism is the only religious party in Jewish life whose origins are entirely American."

22. "Personal Reminiscences of My Early Life," reprinted from *Hebrew Union College Monthly,* May, 1918, in Kaufmann Kohler, *Studies, Addresses and Personal Papers* (N.Y., 1931), 475. Leeser published translations of some of Hirsch's writings from *Jeschurun* in the *Occident,* for instance in XIV (1856), 269–81 (comments on a French rabbinical conference) and 332–47 (interpretations of the Fast of the Ninth of Ab.) Leeser did not regard his own and Hirsch's ideologies as essentially different—perhaps he did not comprehend the separatist aspects of the Hirsch viewpoint—but this may be a warning to those who automatically claim Leeser as a member of the Historical School.

23. Drachman says in his biographical sketch (p. xxi) that "the publication of this work . . . showed that orthodox Judaism was not maintained solely by the superstitious, or narrow-minded older generation, who had never been initiated into the science and culture of the age; but that it could be warmly, nay, enthusiastically, upheld by one who had thoroughly acquainted himself with the most daring researches of the new time, and met them with equally bold and open argument."

24. Dayan Dr. I. Grunfeld, *Three Generations, The Influence of Samson Raphael Hirsch on Jewish Life and Thought* (London, 1958), 82–90; Charles S. Liebman, "Orthodoxy in American Jewish Life," *AJYB* 66 (1965), 71–2; the New York firm of Feldheim Publishers issues a leaflet which lists the Hirsch translations thus far sponsored by the Society. Some significance must also be attached to the ongoing and perhaps increasing interest in Hirsch's concepts and attitudes evidenced by four articles about his thought which have appeared in the quarterly *Tradition, A Journal of Orthodox Jewish Thought.* One of these includes a translation by Leo Levi of Hirsch's *halachic* decision that observant Jews must shun "association with any organization which [in the opinion of Orthodox Jews] denies in principle certain fundamentals of Judaism"—*Tradition* IX (1967): 95–102.

Reviews of translations of five of Hirsch's works into English have also been included in *Tradition,* and some of its more scholarly articles, when appropriate, have referred to Hirsch in footnotes. Milton Himmelfarb, in his introduction to the well-known *Commentary,* August 1966, symposium on American Jewish thought, reprinted as *The Condition of Jewish Belief* (N.Y., 1966), perceives most of the Orthodox participants in the survey as being "in the tradition of . . . Samson Raphael Hirsch . . . because Hirsch was not only Rabbi Hirsch, he was also Dr. Hirsch." But as we indicate in the second section of this lecture, the background would seem to be much more that of *Wissenschaft* scholarship, than the theoretical teaching of S. R. Hirsch. Lou H. Silberman, however, in "Concerning Jewish Theology in North America: Some Notes on a Decade," *AJYB* 70 (1969), 53, defines the Hirsch influence upon today's younger Orthodox scholars largely in terms of the fact that "in the 19th century Hirsch began to do Jewish theology from the Bible . . . an unmistakably Jewish foundation, one that was more readily available than the immense *halakhic* literature even to his strictly traditionalist community."

25. No single study in English presents a full description of the growth and achievements of the *Wissenschaft* school in the country of its origin. Meyer, *The Origins of the Modern Jew,* 144–182, traces the inception of the concept. Luitpold Wallach, "The Beginnings of the Science of Judaism in the Nineteenth Century," *HJ* VIII (1946), 33–60, offers a spate of definitions and interpretations, especially from the early period. Schechter, in a lecture delivered at Dropsie University in 1910, "The Beginnings of Jewish 'Wissenschaft,' " included in *Seminary Addresses,* 173–93, presents some pungent antidotes to the exaggerated tributes to the pioneers.

26. Ginzberg on Zacharias Frankel in *Students, Scholars and Saints,* 195. This was a lecture which Ginzberg delivered to the Ohole Shem Society in New York City on Oct. 6, 1901, to mark the centenary of Frankel's birth.

27. Glatzer, "The Beginnings of Modern Jewish Studies," in Alexander Altmann (ed.), *Studies in Nineteenth Century Jewish Intellectual History* (Cambridge, 1964), 32.

28. Voiced very early by Zunz in his 1818 pamphlet *On Rabbinic Literature* (*Etwas über die Rabbinische Litteratur* [*Berlin*]) and reiterated by Geiger and Philippson—see Adolf Kober, "The Jewish Theological Seminary of Breslau . . . ," in Kisch, *The Breslau Seminary,* 264–5—and such successors as Kaufmann —see references to his "Die Vertretung der jüdischen Wissenschaft an der Universitäten" in Lou H. Silberman, "The University and Jewish Studies," in Leon A. Jick (ed.), *The Teaching of Judaica in American Universities, The Proceedings of a Colloquium* (N.Y., 1970).

29. Cyrus Adler, *Catalogue of the Leeser Library* (Phila., 1883). This is not the place to review the development of the great Jewish libraries of America, but it is worth noting that when Judge Mayer Sulzberger contributed part of his library to the JTS, he expressed his confidence that the institution would become "a center for original work in the science of Judaism." *Jewish Theological Seminary Semi-Centennial Volume* (N.Y., 1926), 90.

30. Zunz was actually a correspondent for the short-lived German-American

periodical, *Israels Herold,* which was published in New York City in 1849 by the refugee forty-eighter Isidor Busch (= Bush). The tone of the weekly was too highly intellectual for popular consumption in the United States—but Zunz' collaboration was apparently necessary to put the stamp of approval upon a Jewish intellectual endeavor. See Kisch, "Israel's Herold," *HJ* II: 73, 75–6, for details of Zunz' contributions.

31. Heller, *Wise,* 223, reports that Wise contributed translations of excerpts of the writings of Zunz, Geiger, Frankel, Rappaport, Luzzatto, Krochmal, Holdheim, Jost and Graetz to the *Asmonean* during the period 1852–1854 when he served as editor of the journal's department of "Theology and Philosophy," even before he began to publish his own paper. The translation of a study by Philippson on "The Expulsion of the Jews from Spain and Portugal" is in *Occident* XII (1859): 93–4, 106–7, 111–12, 121–2, 129–30.

32. Biographical data about Mayer is in *Israelite* XIII (1867), Sept. 13; Korn, "Jewish 'Forty-Eighters' in America." *Eventful Years and Experiences* (Cincinnati, 1954), 18–20; Elzas, *South Carolina,* 160, 219. Mayer's publications are as follows: 1) *Ben Sira. Volksbuch über moral und Sittenlehre* . . . (N.Y., 1850); 2) transl. of Isidor Kalisch, *A Guide for Rational Inquiries into the Biblical Writings* . . . (Cincinnati, 1857); 3) transl. of Samuel Adler's revision of Emanuel Hecht, *Biblical History for Israelitish Schools* (N.Y., 15 editions between 1859 and 1874); 4) transl. of passages from Zunz' *History of Jewish Literature* in *Occident* XIX (1861), 471–6. 547–51; XX, 7–10, expanded with notes by Mayer; 5) transl. of Geiger's *Origin and Development of Christianity* in *Occident* XXI (1863)–XXIII (1865); 6) transl. of Geiger's *Judaism and its History* (N.Y., 1865); 7) transl. of Ludwig Philippson's "Did indeed the Jews Crucify Jesus?" *Occident* XXIII (1866)–XXIV (1867), published separately as *The Crucifixion and the Jews* (Phila., 1866), with preface by Leeser; 9) transl. of Fanny Neuda, *Hours of Devotion* (N.Y., 10 editions between 1868 and 1874); 10) a lecture on Jost in *Occident* XIX (1861), 12–17, 58–65.

33. Solomon Grayzel, "Graetz's 'History' in America," *HJ* III (1941), 53–66, revised for Kisch (ed.), *The Breslau Seminary,* 223–37. Grayzel does not attempt to list every appearance of Graetz in America, for instance the article on Spinoza in *Israelite* XIV (1868), 42 and following issues, or young Simon Tuska's translation of his teacher Graetz's *Influence of Judaism on the Protestant Reformation* (Cincinnati, 1867).

34. The best account of the activities of the first two Jewish Publication Societies is Lewis C. Littman's unpublished master's thesis *Stages in the Development of a Jewish Publication Society* (HUC-JIR, N.Y., 1967), 138 pp. At an early point, the AJPS had also considered the publication of translations of works by Geiger and Ludwig Philippson. The *Jewish Times* of New York, however, had begun to publish the first chapter of Gutheim's translation as early as 1869— this means Gutheim's work antedated the formation of the AJPS.

35. Louis J. Switchkow and Lloyd P. Gartner, *The History of the Jews of Milwaukee* (Phila., 1962), 123–7. *Der Zeitgeist* also published an original study by Graetz on "The Stages in the Development of the Messianic Belief," and sections of a volume by Adolf Jellinek (1820–1893).

36. Rabbi Henry Iliowizi in Philadelphia *Jewish Exponent*, Oct. 4, 1889, quoted by Grayzel in Kisch, *Breslau Seminary*, 227. German-Jewish *Wissenschaft* refugees have made notable contributions through the Leo Baeck Institute (organized after World War II in New York City, with branches in London and Jerusalem) and the Schocken Books firm which perpetuates in New York the ideals of its Berlin founder.

37. The most complete sketch of Nordheimer is by David de Sola Pool in *Dictionary of American Biography*, 22 vols. (N.Y., 1946), XIII, 547–8. Blau and Baron, *The Jews of the United States 1790–1840*, II, 429–36, reprints the preface and introduction to Nordheimer's *Grammar*. Hyman B. Grinstein, *The Rise of the Jewish Community of New York* (Phila., 1945), 220, 253, 590, and de Sola Pool, *Old Faith*, 224, 229, give data on Nordheimer's participation in Jewish education and the affairs and interests of the Jewish community. William Chomsky, "Hebrew Grammar and Textbook Writing in Early Nineteenth Century America," *Marcus Fetschrift*, 136–41, regards Nordheimer's *Grammar* as "the most scientific Hebrew grammar of that period and, perhaps, of the century."

38. Matitiahu Tsevat, "A Retrospective View of Isaac Leeser's Biblical Work," *Marcus Festschrift*, 295–313, see especially note 27 in which Tsevat expresses the feeling that "Leeser referred to Philippson and Zunz more than was necessary in an edition for popular and liturgical use." Orlinsky's opinion of Leeser's Bible is from his essay "Jewish Biblical Scholarship in America," *Jewish Quarterly Review* (N.S.) XLV (1955): 380.

39. This fifteen year-long process is described in the Preface to the 1917 Jewish Publication Society translation, iii–vi; additional details are recorded in David Philipson, *By Life as an American Jew* (Cincinnati, 1941), 195–200, including a reproduction of a photograph of the Board of Editors, together with their autographs.

40. Alexander Marx, *Essays in Jewish Biography* (Phila., 1947), in his tribute to Moritz Steinschneider, 141, lists Jacobs as having attended the great bibliographer's lectures at the Veitel-Heine-Ephraim Institute.

41. Robert Gordis, "The Life of Professor Max Leopold Margolis: An Appreciation," in Gordis (ed.), *Max Leopold Margolis, Scholar and Teacher* (Phila., 1952), 3–4; Louis I. Newman, "Richard J. H. Gottheil," *AJYB* XXXIX (1937): 29–46; Gottheil, "Morris Jastrow," *PAJHS* XXIX (1925): 170–3: "Our acquaintance as fellow scholars and as fellow workers in the same field dated from about the year of 1882 or 1883, when he was a student in the Orthodox Jewish Seminary in Breslau, and I at the Reform Seminary in Berlin."

42. Cyrus Adler, *I Have Considered the Days* (Phila., 1941), 12–14.

43. Joshua Trachtenberg, "American Jewish Scholarship," *The Jewish People, Past and Present*, 4 vols. (N.Y., 1946–55), IV, 417.

44. "Dr. Singer at Three-Score Ten," *American Hebrew*, Nov. 8, 1929.

45. Ginzberg was still writing in German when he submitted the second volume of his encyclopedic *Legends of the Jews* to the Jewish Publication Society in 1910.

46. See Koppel S. Pinson's biographical introduction and selection of the historian's essays in *Dubnow, Nationalism and History* (Phila., 1958), especially pp. 22–3, for Israel Friedlaender's championship of Dubnow in the United States; "Israel Friedlaender the Scholar," in Marx, *Jewish Biography*, 280–1, for his translations of Dubnow into German, one of which was, in turn, translated into English by Henrietta Szold, published in 1903, and is reprinted in the Pinson volume, pp. 253–324. Friendlaender also introduced Ahad Ha-Am to the Western world.

47. The name YIVO, which is more familiar to American Jews, in an abbreviation for *Yiddisher Vissenshaftlikher Institut.*

48. Most of the articles in the *Universal Jewish Encyclopedia* (N.Y., 1939–1943) cannot compare in depth, breadth or texture to the *JE;* a high proportion of them were compiled not by scholars but by journalists and students. Its promoters were fortunate enough to receive the support of governmental funds through the WPA, but were still severely disadvantaged by limited financial resources. But most of the important scholars connected with the venture were *Wissenschaft* products . . . see the photo of the leaders in Vol. IV, 106. The new *Encyclopaedia Judaica* (Jerusalem, 1972) stems originally from work undertaken prior to the holocaust in Germany where ten volumes of an *Encyclopedia Judaica* were published (complete through the letter L) under the direction of Jacob Klatzkin, Ismar Elbogen and Nahum Goldmann. When the present writer agreed to prepare one article in the latter part of the alphabet, he received transcripts of original research notes made more than thirty-five years previously, in Germany!

49. Jacob Mann, "Modern Rabbinical Seminaries," *CCARYB* XXXV (1925): 304, 307.

50. Heller, *Wise*, 530–3; Eli Ginzberg, *Keeper of the Law, Louis Ginzberg* (Phila., 1966), 62–3; Schechter, "Higher Criticism—Higher Anti-Semitism," address delivered at a banquet in 1903 in honor of Kohler, printed in *Seminary Addresses*, 35–9.

51. Charles S. Liebman, "The Training of American Rabbis," *AJYB* 69 (1968): 30–1. Revel's dissertation was *The Karaite Halakah and its Relation to Sadducean, Samaritan and Philonian Halakah* (published by Dropsie in 1915). Gilbert Klaperman, in his *Story of Yeshiva University* (N.Y., 1969), 138, says in so many words that "with equal enthusiasm he [Revel] devoted himself to secular studies and hakhmat Yisrael, the Wissenschaft des Judentums (the Scientific Study of Judaism)." Samuel Belkin, the present head of Yeshiva University, is a Ph.D. from Brown (1935), his dissertation having dealt with Philo and the Oral Law. This does not mean that either of these men was a champion of *Wissenschaft,* but it does connote respect for "scientific" scholarship and research in Jewish life and letters beyond the confines of operative *halacha.* Since this was written, Aaron Rothkoff's *Bernard Revel: Building of American Jewish Orthodoxy* (Phila., 1972) has been published, and reiterates our point—see especially pp. 242ff.

52.. Marx, *Essays in Jewish Biography:* studies of Steinschneider; David Hoffman, second president of the Hildesheimer Seminary of Berlin (and Marx' father-in-law); Schechter; Joseph Jacobs; Henry Malter; Max Margolis; Israel Friedlaender.

53. The essay is in *Studies in Judaism* III (Phila., 1924): 84–142. *Jewish Conference Papers* (N.Y., 1887), 9–18, constitute a study of Zunz by M. Landsberg of Rochester; 40–1 refer to the prize.

54. Wise, *Challenging Years* (N.Y., 1949), 133. Wise himself was not ordained at a seminary but, according to report, by Rabbi Adolf Jellenik of Vienna, a distinguished *Wissenschaft scholar*. He had, however, studied with his father, with Kohut at JTS and with Gustav Gottheil. His Ph.D. was from Columbia, under the younger Gottheil. Rebekah Kohut, *His Father's House* (New Haven, 1938), 44–5.

55. Magnes and Morgenstern overlapped for a few years. Magnes spent a year at the Lehranstalt (Hochschule) and at the University of Berlin before going on to Heidelberg, where he received the Ph.D. and where Morgenstern also took the doctorate. In Berlin Magnes was friendly with Eugen Taeubler (1879–1953), who later came to Hebrew Union as a refugee professor, and with Emil Bernhard Cohn (1881–1948) who served a German refugee congregation in New York City after his flight from the Nazis. Norman Bentwich, *For Zion's Sake, A Biography of Judah L. Magnes* (Phila., 1954), 24–5, 31. According to Marx, *Essays,* 140, Magnes also attended Steinschneider's lectures.

56. Baron's first post in the United States was at the Jewish Institute of Religion (1926–30), prior to his call to Columbia. His methodological training was in Vienna, where he took three doctorates at the University, and also was ordained at the Jewish Theological Seminary—an institution which followed the Breslau model, (Joseph Blau et al., eds., *Essays on Jewish Life and Thought Presented in Honor of Salo Wittmayer Baron* [N.Y., 1959], vii–xi).

57. *CCARYB* XI (1901): 93–4.

58. Ginzberg, *Keeper,* 83.

59. Schechter, *Seminary Addresses,* 241–2.

60. Philipson, *My Life,* 197.

61. Ginzberg, *Keeper,* 165–75.

62. Charles S. Liebman, "The Training of American Rabbis," *AJYB* 69 (1968): 31, 50, 57–8, 94, 106–12.

63. "Semitic Studies in American Colleges," *CCARYB* VI (1897): 99–113. See also David Rudavsky, "Hebraic Studies in American Colleges and Universities with Special Reference to New York University," in Israel T. Naamani, David Rudavsky and Carl F. Ehle (eds.), *Hebraic Studies, Education and Methodology* (N.Y., 1965), 3–25.

64. Copies of the very attractive invitation brochures are in the Hebrew Union College Library, Cincinnati. *Menorah Journal* IX (1923), 1–9, 128–31, 216–29, published a lengthy essay on "Leopold Zunz—"Humanist" by S. Baruch, according to Professor Jacob R. Marcus, a pseudonym for Adolph S. Oko.

65. Enelow, "Leopold Zunz: Forty Years After," *Selected Works of Hyman G. Enelow* (N.Y., 1935, 4 vols.), II, 132.

66. *Universal Jewish Encyclopedia* IV: 107, gives Enelow credit for involvement in the establishment of both the Littauer and Miller chairs. This information may be more explicitly and fully developed in a lecture "Jewish Studies at Universities: A Century of Struggle," which Baron was announced as delivering at the Bernard Revel Graduate School on March 19, 1972.

67. Jick (ed.), *Teaching of Judaica*, 135. See Arnold J. Band, "Jewish Studies in American Liberal Arts Colleges and Universities," *AJYB* 67 (1966), 3–27 for an early survey of the field.

68. *Ibid.*, 119.

69. For Mendelssohn's biography and teachings, consult Fritz Bamberger's article in *Universal Jewish Encyclopedia* VII: 471–4; Julius Guttmann, *Philosophies of Judaism* (Phila., 1964), 291–303; Meyer, *Origins*, 11–56; Nathan Rotenstreich, *Jewish Philosophy in Modern Times* (N.Y., 1968), 6–29. Mendelssohn's letter to Deacon Lavater was printed in the first American Jewish periodical, Solomon Jackson's anti-missionary *The Jew: Being a Defense of Judaism Against All Adversaries and Particularly Against the Insidious Attacks of Israel's Advocate* II (1824): 179–87; it was also published in the *Israelite* I (1854), 132–3. *Jerusalem* was printed as a supplement to volume IX of the *Occident* (1852) and reprinted in 1866. Leeser issued the translation mainly to combat the idea then at large that Mendelssohn had favored Reform Judaism—see pp. iv, v, xvi, and xvii of Leeser's introduction.

70. Guttmann and Rotenstreich summarize the teachings of these men. A striking number of scholarly articles on Hirsch has appeared recently: Emil G. Fackenheim, "Samuel Hirsch and Hegel," in Altmann (ed.), *Studies in Nineteenth Century Jewish Intellectual History*, 171–209; Gershon Greenberg, "Samuel Hirsch: Jewish Hegelian," *Revue des Etudes Juives* CXXIX (1970): 205–15; Jacob Katz, "Samuel Hirsch—Rabbi, Philosopher and Freemason," *REJ* CXXV (1966): 113–26.

71. None of Cohen's major works has as yet been published in English, but the first extensive treatment of his philosophy appears to have been Trude Weiss-Rosmarin's *Religion of Reason: Hermann Cohen's System of Religious Philosophy* (N.Y., 1936). Leo Baeck's *Essence of Judaism* appeared in English in Great Britain in 1936, and in the United States in revised form in 1948. The first English translation of Bubers *I and Thou* was published in Scotland in 1937, and in revised form in the United States as late as 1958—but some of Buber's versions of Hasidic tales had already been made available in English in 1931, and Ludwig Lewisohn included excerpts from Buber's writings in his 1935 anthology *Rebirth: A Book of Modern Jewish Thought* (N.Y.). The first major consideration of Rosenzweig in English was by Jacob B. Agus in his pioneering work *Modern Philosophies of Judaism* (N.Y., 1941), which also evaluated Cohen, Buber and Kaplan. Nahum Glatzer was the first to publish substantial portions of Rosenzweig's writings in English, especially in his *Franz Rosenzweig: His Life and Thought* (N.Y., 1953).

72. Only Kaplan can be said to be largely American in educational back-

ground, since he was only eight years old when he came to this country. He entered JTS at the age of twelve, but had already learned much from his father, a distinguished Talmudic scholar. Wiesel is still a spiritual child of his Hasidic home and of the concentration camp; though he spends much of the year in the United States and has an enormous American following in person and in print, it is questionable whether his work has been shaped to any degree by the American environment. Heschel and Soloveitchik are both products of Eastern European traditional learning who pursued doctorates in Berlin, Soloveitchik curiously enough writing a dissertation on Hermann Cohen's epistemology and metaphysics, and Heschel teaching Talmud at the Hochschule, where he also held a fellowship. After Heschel succeeded in making his way from Germany to Poland to England to America, his first teaching post was at Hebrew Union College. (A reliable outline of Heschel's life appears in *Current Biography Yearbook for 1970*, 177–9.) Soloveitchik's intellectual involvement with Cohen's Marburg neo-Kantianism is said to have marked a significant stage in his conceptual growth: see especially his son-in-law Aharon Lichtenstein's biographical and ideological sketch of Rav Soloveitchik in Simon Noveck (ed.), *Great Jewish Thinkers of the Twentieth Century* (Washington, 1963), 284–5.

73. Kaplan, *The Purpose and Meaning of Jewish Existence, A People in the Image of God* (Phila., 1964), pp. 61–252 being an epitomy of Cohen's *Religion der Vernunft*, while pp. 255–86, "A Modern Esoteric Rationale," form a brief evaluation and, to a degree, critique of Buber.

74. Eva Jospe (ed. and transl.), *Reason and Hope, Selections from the Jewish Writings of Hermann Cohen* (N.Y., 1971). See also Henry Slonimsky's touching and tender tribute to his teacher in *Essays* (Cincinnati, 1967), 97–112, reprinted from *HJ* IV (1942): 81–94; and Emil Fackenheim's evaluation, *Hermann Cohen—After Fifty Years* (N.Y., 1969). The April 21, 1972, issue of *Sh'ma* includes three penetrating essays on Cohen, by Mrs. Jospe, Michael Wyschogrod and Steven S. Schwarzschild. Since this was written, the full text of Cohen's *Religion of Reason Out of the Sources of Judaism* has appeared in an English translation by Simon Kaplan (N.Y., 1972).

75. Friedlander, *Leo Baeck, Teacher of Theresienstadt* (N.Y., 1968). On page 268 Friedlander makes the very significant point that among Baeck's students at the Hebrew Union College in the period following the end of World War II and his release from the camp were many of the younger theological writers: Eugene Borowitz, Bernard Martin, Jacob Petuchowski, Steven Schwarzschild and Arnold Jacob Wolf. See also Wolfgang Hamburger, "Teacher in Berlin and Cincinnati," *Leo Baeck Institute Year Book*, II (1957): 27–34, for the observations of a rabbinical student who attended Baeck's lectures both at the Hochschule and at Hebrew Union.

76. The many printings of Will Herberg (ed.) *The Writings of Martin Buber* (N.Y., 1956ff) and the extensive but by now altogether outdated biliography in Maurice S. Friedman, *Martin Buber, The Life of Dialogue* (Chicago, 1955) help to testify to the breadth of interest in Buber. A more complete bibliography appears together with thirty interesting evaluations of the philosopher's work in Paul Arthur Schlipp and Maurice Friedman, *The Philosophy of Martin Buber* (*The Library of Living Philosophers*, Vol. XII) (LaSalle, Illinois, 1967).

See also Herman Hesse's statement, when nominating Buber for a Nobel Prize in 1949, that in his *Tales of the Hasidim* Buber had "enriched world literature more than any other living author," quoted in 1968 edition of *Encyclopedia Britannica*, IV: 337. Everett Fox makes a fascinating attempt to reproduce the Buber-Rosenzweig German Biblical technique in English in "We Mean The Voice," *Response* 12 (1971–72): 29–42.

77. See reviews in *Time*, Aug. 9, 1971, 50–1, and by Jacob B. Agus in *Reconstructionist*, March 17, 1972. *Sh'ma*, Dec. 17, 1971, and *Midstream*, February 1972, both published commemorative articles by Arthur A. Cohen.

78. *The Condition of Jewish Belief*, 2. A "Hillel Lehrhaus" has been organized at Brandeis University in tribute to Rosenzweig's Frankfurt institution of adult education. It is possible also that some relationship exists between the Frankfurt Lehrhaus and the Free Jewish Universities which have developed in a number of communities.

79. *Judaism, Twenty Years, Cumulative Index, 1952–1971* (N.Y., 1972).

7

JEWISH TRADITION IN THE MODERN WORLD
Conservation and Renewal

ROBERT GORDIS

A NY EFFORT TO ACHIEVE a genuine understanding of the contemporary status of Judaism and of the problems confronting the tradition in the modern world must relate it to the millennial experience of the Jewish people, which has been the creator and exemplar of the tradition for thirty-three centuries. More specifically, we shall need to turn to Central Europe, where it was German-speaking Jewry that constituted the great laboratory of the Jewish spirit in modern times. Here the Jewish tradition and the Jewish community first encountered the challenge of the modern world, with all its power, its peril, and its promise. It was in the German *Kulturkreis,* which included Austria, Hungary and Bohemia as well as Germany, that there emerged virtually every aspect of the problem of Judaism and the Jewish people in the modern world. Here every conceivable solution was proposed and every approach tried. As all roads were explored, some led to dead-ends, while others opened into fruitful vistas. With relatively few exceptions every significant movement in modern Jewish life had its origin or found its expression within German-speaking Jewry.

Today German Jewry is virtually extinct as a result of the Nazi holocaust. It is American Jewry that constitutes the largest free Jewish community in the world, and by that token is the bearer of the immemorial Jewish tradition. This responsibility it shares with Israeli Jewry, which lives under conditions radically different from those of the Diaspora. Yet all the branches of American Judaism have their roots in Europe.[1] A century and a half ago, the British writer, Sidney Smith, contemptuously asked, "Who reads an American book?" If it be true that American literature remained virtually subservient to its European antecedents as late as the nineteenth century, it is not astonishing that Jewish life in America continued as a cultural dependency of Europe until the second decade of the twentieth, if not beyond.

During the long expanse of Jewish history, three major types of Jewish community emerged:

The first category was the *natural community,* of which ancient Palestine during the First and Second Commonwealths offers the most striking illustration. This community, which was rooted in its own soil, may be described as both exclusive and inclusive. It was exclusive in the sense that a Jewish child born in Palestine during the period of national independence or autonomy could join no other community except the Jewish, unless he chose to dissociate himself by means of a violent act of apostasy or treachery.[2] Barring such extreme and infrequent departures from the norm, a Jewish child grew naturally into the institutions of Jewish life, which he regarded as his natural environment.

The natural community, too, was all-inclusive, embracing every area of human experience. To be a Jew was to be a member of a group which shared in common all aspects of human life, such as geographical contiguity, economic interdependence, and political unity. Moreover, all the religious and cultural values of life were created and shared in common.

Another characteristic which the natural community possessed is that it was largely self-determining, to the extent to which any people living upon its own soil may be described as being the master of its own destiny. Even during the periods of Jewish subjection to foreign powers —Persian, Greek, Egyptian, or Roman—Palestinian Jewry possessed local autonomy, which included religious and cultural activity and its own legal and judicial system.

With the Roman Exile and the rise of the Diaspora after the year 70 C.E., another type, the *compulsory community,* appears on the stage of Jewish history, taking on varied forms in ancient Babylonia, in Christian Spain, and in medieval Poland. In the later Middle Ages, it takes on the now familiar pattern of the Ghetto throughout Europe. The basic distinction of the compulsory community is that it is not self-determining. Juridically speaking, the basis for the participation of Jews in Jewish community life was not their own volition, but the organized pressure of the state. It is not to be imagined for a moment that there were no inner sanctions in Jewish life, universally felt and deeply rooted. But whether or not the individual Jew wished to associate himself with the Jewish community, he was compelled to do so by the "host" community in which he lived.

The implications of this fact are far reaching. In the medieval state the Jew as an individual had no official existence; he was a cell of the

Jewish community. In levying taxes upon Jews, the government would place the assessment upon the Jewish community as a whole, which in turn would allocate the shares to each individual member. The most important consequence was that the Jewish community had the power to enforce taxation upon its members. The significance of this function can scarcely be exaggerated, for the right to tax means the right to govern, and therefore to organize and influence every area of life, not merely the economic. The Jewish community legislated for its members, maintained a system of courts with power to enforce decisions in civil, criminal, and ritual cases, and supported the synagogues, schools, bath-houses, and slaughtering houses. This was true of the Babylonian Exilarchate, of the Spanish *Aljama,* and of the Polish *Vaad Arba Aratzoth* (The Council of the Four Lands). By virtue of these functions the Jewish community became the all-inclusive agency for all group needs and activities.[3]

Not only is this type of community inclusive; it is, to all intents and purposes, also *exclusive.* While it is true that some Jews, especially of the wealthier and more privileged classes, might be lost to their people through assimilation or conversion, either voluntary or forced, escape for the Jews as a group was impossible. Indeed, for most of them it was unthinkable, since the Jewish community was the only one with which they had any real contact.

More important than the difference between the "natural" and the "compulsory" types of community were their far-reaching similarities. In historical actuality, the natural community was compulsory for the average Jew because no other was within reach, and the compulsory community was natural because no other was conceivable.

Even more significant is the fact that both the natural and the compulsory community were *organic.*[4] The activities that we are accustomed to categorize today as religious, cultural, educational, civic defense, charitable, and administrative were maintained by and for all the members of the Jewish community within a single pattern of organization.

Finally, neither type of community was troubled by what might be described as the hallmark of the modern Jew, the problem of his status and the character of his group life. Nowhere in the Bible or in the Talmud do we find any discussion as to whether the Jews are a religion, a nationality, or a race. Even the medieval Jewish philosophers did not concern themselves with this issue. Until modern times it sufficed to recall the classic formulation attributed to the Zohar, "God, Israel and the Torah are one,"[5] which emphasized the organic relationship linking religion, culture, and peoplehood.

With regard to the hierarchy of values among these three fundamentals, one could go a step further. The Talmud had not hesitated to
declare that God Himself said, "Would that men forsook Me but kept
My Torah."[6] The tenth century philosopher Saadia had enunciated the
view, "We are a people only by virtue of our Torah."[7] By juxtaposing
these statements, one might derive the conclusion that of the three elements of God, Israel, and the Torah, it is the Torah, the tradition, which
is *prima inter pares!* Indeed, normative Judaism as a whole may be described as Torah-centered. Torah, which means "teaching, guidance,
discipline," encompasses the entire law, lore, and learning of Judaism.
Its foundation is the five books of Moses and the Bible; its elaboration,
the Talmud and Rabbinic literature, and its extension the Responsa,
Codes, and religio-ethical literature of post-Talmudic Judaism.

To be sure, there were variations in religious practices among
Jewish communities in different parts of the world, as there were in
their political and economic status. Yet the basic pattern was one of
uniformity. In 1565 the great Rabbinic scholar Joseph Karo published
his compendium of Jewish law, intended for the layman, which he called
Shulhan Arukh, "the Prepared Table." In it he codified the practice of
the Sephardim, or Spanish-Jewish communities. His work was soon enlarged by the glosses of Rabbi Moses Isserles, who in his *Mappah,*
"Tablecloth," added the practice of the German-Polish communities. In
this augmented form the *Shulhan Arukh* became the standard guidebook
to Jewish traditional practice. For a variety of historical reasons the
Shulhan Arukh superseded all its predecessors, including the great
Mishneh Torah of Maimonides, and became the ultimate arbiter of traditional Judaism everywhere. For all Jews segregated within the Ghettos,
the Jewish community constituted the authoritative government, the
Jewish tradition the normative way of life, and the *Shulhan Arukh* its
code of practice.

To an outsider, it might seem unbelievable that within the dark and
forbidding walls of the Ghetto life could be tolerable and even joyful.
Yet that was emphatically the case. Jewish life in the Middle Ages was
vital and beautiful, informed by a sense of unity and a triumphant faith.
Everywhere the Jew followed the same pattern of life as laid down in
the Law of Moses and interpreted by the Rabbis. The Torah governed
his work and his festivals, his food and his family life, his culture and
his recreation, and spiritualized it all. Though he was physically weaker
than his neighbor, the Jew was conscious of his distinction in possessing
this "precious treasure." Each morning he rose to thank God for having
made him a member of Israel, and to reaffirm his conviction that the

Torah and the commandments were his life and the length of his days. His lot was hard to bear but never beyond endurance. His oppressors possessed might, but he had patience. In God's own time, redemption would come, and Israel would be restored to its homeland. Meanwhile, he concluded his daily prayers by proclaiming his perfect faith in the coming of the Messiah, for whom the Jew waited daily, however much he might tarry.

Thus life went on behind the dark walls of the Ghetto, which served as a barrier, to be sure, but also as a bulwark. Then a mighty rumbling arose, and the French Revolution undermined those hitherto impregnable walls. As the victorious French legions carried the slogan "Liberty, Fraternity and Equality" to every corner of Europe, those ideals were applied, slowly and hesitatingly, even to the Jews. The Civil Emancipation of the Jews proclaimed by the French Assembly on September 28, 1791, was no all-conquering tide. On the contrary, it varied with the ebb and flow of liberalism and reaction in the various states of nineteenth-century Europe. With each wave of liberalism Jews were enfranchised and admitted to citizenship; each return of reaction sought to restore the status that existed before the Revolution. But each receding wave of reaction was unable to undo completely the fruits of the Emancipation. In this piecemeal fashion the Jews of Germany, Italy and France were given substantial political rights and civic equality, though the army, high "society," and even the universities gave scant practical recognition to the new ideals.

The enthusiasm with which eighteenth and nineteenth-century Jews greeted the Emancipation and the relative ease with which they severed their relationship to the Jewish community in the Ghetto was due not merely to the promptings of personal advantage. Another influence called them to the brave new world outside: the intellectual impact of the Enlightenment. The philosophers of the Age of Reason in France and England, as well as in Italy and Germany, adopting reason as the instrument of human redemption, had rediscovered the fundamental truth of the unity and equality of mankind. With reason as their touchstone, they subjected every element of the social and cultural structure of their times to rigorous analysis. The state, education, religion, the family, the status of women, the criminal code, and the moral system, all came under their critical scrutiny and were found wanting.

The impact of the ideas of the Enlightenment upon organized Christianity was severe. Upon Judaism it was catastrophic, for behind its ghetto walls Judaism had all but lost touch with contemporary life and thought. Judaism in the eighteenth century was far narrower in compass and much more thoroughly alienated from the philosophy and science of its day than it had been in the twelfth or thirteenth century. The Enlightenment constituted a far more powerful challenge to Judaism than did medieval Aristotelianism or Platonism, but the defenses were now infinitely weaker. When, therefore, the Emancipation demanded the destruction of the organic Jewish community and the diminution of the Jewish tradition as the price for political and civil equality, the Enlightenment offered intellectual support for the conviction that the transaction was a bargain.

From the vantage-point of the twentieth century the limitations of both these great historical processes are clear. The Emancipation was a great step forward in the progress of mankind toward freedom, but it was not the final step. It represented the collapse of the feudal system and the coming of age of the middle-class and transfer of power to the *entrepreneurs* of the Industrial Revolution. Its viewpoint on government and economics was succinctly summed up in the philosophy of *laissez-faire* and in the doctrine of "freedom of contract," by which a factory-hand in Manchester, competing for a job against a thousand other workers, was on a par with the mill-owner, possessing equal rights that were not to be "compromised" by social legislation or by collective bargaining. The Emancipation was a consequence of the spirit of individualism.

Moreover—and this is directly germane to our theme—the Age of Reason lacked a sense of historical development, the slow growth of institutions and practices among men. Nor did it appreciate the non-rational elements of human life, the deposit of customs and attitudes created by human experience both individual and collective. Hence it failed in another crucial respect. In emphasizing the individual rights of man, the thinkers of the eighteenth century looked upon the group relations of man as external, insignificant and artificial. They did not understand that a man's economic position, his cultural interests, his ethnic roots, his religious loyalties, and his social ideals all constitute essential elements of his personality without which he is scarcely human. For the advocates of the Emancipation, the Jewishness of Jews was accidental and therefore expendable. Hence the Emancipation, for all its positive achievements, failed to accord to Jews the basic right of spiritual self-determination.

These drawbacks of the Age of Reason, with their negative effects on Judaism, have led, particularly in the post-Hitler period, to widespread expressions of scorn for both the Enlightenment and the Emancipation. We are told in some quarters that the century and a half of

Jewish history extending from the French Revolution in 1789, to the Nuremberg Laws in 1935, has been a tragic aberration. Quite aside from the debatable proposition whether a period of a hundred and fifty years in the life of a people can be dismissed as a blind alley, it is noteworthy that there have been few applications by the eloquent *laudatores temporis acti* for reghettoisation and for the surrender of their civic, political, and economic positions in Western society. Moreover, it is interesting to note that these glorifiers of the Ghetto tend to use German, English, French, Yiddish and modern Hebrew as the literary vehicles for their discontent, all of which are products of the modern age they are castigating.

There is an even more basic objection to this denigration of the eighteenth century. In our day the menace of unbridled nationalism has been immeasurably heightened by the threat of aggressive totalitarianism. All the more reason for jealously guarding the concept of the inherent and inalienable rights of man proclaimed by the Age of Reason, which remains a bulwark of humanity, that we abandon at our peril.

To revert to our theme, most Western Jews, with some striking exceptions like the Jewish community of Holland, welcomed the Emancipation as ushering in the Messianic Age. As the ghetto walls were breached, Jews streamed into Western society, leaving the age-old Jewish tradition a shambles behind them.

A homely parable may illustrate the process. Traditional Judaism may be compared to a vase, handed down as a precious heirloom from father to son, and set up in the family homestead in a place of honor. An earthquake breaks out, the home is shaken to its foundations. The vase is hurled to the ground and is smashed to bits. Each jagged piece is no longer beautiful, for it is without shape or form. Many of the children now see no reason to cherish the broken potsherds. For them, the only wise course is to sweep the debris out of the homestead.

Thus the first and decisive answer to the challenge of the new age was assimilation. Judaism was no longer a joy, but rather a burden and an embarrassment. Heinrich Heine summarized the attitude of his entire generation when he declared, *Das Judentum ist ein Unglück,* "Judaism is a misfortune."

It is often assumed that this wholesale rejection of Judaism was solely a matter of convenience. Actually, there was a considerable element of conviction, at least on the conscious levels of thought. The eighteenth century with its emphasis on reason, and the nineteenth with its great scientific discoveries, particularly the theory of evolution, seemed to undermine religious ideas and sanctions and make religious practices distasteful and irrelevant. Patriotism, tolerance, modernism, internationalism, and science—all were invoked to justify total absorption in the majority group. For once, intellectual conviction agreed with practical convenience in urging abandonment of the sinking ship. Those who were logically consistent sought release by outright conversion or through intermarriage, so that their children at least might be free. Fortunately for their peace of mind, they could not foresee the fate of their "non-Aryan" grandchildren.

Total assimilation was, however, not the universal answer of modern Jews. To revert to our parable, most of the children were unwilling to part even with the misshapen fragments of the vase. Each one snatched at a bit of clay and guarded it jealously. He clung to it proudly as the patent of his nobility, the emblem of his origin. There was little or nothing he could do with it, but he refused to do without it.

The majority of Jews were unwilling or unable to surrender their Jewish distinctiveness *in toto*. Often they felt a deeply rooted emotional attachment to familiar Jewish ideals or practices. Many Jews were kept within the Jewish fold by a sense of loyalty to parents, grandparents or other kinsmen—an impulse which they often could not justify on rational grounds and of which they might even be ashamed. In many cases, Jews found themselves unable to accept the dogmas of Christianity, while their sense of honor and self-respect forbade their entering the portals of the Church with tongue in cheek. Thus David Friedlander, the acknowledged leader of the Berlin community, addressed an anonymous Epistle to Pastor Teller in 1799, on behalf of "several heads of families of the Jewish denomination" offering to accept Protestantism on condition that they be excused from subscribing to the belief in the divinity of Jesus. When Pastor Teller replied that adherence to Christianity without Christ was meaningless, Friedlander surrendered the plan and became active within the Jewish community. In many instances the motive was a sense of personal dignity, as when the German-Jewish leader Gabriel Riesser declared that it was ignoble to desert the sinking ship of Judaism merely for the sake of personal advantage or convenience.

These subtle inner factors were immeasurably strengthened by far from subtle external conditions, particularly the rise of modern anti-Semitism. As though arranged by a cosmic dramatist, a series of tragic incidents during the nineteenth century—the Damascus Affair of 1840, the Mortara Case of 1857, the six blood-libel trials in Germany, Russia and Hungary between 1882 and 1911, the Russian pogroms of 1881, and the most sensational of all, the Dreyfus Case in 1894—reminded most Western Jews that they shared an ineluctable Jewish destiny.

For all these reasons, the largest number of Jews living in Western Europe, of which America was a cultural dependency, were actuated by two goals. The first was the retention of political citizenship with its concomitants of civic equality, economic opportunity, and cultural acceptance, and the second, the retention of some form of Jewish identity. *From the days of the French Revolution to the present, the ideal for modern Jews may be expressed, in current sociological terminology, as integration without assimilation and acculturation without absorption.*

Analogies are convenient but rarely completely adequate. In tracing the tragedy of the modern Jew, we have compared Jewish life since the Emancipation to the jagged and shapeless fragments of a once-beautiful vase. These bits of clay were all that remained to the children of the glory of their father's house, and they therefore insisted on preserving them with obstinate zeal.

Beyond this point, however, the parable fails us. For Jewish life is best compared not to clay, but to protoplasm. It is not inert matter but rather a living organism, possessing a will to survive and unsuspected powers of recuperation. Hence a better analogy for Jewish life would be those living creatures which have the gift of replacing lost or injured organs by growing new parts or by having their bodily functions taken over by those remaining. As Jewish life was smashed into countless fragments, various schools of thought arose, each determined to preserve one or another element, which it regarded as indispensable for Jewish survival. Nay more, each school tended to insist that its own chosen aspect could be developed and extended so that it would serve perfectly in place of the older integrated pattern of Jewish living that had prevailed before the Emancipation and the Enlightenment.

The earliest attempt at reconstruction was made by a group of young German-Jewish intellectuals who had received a university training. In 1819 they banded together to create *die Gesellschaft für die Wissenschaft des Judenthums.* Their revolutionary hope was that the scientific study of Jewish history, literature, and institutions would bolster the wavering loyalty to Judaism of the younger Jewish generation and win the respect of the larger community for the Jewish heritage and its values. But the high hopes of Eduard Gans, Moses Moser, Heinrich Heine, and their colleagues, turned to dust and ashes. Within a few, short years virtually all the members of the group lost heart in the enterprise and abandoned Judaism completely, in order to advance their personal careers. There was one towering exception, Leopold Zunz, who remained loyal, in Heine's words, to "the great caprice of his soul." Virtually single-handed, he founded the modern science of Judaism.[8] In the century and a half which has elapsed since Zunz' pioneering works began to appear, the science of Judaism has become a multifaceted and far-reaching area of research, recognized as a significant branch of humanistic studies throughout the world. It is today being carried on with zeal and ability in journals, monographs, and books appearing regularly throughout the world. The religion, history, literature, law, institutions, folk-lore, and languages of the Jewish people during three and a half millennia continue to be the subject of dedicated and gifted research by Jews and non-Jews in every civilized country.

Had the science of Judaism possessed no practical implications, and served only to enrich the boundaries of man's knowledge and understanding of himself through its researches, it would deserve an honored place among the humanities. As a matter of fact, however, *Jüdische Wissenschaft* laid claim to being much more than a branch of scientific study. Its spokesmen insisted that it had exerted a powerful and beneficient influence on the life of modern Jewry. Ismar Elbogen summarized the achievement—or at least the claim to achievement—of modern Jewish scholarship in these words: "The science of Judaism did valuable service in dispelling erroneous notions of the Jews and Judaism among non-Jews. It aided in bringing about the emancipation of the Jews; it made Jews proud of themselves and their people; it improved education, clarified religious views, and played its part in the secularization of Jewish life."[9] Elsewhere he maintained that the science of Judaism also had three important, popular effects: it had broadened the content and range of Jewish education to include the Bible, Jewish history, the Hebrew language and literature; it had served to stimulate the creation of Jewish nationalism, and it had contributed to the revival of the Hebrew language.[10]

By its very nature, however, modern Jewish scholarship was directed to the past rather than the present. It was a method of research, not a philosophy of life. Moreover, the works of the early masters, Luzzatto, Rappaport, Graetz, and Weiss, whether written in Hebrew or in other languages, were accessible to broad sections of the Jewish people and found a place in every cultured Jewish library. Modern scholarly works, on the other hand, which are often marked by exhaustive, and exhausting erudition, are read only by specialists.

The importance of this type of research can scarcely be overestimated. It has, however, proved wholly inadequate as a Jewish way of life or even as a direct factor in Jewish survival. A culture can help preserve a people only if it be a popular culture, drawing its sustenance from the great masses, dealing with their problems and aspirations, and ministering to their needs. That level the science of Judaism never attained. As the defection of its earliest protagonists proved, it could not generate the necessary loyalty for a great renaissance of Judaism. It was perhaps enough that it supplied the tools for the various positive philosophies of Jewish life that arose in the nineteenth and twentieth century.

To be sure, a cultural renaissance took place during the middle and closing decades of the nineteenth century. It was concentrated almost entirely in eastern Europe. It was basically a literary efflorescence, with Hebrew and Yiddish as its vehicles of expression. The Jews of Poland, Russia and Roumania, unlike their Western brothers, lived in large compact masses and had never been exposed to the opportunities and temptations of political equality. They had, therefore, never lost the sense of Jewish nationhood. Even they, however, had felt the impact of modern ideas upon traditional Judaism, and many of the youth were losing their religious moorings under the influence of the "Enlightenment," which characteristically bore a Hebrew name in the East, the *Haskalah*. Its leaders declared, in effect, that the Jewish religion had grown weak and unsatisfactory, and was incapable of safeguarding the life of the Jewish people. On the other hand, they felt that Judaism could still be preserved as a modern secular culture.

In regard to the medium of this culture, there was no unanimity. Some preferred to make Yiddish, which was the language of the masses, the vehicle of modern Jewish culture. Within a few decades a rich literature, a powerful drama, and a living press came into being. S. I. Abromowitch, I. L. Peretz, Sholem Aleichem, Sholem Asch, and I. J. Singer are some of the leading figures in the Yiddish cultural renaissance.

What the future of Yiddish will be is difficult to say with assurance. Indications point to its gradual elimination as a living tongue. In America, Poland and South America, the younger generation tends to speak the language of the country and therefore has no need, and often no knowledge, of Yiddish. Nevertheless, it seems clear that for years to come Yiddish will still survive, especially in large centers of Jewish population, and vigorous efforts are being made to preserve it. All that can be predicted about its future is that it is unpredictable.

Another highly influential group in Eastern Europe espoused Hebrew and succeeded in bringing the ancient tongue back to life. During the past century a group of gifted writers—Smolenskin, J. L. Gordon, Bialik, Ahad Ha'am, Tschernichowsky, and Schneur—created a vital literature in prose and poetry, and demonstrated that the language of Isaiah and Akiba, enriched by its medieval and modern developments, could serve to express every nuance of human thought and emotion.

Today the creative future of the Hebrew language is assured, since it has a flourishing present as the official tongue of the State of Israel. There is an extraordinary literary, scholarly, and scientific output in Israel with significant contributions from the Diaspora, all written in Hebrew. So vital is this influence radiating from the State of Israel that many of its leading spokesmen insist that the Hebraisation of Jews living outside of Israel is all that is required to guarantee their Jewish survival in the Diaspora and the maintenance of its relationship to the Jewish homeland.

The value of this modern cultural renaissance is enormous as a creative and quickening force. Yet it is clear that culture alone cannot constitute an enduring pattern of Jewish living. The cultural revival in Yiddish and Hebrew began in those lands where Jews were excluded from its general life. As Jews became integrated into the dominant culture of their native lands, Hebrew and Yiddish were either crowded out completely or, at best, accorded a secondary position. It may be possible to spread a reading knowledge of Hebrew among increasing numbers of American Jews. Yet, at the most, they will constitute only a small fraction of American Jewry. It is hardly likely that Hebrew can ever be made the spoken every-day tongue for American Jews. For Yiddish the prospects seem even less hopeful. For the meaningful survival of the Jewish tradition, culture is a necessary, but not a sufficient, condition.

At the same time that small groups of Jewish intellectuals were attempting to extract the facet of culture from the totality of Jewish life, far more intensive and extensive efforts were made to isolate and preserve the aspect of religion from the pattern of the Jewish tradition. Early in the nineteenth century a logical formula was evolved designed to achieve the two goals of citizenship and Jewish identity. All that was necessary was to reduce Judaism to the dimensions of a religious denomination and eliminate all those elements of the tradition that were not specifically "religious." Thus, by the side of the German citizens of the Catholic faith and the Protestant persuasion, there would be a third category of *Deutsche Staatsbürger juedischen Glaubens,* "German citizens of the Jewish faith." This phrase was actually incorporated into the name of the central organization of German Jewry.

The first movement to reflect the impact of the new age and to seek to reckon with its demands and attitudes was Reform Judaism.[11] As classical Reform evolved in Germany during the first half of the nineteenth century, it represented a synthesis between the practical demands of the laity and the theoretic formulations of the rabbis. The laymen such as David Friedlander, Israel Jacobsohn, and Jacob Herz Beer, father of the composer Meyerbeer, were concerned with beautifying the service by eliminating the traditional Jewish cantillation and by the introduction of the organ. On the other hand, the scholars sought to establish guiding principles for reform. Thus Samuel Holdheim (1806–60), who had been trained in Talmudic dialectics, was concerned with the problems of Jewish law and sought to justify the changes he desired by evolving a distinction between "religious" and "non-religious" observances and between Biblical and Talmudic enactments. Abraham Geiger (1810–74), perhaps the most brilliant Jewish scholar of the era, validated his Reform outlook by tracing the growth of religious ideas and institutions in historical Judaism, as reflected in the pages of the Bible and the Talmud.[12]

Ultimately a theory of Reform Judaism emerged, which rested upon four cardinal principles:

1. *The separation of the religious and national elements in the Jewish tradition.* By the surrender of its national aspects, Judaism would parallel Christianity as a religious sect pure and simple, so that Jews, like their Catholic and Protestant neighbors, would be recognized as patriotic Germans, Frenchmen or Englishmen, differing from their fellow-citizens only in religion. To prepare for this delicate operation upon the organism of Judaism, the national elements were declared to be transitory and hence expendable, now that the national life of the Jewish people was ended. Only the religious and ethical aspects were held to be timeless and binding. Samuel Holdheim, son of the Age of Rationalism, was the most consistent exponent of this principle, never flinching in applying this principle to the Jewish heritage. Geiger, who had a profound sense of history and a deeper appreciation of Jewish tradition, was considerably less consistent in giving up the particularist practices in Judaism. Thus he opposed the transfer of the Sabbath to Sunday, the practice of intermarriage, the surrender of circumcision, and other logical consequences of the attempted elimination of the national elements from Judaism.

At all events, Reform insisted that of the complex regimen of Jewish practices, only the ethical law was binding, and this, by its very nature, was not enforceable by synagogal authority. As for ritual, the hallmark of Judaism, it was essentially a private affair. Only such ceremonies were to be retained as possessed edifying value, or were in conformity with the esthetic standards of Western Europe. Hence there followed the surrender of the varied traditional modes of chanting the service, the cantillation of the Torah, the Prophets and the Megillot, the use of phylacteries and the prayer shawl, and the Oriental custom of covering the head at worship. The dietary laws, which tended to separate Jews from non-Jews, and which posed practical problems in modern society, were felt to be unnecessary, if not downright objectionable.

2. *The maintenance of the principle of the reality of growth and the legitimacy of change in Judaism.* Here again Holdheim, as a Talmudist, sought to validate the changes he favored by the citation of passages in Rabbinic literature which suggested less rigorous observance. Geiger, as a theologian and historian, enunciated the doctrine of progressive revelation to serve as the foundation for the reforms he felt necessary. He cited the changes in the Biblical text and in the interpretation of Scripture, as well as the stages in the evolution of Jewish law, as evidence for his views. In fact, the entire science of Judaism supplied the scholarly proof for the principle of development in Judaism.

3. *The surrender of the concept of the binding authority of Jewish law.* Basically, the separation of the national and religious elements in Judaism and the changes in personal observance and synagogue ritual favored by Reform were too far-reaching to be achieved within the framework of the Jewish tradition, no matter how liberally it was interpreted. This was true whether these changes were accomplished by the decision of rabbinical synods or, as was usually the case, through a process of nullification by the laity.

It was, therefore, necessary to declare that the traditional Jewish Halachah, which included civil, criminal, and ritual law, and which had been accepted as binding for centuries, no longer had authority in the modern world. The dietary laws were surrendered, as was the strict observance of Sabbath rest. In the field of domestic law, Jewish divorce was abolished, though Jewish marriage was retained through the creation of the untraditional concept that marriage was a sacrament, while divorce was purely a civil matter.[13]

4. *The establishment of a Jewish religious regimen eclectic in character.* Every rabbi, layman, and congregation was free to retain or reject rituals *ad libitum.* To minimize the confusion of such a state of affairs, Geiger and his successors in Germany, like Isaac Mayer Wise in America, attempted to create a Synod or rabbinical council, as a supreme legislative authority for modern Judaism, but with no success. In the strongly individualistic atmosphere of the nineteenth century such efforts were doomed to failure.

The most comprehensive statement of the philosophy of Reform Judaism in its classic phase was embodied in the *Pittsburgh Platform* of 1885, and the most consistent application of the theory of Reform was made in the United States. In Germany, for a variety of reasons which need not detain us here, Reform lost much of its momentum in the second half of the nineteenth century and reverted to a more traditional pattern.

The rapid rise and growth of Reform during the first half of the nineteenth century evoked a very spirited reaction, which crystallized as Neo-Orthodoxy.[14] One of the most gifted of the newer rabbis, who had been trained in German universities, was Samson Raphael Hirsch (1808–80). Deeply mystical in temperament, while conversant with modern thought, Hirsch was as acutely aware as Geiger of the contradictions between the modern world and traditional Judaism. However, he came to a diametrically opposite conclusion. Instead of modifying the tradition to the times, Hirsch called for "bending the times to the Torah." Hirsch was quite willing to concede the truth of the principle of growth and development in all human institutions. But Judaism was divine and, as such, immutable. Biblical and Talmudic Judaism, the product of Divine revelation, constituted one unchanged and unchangeable unit derived from the absolute source of truth, which is God.

As for those practices which seemed to be meaningless or distasteful to the modern temper, Hirsch declared, they needed only to be given a spiritual or symbolic meaning in order to win the allegiance of men. He first presented his views in a brilliant and moving volume which appeared in 1836, entitled, "The Nineteen Letters of Ben Uziel."[15] His subsequent rabbinical and literary career was dedicated to expounding these basic doctrines and establishing separate congregations dedicated to Neo-Orthodoxy. Unlike other teachers of traditional Judaism who favored retaining a large measure of unity and cooperation with the larger Jewish community, Hirsch felt that the purity of his doctrine could be maintained only through separatist congregations with their own houses of worship, schools, abbatoirs, ritual bath-houses, and cemeteries. Though the adherents of the *Austrittsorthodoxie* of Samson Raphael Hirsch were never numerous, they became an articulate and significant minority in the German culture-sphere, which included not only the German states, Austria, Hungary, but outposts in Great Britain and the United States as well. Their unflinching loyalty to all the minutiae of Jewish observance and their readiness to sacrifice for their convictions served as a countervailing force to the onsweeping tide of Reform.

A larger and far more influential challenge to Reform came from a third direction. In response to the same issues as Reform, a third movement arose, called the "positive-historical school" in Germany and Conservative Judaism in the United States.[16] Zechariah Frankel, its leading spokesman (1801–75) was a modern rabbi in training and outlook.

Thus his opinion was solicited with regard to the new and radical Reform prayer book created by the Hamburg Temple, and he attended the Rabbinical Conference convened by Geiger in Frankfort in 1845. Unlike Samson Raphael Hirsch and the other defenders of Orthodoxy, who denounced the prayer book because they denied the legitimacy of ritual change *ab initio,* Frankel defended the right of modification on the basis of his historical studies. He insisted, however, that the changes made in the Hamburg prayerbook were not in accord with the spirit of Judaism. In eliminating all references to the restoration of Zion they were obliterating the sense of national loyalty which was integral to the Jewish religion. As he wrote, "A people without a center or government of its own can never attain to honor among the nations of the world. We must therefore demonstrate that the desire for rebirth still lives within us. Is not this hope better than the undignified efforts to imitate and assimilate ourselves to our neighbors?"[17]

At the Frankfort Conference Frankel listened without enthusiasm to many proposals advanced for changes in the Sabbath, the dietary regulations, and the laws of marriage and divorce. Nevertheless he remained in attendance until the discussion turned to what seemed a comparatively minor matter. When the delegates voted that the Hebrew language was not "objectively" essential to Jewish prayer, but should be retained only to meet the "subjective" needs of the older generation, Frankel walked out of the Conference. Frankel, who was a distinguished Talmudist, did not need to be reminded of the Rabbinic dictum, "You may recite the *Shema* in any language you understand."[18] It was not a matter of Halachah, but of the entire approach to the Jewish tradition. Frankel was no theologian; he lacked the taste and probably the capacity for the formulation of principles, which Geiger possessed in pre-eminent degree. Yet his reaction to the Hamburg Prayerbook and the Frankfort Conference, which were both landmarks in the history of Reform, was highly revelatory of the new trend of which he became the acknowledged leader.

It was a foregone conclusion that he would be accused from both the right and the left. Both Geiger and Hirsch regarded him as a temporizer, lacking either the courage to implement his secret Reform convictions or the self-sacrifice to adhere to his stubborn Orthodox prejudices. Actually, however, the positive-historical school had a point of view or, what is at least equally important, a climate of attitude with very respectable antecedents. In the judgment of a distinguished contemporary Jewish historian who through the greater part of his career has not been identified with the movement, Conservative Judaism, both in its positive attitudes and in its omissions, is most directly in the mainstream of traditional Judaism. To cite Professor Salo W. Baron: "Neo-Orthodoxy, equally with Reform, is a deviation from historical Judaism. No less than Reform, it abandoned Judaism's self-rejuvenating historical dynamism. For this reason we may say that the 'positive-historical' Judaism of Zechariah Frankel and Michael Sachs and the 'Conservative' Judaism of America have been much truer to the spirit of traditional Judaism. By maintaining the general validity of Jewish law and combining with it freedom of personal interpretation of the Jewish past and creed, Frankel and his successors hoped to preserve historical continuity. It is Conservative Judaism which seems to show the greatest similarities with the method and substances of teaching of the popular leaders during the declining Second Commonwealth, inasmuch as clinging to the traditional modes of life, it nevertheless allows for the adaption of basic theological concepts to the changing social and environmental needs."[19]

Frankel agreed with Reform on the existence of development in the past and on the need for growth in Judaism in the present. But the school he founded parted company on three fundamentals. *It opposed the elimination of the national elements of Jewish tradition as embodied preeminently in its ceremonials and legal system,* which rest, in turn, upon two basic postulates, *the authority of Jewish law* and *the peoplehood of Israel.*

Obviously Frankel and his successors, both in Germany and in the United States, have not solved all the problems inherent in their position. The crucial difficulty has lain in determining *the source and nature of the authority behind Jewish law,* since Conservative Judaism accepts the result of modern scientific scholarship regarding the past development of Judaism and believes that its growth in the present and future is both inevitable and necessary. Both Zechariah Frankel in the nineteenth century and the great exemplar of Conservative Judaism in the twentieth, Solomon Schechter (1850–1915), sought to meet the problem by proposing that the basis of authority lies in *kelal Yisrael* or Catholic Israel, which determines what elements of Judaism are vital, obsolescent, or obsolete.[20]

It was not difficult to demonstrate that this process had been at work throughout the history of rabbinic and medieval Judaism, giving the Jewish tradition its protean capacity for growth and adjustment, while retaining its sense of continuity with the past. On the other hand, it was not easy to indicate how the process is to operate in the present, seeing that Jewish tradition is being honored far more in the breach than in the observance by most Western Jews, who, thanks to Hitler, now constitute the majority of World Jewry. If we were to follow literally the verdict of the practice of the majority of contemporary Jews, it would mean the abrogation of such basic fundamentals as the Sabbath and festival observances, the regimen of daily prayers and dietary laws, and much else besides that is basic to traditional Judaism.

It is therefore clear that while the concept of Catholic Israel is both fruitful and true, being validated by centuries of Jewish experience, it cannot suffice today in its original form. Elsewhere I have sought to re-interpret Schechter's theory of authority being vested in *kelal Yisrael*, in order that it may be relevant and practicable in our present situation.[21]

Undoubtedly ambiguities, unclarities, and differences of viewpoint still to be resolved remain within the movement. Nonetheless, the basic retention by Conservative Judaism of traditional practices, its flexibility with regard to necessary changes, its liberalism with regard to the body of doctrine and belief, and its tolerance of differences have united to make it the most rapidly growing movement in contemporary Judaism, with a strong impact upon its sister movements to the right and to the left.

The basic outlook of the three movements in their classic forms may now be set forth schematically as follows: *Reform declares that Judaism has changed throughout time and that Jewish law is no longer binding. Orthodoxy denies both propositions, insisting upon the binding character of Jewish law and negating the view that Judaism has evolved. Conservative Judaism agrees with Orthodoxy in maintaining the author-ity of Jewish law, and with Reform that Judaism has grown and evolved through time.*

A momentous century has gone by since the three movements arose in Germany and spread throughout the Western world. This period has seen the bloody extermination of European Jewry, the rise of a new, populous center of Jewish life on the American continent, and the es-tablishment of the State of Israel as an independent and viable member of the family of nations. These three major events, virtually without parallel in Jewish history, have had a powerful effect upon the directions these movements have taken, particularly in the last two decades.

While therefore the theoretical differences among the three move-ments are still valid, in practice the gap has been narrowing. To the un-biased observer, it is clear that Orthodoxy, Conservatism, and Reform in America have, by and large, been drawing together and developing a larger degree of similarity than existed four decades ago. Paradoxically, the greater homogeneity of outlook and practice among the three groups has been accompanied by a strengthening of denominational loyalties and a sharpening of organizational rivalries, due in large measure to the development of elaborate central agencies in Reform, Conservatism, and Orthodoxy. For the foreseeable future these groups will retain their identity.

It should not be astonishing that the American scene has played a decisive role in developing a greater similarity among all three groups. The impact of American conditions and attitudes on the various denominations of Christianity has been frequently studied and expounded. It was not to be expected that exposure to the American environment, its opportunities, temptations, and problems, would leave Judaism any less affected than it has the Protestant churches. That the impact of the American way of life in Catholicism has been far more substantial than was believed, becomes clearer each day.

The second great factor was the emergence of the Zionist ideal, which achieved a modern miracle in the creation of the State of Israel. In 1897 when the Basel program was promulgated, calling for "the securing of a publicly secured, legally recognized homeland for the Jewish people in Palestine," several American rabbis, of the Reform group incidentally, participated. While Reform Judaism officially continued to oppose Jewish nationalism for decades, Zionism increasingly captured the loyalty of both the rabbinate and the laity. It was, of course, particularly congenial to Conservative Judaism and to most segments of Orthodoxy, since in traditional Judaism there is no line of demarcation between the religious and the national, the particularistic and the universalistic. Today, the vast majority of adherents of all three groups accept the peoplehood of Israel, with Israel as the spiritual homeland, as fundamental postulates of their religious world-outlook.

This basic principle of Jewish peoplehood was underscored both negatively and positively during the past two decades. The Nazi holocaust, which destroyed six-sevenths of European Jewry, was a bloody reminder to Jews—of all religious persuasions and of none—that they shared a common destiny and were members of a single people. The establishment of the State of Israel seventeen years ago, its heroic defence, and its steady progress and development, have brought to virtually all Jews a new sense of pride and identification with the traditional homeland of the Jewish people. From it has emerged a greater concern with the teaching of the Hebrew language and a higher measure of appreciation of Jewish observances, even in Reform. In the other groups, the impact has been even more striking.

To understand the present condition of Judaism, it must be kept in mind that each group represents a coalition of forces. Orthodoxy contains many varieties, particularly on the extreme right. As one studies Jewish history, one is struck by the fact that after each great calamity, a wave of extreme pietism has swept over significant segments of the community. This was true after the Crusades, the Spanish persecutions of 1391, the Expulsion in 1492, and the Chmielnicki massacres in Poland in 1688. A similar phenomenon is in evidence today. Right-wing Orthodoxy has become active and articulate in the United States with the influx of surviving members of Polish Hasidism and German ultra-Orthodoxy. They have zealously attempted to establish the concept of isolationism, both *vis-à-vis* the majority of American Jews and the larger American community. In a few instances, they have created viable communities of their own, as in the older Brooklyn neighborhood of Williamsburgh and the new settlement of New Square, near Spring Valley, New York.[22] Generally, they look askance at forms of cooperation either in the practical or the theoretic sphere with those who do not share their viewpoint.

While the pressure they exert upon the mainstream of American Orthodoxy is considerable, they are less significant in numbers and in influence than the more moderate elements grouped round Yeshiva University in New York and the Hebrew Theological College in Chicago. The rabbis trained in these seminaries and the laity to whom they minister are acutely conscious of the demands of modern life. In their congregational as well as in their personal lives they represent various degrees of accommodation between the tradition and the contemporary scene. Often they prefer such terms as "traditional" and "modern Orthodox" to describe their standpoint.[23] Several years ago, shortly after the establishment of the State of Israel, many members of this group hoped for the establishment of a Sanhedrin, a central religious tribunal in Israel, which would serve as the supreme arbiter in religious law. The idea of the Sanhedrin was propagated with great vigor and learning by the late Rabbi Maimon, but the manifold difficulties facing the project are now generally recognized to be insuperable. The largest sections of American Orthodoxy continue to insist upon the immutability of the Torah, but through a process of conscious interpretation and unconscious adaptation they are drawing closer to the center.

Reform Judaism contains within its ranks a small splinter group which represents the standpoint of early nineteenth-century Reform, totally oblivious of the last century of Jewish experience and thought. The strongest article of faith of this group is its negation of Jewish peoplehood and its hostility to the State of Israel. Its members are affiliated with a small but highly vocal organization called the American

Council for Judaism, which has been repudiated time and again by the vast majority of responsible Reform leadership. As we have noted, the peoplehood of Israel is basic to Jews of all persuasions, and the State of Israel is a source of prideful identification.

The Columbus Program of 1915 drastically modified the earlier Pittsburgh Platform, not only with regard to the concept of Jewish peoplehood, but in adopting a more affirmative attitude toward Jewish traditional practices. In the half-century that has elapsed since the latter document was issued, Reform synagogues have introduced many practices of a traditional character and have often intensified their educational program. Some Reform leaders have been calling for a ritual code for Reform, and others have gone so far as to urge the establishment of Reform day schools for maximum Jewish education. This increasingly sympathetic attitude toward Jewish tradition has not, it should be understood, meant a return to the principle of the binding character and authority of Jewish law, but it has created a far closer sense of identification with *kelal Yisrael,* the totality of Israel.

Conservative Judaism, like its sister movements, includes several trends within its ranks. At the left is a highly influential movement in contemporary Jewish life known as Reconstructionism. It was founded by one of the seminal thinkers of modern Jewry, Professor Mordecai M. Kaplan, and draws some of its adherents from Reform and from secular circles as well.

Reconstruction is best conceived of on two levels, as a broad sociological theory of Jewish life and as a more limited, theological reinterpretation of Jewish tradition. Its sociological approach to Jewish life is set forth in its credo—"Judaism is the evolving religious civilization of the Jewish people." This affirmation is no new doctrine in Judaism. In its emphasis upon Jewish peoplehood, the all-embracing character of the Jewish heritage and its evolving nature, Reconstructionism is basically a restatement of a position congenial to many, if not most, modern Jews. In its narrower, theological aspect, Reconstructionism, as expounded in the writings of Professor Kaplan and several of his disciples and associates, may be described as Jewish religious naturalism.[24] It espouses a humanistic conception of God and has surrendered such traditional Jewish doctrines as that of the election of Israel, Revelation, and the binding character of Jewish ritual practices, which it regards as "folkways," and not as "law."

At the furthermost pole from Reconstructionism is the right-wing in Conservative Judaism. This group seeks to avoid any clear-cut definition of the content of the movement, alleging that it wishes to avoid further divisiveness in the Jewish community. In practice and to a lesser degree in theory, it adopts a negative position toward any proposed modifications in Jewish practice. Because its members occupy positions of authority in the institutions of Conservative Judaism, the group has a substantial measure of influence and power today.

The majority group belongs to the center, which believes that Conservative Judaism possesses its own distinctive viewpoint, which it should articulate clearly and unequivocally. This does not exclude seeking points of contact and areas of cooperation with other schools of Jewish thought. Most Conservative congregations have adopted such practices as family pews and various lesser changes in ritual observance. Most of them use the *Sabbath and Festival Prayer Book* published by the Rabbinical Assembly and the United Synagogue. This official prayerbook has slightly rephrased the traditional prayers for the restoration of sacrifices in the Temple, so as to express a reminiscence of ancient glories rather than a goal for the future. It has also modified several other passages, such as one of the traditional blessings that implies an inferior status for women. Nor has the Conservative movement excluded congregations which use the organ at services, or have abridged the Torah reading, or have officially permitted travel to synagogue services on the Sabbath. On the basic regimen of Jewish traditional practices, there is substantial agreement among all Conservative congregations.

Not satisfied with a purely practical consensus, individual scholars and teachers in the movement have sought to formulate the philosophy of Conservative Judaism in terms of their needs, aspirations and outlook.[25] In spite of variations in detail, they would, I believe, agree that the philosophy of the movement may be formulated in two propositions: *Growth is the law of life,* and *the Law is the life of Judaism.*

In sum, the rise of modern tendencies in Orthodoxy and the growing appreciation of tradition in Reform, coupled with the all-but-universal recognition of Jewish peoplehood, have given American Judaism, within the short space of a half-century, a far greater degree of homogeneity than seemed possible at the turn of the century. Today most devotees of Orthodox, Conservative, and Reform Judaism would agree that the noun is more important than the adjective. The various contemporary theological currents of naturalism, rationalism, and existentialism cut across all groups. In their devotion to the State of Israel and their pride in its achievement, all schools are united. They are also increasingly conscious that the future of Judaism requires an intensification of the quality and the quantity of Jewish education for children, adolescents, and adults.

There is, too, a greater determination to emphasize the ethical content of Judaism and its relevance to the problems of modern man in the twentieth century. On the perennial issues of man's nature and destiny, the purpose of life, the meaning of suffering, death, and immortality, the basis and nature of the moral law, sex and the family, scholars in all groups have sought to present the Jewish world-view. Some have elucidated the insights and attitudes of the Jewish tradition which bear upon group relations, racial, religious, and national, and upon crucial world issues like poverty, war, and peace. Even in the sphere of Jewish law and ritual, and its relevance and applicability to modern life, where the differences among Orthodoxy, Conservatism, and Reform are most fundamental, there is a fruitful interaction among the three groups.

The problems involved in the conservation and renewal of the Jewish tradition are more, not less difficult today than in the eighteenth or nineteenth century. For Judaism must confront all the challenges that threaten Jewish particularity in an increasingly impersonal and technological world. In addition, like all religion, it must speak to the mind and heart of modern man in his agonizing search for meaning in life, in his quest for goals in an age when all standards of conduct seem eroded, and in his yearning for hope in a world poised on the brink of destruction. In other words, the Jewish religion faces grave problems today, both because it is Jewish and because it is religion.

Assimilation, which in its various forms was the initial response of Western Jewry to the opportunities and temptations of the Emancipation, continues to take a heavy toll from the Jewish community. It is the price that modern Jewry must pay for life as a minority in an open society, which is striving, however hesitatingly, to divest itself of the last vestiges of discrimination on racial or religious grounds. By its very nature, assimilation is not an organized group movement with an articulated rationale. It generally takes the form of a decision by an individual to minimize or sever completely the ties binding him to the Jewish community. The motivations for assimilation are nearly as numerous as the individuals involved, and the patterns run the gamut from outright conversion through intermarriage to spiritual and cultural alienation from the Jewish tradition, unaccompanied by a formal break with the Jewish group.

The Jewish population of the United States is generally estimated at about five and a half million. No statistics, or even trustworthy estimates, are available with regard to the incidence of assimilation in its principal categories.[26] Most sociologists would agree that the process is ubiquitous and powerful, so that it is quite likely that the American-

Jewish community will not grow in numbers. Indeed it may even decline somewhat in the next few decades, depending on whether the natural increase will be able to compensate for conscious or unconscious defections.[27]

In order to minimize its losses through assimilation, American Jewry is seeking to mobilize its resources to strengthen Jewish loyalty. *The goal is the building of a voluntary community dedicated to organic Judaism.* Thus the circle comes complete, and the basic characteristic of the natural and the compulsory Jewish communities of earlier eras must be renewed—with one fundamental difference: while its organic character must be restored, allegiance must be voluntary and not compulsory.

This new stage in the evolution of the Jewish community will not emerge tomorrow or the day after. Indeed, the organizational problems are at present insuperable. But the lineaments of this voluntary community dedicated to organic Judaism may be set forth as an ideal goal if not yet as a blueprint. It will affirm the character of the Jewish peoples, as an *'am 'olam*, a world-people as well as an eternal people. It will underscore the centrality of the State of Israel as the spiritual homeland of world Jewry, *pari passu* with its faith in the survival of American Jewry as a vital, active and potentially creative center for Jewish life. It will, at the same time, reaffirm wholeheartedly the role of American Jewry as an integral element of the American people, since group loyalties, morally conceived and culturally expressed, are not mutually exclusive.

It will actively encourage all manifestations of Jewish creativity in art, literature, music, drama, philosophy, and scholarship. Yet it will recognize the centrality of the Jewish religion as the heart of Jewish expression and of Jewish brotherhood. At the same time, it will emphasize the right of all Jews, affirmed by Jewish tradition, to fellowship in the Jewish community, however far removed they may be at present from an affirmative attitude toward Jewish tradition. Accordingly, it will welcome all individuals and groups unable to give their assent to Jewish religious beliefs and practices, to participate in whatever positive phase of Jewish life elicits their concern and interest.

It will underscore the ethical and universal ideals of Judaism which its religious teachings and national consciousness have sought to perpetuate and intensify. It will therefore emphasize the duty and destiny of the State of Israel, and of world Jewry, to advance the messianic ideals of the One God and of the One Humanity, embodied in a world order of social justice, individual and group freedom, and universal peace. This is undoubtedly an ideal, but without the vision, the people must perish.

To achieve these goals, the voluntary Jewish community of the future will give, in deed and not merely in word, the highest priority to Jewish education for children, adolescents, and adults, conceived in the broadest terms and based on the three pillars of faith, culture and peoplehood.

The modern Jew has inherited a rich tradition from the three-thousand year-old experience of his people, which has been shattered into fragments. His tragedy is that he does not know what to do with it; his glory, that he is unwilling to do without it. The history of world Jewry in the last two centuries is the record of various creative if unconscious attempts to restore the organic character of Judaism. In struggling for meaningful survival, the Jewish tradition wishes to make its contribution to the solution of the problems confronting the free society of today and the world community of tomorrow. The various movements dedicated to a revival of Jewish religion, to a quickening of Jewish culture, and to a rebuilding of the Jewish people both in the State of Israel and throughout the world, are not ends in themselves, but instruments for the fulfillment of the prophetic injunction to "be a light to the nations, a covenant to the peoples."

(1965)

NOTES

1. This classification was first proposed by the writer in *The Jew Faces A New World* (New York, 1941), pp. 12–31. *Cf.* also my papers "Toward A Creative Jewish Community in America" in *Proceedings of Rabbinical Assembly of America* 1949, and "Creating An Organic Community" in *Commentary* 1950, pp. 23–33.

2. Two instances are known to us from the Greco-Roman period, aside from the Hellenizing priests of the pre-Maccabean era. Tiberius Alexander, the nephew of Philo of Alexandria, who became a pagan, served as Roman procurator of Judea (until 48 CE), and later advised Vespasian in the siege of Jerusalem. The historian Josephus defected to the Romans during the war and settled in Rome, where he wrote his *Antiquities, History of the Jewish War,* and his tract, *Against Apion,* a defence of Judaism against the attacks of a contemporary anti-Semite. These writings of Josephus point to his pride in his heritage and his identification with his people, which impelled him to try to justify his weak, if not traitorous, behavior during the war against Rome.

3. On the history and development of the types of Jewish community and the variations among them, cf. S. W. Baron, *The Jewish Community* (Philadelphia, 1942) 3 vol., A. A. Neuman, *The Jews in Spain* (Philadelphia, 1942), and Fritz Baer, *Die Juden im Christlichen Spanien*, 2 vol. (Berlin, 1929, 1936). The first volume has appeared in an English translation by Louis Schoffman under the title of *A History of the Jews in Christian Spain* (Philadelphia, 1961).

4. Cf. Mordecai M. Kaplan, "The First Step Toward Organic Community," in *The Reconstructionist*, vol. 15, No. 7 (February 18, 1949), "The Conference on Organic Community," *ibid.*, No. 2 (March 4, 1949), and his book, *The Future of the American Jew* (New York, 1951). See also Carl Alpert, "Toward an Understanding of Organic Community," *ibid.*, vol. 15, No. 8 (May 27, 1949). Kaplan's influence stimulated the application by Max Kadushin of this concept to the study of Rabbinic Judaism; cf. his *Theology of Seder Eliahu* (New York, 1932), pp. v, vi, 17–32; *Organic Thinking* (New York, 1938), pp. v–x, 1–15; *The Rabbinic Mind* (New York, 1952).

5. *Idra, Zohar.*

6. See *Palestinian Talmud, Hagigah* 1:7.

7. See *Emunot Vedeot*, chap. 3 (Leipzig, 1851; photographic edition New York, 1947, p. 80). Curiously, the text uses the plural, *torotheha*, "its Torot, teachings."

8. For a discussion of the history of modern Jewish scholarship, its achievements, limitations and prospects, see the writer's Leo Baeck Memorial Lecture 6, "Jewish Learning and Jewish Existence—Retrospect and Prospect" (New York, 1963).

9. Cf. for example, his *A Century of Jewish Life* (Philadelphia, 1944) p. xxxvii.

10. Cf. his Hebrew essay, *"Hokmat Yisrael"* in *Debir* (Berlin, 1924), vol. 1, pp. 1–16.

11. The fullest treatment of the history of Reform Judaism in its earlier "classical" phase is David Phillipson, *The Reform Movement in Judaism* (New York, 1907). See also Emil G. Hirsch in *Jewish Encyclopedia* X, s.v. Reform Judaism. For the subsequent history of the movement and its newer tendencies, the *Yearbooks of the Central Conference of American Rabbis*, published annually, are an invaluable and indispensable source. The basic documents are collected in W. Gunther Plaut, *The Rise of Reform Judaism* (New York, 1963).

12. See Max Wiener, *Abraham Geiger and Liberal Judaism* (Philadelphia, 1962).

13. Cf. the Introduction in the valuable work of S. B. Freehof, *Reform Jewish Practice and its Rabbinic Background* (Cincinnati, 1944) 1; 2 (Cincinnati, 1952); *idem, Recent Reform Responsa* (Cincinnati, 1963).

14. See Herman Schwab, *The History of Orthodox Jewry in Germany,* translated by I. R. Birnbaum (London, 1950).

15. An English version of *The Nineteen Letters of Ben Uziel,* translated by B. Drachman, appeared in New York in 1899. A revised translation, prepared by

Jacob Breuer, was published in New York in 1960. During the last decade many others of Hirsch's works have been translated into English.

16. Among earlier works on the movement, Saul Phineas Rabinowitz' Hebrew biography of *Rabbi Zechariah Frankel* (Warsaw, 1898) may be cited. More recent works concentrating on the American scene include M. Sklare, *Conservative Judaism* (Glencoe, Ill., 1955), which is primarily concerned with the socioeconomic background of the movement; R. Gordis, *Conservative Judaism, A Modern Approach* (New York, 1956); M. Davis, *The Emergence of Conservative Judaism* (New York, 1963); H. Parzen, *Architects of Conservative Judaism* (New York, 1964).

17. *Cf. Orient*, 1842, nos. 7, 8, 9.

18. *B. Berakhot* 13a.

19. *Cf. A Religious and Social History of the Jews,* (1st edition, New York, 1937), pp. 393f.

20. *Cf. Studies in Judaism* (Philadelphia, 1896) Series I, pp. xi–xxv, and Bernard Mandelbaum, *The Wisdom of Solomon Schechter* (New York, 1964).

21. *Cf.* R. Gordis, "Authority in Jewish Law" in *Proceedings of the Rabbinical Assembly of America* (1942–47), which was published also as two papers in *The Reconstructionist*, Nov. 13 and 27, 1942, and *Judaism For The Modern Age* (New York, 1955), pp. 127–85, esp. pp. 166ff.

22. Two studies of the Williamsburgh Community have recently appeared: Solomon Poll, *The Hasidic Community of Williamsburgh* (Glencoe, Ill., 1962), and Gershon Kranzler, *The Hasidim of Williamsburgh* (New York, 1963). A study of the New Square settlement is now in process by Edith Freedman.

23. A prime source for the outlook of this predominant group in Orthodoxy may be found in the journal *Tradition,* published by the Rabbinical Council of America.

24. In addition to many papers by M. M. Kaplan, see the basic presentation of his outlook in *Judaism as a Civilization* (New York, 1934), which has been followed by many other important works, notably *The Meaning of God in Modern Jewish Religion* (New York, 1937); *The Future of the American Jew* (New York, 1948); *The Greater Judaism in the Making* (New York, 1960); and *The Purpose and Meaning of Jewish Existence* (Philadelphia, 1964). Other expositions of Reconstructionism are to be found in the writings of Eugene Kohn, Milton Steinberg and Ira Eisenstein.

25. For a collection of papers by many of the leaders of the movement reflecting its philosophy, see the excellent volume edited by Mordecai Waxman, *Tradition and Change: The Development of Conservative Judaism* (New York, 1958), which contains a valuable introduction. The reader may be referred to the varied writings of Israel Friedlander, Solomon Schechter, Louis Ginzberg, Solomon Goldman, Louis Finkelstein, Max Kadushin, Max Arzt, Simon Greenberg, Jacob Agus, Robert Gordis, Ben-Zion Bokser, and others, for varying interpretations of the basic viewpoint of Conservative Judaism.

26. For a classification of the assimilatory process under seven categories see Milton M. Gordon, *Assimilation in American Life* (New York, 1964). The implications of this study for Jewish group survival in America are trenchantly analyzed by Marshall Sklare in "Assimilation and the Sociologist" in *Commentary*, May 1965, pp. 39, 63–67.

27. Intermarriage, which is more amenable to statistical investigation than conversion or "alienation," is the subject of a growing literature. *Cf.* Hershel Shanks, "Jewish-Gentile Intermarriage," in *Commentary*, vol. 16, October 1953; Erich Rosenthal, "Studies of Jewish Intermarriage in the United States," in *American Jewish Year Book*, vol. 64, 1963; Werner J. Cahnman, ed. *Intermarriage in Jewish Life, A Symposium* (New York, 1963), the volume *Intermarriage and the Future of the American Jew*, proceedings of a conference sponsored by the Commission of Synagogue Relations of the Federation of Jewish Philanthropies (New York, 1964), and Albert J. Gordon, *Intermarriage* (Boston, Beacon Press, 1964).

8

THE SABBATH AS PROTEST
Thoughts on Work and Leisure in the Automated Society

W. GUNTHER PLAUT

A CHANGE OF CONCEPT

THE DIFFICULTY of approaching our subject lies to no small degree in the fact that all its important terms—Sabbath, work, leisure—have undergone changes of meaning. These changes are not merely semantic novelties. They contain changes of subtle or not so subtle emphasis revealing shifts in cultural outlook. One of the great problems of any contemporary discussion involving religion and society is that such changes of terms and concepts are not always sufficiently recognized. Let me give you an example which will serve as an opening illustration.

A few years ago a young woman called at a home in an upper-class neighborhood. She represented a university-sponsored survey to gather materials for a family study. The surveyor was courteously received by the lady of the house who, having been assured that complete anonymity of the respondents would be observed, gave her answers with total frankness. She answered questions about her parents and children, and about sexual relationships with her husband as well as her and his extramarital ventures. The interviewer then asked: "Incidentally, what is your husband's income?" The answer: "Now listen, aren't you getting a little personal?"

This story, which I am assured is not apocryphal, tells us not only about the way in which sex and money may or may not be discussed in our time, but also reveals something far more significant: where formerly the family sphere defined the man and his status, and his finances were an external additive, today money, that is, possession and the social status which derive therefrom, primarily describe a man. Which is to say that the meaning of the words *private* and *public* has changed because the very structure of society which defined these terms has undergone revolutionary changes.

So it is with the terms *work* and *leisure* with which I am concerned in this lecture. Everyone seems to be quite clear when he is told by someone else, "I have little leisure." Yet, the speaker may convey something altogether different from what his counterpart using the same words and the same sentence structure would have meant one hundred years ago. What is "little" today would have been "much" then; and "leisure" itself has changed its content.

We no longer live in Puritan times when idleness was considered one of the seven deadly sins and the word *sloth* a favorite opprobrium. Today idleness appears, to many, as one of life's most desirable blessings and, when it is achieved, often as its greatest threat. I do not know whether a Puritan could have understood the term "killing time," but we certainly can.

Similarly with the term *work.* If the story of the Garden of Eden means anything, it means that work was at one time considered a curse— although later Jewish and Christian theology strenuously denied this and turned it in fact into its opposite, so that work became the very essence of living and labour its own fulfillment. We shall have more to say on this later on, but let it be noted now that work no longer has this implication today. For most of us it is a means to an end; it implies not life but livelihood. And if the latter can be obtained in some other way, by investment or pension, then most of us would like to be done with working, only to tackle the even more difficult problem of leisure.

Even time itself is a relative concept, and not merely since the days of Einstein. It has had different meanings in successive ages, and often in different places and cultures at the same time. In our society, we save time, spend time, waste time, in the same way in which we waste, spend and save money. In fact, time *is* money. But it is not so for everyone.

A study of contemporary Greek society reveals this analysis:

> Greeks 'pass' the time; they do not save or accumulate or use it. . . . The clock is not master of the Greek: it does not tell him to get up, to go to the field. . . . At church the people are not impatient while waiting for Mass to begin; and the church fills only gradually. They know when to go to church; yet when a foreign visitor inquires as to the time of a certain Mass, the subject creates a discussion; and eventually the answer will be something like: "Between 2 and 3." And when Greeks who follow their traditional ways invite, they say, not: "Come at 7 o'clock," but: "Come and see us." To arrive to dinner on time is an insult, as if you came just for the food. You come to visit,

and the dinner eventually appears. . . . For the Greek traditionally, to work against time, to hurry, is to forfeit freedom. Even in the cities, people are called 'Englishmen' when they turn up on the dot at meetings or appointments.[1]

Examples can be multiplied. When I went to university in Germany, a distinction was always made between standard time and academic time. When you said "two o'clock" without any additive, you meant two sharp. When you said "two o'clock academic," you meant 2:15. Every Jew knows that we have, or at least had in the very recent past, something called "Jewish time." A Jewish fraternal or Zionist meeting may be called for 8:30 P.M., but it is understood that it will not start until 9. There are still some people in Toronto who are shocked to find that when they come to my synagogue at 6:30 for a wedding that has been called at 6, the ceremony is already over. Not a few have been quite incensed over this breach of what they consider a Jewish cultural convention. In Toronto a dinner invitation for 7 o'clock on a weekday, means 7 o'clock sharp or shortly thereafter; on a Saturday night it would be perfectly alright to arrive at 7:45 or even 8 o'clock.

What I have been trying to say in this somewhat lengthy prolegomenon is that in approaching the problems and opportunities of the Sabbath we must be aware that we are dealing with variables. Further, if we are to make a radical reassessment of our time and value structure, as I believe is urgently necessary, it is both instructive and useful to take the Sabbath as paradigmatic. The revolution which it set off when it first made its appearance amongst the Jews has not yet ended, and its potential function may yet be as great as it has ever been. For the Sabbath is indeed a ubiquitous institution. In one form or another, it now exists amongst all people in the West. Its neglect, misuse, and abuse are in themselves significant bellwethers of social problems, even as its radical reassessment may become a window of hope and progress.

THE SABBATH IN HISTORY—*A Partial Survey*

Much has been written on the relationship between the biblical Sabbath and the Babylonian *shappatu,* which was considered an unlucky day on which certain labors and procedures were proscribed. Just what the connection was between these taboos and the work prohibition of the Bible is no longer clear. Suffice it to say that somewhere in history there appeared a revolutionary observance of religious time which was not dependent on any natural phenomena in the heavens or on earth.

The significance of the Sabbath as opposed to the earliest festivals in Israel and in all nations was precisely that it was not dependent on the position of sun or moon, on planting or harvest time. To be sure, both in Genesis and Exodus, the Sabbath is related to Creation, that is, to a cosmic event. But its celebration week after week becomes remembrance and is not based on contemporaneous observations or happenings. Thus, the Sabbath becomes God's time, the God who created the world and also created Israel. Every Sabbath, when the Jew lifts his Kiddush cup for blessing, he remembers the One who created the Universe out of primeval darkness and led His people from the night of Egyptian slavery.

At a later age the Sabbath became "humanized," if one may so call it. It became social time devoted to the liberation of every man from the fetters of work, a liberation which included the freeman as well as the slave. Thus the Sabbath acquired a dual aspect which it has maintained throughout the centuries and which can best be explained by the differences between the Ten Commandments in the Books of Exodus and Deuteronomy.

The command in Exodus (20:8) opens by saying *zachor*—"*Remember* the Sabbath Day*." Remembrance is an act of cognition, of reason, of the mind. The Deuteronomic command (5:12) begins with *shamor*—"*Observe* the Sabbath Day." Man is here called to an act of will rather than reason. Thus cognition and obligation form the twin aspects of this day, which is God's time and man's time and finds a place for both.

Or put it another way. *Zachor* demands spiritual effort, *shamor* physical observance. We may state here the distinction which Isaac Arama made centuries ago. "Remember," he said, is a reference to rest as sanctification; "Observe" to rest from physical labour.[2] We shall return to this proposition at a later time, but lest the differentiation is driven too far, I may also quote another tradition, which emphasizes the need to consider *zachor* and *shamor* as two sides of the same coin: "The two commandments 'Remember' and 'Observe' were spoken by God in one single moment."[3]

Like any vital religious system, Judaism became deeply concerned with the need to translate the Sabbath command into Sabbath reality. The Talmud developed thirty-nine different categories of labor, with many subdivisions arising therefrom, so that to the superficial observer it might appear that the Sabbath was indeed a great burden laden with taboos and prohibitions. Prohibitions there certainly were and many of them, but a burden?—no, that the Sabbath was not, at least not in those days when work and rest still meant what since biblical times they had meant. Only when the cultural environment, in fact the whole context of civilization, changed to such a degree that labor and idleness, leisure and work, assumed different meanings, only then were the ancient categories of the Talmud first drawn into question and then largely abandoned by the multitudes of the Jewish people.

It is not essentially different with the Christian observance of the Sabbath. We here in North America are to a large degree inheritors of the Puritan tradition, and while the younger generation may recall Blue Laws only from the history books, we older ones still remember them very clearly. A mere nine years ago when I moved to Toronto you could not see a movie on Sundays, a prohibition which has since been abandoned. In many American states there are similar left-overs, covering sports events or the purchase of alcohol.

The disappearance of the Blue Laws signals the abandonment of certain old ideas and values. It highlights the break-up of traditional society, just as the dissolution of the Jewish ghetto was highlighted by the disregard of the thirty-nine categories of forbidden Sabbath labor.

Here too, then, the Sabbath has become paradigmatic. It has heralded the shattering of personal observance. Not by coincidence, attendance at Sabbath services is falling to ever lower levels.

People concerned with the religious enterprise are, however, quite mistaken when they believe that attractive services, fine music, comfortable pews, air-conditioned halls, and other esthetic and physical stimuli will return church and synagogue to their erstwhile pre-eminence. Nothing of the sort. People will return when the Sabbath and what it means become important to them, not the other way around. And in our day the Sabbath cannot become important to people until it has been radically restructured, its foundations reexamined, and its opportunities thoroughly reassessed in the modern context. The old Sabbath may be alive for the few; for the many it is a shell without substance. A new Sabbath observance must begin with real and realistic relationships, with people where they presently are in their daily lives.

NEW APPROACHES

Quantitatively, the work week is constantly getting shorter. In Canada a union recently demanded that its work week be reduced from 32 to 28

hours. While such demands will be made and granted more and more frequently in the next decade, they no longer form the major concern of
the working public. No longer will it be the *right not to work* which
people will worry about, but the *right to work*. The very concept of a
negative income tax indicates this inversion. Fifteen years ago it was
estimated that there were 500 billion leisure adult hours to be disposed
of in the United States. Now, the figure may easily be double.

Concurrently, leisure has become a problem. Where formerly man
was concerned with surcease from work, he now wonders how to get
surcease from leisure. Furthermore, our rapidly increasing geriatric population needs everything except physical rest. Doing nothing was for
centuries the acme of pleasure, and too much work a curse; now too
much leisure is a curse and doing something a pleasure.[4]

In 1952, Josef Pieper called leisure one of the foundations of
modern western culture, and claimed that we had entered a new era in
which one would have to set aside the prejudices that come from over-
valuing the sphere of work. Work alone, he emphasized, could no longer
define our concept of human life. Leisure had to be recognized as a
source of value and perhaps its primary source.[5] A few years after
Pieper first gave the concept of leisure a new dimension, the Jewish
Theological Seminary of America called a "Conference on the New
Leisure" and subsequently published a volume of its findings.[6] Leisure,
the Conference held, must now be incorporated into the theological and
philosophical thinking of church and synagogue.

What these new approaches tried to do was to remove work from
the center of our attention and put leisure in its place. They intended to
replace the traditional work ethic of Western culture with a leisure ethic.
But despite all the quantitative changes in our work-and-rest habits we
still continue—at least for the present—to consider work as central to
human existence. The important change which has taken place is that it
is the *quality* of work—and no longer its quantity—which determines the
structure of our civilization. The question that men ask is no longer
"How long do I have to work?" or "How much leisure can I get?" That
is the surface question which is asked in labor negotiations. The human
question below, however, is asked with ever greater urgency: "How can
I do significant work? How can I do work which fulfills not only the
needs of my pocket book, but also the needs of my ego?" French young
people were recently asked: "What is most important in choosing your
job?" The answers were as follows: The job must be interesting—65%;
it must pay a high salary—24%; it must provide much leisure—10%.[7]

Pieper and his successors were of course right in one important area and therein lies their chief contribution: leisure *is* a potential source of significant living, and this is the area to which we now turn.

We can begin with an old definition to which I have already alluded, that of Isaac Arama who differentiated between Sabbath rest and sanctification. This definition was taken up in the nineteenth century by the Jewish religious Reformer Samuel Holdheim and his successors.[8] Definitions, of course, do not a Sabbath make, and so the rabbinical Reformers had little success in rescuing the Sabbath from neglect, for they approached its problems in an ideological rather than a structural way— that is to say, they believed that by providing their new definition they could also radically alter the habits of their contemporaries. That was a delusion which we ourselves must take care not to emulate.

But it is important to realize that all living consists of doing and not doing, of positive acts and of abstaining. The opportunities of the Sabbath still lie in turning doing and not doing toward rest and sanctification. Only we must understand these opportunities in the context of our time. We still need rest, but not primarily from work. Rather, *we need rest from unrest.* We do need sanctification in our lives and particularly *a sanctification of freedom,* the cry for which is urgent in our time.

Two questions arise here. For one, why must rest and sanctification be linked to the Sabbath? Young people especially suspect that tying these objectives (of which they generally approve) to one particular day is another way of shoring up the institutional religious enterprise. I do not deny my hope that such might indeed be a result. But the argument needs to be met on its own merits. Now, experience teaches that while occasional and intuitive actions are in fact often more authentic religious responses than the regular and patterned practices of traditional religion, the former will tend to occur so rarely that their effect on one's life becomes negligible. The repetitive occurrence of the Sabbath is more likely to encourage rest and sanctification than the once-in-a-while, whenever-it-may-be spontaneity which sounds ideal and turns out to be Utopian.

Second, must our response be couched in prescribed acts and abstentions? Alvin Reines, in opposing such codification, pleads for an "open symbolism," a framework vague enough to permit each person his own understanding of and response to the opportunity, because the set responses of traditional religion are most likely no longer meaningful to him.[9] However, in the Jewish context group observance has its own motive force in addition to its indigenous merit: it is good for the enhancement of Jewish identity and in turn encourages others to join in these particular forms. But Reines is right when he suggests that there must be openness, and, indeed, contemporary guides to Sabbath observance should emphasize choices and opportunities.[10]

REST FROM UNREST

If the Sabbath is to have any significance it must confront one of modern man's greatest curses, his internal and external unrest. This unrest arises from the fact that today he leads a life without goals and, as a consequence, that he is involved in competition without end.

Life Without Goals

Formerly, both the physical and spiritual goals of man were clear. He needed to survive physically and do everything and anything that would help him achieve this goal. He tried to survive in nature's as well as in society's jungle. He had to fight the devils of sickness and starvation and whatever else was his lot. If only he could survive he had achieved life's major physical goal. Spiritually, the matter was even simpler. With Jew, Christian and Mohammedan, living the good life or the life of faith was sure to bring some form of salvation: Paradise, Heaven, or Life in the presence of God. It was happiness postponed, but as a goal it remained quite clear.

In today's Western society purely physical survival is no longer the clearly defined physical goal (although for a good portion of mankind it still is, and therefore their Sabbath needs would be entirely different from ours). For us, to keep from starvation is no longer the problem. Rather, if I may so put it, the problem is that we no longer know what the problem is. We no longer know what life's physical goal might be or even if there is one altogether. Further, except for those who truly believe in salvation in the old sense, few men are sure what life's spiritual goals are. So they talk of happiness or use similar empty phrases with which to cover their aimlessness.

I often ask young people who come to me to discuss their marriage plans just what their goals are. The two outstanding answers are "happiness" and "security" (the latter is the preferred answer of women). But when I press my visitors further and ask what they mean and how they aim to achieve these goals, they become very vague. The fact is that, like their parents, they have no clear goals, a lack of which from the outset is a built-in cause of marital unrest.

Added to the general conundrum is the ever-increasing infantilization of our culture. The child wants his satisfactions now and not later. The "now" dimension has become the over-riding aspect of our youth culture and has increased their sense of unrest (which in turn affects their elders), because the moment now is experienced another now is at hand. Thus now becomes never, and never is the feeding place of restlessness.

I therefore view the Sabbath as potentially an enormous relief from, and a protest against, these basic causes of unrest. Once a week it provides us with an opportunity to address ourselves to the who-ness rather than the what-ness of life, to persons rather than things, to Creation and our part in it, to society and its needs, to ourselves as individuals and yet as social beings. That is what Pieper called "the inner source of leisure," the setting of goals which are both realistic and within one's reach, yet also beyond one's self.

I rarely find a better place for such redirection than a religious service, whose major function ought to be not just the repetition of well worn formulae but the celebration of human goals, setting them within the context of Creation. If nothing happens to us during this or any Sabbath experience except an enlarging of our vision, we will have gained a new perspective of life's meaning and will have diminished our sense of unrest. That will be Sabbath rest, in the sense required by our time.

Competition Without End

Endless competition is a specific form of goal-lessness. Formerly there was probably not as much economic competition as there is today, but however much there was had a clearly defined objective. For most people it was to gain a livelihood. In today's Western civilization that is simply no longer enough.

Nowadays, everything is competitive, but the end is never quite defined. Our culture asks us to acquire and acquire ever more, but we are never told when we will have enough. Women are urged to beautify themselves, for the sake not only of other women but also of other men, but are never told to what end such competition is entered into.

I view the Sabbath as a surcease from and a protest against all forms of competition, even when they come in attractive packages marked "self-advancement" or "self-improvement." I view the Sabbath in this respect as a "useless" day. Our forefathers had a keen understanding of the fact that sleep on the Sabbath day was a form of coming closer to God. We must once again understand that doing nothing, being silent and open to the world, letting things happen inside, can be as important as, and sometimes more important than, what we commonly call the useful.

I am often asked why we have more than the necessary number of Torah scrolls in the synagogue. Actually, only one single scroll is needed; two and on rare occasions three are useful in the sense that when various passages are required to be read at the same service the congregation need not wait until the single scroll is rolled back and forth. But many congregations have ten, fifteen, twenty, or even more scrolls in the Ark, more than they can possibly use—and these scrolls are considered the prize possessions of the synagogue. That to me is a marvelous example that the House of God is essentially not useful. Besides, it does stand empty a great deal of the week, its facilities are not always used, nor are the activities that take place there useful in the ordinary sense.

Formerly, a person who did not work was considered useless; what we need now is a *purposive uselessness,* an activity (or non-activity!) which is important in that it becomes an essential protest against that basic unrest which comes from competition without end.

In the Jewish context I would therefore suggest that on the Sabbath one ought to abstain from everything which on one level or another is considered *usefully competitive.* For instance, going to the hairdresser's on the Sabbath is in my view a form of sexual or social competition and ought to be left to other days. Equally, going to classes at night to advance oneself usefully would fall into the same category of Sabbath prohibition. Let there be some special time during the week when we do for the sake of doing, when we love the trivial and in fact simply love, when we do for others rather than for ourselves and thus provide a counterbalance for the weight of endless competition that burdens our every day.

THE SANCTIFICATION OF FREEDOM

The Sabbath gives us a quantity of free time and thereby a quality potential of freedom time, when a man can be himself and in some area do for himself and for others what in the workaday world he cannot. Such Sabbath observance is a sanctification of freedom.

Part of the hopelessness of our age is our sense of imprisonment.

This comes not merely from the increasing complexity of society and our experience of marginality, but from the ever growing importance of machines and the advance of automation. Everyone can add to the stories that illustrate this experience. For example, this exclamation by an adult: "See that beautiful flower! It looks as perfect as if it were artificial!" Or the marvel of a child who upon seeing a pianist says: "Look, Daddy, he is playing with his own hands!" Automation not only removes men further and further from their work, but also from the opportunity of making decisions. And a man who makes no decisions is ultimately a man who is bereft of a basic freedom.

It is for this reason that, on the whole, spectator sports and other spectacles which now fill much of men's free time too often represent missed opportunities. True, when we sit and watch we may celebrate the uselessness of the day. But is this the only way to escape the time machine, or can we put something else in its place? There ought to be occasions when free time becomes sanctified freedom time.

In contemplating these matters I have come to wonder why baseball, formerly America's favourite spectator sport, has lately fallen from grace. Is it because it is too slow for today's taste? Perhaps, but there may be another, subtler reason. Over the decades the record book has become such a major factor in the game that it has begun to overwhelm spectator and player alike. What a man does is at once measured against the performances of the book; his own individual effort in the framework of the game is frequently dwarfed by the record of the ages. And somehow, somewhere, deep down in the public's mind there may be some doubt that their own needs of escaping from the machine and its pressures are sufficiently served by this constant recourse to statistics.

It is perhaps this very fact which attracts so many to the game of golf, both in the doing and in the watching. For here a man competes ultimately not for the money (that is reserved to the few professionals) and not even primarily against others, but essentially against himself and his own potential. Thereby he opens up a measure of freedom which may give him some relief of the soul—despite the ulcers and other frustrations which the game may otherwise produce. (Of course, I am not unaware that people might come to any game or program "with many different attitudes and approaches. And what might look like the same activity because it has a similar format, might have an entirely different value with respect to whether the person is increasing his or her personal freedom through the experience."[11])

The words "sanctification of freedom" imply yet another dimension. It has to do with that hope which attempts to make possible what is apparently impossible. There is a special kind of freedom which enables us to strive for the perfection of the essentially imperfect and thereby to enter the dimension of the Divine into a segment of human time. Abraham J. Heschel speaks of Judaism as "a religion of time aiming at a sanctification of time. Unlike the spaceminded man whose time is unvaried, iterative, homogeneous, to whom all hours are alike, qualityless, empty shells, the Bible senses the diversified character of time. There are no two hours alike. Every hour is unique and the only one given at the moment, exclusive and endlessly precious. Judaism teaches us to be attached to holiness and time; to be attached to sacred events, to learn how to consecrate sanctuaries and emerge from the magnificent stream of the year. The Sabbaths are our great cathedrals. . . . Jewish ritual may be characterized as the art of significant form in time, as architecture of time."[12] To the religious person God is the source of holiness, and the Sabbath therefore a truly sanctified segment of hope which lights up the dark horizon of pessimism. It is not only useless time, but non-rational time, for in the final analysis hope like faith is non-rational (to be distinguished from irrational).

A fascinating number of parallels suggest themselves, especially from the world of psychology.

The English psychologist R. D. Laing, for instance, has suggested that man's true liberation might have to come from a temporary retreat into schizophrenia. That is to say, with the world being what it is, one must experience unreality in order to both understand and master reality. In order to be oneself one must so to speak learn to get outside oneself. In his book *The Divided Self,*[13] Laing suggests a retreat into simulated insanity as the extreme means of liberation, to propel us out of the box in which we are imprisoned. I am in no position to comment on these latest theories, but it occurs to me that since ancient times religious people have often been closely linked to what were considered the crazy and the insane—only we used more pleasing words such as vision and mystic trance for otherwise dubious experiences.

However, we do not have to go to extremes of religious apprehension to understand that the religious man who escapes from the machine does indeed escape from the normal. The man who attains freedom on any level in our day is, in effect, abnormal when measured against the normalcy of automation. Because it encourages this kind of non-rational escape the Sabbath may therefore be described as an opportunity for "religious schizophrenia," a pious *meshuggas* which R. D. Laing would find a source of real hope. I use this terminology only to indicate again how closely the concerns of religion may be related to those of psychology and how closely the prescriptions resemble one another.

In pursuing yet another avenue of psychological inquiry one can consider all religious ritual a kind of sacred play or game, a retreat into the "as-ifness" of our soul. Johan Huizinga describes three qualities which religion and play have in common: Both strive seriously for perfection; both have specially assigned spaces with their own rules and sanctions; and both religion and play rely on symbols, pageantry, vestments, and special languages.

Both religion and play, we might add, are important retreats from the realness of the machine and the pressure of the everyday and are on their level avenues of hope—whatever that hope may be: either to win a game, or to score, or perchance to win salvation. To put it yet in a different way, prayer may be regarded as a form of sacred recreation—and saying this does not demean either prayer or recreation. Frequently, study belongs to the same category. Judaism has always encouraged study in every form and on every level. Study for its own sake and not for the sake of self-advancement is basically an exercise in "as-ifness," a sacred kind of game where thought takes wings and imagination replaces automation.

For where hope exists decision exists, and where decision exists there is freedom. And freedom comes in many packages. It comes alone or in groups, it comes in effort and doing, or it comes in openness and in silence. It comes in retreat from men as protest against the oppression of man and machine. It may fill a day or only a portion of it. However much or little, it is a precious time to sanctify freedom. And for him who knows this day to be beloved of God it is indeed a very special day with special opportunities. To celebrate it let a man do those things which liberate him from the ordinary and give him areas of free decision, of doing for himself and for others those things he wills to do rather than those which he must do; where he indulges in recreation both sacred and other which will help him to escape from the oppression of our civilization.

THE PROTEST

I titled my lecture "The Sabbath as Protest"—but it is not only the Sabbath which does the protesting; it is also that which it represents, namely, the religious venture of man. For religion itself at its best is a protest. It is the unusual that denies the ordinary; it is standing still and sitting down; it is doing something and nothing; it is hoping and being.

The Sabbath can be the paradigm of this understanding of the religious quest.

Two French psychologists, André Virel and Roger Frétigny talk about four states of human consciousness: imaginative, active, reflexive, and contemplative.[14] The two middle states (activity and reflexive response) characterize our automated society; the two other (imagination and contemplation) are the redeeming features which make life livable. These are the qualities to which the Sabbath addresses itself, for imagination is a form of freedom, and contemplation is rest from unrest.

I have spoken from the vantage point of a Jew, but the problems and the opportunities are not Judaism's alone. Everyman, and not just a Jew, needs rest from unrest, needs surcease from goal-lessness and endless competition, and in the face of automation needs to sanctify his free time as freedom time. In the process, work and leisure will have to get themselves new vestments so that the increasing quantities of free time which society will have in the years to come may become true freedom time for many—until that day when the protest will no longer be necessary and when the Sabbath will have become the antechamber to the Messianic era. Until then, I fear, it will have to be a protest against what is, and a celebration of what may yet come to be.

(1970)

NOTES

1. Margaret, Mead, ed., *Cultural Patterns and Technical Change* (New York: Mentor, 1955), pp. 70ff.

2. *Akedat Yitzchak,* Vayak'hel.

3. *Mekhilta,* Yitro.

4. See the comprehensive study by Max Kaplan, *Leisure in America: a Social Inquiry* (New York & London: 1960).

5. Josef Pieper, *Leisure, the Basis of Culture* (New York: Pantheon, 1952).

6. Moshe Davis, editor, *Conference on the New Leisure,* Jewish Theological Seminary of America (Dec. 1956).

7. From *Paris Match,* reprinted in *Atlas* (May 1970), p. 22.

8. Holdeim argued that the true objective of the Sabbath was to achieve

sanctification. Rest was but a symbolic means to the end of ethical sanctification, not an end in itself. See W. Gunther Plaut, *The Rise of Reform Judaism,* (New York: World Union for Progressive Judaism, 1963), pp. 190ff.

9. "Halachah and Reform Judaism," *Dimensions* IV (3) (Spring 1970): 20ff; also *idem*, "Sabbath as a State of Being," *CCAR Journal* (January 1967): 29ff. His suggestion that the Jewish Sabbath be shifted to Sunday and that the observance and the character of other Jewish holy days be changed has ample precursors in Reform History; see W. Gunther Plaut, *The Growth of Reform Judaism* (New York: World Union for Progressive Judaism, 1965), pp. 269ff.

10. *A Shabbat* (New York: Ktav, 1972), prepared by the Central Conference of American Rabbis, is structured on the principle of choice.

11. Kenneth Benne, *Conference on the New Leisure*, part II, p. 74.

12. *Man is Not Alone* (Philadelphia, Jewish Publication Society, 1951), pp. 28–29.

13. R. D. Laing, *The Divided Self* (New York: Pantheon, 1970).

14. *Imagerie Mentale* (Paris, 1968).

9

MUTATIONS OF JEWISH VALUES
IN CONTEMPORARY AMERICAN FICTION

LEO W. SCHWARZ

C ontemporary American novelists are preoccupied with man's condition and his attempts to find meaning in it. This preoccupation has elicited opposite responses: no one is less capable than the writer of describing his times and his contemporaries; no one has this capacity in greater degree than the writer. The literary artist, it is argued, cannot be trusted as an elucidator of man's condition and fate because on the one hand he has escaped into incomprehensible imagery and symbolism, and on the other hand he sees in man only absurdity, self-deception and insignificance. No doubt something like this has happened, but it does not follow that a writer who despairs of a world in which he sees no meaning must fail to lend reality to the segment of life he has chosen to record. True as it may be that a scientific and technological society is creating a man without values, it is also true that, science and technology notwithstanding, there are men who cherish traditional values.

Of course the probing of man's situation and his search for self-significance is not the walled-in preserve of the literary artist. Critics, philosophers, sociologists, and theologians are there to testify to the contrary, but the point is that they are concerned in the main with mankind and society; that is to say, with man collectively and metaphysically. The case is different with the literary work. It deals with individual human beings in their infinite variety and complexity, their dilemmas and delusions, their frauds and failures, their fears and faiths, their degradation and ennoblement, their coarse malignancy, and lyric tenderness. The writer's province is not statistical tables or clinical experiments or subcommittee meetings or press relations. His aim is insight, not manipulation. No one is more sensitive to the self-righteous, the sanctimonious, the fraudulent, the obscene, and quicker to express them. He uses his gifts—his sense of irony and his sense of pity—to hold the mirror up to our face, to project images of human life. He persuades us to think, wonder, feel, and, in his best creations, to confront life at its most real levels.[1]

All this is general, but it establishes the context in which I propose to examine traditional values and the changes they have undergone in contemporary American fiction. I mean by "values" the beliefs, ideas, and lifeways which give human life and human beings significance and meaning. I shall confine myself to certain moral values which, though not peculiar to, are essential to the Jewish structure of beliefs. It may be well to point out here that in speaking of values I employ the term "moral" rather than "ethical." Ethics is concerned with the theoretical formulation of a system of values—a speculative task for philosophers and theologians. Morality has to do with commitment to standards of conduct. You can solve ethical problems in an armchair. Moral problems are resolved in life.

I

The novels of Philip Roth and Saul Bellow provide numerous illustrations of the present-day change of values.[2] Whether the vogue of these writers is owing to their literary talent or their ideological bent, or to their appearance at a time when literature has become big business, I do not know. That they are epicures of psychopathology and sex is doubtless part of the explanation. In any case, the characters who people their novels project a view of man and society which emphasizes that the individual is alone, forsaken, and alienated by powerful impersonal forces that grind him down to anonymity and hopelessness. Coupled with a passion for introspection and a sense of disillusionment, the positive non-belief of these novelists has made for a version of American reality that negates tradition and religion. Their books present an American version of the *Luftmensch,* Americans wallowing in confusion and misery without an ideal or value to their name. Specifically, these writers are engaged in assaulting the American middle-class and middle-brow, and since American Jews are practically or potentially middle-class, and Jewish characters fill their pages, the gallery of Jews they portray seem like figures embalmed in pop art—rootless, neurotic, frozen in a scatological daymare. They see in man only absurdity, self-deception, and insignificance.

Philip Roth has given us, in his *Letting Go,* the alphabet and syntax of the alienated American, both Gentile and Jewish. All the characters in the book are trapped in lives of noisy desperation. Whether in Chicago or New York, the atmosphere in which they live is polluted to the point of suffocation. Roth shows with remarkable psychological insight how the involvement of the four principal characters with each other is a process of pushing and pulling in which each is letting go of his past and of the values associated with that past. They are like young teenagers who are torn between self-dependence and over-dependence, and haunted by excessive feelings of personal guilt. As the emotional intensity is built up to a nerve-wracking pitch, childhood values and loyalties disappear as if in a cauldron. Paul Herz says, in talking of his planned marriage to a Catholic girl, "She's a Catholic like I'm a Jew. It's not the kind of thing that'll have much to do with our lives. It hasn't to do with us. It's another ruse."[3] The protagonist, Gabe Wallach, intelligent, rich, and well-intentioned, who is drawn capriciously into the lives of the Herzes and Martha Regenhart, avoids full involvement and is conscience-stricken because he cannot let go and become responsible for the health and security of others. In the last pages of the book, Gabe is free of his involvements: he has escaped to London, but he remains the slave of his incapacity to cope with his guilt and has nothing to cling to. He has no values and hence no moral choice.

Although Bellow's *Herzog* appears to be a more philosophical work, it is nevertheless just as clinical as *Letting Go*. The mind of Moses Herzog is a willed chaos—a chaos that is death to human relationships; his utterances are piffle rather than philosophy. He is frustrated, angry, defeated, or more to the point, self-defeating. He wallows in emotional and intellectual sludge. He thinks freedom is only "a howling emptiness."[4] He, too, has "let go" of traditional values, and he has nothing with which to replace them. The best he can do is to investigate "the social meaning of nothingness."[5] Man has made his bed of neuroses, and he must lie in it. Herzog's definition of truth reveals his distorted sense of life. "Truth is true only as it brings down more disgrace and dreariness upon human beings," he writes, "so that if it shows anything except evil it is illusion."[6] Is Herzog searching for truth or succumbing to chaos? What is evident in his neurotic epistoloquacity is something other than rebellion, skepticism or iconoclasm. It is his failure to accommodate to the human community. The world of Herzog is first bent and then broken.

Alienation is the child of nihilism. Paradoxically, these writers regard alienation as the condition of being Jewish. Leslie Fiedler has stated this pointedly: "Jewishness means . . . not to belong; to be alienated."[7]

This, in essence, is a new kind of *galut,* a *galut* that rejects everything including the Jewish doctrine of *galut.* No wonder the alienationist writers regard Judaism as an anachronism. Knowingly or not, they are engaged in devaluating all human values. They are unable to believe in a reality that is not physical, sexual, or visceral. If the identification of Jewishness with nihilism has a precedent in the 3,500 year tradition of Jewish literature,[8] I do not know of it.

II

If the apostles of the doctrine of alienation have expressed the dejudaization of the American Jew, certain other novelists in vogue can see the Americanization of the Jew in the light of what amounts to caricature. Writers who came to the fore in the fifties and sixties seem to expressed the condition portrayed in Meyer Levin's *The Old Bunch* (1937), showing perhaps a deepening of the process of accommodation to American mores and morality. Two instructive examples are Marjorie Morningstar, the coed who wants to make the borscht circuit and have suburbia too, and Richard Amsterdam, a kind of male Marjorie Morningstar and Harvard playboy whose ideals are the Hasty Pudding Club and having a beautiful gentile wife and ten thousand a year (*Remember Me To God,* 1957). The worlds of Herman Wouk and Richard Kaufmann swarm with Americanized versions of *schlemeils, schleppers,* and *paskudnyaks.* Those who speak for traditional Jewish ideals, like Richard's father and Marjorie's uncle, are the only characters who win the reader's sympathy. But their views are deprived of any intellectual or moral force.

Few observers will deny the impact of American mores upon Jews, as portrayed by Wouk, Kaufmann and dozens of other popular novelists. Richly illustrative in this regard is Broadway's fiddling with Sholom Aleichem. *Fiddler on the Roof,* certainly an amusing, successful musical, is nevertheless false to Sholom Aleichem's *Tevye the Milkman.* The Broadway Tevye is made over into a permissive father who blesses the marriage of his daughter to an apostate. The original Tevye would neither have blessed nor condoned the marriage, however painful his decision. The Broadway Tevye is transformed into an oafish, peasantlike, hip-swinging, hen-pecked fellow whose faith is tailored to titillate the *amharazus de luxe* of the devotees of musicals. He is a purveyor of wisecracks rather than sober wisdom. The line spoken to God on Broadway,

"I don't have to tell you what the Good Book says," is jazz for "I don't have to tell you what the *Gemora* says." The original Tevye is a spiritual descendant of the Biblical Job, protesting life's injustice and affirming man's moral integrity—an affirmation enshrined in Jewish tradition and traceable to Mt. Sinai, as Tevye knows and his bellowing Broadway counterpart does not.[9]

We shall have to look elsewhere for that part of American reality which reveals the attempt by Jews to establish traditional Jewish values on American soil. An illuminating example is the series of engrossing novels by Charles Angoff, which began with *Journey to the Dawn* in 1951 and passed its middle point with the sixth volume, *Summer Storm,* in 1963.[10] The protagonist, David Polansky, and his proliferating family emigrate from Russia to Boston, where they endure the trials of economic hardship and social adjustment. Angoff is no less aware than Bellow and Roth of the corrosive effect of American life upon the Jewish family and tradition. Yet the Polanskys, for all the diversity of their viewpoints and the new roles of the second and third generations, remain rooted in Jewish life. They have regard for the Puritan-oriented culture of Boston. They revere the great representatives of American liberalism —figures like Woodrow Wilson and Louis D. Brandeis. In no way does this accommodation to American life obscure or downgrade Jewish culture and values. The Polanskys maintain their family integrity, employ Hebrew and Yiddish as living tongues, venerate education, respect law and justice, and are deeply mindful of human dignity. By a natural and healthy identification with Jewish values, the Polanskys are, according to their endowments and talents, conservators of Jewish cultural values.

Moreover, the Polanskys are not grotesque aberrations or wistful abstractions. Whether they are secularist or religious, their lives are informed and inspired by the traditional values—freedom, justice, law, goodness, learning, and compassion with its religious and moral bearings. These values are real and are expressed in human and communal relationships. Ben Gurion and Eric Fromm notwithstanding, the perpetuation of the structure of Jewish values requires something more than that we be upright and humane. The moral essences of Jewish culture, whether sanctioned by religion or humanism, require an institutional expression of shared beliefs and values.

How these values become merely verbal labels, emptied of their essence, can be illustrated by the present vogue of "compassion" in American fiction, especially in the tough, realistic novels. It would seem that compassion is lavished on the neurotic, the hipster, the whore, and an assortment of "sad cryptograms." What these practitioners of realism suggest is a phony compassion for ineffable delinquents. This amounts to the exploitation of human degradation for commercial ends rather than the sense of human tragedy. For compassion, in the traditional sense, is *rachmanut:* derived from *rechem,* the womb, the very matrix of life, compassion is a discriminating sympathy for human suffering, tempered by an understanding of pain and tragedy. True compassion requires a generous view of life and a standard of values. The compassionate man lives within a moral framework. He recognizes the gap between the man that he is and the man he can be.

All this is especially evident in the stories of Bernard Malamud. His characters are inept, hard-pressed, and sometimes obnoxious, yet they rise above the cruel pressures of their existence. They have an indomitable will to survive. Malamud invests these sad failures with pathos and dignity. His writing is instinct with the profoundest virtue of the Jewish spirit—a healing tenderness and loving compassion.

III

The world of Isaac Bashevis Singer's novels and stories[11] is rooted in the soil of Jewish tradition. His symbolism is of a pre-modern culture, but his themes are as fresh as the dialogues of our time. The major characters of his stories and novels, despite the blend of mysticism, superstition, and eroticism in them, are deeply religious and moral. Singer has come to terms with himself; he is committed to the hallowing of man and life. In his novel *The Slave,* Jacob, a pious scholar of Josefov, is sold as a slave to a Polish peasant. At first Jacob regards the peasants as debauched and soulless creatures. But in time he discovers that they are in reality human beings, created like himself in the image of God. In this way he learns from actual life his own affinity with "all living things: Jews, Gentiles, animals, even the flies and gnats." As a consequence he eats no flesh, "neither meat nor fish nor anything else from a living creature, not even cheese or eggs." He is ultimately ransomed and busies himself obsessively with the 248 commandments and 365 prohibitions of the Law. But he sees all around him Jews obeying every injunction and practicing every ritual, yet mistreating their fellow men. Ripening into an inner maturity, Jacob discovers that the essence of his religion is the relation between man and his fellows. Singer's theme, then, is the Jew and his faith in their universal character; his message is that all creatures, man and beast, are God's chosen. Singer's allegory of man enshrines other essential Jewish values. Jacob's marriage to a Gentile woman made him subject to excommunication and subject to death by burning. But Jacob and his wife loved each other, hoped, endured, and kept their faith. Like Job and the Berditchever Rabbi, he engaged in a perpetual debate with the Almighty. Despite the evil he saw in his fellow Jews, he recognized that there were many kind and good Jews. No matter how cruel he found the Gentiles, he found that there were many good Gentiles. It is the practice of human goodness that gives nobility to the religion they all profess. Singer shows, by way of acts of faith and kindness, that the mind and the heart are human instruments which must be played upon together in order to produce the true music of life, that the secrets of the heart are as real and powerful as the secrets of the atom. The words are the words of Singer, but the message is the message of Judaism.

A similar validation of Jewish values, based upon the experience of the present, may be found in the fiction bequeathed to us by Edward Lewis Wallant (1926–62). Deeply concerned with the problems of human guilt and responsibility, Wallant's stories of emotional crises penetrate to the essence of the human personality. The hero of *The Human Season* is a hero and not a victim. Joe Berman is a plain, rough-hewn, unselfconscious Jew. He exults in being alive. He accepts hard labor with equinimity. His Irish boss is a bully, but Joe does not crawl or cringe before him. Nor is he overawed by the bully's physical prowess. He meets insult and challenge head-on, without fear of the mauling he knows awaits him. Berman's head is bashed, and he loses a finger. When he awakes and discovers that his head is swathed in bandages and his finger gone he laughs. His brother thinks the beating has affected his head. "It's affected my head and my hand, too," Joe says, "but you should see the other guy." His humor is an expression of his love of life. "His heart sang with that mysterious exaltation that had no basis in reason." Later, in the face of the death of his wife, he is driven to the depths of melancholic grief and suffers the torments of what Freud calls "the work of mourning." He rises out of his bewildering sorrow with a deepened sense of family and faith, and achieves a dignity hewn out of a poignant encounter with life and man, with death and God. There is no ambiguity about his ultimate affirmation of life. Joe Berman is an imperfect man whose very imperfection gives the reader hope that the good in man as well as the evil is amenable to human need. Wallant's view of man, as expressed through Berman, makes man comprehensible without making him contemptible, just as Wallant's view of life makes life compassionate without making it cruel.[12]

Nothing has been more corrosive of traditional values than modern science, and its offspring, technology. In this regard, it is science fiction that portrays the struggle of God versus Golem. In his gem of a story, *The Golem*,[13] Avraham Davidson pictures a humanoid robot, which a scientist has created to displace mankind, making his first assault on a plain, middleclass Jewish couple, the Gumbeiners. They are unimpressed by his highfalutin scientific vocabulary and his pretensions to mastery. Their main concerns are the ordinary problems of everyday life. They quickly recognize a *golem* when they see one. Mr. Gumbeiner, drawing on his knowledge of Jewish folklore, employs the old device of marking a mystical formula on the robot's forehead and then puts the robot to work on household chores. The author mixes humor with satire to expose the intellectual smugness of technology. The use of ordinary people to project the conflict between man and technics is an expression of faith in the capacity of plain people to expose the protective devices of intellectual humbug. Davidson reasserts the Jewish belief that humor is the great solvent of life.

More than any other contemporary American writer Meyer Levin has explored the Jewish psyche in all of its bearings. Very early in youth he discovered his roots in Zionism and Hasidism and employed his art in the service of his American and Jewish heritage. One of his early novels, *Yehuda,* is a splendid evocation of life in a Palestinian kibbutz in the twenties. *The Golden Mountain,* published in 1932 before Buber's books were available in English, beautifully brought to life the legends of Israel Baalshem and Nachman Bratzlaver. His realistic portrayal of second-generation American Jews in *The Old Bunch* reveals clearly and memorably the paradoxes of American Jews. During the past two decades Levin has plumbed the psychopathology of violence in crime and war and their consequence for his own people and mankind. He sees in the emergence and growth of the state of Israel a catalyst for Jews and Jewish culture and feels that Jewish fate is bound up in the development of an organic relation between American Jews and Israel. Fostering such a relation is therefore a work of supreme importance. He writes: "If there was a Messianism in the Jewish folk that enabled it to rise out of death to attain Israel, then humanity as a whole must possess the fuller Messianism, and contain within itself the force to attain universal peace and justice."[14]

Levin's recent novel, *The Stronghold,* continues this grand theme. In a Bavarian castle a dozen renowned Allied hostages, including a

Jewish ex-Premier of France, await liberation by the American forces. During the few days when they are suspended between life and death, there is a dramatic confrontation between the prisoners and their Nazi jailors. All the subconscious forces in the protagonists come to the surface, and the questions of motive, responsibility, identity, and faith are explored. The book is a consummation of Levin's personal and moral quest and of the meaning of the Jewish experience in our time. "The story is developed," he writes, "as a thriller, but it is in reality a confrontation, a distillation, I hope, of the morality of Judaism, Christianity, and Nazism. The story is as far as I have got, in my sixty years, to an understanding of what we in our amazing time have lived through, in relation to our Jewish tradition and history, and in relation to the behavior of mankind."[15] Levin has made his home in a villa in Israel, overlooking the Mediterranean. His odyssey over the past forty years, from Chicago to Herzliya, has deepened his Jewish roots and enlarged his vision. The humane values of Jewish culture, which inform his life and art, work to offset the barbarities of alienation and to transform the suffering of our time into something tonic and healing.

IV

By way of conclusion, I shall try to point out objectively a few of the implications of the changes of values described above. But being objective does not mean being impartial.

The novelist is neither scientist nor philosopher nor sociologist. He is primarily an artist, and as such he must remain a stranger within our gates. He has his own net and his own draught of fishes. The images of Jews enshrined or embalmed in his writing are in part the image of the writer himself and in part the composite image of the people and the world he knows—and hates or loves, debases or ennobles. Either the novelist is confused, bitter and ill at ease ("alienated") in Zion; or he has come to terms with himself and his moral and spiritual tradition. In the one case he tells us what it is that makes our Sammies run; in the other, what makes our Davids and Ruths walk and think, despair and hope.

It is significant that writers like Angoff, Singer, and Wallant, whose writings convey a sense of immediacy and warmth in human association, were rooted in Jewish tradition in their childhood. They were reared in a milieu where the passion for kindness and justice took precedence over the lust for wealth and success. Jewish education taught them, not merely about Judaism, but, above all, to be a Jew. In a sense, they are the true rebels. The true rebel is a person who refuses to be what he is and attempts to become what he can be. This means, not copulating with death but coping with life, and this, in turn, means facing the crises and paradoxes of existence and making hard decisions on questions of right and wrong.

Most of the living novelists, whether specialists in tradition or alienation, are dissenters, and on this count they deserve the attention especially of those who live within the fortress of convention. What are the implications of the reality they describe? Their charge is that Jews live on the principle of When-in-Romism, and their adoption of American mores is so complete that they have become indistinguishable from their non-Jewish neighbors; and that this attenuation of the cultural and religious values of the Judaic tradition is bringing about a spiritual abortion. Within the Jewish establishment, one notes everywhere a Gallup-poll mentality, a reliance on quantity rather than quality, a yielding to expediency instead of an embracing of faith, a substitution of research for fact rather than a search for values. Like other Americans, Jews are satisfied with a slip-cover religion and confuse mores with morality. And finally, they tell us that Jewish values, like the Jewish faith, once a substantial part of life, are now a ceremonial aspect of it.[16]

It will serve no purpose to look upon the alienationist writers with an oblique eye or to turn from or on them in anger. To call them "self-hating Jews" is neither honest nor useful. Of course, the process of alienation is a fact of life in our technologized, middle-class society. It is expressed by American novelists of every background and persuasion— perhaps most poignantly by Negro novelists—for example, in Ralph Ellison's superb novel, *The Invisible Man.* For Jews, alienation is part of the process of the recent naturalization of Jews and Judaism in American society, and committed Jews should consider seriously what these gifted, free-wheeling writers are saying. They should be faced with historical and psychological candor.

It is our obligation to counter their doctrine of nothingness and meaninglessness on rational and moral grounds. The principle that all men are strangers is no adequate substitute for the principle that all men are brothers. To hallow human estrangement and to sanctify the emptiness of life is, in terms of the consequences of this doctrine, to justify inhumanity. A writer cannot be absolved of the responsibility for the consequences of his ideas any more than the scientist can be absolved for the consequences of nuclear fission.

There is in our best fiction an indefinable note whose burden is that the inhuman and destructive elements in life today are evidence of human inadequacy and moral failure. Even the philosopher of the absurd, Albert Camus, has written, "The meaning of life is the most urgent of all questions."[17] And he has carried the thought further. Here is a passage from an address delivered in New York in the spring of 1946, a little less than two years after he emerged from the French underground:

> We all sanctify and justify [murder and terror] when we permit ourselves to think that everything is meaningless. This is why we have sought our reasons in our revolt itself, which has led us without apparent reasons to choose the struggle against wrong. And thus we learned that we had not revolted for ourselves alone, but for something common to all men. . . . There was in this absurdity the lesson that we were caught in a collective tragedy, the stake of which was a common dignity, a communion of men, which it was important to defend and sustain.[18]

Thus speaks a voice of honesty, courage, and moral vision. And a voice which should remind us that the latest literary fashion is not necessarily the last word.

(1966)

NOTES

1. Of the critics who are concerned with the matter as well as the manner of the contemporary American novel, I have found the following stimulating: Edward Dahlberg, *Do These Bones Live?* (New York, 1941); Edmund Fuller, *Man in Modern Fiction* (New York, 1949); Granville Hicks, ed., *The Living Novel* (New York, 1957); Alfred Kazin, *Contemporaries* (Boston, 1962); Walter Allen, *The Modern Novel in Britain and the United States* (New York, 1964); Marcus Klein, *After Alienation* (New York, 1964); Irving Malin, *Jews and Americans* (New York, 1965). Most of the important essays and reviews about the authors treated in this lecture are mentioned in the notes and bibliographies

in the books of Klein and Malin mentioned above. A growing number of writers are attempting to "correlate" theology and contemporary literature. The attempts thus far appear to overlook the fact that if a writer treats of religion it is simply because it is an ingredient of life and not because he intends to theologize. A few examples are Nathan Scott, Jr., *Modern Literature and the Religious Frontier* (New York, 1958); Randall Stewart, *American Literature and Christian Doctrine*, and John Killinger, *The Failure of Theology in Modern Literature* (New York, 1963).

2. The view expressed here applies with minor qualifications to other writers in vogue, for example, J. D. Salinger, Herbert Gold, Norman Mailer and Leslie Fiedler.

3. Original edition of *Letting Go*, p. 91.

4. Original edition of *Herzog*, p. 39.

5. *Ibid.*, p. 39.

6. *Ibid.*, p. 93. For a searching critique of *Herzog*, see Maurice Samuel's fantasy, "My Friend, the Late Moses Herzog," *Midstream*, Vol. XII, No. 4 (April, 1966), pp. 3–25.

7. Here is the full quotation: "I think the essential nature of Jewishness—this is my notion, but I think it is not a notion which is completely unshared; I think of it as a notion which is both deeply traditional and deeply contemporary—is, quite simply: *not to belong*. Not to belong; to be an exile; to be alienated; to know at every moment that wherever one is one does not belong; to know at every moment that wherever one finds himself he is alienated." The statement comes from a dialogue in Israel in which American and Israeli writers participated. For the proceedings see "Second Dialogue in Israel," *Congress bi-Weekly* 30 (12) (September 16, 1963): 24.

8. Critical discussion of the American Jewish or Jewish American writers has been complicated and obscured by the various meanings given to or implied by the word alienation. Estrangement from society, whether suffered by an artist or a delinquent, by a minority group or marginal man, is known to all human societies from biblical Israel to neotechnical America. Quite different is the estrangement of an individual from both society, and himself, the individual who is presumably a victim of the human condition—the faceless man whose interior life is a vacuum. Alienation is also used to describe the estrangement caused by technological "mass culture." One of the few works which attempts to make valid distinctions is Ehrich Kahler's *The Tower and the Abyss* (London, 1958). An example of the undefined use of the word is the anthology edited by Gerald Sykes, *Alienation: Cultural Climate of Our Time* (New York, 1964).

A book bearing directly on the subject of this essay is Irving Malin's *Jews and Americans*. He deals thematically with the work of seven writers—Karl Shapiro, Delmore Schwartz, Isaac Rosenfield, Leslie Fiedler, Saul Bellow, Bernard Malamud, and Philip Roth—and attempts to show, in chapters devoted to themes ("Exile," "Time," "Irony," "Parable," etc.), its relevance to Jewish experience, American experience, or by analogy to both. The procedure is pat, the interpretations are subjective and impressionistic. His terminology is vague. He asks important questions—for example, "Why is the Jew a new culture hero?"—which he never answers. He is unconscious of the fact that his conception of what makes a writer "Jewish" is no different from what makes him an American. Philip Roth has stated with honesty that he does not consider himself a Jewish intellectual. "The biggest passion in my life is to write fiction, not to be a Jew," he is reported to have said (*New York Times,* June 19, 1963, p. 31).

Actually the book is an enlargement of the introduction by Malin and Irwin Stark to their anthology *Breakthrough: A Treasury of Contemporary American-Jewish Literature* (New York, 1964), in which the thesis is more clearly stated. The view it expresses and documents is that the writers included represent a gifted group who have "broken through the psychic barriers of the past to become an important . . . influence in American life and letters." However, the barriers were only in part psychic; they were in greater part social. What we have been witnessing in the past few decades is the naturalization of Jews in American society, and one result has been the overidentification of Jews with American life and values. For example, the fiction of Roth, Fiedler and Bellow is filled with protagonists who are only nominally or tribally Jews but "spiritually" and culturally Americans. This seems to me, not a breakthrough, but a breakaway.

Malin's premise of the so-called breakthrough writers is that "the absurd is the condition of being." Their search for identity and personal freedom has alienated them from both conventional American society and from the Jewish Establishment. They leave Jews dangling, like Mohammed's coffin, in mid-air, with no home to go to. While this new self-definition is at bottom self-delusion, this collection of writing is evidence that alienation is the opiate of certain Jewish American intellectuals.

9. For a thoroughgoing analysis of *Fiddler on the Roof,* see Joseph C. Landis, "Fiddling with Sholom Aleichem," *Arts and Sciences* (New York University Bulletin, Vol. LXV, No. 24, June 14, 1965), pp. 29–33.

10. The series comprises *Journey to the Dawn* (1951), *In the Morning Light* (1952), *The Sun At Noon* (1955), *Between Day and Dark* (1959), *The Bitter Spring* (1961), and *Summer Storm* (1963), all published by Thomas Yoseloff, New York. The reader will find his appetite whetted by two collections of short stories, *When I Was a Boy in Boston* (New York, 1947) and *Something About My Father* (New York, 1956). For appreciations of Angoff's fiction, see Sholom J. Kahn, "Angoff's Polansky Chronicles," *Jewish Heritage* 3 (2) (Fall 1960): 35–44, and Sol Liptzin, "Angoff's Polansky Saga," *Congress bi-Weekly* 32 (17) (December 27, 1965): pp. 27–29.

11. Certain American critics have spoken of Singer as "a great American writer" but he has told me that he prefers to be considered a Yiddish writer. He has achieved fame in a dozen languages, a phenomenon which needs exploration. For a major Yiddish writer's view, see Jacob Glatstein's "The Fame of Bashevis Singer," *Congress bi-Weekly* 32 (17) (December 27, 1965): 17–19. Irving Howe gives a balanced critical estimate in "I. B. Singer," *Encounter* (3) (March 1966): 60–69.

12. Wallant's books are not as well known as they deserve to be, but the powerful movie version of *The Pawnbroker* is bringing him to the fore. Seymour

Epstein has written a perceptive appreciation, "Wallant's Literary Legacy," *Congress bi-Weekly* 32 (9) (May 10, 1965): 8–10.

13. *The Golem* is most easily accessible in the revised version of Leo W. Schwarz, *The Jewish Caravan* (New York, 1965), pp. 647–654. No more interesting expression of the problem of the individual's sense of identity and reality can be found than in contemporary science fiction. While it has won for itself a niche in imaginative literature, its profound social vision has been ignored. The twentieth-century writers are creating a new myth for their age, and their conceptions of the relations of Earthmen and Spacemen in their interplanetary experiences combine the fantasies of world-creation and world-destruction. The best of its practitioners are concerned with the nature of man and the meaning of his world. They are at the bottom moralists, insisting that human values must be preserved and defended against the encroachment of whatever is inhuman and mechanical.

14. *In Search* (Paris: Author's Press), p. 524.

15. "Crossing Sixty" in *The Kansas City Jewish Chronicle*, Friday, October 15, 1965, p. 8. For a sympathetic appreciation of Levin's work, see "The Jewishness of Meyer Levin" by Charles Angoff in *Congress bi-Weekly* 32 (17) (December 17, 1965): 13–14.

16. This criticism is implied in the studies of the contributors to Oscar I. Janowsky, editor, *The American Jew: A Reappraisal* (Philadelphia, 1964). See also Marshall Sklare, editor, *The Jews: Social Patterns of an American Group* (Glencoe, Ill., 1958).

17. *The Rebel: An Essay in Revolt* (New York, 1954), p. 89.

18. As quoted in the *New York Times*, March 19, 1946, p. 11.

10

AFTER THE GHETTO
Jews in Western Culture, Art, and Intellect

SAMUEL SANDMEL

I

The subject of this lecture is a phenomenon with which we are all acquainted: Jews in the modern world have included a noticeably disproportionate number of individuals of high and distinctive personal attainment. Lord C. P. Snow has spoken of a record that is "remarkable, and quite outside any sort of statistical probabilities." I hold this to be true. Let me mention a few names: Gustav Mahler, Sigmund Freud, Max Reinhart, Lord Solly Zuckerman, Ferenc Molnar, David Sarnoff, Albert Einstein, Henri Bergson, Jacob Javits, Albert Sabin, and Saul Bellow.

What these men have in common is that, had the ghetto walls not fallen, none of these men would have been able to realize their innate potentials, nor have come to that admiring notice which the modern world has taken of them. Perhaps we might emphasize how totally unexpected it was that Jews could rise to such attainments by recalling Christian Wilhelm Dohm. This German clergyman, whose dates are 1751–1820, wrote a two-volume work in 1781, *On the Political Amelioration of the Jews,* in behalf of Jewish political emancipation. His wholehearted advocacy of civil rights for Jews included his expression of a conviction that, were German Jews accorded the rights of citizenship, they might in three or four generations cease to be unproductive and begin to make some contribution to the general culture of Germany. About a hundred years later, the predecessors of Adolf Hitler complained that Jews had come, to use his later phrase, to dominate or even control the cultural life of Germany. It is, of course, a bitter irony that under Hitler Germany, rather than being grateful for the contributions of its Jews, chose to follow the diabolic demagogue and either to drive its Jews out of their Fatherland or else to kill them. But even this dreadful calamity only underscores the reality that Jews were able to enter the western world and to distinguish themselves in its intellectual and cultural streams in an unusual way, and in unusual numbers, and with unexpected rapidity.

Our direct query is this: how can we explain this phenomenon? More precisely, in what way did the ghetto experience of Jews lay the foundation for this ultimate aggregate of rather speedy individual achievements?

Two explanations for the eminence of Jews are recurrently offered. One of these stems almost exclusively from Gentiles. It is a very simple explanation. Jews are God's chosen, and hence Jews are better endowed than Gentiles. I personally know of no Jews who seriously support this explanation. In general, Jews shy away from a theological view of this kind, however flattering it is, simply because we have had no marked disposition towards theological explanations. Moreover, we Jews are realistic enough to recognize that among us, unhappily, mediocrity and even incapacity abound, and we would need to be honest and say that if, indeed, God chose us, he rather stingily abstained from endowing each and every one of us with the full benefits of his otherwise boundless grace.

A more naturalistic explanation is offered by Van der Haag in *The Jewish Mystique,* in what might perhaps be called a novel and revised version of Darwin's theory of the "survival of the fittest." Persecution winnowed out of Jewish life those unfit to survive, and hence the survivors were necessarily fit. On the Christian side, the best human material gravitated into the clergy, who were celibate, with the result that Christians did not reproduce their best, but only something less. Accordingly, we Jews reproduced human specimens markedly superior to what the Christians reproduced.

Now, the attainments of Jews have been minor in the realm of physical prowess, and I fear we have been somewhat underrepresented among boxing champions or all-American football players, and I wonder if Van der Haag sees the clear difference he should have seen between the physical and the mental. His book flatters us Jews, and wondrous as have been our endowments and attainments, they are somewhat less wondrous than he has made out. My children recurrently use an expression that may be apropos: Flattery will get you nowhere.

II

Is there some rational, commonsense explanation for this factor of Jewish eminence? I am persuaded that there is. To provide it, I need to draw on some broad generalizations which, if in part they may be a bit fallible, are still true enough to guide us.

The separatisms which dominated Jewish life in the ghetto are readily to be summarized: Jews ordinarily lived under rabbinic, rather than state, civil, law; often, indeed almost usually, they dressed differently, or, when they dressed similarly, needed—at various times and places—to wear the "Jew badge." Ordinarily they differed in language, speaking in Germanic or Slavic Europe that German dialect known as Yiddish, or in Turkey and Grecian lands that version of Spanish called Ladino. Perhaps we might summarize matters by saying that Jews lived in their own Jewish world.

The inner life of Jews was shaped by certain idiosyncracies of the Jewish religion. One of them was a ritual prayer book. Though an ancient rabbinic dictum had cautioned against fixed prayer, advocating instead the spontaneity of the heart, nevertheless the Jewish prayer book developed, and through the centuries grew in bulk and in a certain complexity. There has been a general, recognizable format in the worship, but this format has required constant variation. In a certain portion of the year, a prayer for rain is obligatory, and in the other portion it is to be omitted. Again, the core of the service has been the "eighteen benedictions," which turn out to have been increased in the daily worship to nineteen, but reduced on the Sabbath to seven. The end result of these variations was that one needed to be instructed in the use of the prayer book, in order for one to omit what was to be omitted and to traverse what was to be added. The Yiddish phrase put it in this way, that one needed to learn to *davven,* to pray.

The ghetto had its educational system. On the lowest level there existed the need for some minimum of literacy, for one could not pray out of a prayer book unless one could read the prayer book. I speak of "lowest level"; the prayer book was in Hebrew and Aramaic. The lowest instruction was in what we Jews have called *ivre,* which simply means an ability to read Hebrew—to read it, mind you, without necessarily understanding it. If one questions the value of such un-understanding reading, one nevertheless needs to observe that, among Jews, there existed an obligatory requirement of literacy, a literacy incumbent universally on males.

At the age of thirteen, a boy became *bar mitzvah*. The theory was that up to that age his parents were responsible for his misdeeds; after bar mitzvah, the lad himself became responsible. The occasion was observed in the synagogue, with the father instructed to acknowledge the son's arrival at maturity by reciting the formula which I paraphrase: "Blessed is God who has now relieved me of liability for my son's trespasses."

The bar mitzvah ceremony required the lad to master the reading of the scriptural portions assigned for the two lections, Pentateuch and Prophets, for the Sabbath nearest his thirteenth birthday. True, he might not understand the Hebrew he was intoning, but it was unthinkable that a lad at thirteen not appear before the congregation and not read his scriptural portions. Indeed, Jews often gave their significant dates, of birth or marriage, by the titles of the Pentateuchal segment.

Literally, *bar mitzvah* means "son of the commandment," though its import is "obliged to the commandment." No term that I know of is as apt in description of pre-modern Judaism as the phrase, a mitzvah system. If we are to understand it, and its influence, we need to go back into history, to the late pre-Christian period. By that time, surely the Pentateuch, the Prophets, the Psalms had come to be regarded as canonical. The Pentateuch was the sacred book par excellence. Genesis had come to be viewed as divinely revealed exhortation and edifying teaching. The laws of Exodus, Leviticus, Numbers, and Deuteronomy were the *mitzvot* (plural of *mitzvah*) by which man lived in conformity with the revealed will of God. A passage in Deuteronomy 29:10–30 reads: "You stand today before the Lord your God, your tribal leaders, your elders, all the men of Israel, your children, your wives, and the range from those who hew wood through those who draw water, in order that you may enter into covenant and vows with the Lord your God on this day. Not alone with you do I make the covenant and vow, but also with the generations not yet here . . . For this commandment I enjoin this day is not hidden from you nor far off. It is not in heaven that you should say, 'Who will ascend to heaven and bring it to us that we may hear and obey it?' nor is it beyond the sea, that you should say, 'Who will traverse the sea for us and bring it to us that we may hear and obey it?' Rather, the matter is near to you, in your mouth and mind, for you to observe . . . I have set before you this day life and the good, and death and evil . . . Therefore choose life that you and your descendants may live."

The supposition that the Pentateuch provided the guide for affirmative living meant that the Jews had a literary mentor, a source book which one could refer to for his personal guidance. It became natural for Jews to found that institution, unique in the history of religions, called in Greek the synagogue. Jews gave it two kindred Hebrew names, "the house of study" and the "house of assembly," and a phrase in Isaiah, "house of prayer," added its own dimension. There was, then, a sacred book, with access to it possible only through literacy, and a place of study. Study and learning became the key to piety, with prayer a concomitant of both. When in the year 70 the Temple was destroyed by the Romans, the priesthood for most practical purposes ended. When the sacrificial system over which priests presided then terminated, there were already at hand those resources by which the religion with its literary possession could survive and be perpetuated. Judaism became enshrined in synagogue and home in place of in Herod's refurbished Temple; prayer was declared a sufficient replacement for animal sacrifice; the sage, the learned man, supplanted the priest. To be a priest one needed to be born into the right family, but to be a sage, a rabbi, one needed to have acquired rich learning.

The Pentateuchal laws relating to animal sacrifice were outmoded, but still they merited study. Other laws required equally intensive study, for at times Scripture was vague, or apparently repetitious—and such repetition could not be deemed merely idle. Again, at times Scripture supplies particular laws without furnishing a general principle, and elsewhere a general principle without the particulars. The repetitions needed inquiry and explanation. Moreover, the setting had now changed from the early times when the laws had originated, and hence adjustment, or application, or even modification, might be desirable or necessary.

Out of this welter of currents and cross currents, rabbinic Judaism fashioned itself into an at-times amorphous, yet coherent, entity, with some system entering in to provide the bare rubrics of organization. That coherent entity, when it was made tolerably well arranged, became the mitzvah system.

This mitzvah system conveyed to the communicant what were the ongoing viable requirements now that Temple, priest, and sacrifices were obsolete. Rabbinic requirements were known by a special term, *halacha*, meaning "the way to do things," but in effect *halacha* was as obligatory as Scripture itself. Indeed, Scripture was intelligible only as it was refracted through the prism of the rabbinic halacha.

One could observe the mitzvot only if one knew them, and one could know them only by study. Moreover, Judaism ascribed authority solely to Scripture and to its ancient interpretation, and it never developed, as Christians did, a theory of persons in themselves authoritative. The sage, the rabbi, was an authority *in* Scripture and *in* rabbinic lore, and never an authority *over* them. Judaism never knew popes, cardinals, bishops, or councils such as Nicea or Chalcedon. Authority lay only in what had been long ago written and recorded, and not in contemporary persons. One could consult a sage for guidance, but such a sage guided the one who consulted strictly on the basis of his fidelity to and mastery of the written specifications of the literature. Whatever authority he possessed to guide was rooted completely in his learning.

He who learned possessed the key to the authority of the religion. When the ancient rabbinic traditions became recorded, in the fifth century version we call the Talmud, its bulk came to suggest that handy compendia might serve a useful purpose. A succession of such compendia were created, digesting for the ordinary Jew the major substance of the mitzvot. The compendium which gained universal eminence was the Shulchan Aruch of Joseph Caro in the sixteenth century; Germanic Jews utilized it with annotations by Moses Isserles, adapting the work for north European Jews.

In the ghetto, all male Jews learned to read Hebrew. Most also learned their bar mitzvah Scripture portion. An abundance of Jews, by no means learned, could make their way through the Shulchan Aruch. One also studied the Pentateuch along with the ingeniously eclectic commentary of the French rabbi, Rashi, Rabbi Isaac Shelomoh of Troyes (1040–1105). Through Rashi, one gained some good reflection of the contents of rabbinic literature. The truly learned proceeded beyond Rashi on the Pentateuch to the rabbinic literature itself.

The keynote to the mitzvot system is its realism, its practicality. The mitzvot informed a person about what he had to do today, do this very morning, do this very evening. The instructive lessons were neither in heaven nor across the ocean, but near at hand. Paradoxically, Jews studied the rabbinic expansions of the obsolete sacrificial system mentioned above, but on the premise that some day God would miraculously restore scattered Israel to the Holy Land and have the Temple rebuilt; hence, one needed to know the sacrificial laws in order to be prepared for the restoration of the cult.

Feasibility and practicality, then, were the keynote of the mitzvot. He who was to heed them could revert to the words of Deuteronomy, "Choose life that you may live." At times Jews spoke of God's providence, but they never developed any deep or widespread view of predestination. Rather, the individual was a free agent, and the sacred tradition was his to learn, if he had the time and capacity for it. Poverty could impede him, and persecution harass him, and expulsion uproot him; hence, he faced the acute problems of an insecure existence. While in the world to come there was some hope that the inequities of this age would be rectified, one's major preoccupation was in earning his meager livelihood, or in evading the persecutor, or in sinking new roots when he was driven from one dukedom into another. The response to persecution was an acute sense of responsibility for other Jews. If a pirate ship kidnapped five Jews from Bordeaux, the Jewish community of Venice responded to the demand for ransom money. When girls were too poor to possess dowries, the ghetto community provided charitable dowries. He who on dying left a family unable to buy the simple wooden casket could be sure that the *Hevrah Kaddisha,* the burial society, would meet the urgency. Moreover, one could cope with persecution and expulsion only by some elasticity, some resilience. Excessive rigidity was self-defeating, almost a death sentence.

I have mentioned the world to come. Jews inherited and bequeathed ideas about it. They also prayed daily for the Messiah whose appearance would usher in a golden age. I mention these matters in the interest of commenting on a frequent but somewhat distorted contrast alleged to exist between Judaism and Christianity, one which contends that Judaism was this-worldly and Christianity other-worldly. It is a viable contrast only if one overlooks the other-worldliness in Judaism and the this-worldly elements in historic Christianity.

The true contrast is not one of absolutes, but rather one of emphases. Perhaps I might epitomize matters by suggesting that the Christian has conceived of salvation as God's redemption of man *from* this world, while Jews conceived of it as redemption *in* this world—redemption from oppression, poverty, disease, persecution.

Modern Jewish sentimentalists have recently waxed eloquently nostalgic about the ghetto, the *shtetel.* My father, if I may inject a personal word, had no patience with such nostalgia. "I was born there," he would say. "I remember the mud, the filth, the poverty, the insecurity. Values there? Yes—men were desperate, and managed to create values. But go back there from free America? Never, never, never!"

Of course there were values, and one of them was so innate to my father that he never challenged or even questioned it. Had there been a Jewish catechism that he might have written, to the question, "For what purpose is a man born?" my father would have answered, "To become learned." His assessment of his associates, whether he liked them or not, was first and foremost, "Did they become able to learn?" I am not sure the English word *learn* carries the full connotation of the Yiddish *lernen.* When my father asked, "Does he know how to learn?" what he meant was, "Is he adept at a constantly deepening study?"

A clue in ghetto life to this apotheosis of learning was its social system. We Jews have had, as humans are bound to, our own snobbery. One's social standing might be influenced by his having acquired some wealth, but wealth alone did not determine it. At the bottom of the scale were those who had never progressed beyond mere *ivre;* at the top was the scholar, the rabbi. He who began as a tailor or a shoemaker but managed to gather some money could rise in the social scale if by chance he had a daughter for whom he could acquire a rabbinic student as a groom. We Jews fashioned an aristocracy of learning. Our folk song— *Rozinkes und Mandlen* ("Raisins and Almonds")—portrays a mother singing her baby boy to sleep. What will his golden future be? Will he study Torah, will he write books? What is the best of all "merchandise"? Learning, of course!

III

The world outside the ghetto can best be quickly summarized by certain key words: the nobility, the landed aristocracy; feudalism; the farmer peasant; the urban poor. If it was a freer world than that in the ghetto, it was a better world only for royalty and the nobility or the artisans.

Indeed, we can perhaps understand the Christian other-worldliness by recalling the poverty, violence, disease, and dangerous superstitions of medieval times. It was a world one would do well to escape from, and Christian salvation was a desire we should sympathetically understand. Moreover, it was a corrupt world, even within Christendom, for all too often the papacy was a prize to be bartered for by kings, or controlled by bold emperors. No historians I have read are quite as severe on the misdeeds of some popes as Roman Catholic historians. Popular storytellers like Boccaccio told droll tales about the lower clergy. Continence was by no means universal among the celibate clergy, and the monasteries of the orders founded to magnify the virtues of poverty became great centers of wealth. Cathedrals were lavish, all the while lower classes were harrassed and underfed.

Because our modern world has changed so drastically in so short a time, we tend to lose perspective about how slow were the changes before modern days. Some alterations matured only after centuries. It is some of these very slow alterations that we must look at.

When universities began to be founded—about a thousand years ago—they were basically what we would call divinity schools, dedicated primarily to theology, the queen of the sciences. They were conceived and dedicated to the same aggrandizement of the Church as the cathedrals. But out of the universities arose that aggregate of men whom we call "humanists," who for the most part were laymen rather than clerics. The revival of ancient learning—or, if one prefers, the intensification rather than the revival—brought into being an array of individual scholars, some of whom turned their attention to those secular studies, such as astronomy and physics, which the Greeks and Romans had pursued. These Christian humanists were, we may say descriptively, the elite of the time.

Faithful as the overwhelming majority of the humanists were to the Church, tensions arose even before the Reformation between the learned layman and the less learned, or even ignorant cleric. On a local level in 1509, Johannes Reuchlin defended his scholarship in Hebrew against ignorant clerics in Cologne. A Galileo was compelled by a church court to recant about his astronomy; a Giordano Bruno was burnt at the stake. Heresy, for which, too, one might be burnt, was not confined to an improper view of some religious doctrine, but to some opinion in astronomy which, in a system of authorized persons, was deemed by them to go counter to the Church's teachings. The point is that in a sense the Christian religion, even though Christians had founded the universities, was diverted into becoming an obstacle to study, on the premise that study might jeopardize Church doctrine. Perhaps it is an unfair contrast, but there is some possible illumination in the veneration in which Jews held Saadya Gaon of Bagdad who translated Scripture into Arabic and the execution of William Tyndale in 1536 for the crime of translating the Bible into English.

Christianity, in its ambivalence to education, promoted yet feared it, even as Christians continued to found more and more schools, colleges, and universities. Virtually all the oldest American universities were founded and maintained by church groups. But virtually all such major universities ultimately loosened or broke their ties with religious communions.

There is only a minor Jewish analogue to the Christian anxieties about the dangerous, corrosive effect of education. We have had, indeed have, and shall have, our marginal groups who repudiate what they call modern secular learning, and withhold themselves from it. We too have had obscurantists who attempted to impede the entry of Western enlightenment into East European ghettos in the late eighteenth and early nineteenth centuries. But it would be difficult to the point of impossibility of uncovering a tension between Jewish and humanistic learning such as has recurred in Christendom, for the simple reason that Judaism seldom, and never decisively, interpreted learning as a threat to it, as did upper echelons of Christian leadership.

What I trust can now begin to emerge is that there has been a greater sense of congruency between Judaism and the modern world of science, history, technology, than between Christianity and the modern world.

There are some particulars involved in this matter of congruency and incongruency. Christian theology, by far exceeding Jewish theology in profundity, while it included elements that were this-worldly, was nevertheless other-worldly. Again, though Christendom manifested a social concern, it was not as intense and rounded as the Jewish social concern necessarily was. Again, the celibacy and poverty of the clergy in the Roman Catholic Church so emphasized the special nature of the Catholic religious ideal about the highest form of religious life that Protestants were compelled to express the doctrine of vocation, that God calls men for varieties of noble service apart from the monastic existence. Jews had no need for such re-definition.

In sum, to the extent that Christian life might be loosely termed a reflection of a renunciation of this world, and illiteracy prevalent among Christians, and a respect for universal education absent from them, to that extent Jews were better prepared for the modern world than Christians. Add the factor of resiliency, and one sees a further facet of the better Jewish preparation. The resiliency of Americans in the eighteenth and nineteenth centuries prepared them for the modern world in a way in which many European societies were not prepared. European society had its classes, the upper and lower, the nobility, the landed gentry and the peasant and, after urbanization, the working man. While in Western Europe these classes tended to disappear, especially after World War II, vestiges still abide. Within the classes, not only did the upper ones maintain a supposition of their innate superiority, but the lower classes preserved a supposition of their unalterable inferiority. Though Jews in the ghetto had their social gradations, they possessed no full analogue to fixed upper and lower classes. Moreover, having been excluded from Christian society, they had little or no sense that marked poor Christians of belonging to a lower class, destined always to remain lower. Free of a sense of predestination to poverty and subordination, Jews could feel themselves eligible for whatever personal rise was commensurate with individual talents and opportunity.

When universities ceased to be divinity schools and became broader in their scope, when the industrial revolution, prompted by the new sciences, revolutionized European life and led to the growth of large cities and complexities of economic life, Jews were more prepared to adjust to the new age than were Christians. Forgetting momentarily about Jews, we can discern this in the way in which the hereditary nobility gradually surrendered the actual leadership in Western countries to the emerging giants of industry. Even though countries like Britain lagged in granting civil rights to Catholics and Jews, and even though the German states granted Jews civil rights only partly and only temporarily, in the modern society there was nevertheless a sense in which Jews, entering commerce, industry, and the arts, began with a head start over comparable Gentiles. When advanced education and technological learning became the characteristics of the best of western civilization, Jews were prepared for this new world of modernism.

What is notable about this better preparation on the part of Jews takes us back to Christian Wilhelm Dohm. The adjustment to the modern world does not necessarily involve the need for the passing of generations; it is an adjustment that can be made by some in one generation or even less. A country full of immigrants such as the United States exhibits this in the way in which first-generation Americans, whether of German, Scandinavian, Armenian, Italian, or Czech origin, can enter fully into all phases of the resilient life of America, provided they accommodate themselves to urbanization and the demands of advanced education and high culture. Rural groups, of whatever national origin, have tended to lag behind. Individuals, whatever their innate gifts, who were not spurred to take advantage of the educational opportunities, have not made the transition quickly. But the transition is not truly impossible or formidable. If Jews, by virtue of the values they ascribed to education, were individually more profoundly spurred by abiding discrimination than were Gentiles, then motivation simply buttressed the innate capacity. Broadly speaking, individual Jews have been more significantly motivated than Gentiles have needed to be.

IV

Jewish eminence is explainable neither by a theological doctrine of election nor by some vague mystique á la Van der Haag. It is an eminence that has been disproportionate only because of special circumstances. To believe otherwise is to believe in racism.

One need look only at the plight of American Negroes to underscore the natural character of Jewish eminence. In our time the word *ghetto* has become detached from Jews and become a term to describe black urban existence. It has connoted poverty, poor housing, and minimal economic opportunity. Since American Negroes traversed a period of literal slavery, something Jews did not experience, they had no opportunity to develop the cultural and social institutions that Jews did. They had no urgency or opportunity to fashion a general literacy. The slavery period destroyed whatever oral tradition of a past collective greatness; they had no Bible, no Talmud, no legacy of medieval scholasticism to fall back on and to perpetuate.

To skate on thin ice, there exists today a current of debate, or abortive efforts at campus debate, on the question of blacks and their IQ's. I have no information of any consequence on this unpleasant debate as far as substance is concerned. My nearly ten years as Provost of my institution included a responsibility for admission requirements, such as SAT's, ACT's, and GRE's, and even others. I am not prepared to deny that these tests reflect some aspects of a candidate's potential academic achievement. I have to say, though, that other facets of a candidate's personality cannot be measured, for example, pertinacity and motivation. I am by no means sure that a respectable IQ, such as 110–120, is a worse basis for predicting achievement than an IQ of 140 or 150. To my mind, achievement rests on an adequate IQ, plus other traits, and not alone on an extraordinary IQ.

Can blacks catch up with whites in the white man's world? To my mind the only obstacles are the abiding poverty, abiding discrimination, abiding unfavorable social and cultural impediments and discouragements.

What the experience of the Jews should teach us is that, if there is some match between preparation and the opportunities which have become available in the modern world, then no segment of world society is ruled out. What some people today say adversely about blacks is little different from what Christopher Wilhelm Dohm said about Jews.

The reality is that the Catholics, and the Protestants, and the Eastern Orthodox have also had their own types of ghettos. So have the farmers and the urban poor. We Americans have continuing ghettos of backwardness, Appalachia, for example, or Mississippi rednecks.

Virtually all of us assembled at a university function have emerged from our diverse ghettos. Universities were once for the privileged, for the aristocracy, the landed gentry. We today are not very remote from a time when most of society was primarily rural, or poverty-stricken urbanite, or primarily uneducated.

Since I have lived in Britain, I can speak a bit about differences in education. Until very recent years, British education in the grammar, high school, and college levels was better than ours, for it was an education for a select class. We Americans caught up, and even passed the British on the graduate and professional level, for, out of our commendable mass education, our advanced education emerged as a matter of individual quality, not as a consequence of noble birth, or extraordinary family wealth.

We American Jews have been abundantly represented in this advanced education. Are graduate students today reflective of the total country, rural, mountain, small cities, huge cities, whites, blacks, Chicanoes, and others? Or have our graduate students come from a more restricted part of the population? If Jews are 3 percent of the American population, are they possibly 10 percent, or even more, of that urban, motivated group from which advanced students came? Is the Jewish eminence as completely disproportionate as we have thought? My hunch is that we are not so disproportionate.

Eminence is the achievement by a single person, not by the corporate society one comes from. Eminent as individual Jews have become, such individual eminence is certainly not restricted to us Jews. Not by any means. Rather, despite all the confusion and disasters, the world seems to be rounding some corner, and the future will disclose that potentialities capable of realization exist in individuals of all peoples. We Jews have no exclusive possession or monopoly of innate gifts. The world will catch up with us, and that is well and good, for when that comes about, it will have been to our credit that in large measure we showed what all people are capable in a world in which potentialities can be realized.

(1974)

11

ANTI-SEMITISM AND JEWISH UNIQUENESS
Ancient and Contemporary

ARTHUR HERTZBERG

O NE OF THE FIRST SCHOLARLY TASKS that was ever set before me was given me some twenty years ago by my great teacher, Levi Ginsberg. He asked me to translate into English the famous lecture that he had given in 1930, when he had come as visitor to the Hebrew University to inaugurate the Chair in Talmudic Studies. He there propounded the thesis that the changing patterns of Talmudic Law cannot be understood unless they are seen against the background of changing social and economic circumstances and of the new political situations to which they were responding. This thesis has by now become so accepted that it amounts to a cliché, but when it was first stated it amounted to a revolution.

To understand anti-Semitism means to deal not in abstractions but in the concrete reality of the encounters and difficulties between Jews and Gentiles. Only by paying precise attention to the facts, by seeing them as they are and not as some preconceived abstractions would have us interpret them, can we arrive at generalizations that rest solidly on foundations of truth.

This subject, anti-Semitism, is not an antiseptic one. No matter where it is raised and no matter who talks about anti-Semitism, it is a matter that cannot be dealt with with the usual poses, or even realities, of scholarly objectivity. Anti-Semitism has been the single most disastrous phenomenon of the twentieth century, and of many earlier centuries, and we continue to participate, as Jews and as human beings, in the very conflicts from which we are trying to stand back in order to understand. Our senses of our own identity, our religious and political positions at this very moment and for the future, are deeply involved in our estimate of anti-Semitism. All of us can bear important witness to this subject out of the reality of our lives.

211

I do not at the outset want to use the word *anti-Semitism* at all, because the term itself has, at the very least, the connotation that the conflict or conflicts in question are of a different order than all other quarrels between communities and people. This may indeed be true of the contemporary difficulties between Jews and others, but we can arrive at such a judgment only later, on the basis of analysis, and not *a priori*.

One basic distinction must, however, be made between anti-Semitism and group conflict. The French and the Germans were engaged for centuries in wars and lasting antipathies; so were the Christians and the Moslems. These are conflicts of a different order than the age-old problems between Jews and Gentiles. The difference is, in essence, that group conflicts are battles between people who regard themselves as species of the same genus, and who really expect that, at the end of the battle, each of the contestants will essentially remain and be the same. Anti-Semitism presupposes that the Jews are radically other. Its purpose has usually been the attempt to remove them utterly from the scene of the battle, by expulsion or forced segregation, by pogroms or ultimately by death camps. This distinction between anti-Semitism and group conflict has been obscured in our century by the tragic reality that many of the more usual conflicts even among Gentile powers have, in the age of ideologies, acquired new, demonic dimensions. Otherwise kindly men can still in our day make distinctions between murder and the shooting of their political enemies. The destruction of the kulaks by the Russian Revolution had been foreshadowed by the guillotines of the Terror during the French Revolution. Modern ideological conflicts have tended to become religious wars, with inquisitions and demons to be fought, and have thus begun to approximate the age-old problems between Jews and Gentiles. Nevertheless, the Cold War rhetoric of the 1950s has receded, and the major contestants in the battle between democracy and communism are talking less and less in ideological terms and more and more in the language of old-fashioned power accommodations. The recent movement of international politics has been away from ideologies and towards return to group conflict as the only tolerable limit for disagreement among people and communities. It is clear, at first glance, that this tendency has not yet redefined "the Jewish question," but there are signs that some change has been taking place here, too.

There is no need to describe even with minimum precision the major current conflicts between Jews and Gentiles. Let us merely list them, without suggesting that there is any order of priority in the listing. Clearly, there is serious conflict, not merely between Israel and the neighboring Arab states, but between the Jewish world as a whole and the Arab world over the very creation and continued existence of the State of Israel. This quarrel has occasioned the use by Arab propagandists of such anti-Semitic tracts as the Protocols of the Elders of Zion, and the language of Jehad has been used. Nonetheless, not all of the Moslem people have been actively involved in this quarrel, and it is becoming apparent that Arabs are at least having to admit to themselves, even in public, that the State of Israel is a fact, though they no doubt continue to harbor the hope that the day may yet arrive when this fact will be no more.

Another major conflict involves all of the Jewish communities of the world in battle with the Soviet Union. Part of this quarrel is in the fact that the Soviet Union has been and remains the chief supporter of the Arabs against Israel. More pointedly, the repression of Jewish religious and cultural life in Russia and the denial of permission for Jews who want to emigrate is, at this moment, by Jewish choice, a major international issue.

A third quarrel involved Jews with the New Left. From the perspective of these political circles, the existence of Israel is a retrograde phenomenon. It is supported by the United States, which is for the New Left the major source of evil in the world, and the very existence of Israel stands in the way of the triumph in the Middle East of those Arab forces which the New Left identifies as the proper representative of their favorite cliche, the Third World. Part of the anger of the New Left is directed not only at Israel but also at the Jews of the world. Having provided so many of the battalions which have fought in our century for internationalism, the New Left now finds that Jews are involved in the parochial task of supporting a specifically Jewish country in its insistence on its rights to be just that.

In the fourth place, the involvement of the Jews of the world in Israel, especially in its most heightened form after May 1967, has been attacked in circles other than those of the New Left. In the Soviet Union, and elsewhere in Communist Eastern Europe, though not everywhere, Jews continue to be accused of Zionism, that 'ism' of harboring a primary loyalty to their Jewish identity and to the state of Israel. Comparable sentiments were expressed in some church circles in the United States, which sided and continue to side with the Arabs.

In the fifth place, an older alliance in the United States between Jews and blacks, which lasted into the mid-nineteen sixties, has disintegrated in recent years. It has been widely noted that those positions in American society which blacks want, because they are seemingly attainable, are very often occupied by Jews; that Jews are major landlords and storekeepers in the black ghetto; and that, in general, the vision of a society of individuals with opportunity equal to their merit is comfortable for Jews but discomforting for blacks. They are demanding unequal opportunities as "recompense" for their past deprivations, and much of this price is at the moment being paid by Jews. Some of the rhetoric of this quarrel, too, is couched in the language of old-fashioned anti-Semitism, but there are also newer additions of supposed identification of Black Panthers with the Arab and Third World enemies of Israel.

This, in major outline, is an inventory and sketch of the most important contemporary attacks on Jews by their enemies. It, of course, needs to be remembered that all is far from well on the South American continent, and that there the Catholic Church is still dominated by prelates who belong to the older traditions of Christian anti-Semitism. Even in that region, however, Arab communities resident in the region, refugee Nazis, and Left-Wing forces are the more disturbing part of the picture.

What therefore comes immediately and unmistakably to our eyes from this list is two facts, of the most profound importance: the issues between Jews and Gentiles have little or nothing to do with the age-old quarrel between Jews and Christians. It may be argued, as some do and will, that the current issues are but contemporary secularizations of that older quarrel, but it is undeniable that the overt battle lines are quite different. For that matter, Communists, spokesmen of the New Left, and blacks are all former Christians (or Jews), but this is certainly not true of Arabs. It is too bold an assertion to maintain that Christian anti-Semitism is now irrelevant, but it is clear that, if Jews were at peace as a people with all our secular enemies, what remains of Christian hatred would not worry us overly much.

The second obvious observation is that at the center of almost all the quarrels in which Jews are involved today stand the existence of the state of Israel, the support that it draws from all the Jews of the world, and the emotions that it evokes among them. This question is crucial to all of the current battles that I have mentioned except the one between Jews and blacks in America, and even there it plays a minor role of some importance. Here, too, it might be argued that the contemporary angers are but retranslations of older hatreds. Did not Haman once say that the Jews were a peculiar people, spread out in all the world, which behaved in different modes from that of all others? This definition of the justification for anti-Semitism has been termed in contemporary social theory "the dislike of the unlike." Pinsker and Herzl, the founders of modern Zionism, held this view, for they saw anti-Semitism as a rational phenomenon, as the hatred of the world for the "eternal minority" and the "eternal stranger." The creation of a Jewish State was proposed as a cure for this disease, by making the Jews a host somewhere in the world, in a country of their own. In theory, therefore, the existence of the State of Israel should be making an end of anti-Semitism. That its very existence and all the relationships with world Jewry that this existence involves, are now at the center of the conflict requires explanation.

It is possible to complicate the question even more. As conflicts with other groups have become sharper, the Christian church has been the only major contestant with Jews which has been willing and often eager, during the last few decades, to come to some kind of accommodation. This has involved most of its major branches, though, to be sure, the Orthodox have been less willing than either the Protestants or the Catholics. The marked Christian willingness to issue statements against anti-Semitism has been, of course, largely rooted in the guilt of their silence during the Holocaust. It is true that in not a single one of these declarations has the dream of the Church to proselytise the Jews ever been abandoned. Indeed, in the very first meeting after the Holocaust, when the Protestants gathered in Amsterdam in 1946, the still smoking death ovens did not stop them from saying that the highest testimony of their contrition for the murders and the sign of their love for Jews was to continue to bring them the greatest gift in their possession, salvation through the founder of their religion. Nonetheless, even on this most sensitive of issues, the Christian mission, there is today in actual fact large accommodation in practice. In my own personal experience in the United States, in 1959, a public Jewish protest in the form of an article that I wrote in one of the Christian journals led almost immediately to the abolition of a bureau of Christian Mission to Jews that had long existed in the central body of American Protestantism, the National Council of Churches. Much more vehement and powerful protests by the most responsible Jewish bodies in America and elsewhere in the world have had no comparable success in breaking the ongoing alliance between powerful elements in international Christianity and anti-Israel opinion and activity. The reality of our present relationship with the highest bodies of Christianity is that there are no difficulties on all those issues, such as race and poverty, on which we are prepared to behave as an international, religious community, "just like them." Official Christianity continues to deplore older forms of theological anti-Semitism, and is even willing to remove them from its textbooks. The stumbling block, the rock on which the new unity breaks, is the singularity as religious phenomenon and the intensity as present policy of the Jewish involvement in Israel.

Here too, as in almost all the other conflicts today, Israel and Zionism are the crucial issues. There is something more here than a rationalization of the Christian missionary relationship to the Arab world and the desire of various communions to protect their stakes in "holy places." Mid-nineteenth century Reform Judaism was already responding, at its very birth, to the Christian question which suggested that the Jewish religion in the era of Emancipation had to abandon its peculiar identity, as exemplified particularly in its national hopes and longing for the land of its ancestors. The question had been asked very pointedly, even earlier, by Napoleon at the Sanhedrin that he called together, to assure him, among other things, that the Jews of his empire had no patriotism now and in the future for Eretz Israel. At the very dawn of the era of Emancipation, in the first debate about Jews in the French Revolutionary Parliament in September 1789, a liberal deputy from Paris, Clermont-Tonnerre, pronounced the famous sentence: "To Jews as individuals everything; to Jews as a distinct community, nothing." It is in the light of this past, rooted very deeply in the beginnings and in the whole movement of the new encounter between Jews and Gentiles in the modern era, that we can perhaps begin to understand the paradox that all of the anti-Jewish movements of this day, including the overt attacks from Christian quarters, are divorced from religious motifs, and that their central target is the great endeavor of Jews really to behave like conventional modern men in a national state of their own.

There have been generations of argument and bitter exchanges about whether there was a "social compact" as part of the legal emancipation of the Jews under which the Jews agreed to give up every element of their own ethos and disappear as individuals into the wider society. No such formal social compact ever existed, but it is impossible to study the century of battle for Jewish rights on the European continent without concurring that an informal agreement of this nature largely did exist. The best friends of the Jews, those who obtained equal rights for them, expected that Jews would disappear, or, at the very least, become completely inconspicuous. They did not anticipate the kind of Jew who would, even in some new form, make unique and singular demands on society.

It is this last point that has never been clear to Jews themselves. The reigning presumption in all the schools of Jewish thought and action in the modern era, including classic Zionism of the political kind, has been the notion that Jews must now cease being *sui generis,* and that their becoming "just like everybody else" could indeed be realized in life. I would indeed now suggest, as the second premise on which to base an understanding of contemporary anti-Semitism, that the whole movement of Jewish history since the beginning of the Era of Emancipation has therefore had as its purpose such a reordering, such a "normalization" of the relationship between Jews and their environment so as to make an end of anti-Semitism. In the most hopeful dreams of those Jews who fought for equal rights and acceptance in Gentile societies, their purpose was to help bring about a new society, a new age of heaven-on-this-earth, for the modern era was conceived at a time when man could, and would, remake his immediate world into the messianic era. These were the most ecstatic visions of love and brotherhood. In prosaic daily life, what Jews wanted to achieve was sufficient equality and likeness to others, to become species of the same genus as all other individuals or groups, so that the difficulties would become the normal day-to-day problems among equals. Knowing full well that in their most recent ghetto forms Jews appeared to be radically different, every version of emancipatory thinking, including all the major theories of Zionism, accepted the proposition that Jews had to change in important ways in order to enter the modern world as full equals. The presumption is that once this occurred anti-Semitism would be over.

As is well-known, this did not work out as planned, for anti-Semitism did not disappear in the nineteenth century. On the contrary, it attacked Jews with renewed fury, and its targets were not only alien Jews still mostly in the ghetto, such as those of Czarist Russia, but also very Westernized and fashionable ones, the "new men" such as the Rothschilds and Captain Dreyfus. It is nonetheless superficial to interpret Jewish reaction to the pogroms of 1881 in Russia and to the Dreyfus Affair as a turning away from dreams of emancipation and equality in the Gentile world to a renewed, somber awareness that the hatred between Jacob and Esau was unavoidable and eternal. Great as was the shock that these events administered, they did not destroy the peculiarly modern Jewish faith that somewhere, in some attainable situation, through some more exact reordering of the identity of the Jew and of the society in which he was to live, Jews would become species of the same genus as other men and anti-Semitism would end.

In the twentieth century each of the major options offered by the Era of the Emancipation has not only been attempted, it has even been realized at very nearly its optimum. The West European dream of the personal emancipation of the individual in a society in which, in legal theory, group and tradition did not matter, and whatever remained of such loyalties was a private matter, was realized under the most favorable circumstances in the United States around 1960. Communism stunted the opportunity that it afforded for Jews to have complete equality as a national minority among the many in Russia, but for at least a decade in the 1920s until the mid 1930s it seemed that a Yiddish-speaking national culture of great range was being fostered, and it has been said that only the paranoia of Stalin made an end of this success. The normalcy of the State of Israel since its creation, including the re-creation of Jewish military capacity, has been apparent for all to see. The whole drive of Israeli statesmanship, since the beginning of Israel's independence to this very day, has been to change the relations between Israel and its Arab neighbors into one of normal recognition and acceptance. While not forgetting that Israel's creation owed something to the claim that Jews were making on the bad conscience of the anti-Semitic world, Israeli statesmanship has wanted to move away from the presumption that this State remains special, a unique creation of the United Nations and therefore uniquely bound by its tutelage and its decisions.

Only in relation to the Jews of the world has Israel continued to insist on emphasizing ever more throughout the years of its existence that it holds a unique relationship and special responsibilities—and it is this relationship which is under special attack. In reverse, very little of Jewish religion and culture and of the integrity of the Jewish family remains in the Soviet Union, and nonetheless an otherwise unparalleled connection remains between this community and a country outside the borders of Russia. All of the studies of the American Jewish community showed that the opposition to intermarriage had dropped in a few short years among American Jews from over 80 percent to half that, and that most of those still opposed were over 45, that is, preponderantly, the children of immigrants who retain ties to Jewish religion and culture. Nonetheless, the connection with Israel is overwhelmingly strong in all segments of the American Jewish community. The conclusion is simple and inescapable: the very secular, "like all the nations" State of Israel has become the contemporary equivalent of the older Jewish religion; that is, the loyalties that it evokes throughout the Jewish world is the contemporary factor of Jewish uniqueness and Jewish distinctiveness. This is the contemporary embodiment of "their ways are different from those of all other people."

This relationship to Israel is not a factor evoked primarily by anti-Semitism, of either the older, theological kind or the newer, racial and economic conflict between Jews and some of their neighbors. On the contrary, at the very height of its power and integration into the American community, before Jewish-black relations had deteriorated seriously and at a time when Aliyah was at its lowest ebb, the American Jewish community in 1967, and even more in 1973, supported Israel with a vehemence that astonished itself. It was an assertion of their contemporary Jewish ethos.

To say this with pride requires that we remember that it is precisely this kind of Jewish self-assertion which our enemies have attacked repeatedly since near the beginning of our history. Hellenistic anti-Semites found us unsocial, because we would not eat or drink with others or be hospitable to their gods; Christian ones found that we were the one community that rejected the "new light" for all mankind; contemporary ones see us as a peculiar international socio-political entity. In utter honesty, we have been all of these things, and we continue to be them, in secularized forms. I, for one, even harbor the hope that the persistence of this uniqueness will yet lead within the Jewish world to some revival of the spirit—but let us at least understand that the quarrel with our enemies is about a unique Jewish people, that we do not widely differ from some of our critics on the actual facts, and that the quarrel is about moral judgment, the value of what we are, and the meaning of a true human society.

My third, and concluding, premise about the understanding of contemporary anti-Semitism is that if the Israel-centered relationships are the equivalent of the older Jewish religious uniqueness, the economic profile of Jews, not as forced by anti-Semitism but as willed by Jews themselves, is the contemporary equivalent of the ghetto.

From the very beginning of the Era of the Emancipation, indeed, even as a preamble to it, in the thinking of such men as Naftali Zvi Weisel, the restratification of the Jews into a "normal" economy, in which they engaged in all the pursuits, was propounded as necessary to the true integration of Jews into the larger society. What this meant, in actual practice, was a series of repeated attempts on most of the continents to create a class of Jewish farmers and to foster, in many places, Jewish artisans and Jewish industrial proletariat. This has met with substantial success in Israel, though even here there are signs that the older, Askenazi element of the Zionist resettlement is moving away from the farm and from physical labor towards becoming a white-collar elite. In the two great Jewish diasporas, those in the Soviet Union and in the United States, it has been crystal clear in the last half century that the movement of Jews has been away from proletarian pursuits, away from direct involvement in primary production, and towards fighting their way into the intellectual, scientific, professional, and managerial elite. Again, it is an untrue cliche to say that this happened as a direct result of existing anti-Semitism. Precisely because the movements in the United States and in the Soviet Union have been in reverse, they provide us with comparative material and enable us to see what has actually happened. In the United States, the Jews began as a depressed, immigrant proletariat in sweatshops in a few pursuits, largely in the needle trades. There was no real bar to their spreading out horizontally into other industries, such as steel and coal, which were hungry in the early decades of the century for any kind of labor; those who chose to farm were even assured of large subsidies from the fund created by Baron de Hirsch. Nonetheless, Jews chose to remain in the largest American cities and to do battle with economic anti-Semitism for upward mobility into those pursuits which required maximum education and, at least in some of them, brought Jews closer to the very center of intellectual, business and political life. It was not anti-Semitism which has created in the United States the marked and radical otherness of the economy of Jews from the rest of the country. On the contrary, several generations of Jews have fought their way successfully towards this otherness.

In the Soviet Union, the more than fifty years since the Bolshevik Revolution have been marked by a reverse phenomenon. Jews began as a major element of the revolutionary elite. They were prominent at the very center of power, in the early central committees of the Communist Party, in diplomacy, in the press, and in every other pursuit which required training of the mind and the capacity to adjust rapidly to changing situations. In the early decades of the Bolshevik Era, when admission to universities was available by and large on the basis of merit, Jews preferred that avenue to self-realization to settling in Birobidian or in the Crimea, or going to work, except as a project engineers, on the great new dams and power stations being built in the "five-year plans." The point and thrust of Soviet anti-Jewish policy has been in the last two decades the removal of Jews from their most prominent place in the elite and their proletarianization, especially through the denial of places in the universities to which their merit entitled them. Even those Jews in Russia who have no Jewish survivalist sentiments of any kind continue to fight against this and to refuse to accept the notion that they must be "normalized." Such a battle between the Jews and the reigning majority in society is not new in Russia nor unprecedented. *Numerus clausus* was the slogan of Polish anti-Semites between the two wars, and their announced purpose, too, was to make the Jews of Poland into a "normal" economic element. A reverse version of this slogan, the notion that as a depressed group in America the Blacks should now be given "normal," that is proportional, representation in all the economic pursuits from professor in the sciences to editorships of literary magazines, is the immediate "principle" in the name of which Blacks are now doing battle against the preponderance of Jews at or near the top.

There is considerable truth in the explanation which argues that Jews moved in the modern era into certain kinds of capitalist pursuits, into the free professions, and into the intellectual world because the kind of economic experience that had been forced on them by the ghetto predisposed them to such endeavors; because persisting anti-Semitism excluded them from pursuits except those which depended on highly personal, easily transportable skills; and because the inherited Jewish tradition laid great emphasis on the culture of the mind. I am not persuaded by these explanations. It is simply not true that Jews have had in their medieval and early modern past a continuing distance from physical labor and a continuing pervasive intellectuality. Whatever else the Chassidic phenomenon might have been, it was certainly at its origins anti-intellectual. The rich Jewish businessman did exist, but as the pervasive expression of Jewish economic endeavor he is a myth of Karl Marx and Werner Sombart. We need not enter into these vexing issues in order to establish the point that is necessary for our argument. There can be absolutely no doubt that throughout the modern era Jews have had ample and recurring opportunity to turn proletarian and become economically "normal." It was to go in the reverse direction, away from primary production and towards the contemporary secular "priesthood" of intellectuals, managers and technocrats—those figures who were first recognized as a "priesthood" by Saint Simon in the early years of the nineteenth century—that Jews have fought against their enemies in every modern society.

Economic and social integration into a new society of equals, to settle in as individuals throughout all the countries of their dispersion, has been the other, non-Zionist dream of Jewish modernity. Feudal and guild societies denied Jews this opportunity, and so "the career open to talent," promised by the liberal revolution, found its most devoted partisans among Jews. It is not accidental that counter-revolutionary forces, such as the Royalists in France in the nineteenth century, or new groups now bidding for a place in the sun, such as the Blacks in America today, should center their attack on Jews. Let it also be remembered, however, that men of the social and political left, not all of whom can be termed vulgar anti-Semites, insisted throughout the nineteenth century and into our own that Jews must enter proletarian pursuits in order to be truly emancipated and that their refusal to do this in any great numbers meant that they were insisting on a "priestly"—or demonic—role in society.

There are many obvious answers to such demands and such attacks. It is clear, at the very least, that every group in society must not behave exactly like every other group. We even know by now that the notion of physical labor as the only guarantee of personal virtue is a romantic myth. For the purpose of our present analysis it is enough to assert the undeniable, that there was Jewish drive and will and choice in the creation of the otherness of Jews in the open society, and that, indeed, the more open that society has been, the more "other" Jews have become.

We must now, inevitably, confront the question of meaning and of interpretation. I am completely persuaded that contemporary anti-Semitism, even of the most immediate secular kind, is rooted psychologically and emotionally in many centuries of training given to Western men by the Christian church. Let me be even more forthright: I know that to emphasize the secular and the non-Christian in modern anti-Semitism is often disturbing, because it seems to provide too easy an absolution of Christians for their past. Let me also admit that the anti-Semitism of the past has had a major hand in fashioning the intellectual stereotypes of the dangerous alien in all its forms, with which the Jews have had to contend in new guises in the modern era. What I am leaning against in this paper is a premise that was enunciated most clearly by Sartre and has been morally comfortable and comforting to generations of Jews in the last two centuries, that whatever is peculiar and attacked, in the case of Jews, is a creation of anti-Semitism, and that is therefore chargeable entirely to the account of negative, external circumstances. Quite apart from the facts, there is an enormous inherent difficulty with such a premise, for it contains inevitably a negative estimate of the inherited Jewish culture. This must be judged by such thinking as a response to a stunted life, and such attitudes towards anti-Semitism involve the presumption that true freedom for the Jews means that they should and will cease being specifically Jewish. My immediate difficulties with this thesis are not moral or theoretical; they are rather that such explanations do not fit the facts of the modern era.

Whatever might be true about medieval Jewry and the anti-Semitism that it faced, the national peculiarities of contemporary Israel as the center of a world Jewish community and the socio-economic peculiarities of world Jewry are not disfigured responses to Jew-hatred. Anti-Semitism, ancient and modern, has had something to do with this history, but the essence of its meaning is not that what we have been doing is forced on us, but rather that it is willed by Jews. This people of ours is a peculiar people in the modern era not only because the greatest of tragedies, the Holocaust, has happened to us, but because the whole direction of our activity has been, by choice, towards creating a world-wide society of our own like no other. If contemporary anti-Semitism is a re-echo, in the rhetoric and conflicts of this day, of the age-old Gentile impatience with our otherness, the will and passion with which we have created this otherness again is our own contemporary version of the ancient voice which once echoed in our ears commanding us to be "unto Me a peculiar people among the peoples."

It is pretense not to admit that Jews discuss anti-Semitism for more than purely theoretical purposes. We keep retesting the temperature of the waters in which we must swim and the indices of our own strength to survive, because these are everyday matters of the most profound and personal concern. Here we enter a realm that is beyond historical description and analysis into an attempt to see beyond the present. On the simplest level, we know already that wherever the position of Jews in society has become relatively "normal", anti-Semitism has indeed ceased, and group conflict has taken its place. For example, the political policy of Willy Brandt, former Chancellor of West Germany, was less pro-Jewish and pro-Israel than that of his predecessors whose personal pasts were far more questionable. I have no doubt that when he publishes his diaries there will be recurrent entries about his feeling that it is possible to differ strongly with the contemporary policy and needs of the Jewish people and to regard that as a conflict among present equals rather than as anti-Semitism. I sometimes wonder whether King Hussein looks across the Jordan through the binoculars of an anti-Semite or those of a ruler whose very personal existence depends, in some measure, on the good will of a far more powerful and advanced society across the way. What inheres in these examples is that, especially since 1967, a substantial amount of "normalization" has indeed taken place in the image of Israel as a state and society. It ceased in those glorious days being the symbol of a haven of the weak and the persecuted; the counter-myth, of superhuman strength (which owed something to old anti-Semitic ideas and notions about the Jews as both very weak and powerfully demonic), has by now also receded. Certainly political peace in the region, which now seems a possibility, will help translate anti-Semitism into group conflict.

On the other hand, the ingathering of the exiles seems still a far-off dream. The peculiarity of Jewish inner relationship will long remain, and only the most doctrinaire of classic Zionists would argue that the diaspora will soon either come to Israel or disappear entirely. We may be living in a period of "time lag", that is, in an era in which the normalization promised by Zionism and the end of anti-Semitism that will come with it is not around the corner in this immediate generation. The Zionist "End of Days" will come in, let us say, a century or so. I am prepared to believe that it will, and I certainly think that it should. Nonetheless, I wonder whether those voices which are already being raised, even in Israel, about the nature of our contemporary Jewish culture will not continue to insist in future generations with ever greater vehemence that to be either Belgium or Switzerland in the Middle East is not what being Jewish is all about.

In the immediate present I have another suspicion. Every study in recent years of economic pursuits and intellectual level in advanced societies tends to establish not that Jews are becoming more like Gentiles, but that Gentiles are becoming more like Jews. For example, there are ever fewer people in primary education in the United States as a whole nowadays and, proportionately, ever more in the colleges. The best projections for the end of the century are that in America as a whole about 4 percent of the labor force will be engaged in physical labor and about 80 percent of the young will be receiving a college education—but this is precisely the present profile, to the decimal point, of American Jews. On the global scale, societies are beginning to have to deal with one another much more flexibly than on the nineteenth century presumption that all political identities are determined by nation states. Indeed, some of the most pernicious things that have happened in recent years, such as the tragedies during the partition of India and the horror of the Nigeria-Biafra conflict, have resulted from attempts to avoid the living together of different peoples. The very same General Charles de Gaulle who objected to the loyalties of French Jews to Israel tried to evoke such loyalties to France among French Canadians.

Nonetheless, it would be far too hopeful to imagine that anti-Semitism will soon end. It will clearly persist to the degree to which Jews remain a unique entity in the world, and I do not think that we Jews are really prepared completely to surrender our distinctiveness even in the days of the Messiah. At least, so I read the ancient Midrash which insisted that the commandments which were given specifically to Jews would not end even in the Apocalyptic Era. Our internal Jewish problem remains the giving of content to this uniqueness. The larger and more searing question is whether, in the century that has witnessed Auschwitz, which has now secularized almost completely its conflicts with Jews, new definitions of human society as a whole are indeed arising.

At root, the question of anti-Semitism remains not one of Jewish behavior, now balanced between its own uniqueness and accommodation with the world, but of the Gentile conceptions of society. So far the ancient Greek notion that "barbarians" must become Hellenised to be accepted—that no radically dissenting group can be allowed to maintain itself—has dominated in the Western world. This is the age-old social principle from which anti-Semitism has sprung. This "hellenistic" vision is now questionable, both morally and in its practical capacity to deal with the future. In the next century, as East and West encounter each other, many unlike communities will have to live together in decent peace, or the world will be in the deepest trouble. Anti-Semitism is indeed now indicative of the basic, persisting *hubris* of the West. Jews can survive anti-Semitism, but can the West survive its persisting nature?

Jewish history has always been an interweaving of what we are and what we have learned from the environment, of what we have fought for and of the attacks that we have resisted. So it is today. The journey is not yet ended, for the Messiah has not come—but, like all of my ancestors, I hear his footsteps.

(1973)

12

THE HUMAN CONDITION AFTER AUSCHWITZ
A Jewish Testimony a Generation After

EMIL L. FACKENHEIM

I

A Midrash in Genesis Rabbah disturbs and haunts the mind ever more deeply. It begins as follows:

> Rabbi Shim'on said: "In the hour when God was about to create Adam, the angels of service were divided . . . Some said, 'Let him not be created,' others, 'Let him be created.' . . . Love said, 'Let him be created, for he will do loving deeds.' But Truth said, 'Let him not be created, for he will be all falsity.' Righteousness said, 'Let him be created, for he will do righteous deeds.' Peace said, 'Let him not be created, for he will be full of strife.' What then did God do? He seized hold of Truth, and cast her to the earth, as it is said, 'Thou didst cast Truth to the ground.' " (Dan. 8:12)[1]

No Midrash wants to be taken literally. Every Midrash wants to be taken seriously. Midrash is serious because its stories and parables address the reader; they are not confined to the past. It is religious because, while it may contain beauty and poetry, its essential concern is truth. And when, as in the present case, a Midrash tells a story of human origins, the religious truth it seeks to convey is universal. Its theme is nothing less than the human condition as a whole.

Why does this Midrash disturb and haunt us? Not simply because it is realistic rather than romantically "optimistic" about man. Midrash is always realistic. We are haunted because Truth is cast to the ground. This climactic part of the story (as thus far told) does not say that all is well, that the good Lord has the power, so to speak, of indiscriminately

226

silencing all opposition. Were this its message, then Peace as well as Truth should be cast to the ground. That Truth alone is singled out for this treatment suggests the ominous possibility that *all* that might be said in favor of the creation of man is nothing but pious illusion; that Truth is so horrendous as to destroy *everything* for us unless we shun it, avoid it, evade it; that *only* after having cast Truth to the ground can God create man at all.

But then we ask: whom does God deceive? Surely one thing even God cannot do is, as it were, fool Himself. Are we the ones, then, who are fooled? Are we *radically* deceived in our belief that at least *some* of that which we undergo, do, are, is *ultimately* worthwhile—a belief without which we cannot endure?

But such a divine deception (if a deception it is) does not succeed. We can see through it. The Midrashic author *knows* that Truth is cast to the ground. So do all the devout Jews who have read his story throughout the generations. But what is the effect of this knowledge? Can it be other than despair?

The Midrash itself deals with this question when it repudiates despair. It ends as follows: "Then the angels of service said to God, 'Lord of the universe, how canst Thou despise Thy seal?[2] Let Truth arise from the earth, as it is said, Truth springs from the earth.'" (Ps. 85:12) Somehow it is possible for man to face Truth and yet to be. But do we know how?

II

Without doubt to say yea or nay to existence is the ultimate question in all religion and all philosophy. Judaism is firmly committed to being when it sees God Himself as the Creator of the world, and the Creation as good. Yet many a deep religious and philosophical spirit has chosen non-being, and has considered the tragic ultimate. And the most vocal of these in the West, Arthur Schopenhauer, blames all the "vulgar" Western "optimism" on Judaism and its creation story. Is Jewish "optimism" vulgar? Is it blind to the tragic? Must we follow Schopenhauer when he suggests that Jewish and indeed all optimism reflects but a self-congratulatory human "egoism" which is blind to all except our all-too-frail human goals and aspirations?[3] Our Midrash suggests a very different view. Not until Truth is cast to the ground is God able to create man.

And not even God Himself can despise His own "seal" of Truth. "Jewish optimism" affirms existence while at the same time confronting a Truth which is tragic. Yet, in our Midrash at least, the grounds for this togetherness remain inscrutable. "Jewish optimism" is not a "vulgar" optimism. It is an enigmatic optimism.

III

When Judaism came to North America the enigma became obscured. Faith in God often became faith in ever-evolving Reason, with idolatry becoming superstition gradually vanishing in an age of enlightenment. Halakha—the discipline of divine commandments which recognizes both the greatness and the misery of man—moved toward "customs and ceremonies" which had no discipline and no authority, and which stood in no need of them since man himself stood in no need of them. Radical evil, if recognized at all, was considered left behind in Europe. Wars and colonialism were European affairs; poverty was an evil progressively conquered by American conscience, initiative and know-how; antisemitism shrivelled into a "medieval prejudice."

In retrospect, this American Jewish optimism simply is a version of American optimism. Who but an American political leader could ever have seriously and sincerely waged a war to end all wars, when all experience shows that even "just wars" serve at best but limited ends? Who except Americans could still hope, in this century, that the complex Arab-Israeli conflict would vanish if only American know-how came on the scene and irrigated the Jordan waters?

That this and indeed all American optimism was always shot through with illusion is obvious today. Indeed, to scorn it as superficial has become the fashion. Yet the paramount task of the hour is not a rehearsal of the obvious, but rather a discriminating search for such truth as may remain behind all the superficialities and illusions. For a robust, ebullient affirmation of life is of the American essence. And if "American optimism" were ever *wholly* lost, America itself would be lost.

That such discrimination is hard to come by is evident on every side. If traditional American optimism was sweeping and indiscriminate, it has now found a nemesis which shows these same qualities. No political, religious or philosophical quarter has remained exempt. Only in a single camp does the old American optimism seem to survive wholly intact, and this, ironically, is the camp that would destroy America. Where except in America has a group of revolutionaries arisen which does not ask what social forces might be available to build the new world on the ruins of the old—which speaks and acts as though, with the act of destruction accomplished and "the system" destroyed, paradise will come of itself? Perhaps alone of all the present groupings, the American New Left has not abandoned the American Dream. It has merely transformed and postponed it.

IV

No professional historical expertise is required for the discovery of the causes of our present crisis. Hiroshima made known that America had lost her political innocence; and while the Vietnamese war was a daily, tragic reminder that indiscriminate international involvement is neither politically nor morally tenable, retreat to the idyllic isolationist view that the problems of power politics are confined to Europe has become, in a shrinking world, quite impossible. At home, all America now recognizes that in in her collective affirmation that all men are created equal the black man was somehow forgotten; and the nemesis of this past forgetfulness is a racial conflict which seems insoluble. For all their traumas, these two experiences are overshadowed by yet a third, for this assails at its roots the very mainspring of the traditional self-confidence of America. No nation has matched America in the modern certainty that, whatever nature and history have set wrong, human ingenuity and initiative can set right. No nation has staked greater faith in modern technology or has shown greater ability to develop it. Indeed, to this day the word "know-how" has American connotations. Yet this know-how, in no way diminished in energy and ability, has now produced a nemesis of which we read daily in our newspapers. Nature, subdued for human use, is becoming increasingly unusable. The city, built for human habitation, is becoming increasingly uninhabitable. Man himself, the sovereign creator of all the machinery, is being turned himself into part of it: as his power over nature and society increases, so diminishes his ability to be human. And we somehow seem unable to stop the process or to alter its course.

The search into causes is the task of the historian. The search for remedies is the task of the leaders of society. The philosopher's task is the critical examination of our collective human self-image. *A virtually all-pervasive human self-deprecation is today abroad in the land. It is as*

indiscriminate, or even enthusiastic, as was the former human self-eleva-
tion. And just as the one once called for philosophical discrimination and
criticism, so, now, does the other.

Two illustrations must suffice. Once the characteristically American movie was the cowboy picture. With clear villains and clear heroes, it was a morality play whose happy end was foreordained. (In Europe it used to be a bit of a joke that all American movies, cowboy or not, had to end happily.) Today, only the midnight cowboy remains. And foreordained are gloom, disaster, and every kind of degradation and depravity. The odd movie may still dare to portray heroism. It then still remains foreordained that, regardless of the merits of the movie, the critics will pan it. Are there no heroes left?

From the down-to-earth sphere of popular culture we turn to the rarefied sphere of theology—nearly always a sound indicator of the general consciousness even when it is bad. That Harvey Cox's celebration of the secular city should have been a theological bestseller is hard to believe less than ten years later, when this very city is obviously so near to the core of our technological despairs.[4] The phenomenon clearly reflects a religious consciousness which runs hither and thither in search of hope and light but seems unable to find it. Hence, in quick succession, the God-is-dead theology, already itself dead except for one lone, dark voice which moves us but cannot guide us;[5] the theology of hope which, arousing hope if only because its place of origin was post-Nazi Germany, could find no grounds for hope because the grounds of our despair were not confronted;[6] and, finally, a political theology which, derive as it does most of its strength from the well-warranted militancy of black Americans, seems at best either a confession of guilt on the part of the ex-Constantinian white Christian, or else a mere theological endorsement of a black American militancy which is able to dispense with all theological endorsements. In short, current American theology (its core, of course, is Protestant, but Catholic and Jewish representatives are not lacking) may seek to transcend our present crisis; in fact, however, it seems merely to reflect that crisis.

V

The above observations should be taken as a description of our present state of affairs, and not without further ado as a criticism arrived at from some superior standpoint—as if such a standpoint were readily available.

For many centuries this availability was taken for granted. Theologians would resort at once to the Word of God, with or without the
help of ecclesiastical authority. Philosophers would affirm a human
"nature" immune to the vicissitudes of history—an immunity which in
turn guaranteed a timeless access to the True, the Good, and the Beautiful. And a long alliance between these two disciplines produced a firm
stand in behalf of "eternal verities" against perpetually shifting "arbitrary
opinion."

These centuries are past. Theologians (Jewish and Christian)
should always have known that the Word of their God is manifest *in*
history if it is manifest at all: because of the historical self-consciousness
of contemporary man, this knowledge can now no longer be evaded. If
nevertheless seeking refuge in the eternal verities of philosophy, they
find that these, too, have vanished. For modern philosophy has found
itself forced to abandon the notion of a permanent human nature—and
along with this all timelessly accessible visions of the True, the Good
and the Beautiful.

This fact is most profoundly if not uniquely manifest in the philosophies arising from the work of Immanuel Kant. These philosophies do
not deny aspects of the human condition which remain more or less
permanent throughout human history. Such aspects, however, are now
confined to man's natural constitution. What makes man *human* (we are
told) is neither given nor permanent, but rather the product of his own
individual or collective activity. *Man qua man is a self-maker.* This
formula sums up the deepest of all the many revolutions in modern
philosophy. We may wish to quarrel with its central thesis. We may wish
to qualify it. We may even wish to reject it outright. One thing, at any
rate, seems for better or worse impossible—the return to the pre-modern
philosophical wisdom.

Not so long ago theologians of liberal stamp greeted this revolution
in philosophy with rejoicing. Who has not heard sermons (and in particular American sermons) about the "infinite perfectibility of man?"
The notion of man as a self-maker seemed (and in some respects surely
is) far more grandiose than the notion of a human nature given by another—even if this Other was not (rather vaguely) "Nature" or "the
Universe," but the Lord of Creation Himself. Add to this what was said
above about the American tradition of optimism, and it is not surprising
that for a considerable period of time all talk about "the nature of man"
and "*the* True, *the* Good and *the* Beautiful" seemed in many circles to
be timidly conservative, if not downright reactionary.

But now the crisis of American optimism has disclosed for us that the concept of man as a self-maker gives us grounds for apprehension and dread as well as for hope. The lack of a permanent nature may hold the promise that unforeseeable ways of human self-perfection are possible; since this lack is an unlimited malleability, however, it implies the possibility of unforeseeable negative as well as positive developments. And thus the spectre comes into view that man, *qua* unlimited maker, may reach the point of making his whole world into a machine, while at the same time, *qua* infinitely malleable, himself being reduced to a mere part of the machine, that is, to a self-made thing. Nor is this possibility today a mere unsubstantial fancy confined to philosophers. For some of our futurologists have begun to conjure up a future in which man, the proud self-maker, will have lost control over the world he has made, and the reduction to self-made thinghood will be complete. Indeed, even popular consciousness is haunted by the prospect that the whole bold and exciting story of the one being in the universe capable of making his own nature—the story of the only truly *free* being—will come to an end the pathos of which is matched only by its irony.

With prospects so terrifying, it is no wonder that some simply opt out of history; that others hanker after a simpler, more innocent past; and that, as if anticipating catastrophe, we are all tempted even now to deprecate indiscriminately all things human.

The philosopher may not yield to the temptations of escapism or indiscriminate despair. Nor may he simply throw in his lot with the futurologists, for (as we shall show at least in part) their entire approach calls for considerable philosophical suspicion. At this point, we shall be well advised to suspend the future and confine ourselves to the present. Is a genuinely *human* existence possible *even now?* Or, in order to make it possible, must we cast Truth to the ground? Must we suppress all knowledge of a future which is sure to come and force Truth to *stay* cast to the ground?

VI

We have thus far made no reference to Jewish experience in this century. We do so at this point because the direst predictions any futurologist might make have already been fulfilled and surpassed at Auschwitz, Mauthausen, Bergen-Belsen and Buchenwald. One shrinks from speaking of these unspeakable places of unique horror in any context which might invite false generalizations and comparisons. Yet one simple statement may safely be made. In the Nazi murder camps no effort was spared to make persons into living *things* before making them into dead things. And that the dead had been human when alive was a truth systematically rejected when their bodies were made into fertilizer and soap. Moreover, the criminals themselves had become living *things,* and the system, run by operators "only following orders," was well on the way toward running itself. The thoughtful reader of such a work as *The Holocaust Kingdom*[7] reaches the shocking conclusion that here was indeed a "kingdom," that is, a society organized to a purpose; that, its organization near-perfect, it might in due course have dispensed with the need for a "king;" and that such was its inner dynamic and power for self-expansion that, given a Nazi victory, it might today rule the world. This "society," however, was an anti-society, indeed, *the* modern anti-society *par excellence:* modern because unsurpassably technological, and anti-society because, while even the worst society is geared to life, the Holocaust Kingdom was geared to death. It would be quite false to say that it was a mere means, however depraved, to ends somehow bound up with life. As an enterprise subserving the Nazi war effort the murder camps were total failures, for the human and material "investment" far exceeded the "produce" of fertilizer, gold teeth and soap. The Holocaust Kingdom was an end in itself, having only one ultimate "produce," and that was death.

It is not without *prima facie* plausibility that Richard Rubenstein, Jewish theologian long preoccupied with the Holocaust, should in his more recent spoken utterances have characterized the Nazi murder camp as simply the extreme technological nightmare. Taking his cue from Lewis Mumford[8] and others, he in these utterances understands Auschwitz as but the extreme of a technological dehumanization which, to varying degrees, may in the end become the fate of us all. Nazism was simply the machine radically dehumanized, and its millions of victims, its "waste products."[9]

In this view Richard Rubenstein, the Jewish theologian overwhelmed by the Holocaust, is at one with Martin Heidegger, the German philosopher who, so far as is known to us, never mentions the Holocaust in any of his writings. Heidegger omits this subject. He makes much, however, of "world wars" and their "totality," of the human "raw material" of technology, and of *Führers.* Of all these he writes:

"World wars" and their "totality" are mere consequences of a loss of Being. It is only as consequences of this loss that they drive toward securing a stable form of dissipation-through-use. Man himself is drawn into this process, and his condition of being the most important raw material of all is no longer concealed . . . The moral indignation of those who do not yet recognize what is the case often concentrates on the arbitrariness and claim-to-power made by *Führers*. This, however, is the most fatal way of lending them dignity . . . In truth, the *Führers* are merely the necessary consequences of the fact that what-is [cut loose from Being] has gone astray, has spread itself out into the emptiness that has come to pass, and demands a single order and a making-secure of what-is.[10]

In linking Rubenstein with Heidegger we pay Rubenstein a tribute, for of all the philosophical thinking that has thus far been done about the involvement of modern man's very being with modern technology Heidegger's is doubtless the deepest. Heidegger goes beyond the mere external manifestations of technology. He goes to man, the autonomous self-maker, who stands behind these manifestations. Moreover, he goes beyond this self-maker's purported "autonomy" to a modern loss of an original presence of Being, to a *Seinsvergessenheit* and a *Seinsverlassenheit* of which that autonomy, for better or worse, is but a derivative result. And the reward for this search in depth is that, unlike all the far more superficial futurologists, Heidegger offers us at least a glimmer of justified hope.

Yet we are forced, equally by the very depth of Heidegger's philosophy and by the very agony of Rubenstein's preoccupation with the Holocaust, to ask of both thinkers essentially the same question. Can either Nazism or its murder camps be understood as but one particular case, however extreme, of the general technological dehumanization? Or; (to use language which theologians are equipped to understand) does not a scandal of particularity attach to Nazism and its murder camps which is shied away from, suppressed or simply forgotten when the scandal is technologically universalized? To be sure, there have been "world wars"—but none like that which Hitler unleashed on the world. There have been (and are) "total" political systems—but none like Nazism, a truth suppressed when "fascism" is used as a generic term in which Nazism is included. And while there have been (and are) "cults of personality," there have been no *Führers* but only one *Führer*.

Nor is it possible to distinguish between the goals of Nazism-in-general, as one system, and those of the murder-camp-in-particular, as a second system subserving the first. In essence, Nazism *was* the murder-camp. That a nihilistic, demonic celebration of death and destruction was its animating principle was evident to thinkers such as Karl Barth from the start; it became universally revealed in the end, when in the Berlin bunker Hitler and Goebbels, the only true Nazis left, expressed ghoulish satisfaction at the prospect that their downfall might carry in train the doom, not only (or even at all) of their enemies, but rather of the "master race." The mind shrinks from systematic murder which serves no purpose beyond murder itself, for it is ultimately unintelligible. Yet in Nazism as a whole (not only in the murder camps) this unintelligibility was real. And except for good fortune this diabolical celebration might today rule the world.

Even this does not exhaust the scandalous particularity of Nazism. The term "Aryan" had no clear connotation other than "non-Jew,"[11] and the Nazis were not antisemites because they were racists, but rather racists because they were antisemites.[12] The exaltation of the "Aryan" had no positive significance. It had only the negative significance of de- grading and murdering the "non-Aryan." Thus Adolf Eichmann passed beyond the limits of a merely "banal" evil when, with nothing left of the Third Reich, he declared with obvious sincerity that he would jump laughing into his grave in the knowledge of having dispatched six million Jews to their death. We must conclude, then, that the dead Jews of the murder camps (and all the other innocent victims, as it were, as quasi- Jews, or by dint of innocent-guilt-by-association) were not the "waste product" of the Nazi system. They were *the* product.

VII

Despite all necessary attempts to comprehend, the Nazi system in the end exceeds all comprehension. One cannot comprehend but only con- front and oppose. We can here attempt to confront only one miniscule manifestation.[13] When issuing "work permits" designed to separate "use- less" Jews to be murdered at once from "useful" ones to be kept useful by diabolically contrived false hopes and murdered later, the Nazis on occasion issued two such permits to able-bodied Jewish men. One was untransferable and to be kept for himself; the other was to be given at his own discretion to his able-bodied father, mother, wife or one child. On those occasions the Nazis would not make this choice, although to do so would have resulted in a more efficient labor force. Jewish sons, hus- bands and fathers themselves were forced to decide who among their loved ones was—for the time being—to live and who to die at once.

The mind seeks escape in every direction. Yet we must confront relentlessly the Nazi custom of the two work permits, recognizing in this custom not the work of some isolated sadists, but rather the essence of the Nazi system. Hence we ask: where was here Heidegger's "dissipation-through-use?" Where was Rubenstein's technological dehumanization with its human "waste products?" Had utility been the principle of Nazism it would not have left the choice between "useful" and "useless" Jews to its victims. Not utility (however dehumanized), but rather torture and degradation was the principle. Indeed, there is no greater contrast between the technological exaltation of utility (even when out of control) and a celebration of torture *contrary* to all utility when it is not incidental but rather *for torture's sake*.

Why is this scandalous particularity overlooked, denied or repressed by Rubenstein and Heidegger, not to speak of all the other writers who lack the agony of Rubenstein and the profundity of Heidegger? The theologian (Jewish or Christian) may hazard a guess if he falls back on his own authentic resources. For he is himself acquainted with scandalous particularity, for better (in the presence of God) and for worse (in the presence of the demonic). Moreover, he is acquainted with our all-too-human desire to evade or deny each and every scandalous particularity, and he knows this tendency to be pagan. And if he modernizes what he already knows he will understand that in a scientific age the characteristic form of evading or denying scandalous particularity is to explain it away. Hence it may be no coincidence that Heidegger's later thought is pagan;[14] that Rubenstein advocates a Jewish return to paganism; and that the dire predictions of the futurologists have a strong resemblance to ancient pagan fatalism.

We cannot be sure how the ancient rabbis, were they alive, would respond to the death camps. We *can* be sure that they would not explain them away. In their own time, they knew of idolatry, and considered groundless hate to be its equivalent. They knew, too, that it could not be explained but only opposed. Alive today, they would reject all fatalistic futurological predictions as so many self-fulfilling prophecies which leave us helpless. Instead, they would somehow seek to meet the absolute evil of the death camps in the only way absolute evil can be met—by an absolute opposition on which one stakes one's life.[15]

The authentic Jew after Auschwitz has no privileged access to explanations of the past. He has no privileged access to predictions of the future, or to ways of solving the problems of the present. He is, however, a witness to the world. He is a witness against the idolatry of the Nazi murder camps. This negative testimony is *ipso facto* also the positive testimony that man shall *be,* and shall be *human*—even if Truth should be so horrendous that there is no choice but to cast it to the ground.

VIII

The Jew in whom this testimony is unsurpassably manifest is the survivor of the two-work-permit custom. When the torture occurred he had no choice but compliance. Armed resistance was impossible. So was suicide. So was the transfer of his own work permit to another member of his family. Any of these attempts would have doomed the one member of his family who was to live. To save this one member, he was forced to become implicated in the diabolical system which robbed him of his soul and made him forever after innocently guilty of the murder of all his family except one member.

We ask: having survived (if survive he did), why did this Jew not seek blessed release in suicide? Choosing to live, why did he not seek refuge in insanity? Choosing to stay sane, why did he not do all he could to escape from his singled out Jewish condition but rather affirmed his Jewishness and indeed raised new Jewish children? How could even one stay with his God?

These are unprecedented questions. They require unprecedented responses. Why not suicide? *Because after the Nazi celebration of death life has acquired a new dimension of sanctity.* Why not flight into madness? *Because insanity had ruled the kingdom of darkness, hence sanity, once a gift, has now become a holy commandment.* Why hold fast to mere Jewishness? *Because Jewish survival after Auschwitz is not "mere," but rather in itself and without any further reasons or theological justifications a sacred testimony* to all mankind *that life and love, not death and hate, shall prevail.* Why hold fast to the God of the covenant? Former believers lost Him in the Holocaust Kingdom. Former agnostics found Him. No judgement is possible. All theological arguments vanish. Nothing remains but the fact that the bond between Him and His people reached the breaking point but was not for all wholly broken. Thus the survivor is a witness against darkness in an age of darkness. He is a witness whose like the world has not seen.

We do not yet recognize this witness, for we do not yet dare to enter the darkness against which he testifies. Yet to enter that darkness is to be rewarded with an altogether astonishing discovery. *This may be an age without heroes. It is, however, the heroic age* par excellence *in all of Jewish history.* If this is true of the Jewish people collectively (not only of the survivor individually), it is because *the survivor is gradually becoming the paradigm for the entire Jewish people.*

Nowhere is this truth as unmistakable as in the State of Israel. The

State of Israel is collectively what the survivor is individually—testimony on behalf of all mankind to life against death, to sanity against madness, to Jewish self-affirmation against every form of flight from it, and (though this is visible only to those who break through narrow theological categories) to the God of the ancient covenant against all lapses into paganism.

We ask: having survived, why did the survivor not seek both safety and forgetfulness among such good people as the Danes, but rather seek danger and memory in the nascent and embattled State of Israel? Indeed, why do not even now Israeli Jews in general, survivors or no, flee by the thousands from their isolated and endangered country, in order that they might elsewhere find peace and safety—not to speak of the world's approval? Why do they hold fast to their "law of return"—the commitment to receive sick Jews, poor Jews, oppressed Jews, rejected by the immigration laws of every other state? A world which wants no part of Auschwitz fails to understand. Indeed, perpetuating antisemitism, despite Auschwitz or even because of it, it often does not hesitate to resort to slander. Yet the truth is obvious: the State of Israel is a collective testimony against the groundless hate which has erupted in this century in the heart of Europe. Its watchword is *Am Yisrael Chai*—"the people Israel *lives*." Without this watchword the State of Israel could not have survived for a generation. It is a watchword of defiance, hope and faith. It is a testimony to all men everywhere that man shall be, and be human —even if it should be necessary to cast Truth to the ground.

And now, astoundingly, this watchword has come alive among the Jews of the Soviet Union. What makes these Jews affirm their Jewishness against the overwhelming odds of a ruthless system, when they could gain peace and comfort by disavowing their Jewishness? Though we can only marvel at their heroism and not understand it, its mainspring is obvious enough. No American Jew has experienced the Holocaust as every Russian Jew has experienced it. Hence every Russian Jew must have felt all along that to be denied the right to his Jewishness is not, after what has happened, a tolerable form of discrimination or prejudice but rather an intolerable affront; it is, as it were, a secular sacrilege. And if now these Jews increasingly dare to convert secret feeling into public action, it is because of the inspiration incarnate in the State of Israel.

Is heroism in evidence among ourselves, the comfortable, mostly middle-class Jews of North America? In order to perceive any trace of it, we must break through the false but all-pervasive categories of a world which does not know of Auschwitz and does not wish to know of it.

In America this is a time of identity crises. Among these there is a specific Jewish identity crisis which springs from the view that a Jew must somehow achieve a "universal" transcendence of his "particular" Jewishness if he is to justify his Jewish identity. Thus it has come to seem that a Jew shows genuine courage when he rejects his Jewish identity, or when he at least seeks a "universal" justification of that identity by espousing all noble except Jewish causes. And the North American Jewish hero may seem to be he who actually turns against his own people, less because he seeks the creation of a Palestinian Arab state than because he seeks the destruction of the Jewish state.

Such may be the appearances. The truth is otherwise. Just as the black seeking to pass for white has internalized racism, so the Jew joining al-Fatah has internalized antisemitism, and this is true also (albeit to a lesser degree) of the Jew espousing all except Jewish causes. Where is the universalism in this exceptionalism—a "universalism" which applies to everyone with one exception—Jews? There is only sickness. To the extent to which the world still wants the Jew either to disappear or at least to become a man-in-general, it still has the power to produce Jews bent on disappearing, or at least on "demonstrating" their exceptionalist "universalism."

These may seem harsh judgments. They are necessary because Jewish identity crises such as the above have become a surrender to Auschwitz. For a Jew after the Holocaust to act as though his Jewishness required justification is to allow the possibility that none might be found, and this in turn is to allow the possibility, after Hitler murdered one third of the Jewish people, that the rest should quietly pass on. But merely to allow these possibilities is *already* a posthumous victory for Hitler. It is *already* an act of betrayal. And the betrayal is as much of the world as of the Jewish people.

Is there any trace of Jewish heroism among ourselves? The question transcends all conventional distinctions, such as between old and young, "right" and "left," and even "religious" and "secular." The North American Jewish hero is he who has confronted the demons of Auschwitz and defied them. It is the Jew who has said "No!" to every form, however mild or disguised, of antisemitism without and self-rejection within. It is the Jew at home in his Jewish skin and at peace with his Jewish destiny. It is the Jew who is whole.

IX

But if this is the age of heroism in the history of the Jewish people, it is, after all, also an age of unprecedented darkness in world history, and

Jewish heroism itself is possible only at the price of perpetually verging on despair. The question therefore arises what meaning the Jewish *Am Yisrael Chai* might have for contemporary man.

One shrinks from so large a question for two opposite reasons. At one extreme, the singled out Jewish testimony may all-too-easily dissipate itself into a vacuous and thus cheap and escapist universalism. At the other extreme, it may express its universal significance at the false price of deafness to quite different, and yet not unrelated testimonies, such as might come from Vietnam, Czechoslovakia and Bengla Desh. Perhaps one avoids both dangers best by concretizing the question. Earlier we dwelt on the American tradition of optimism which is now in a state of crisis, and stressed that, while much in this optimism was always false, America itself would be lost if American optimism were wholly lost. What may the Jewish *Am Yisrael Chai* reveal about American optimism? What was always false about the American Dream? What—if anything—remains true?

Always false was precisely the "Dream." The innocence which produced that dream is lost. If the saving of America were dependent upon the recapturing of the innocence and the Dream there would be no hope. However, the Midrash which has furnished the text for the present discourse is not the product of a dream. Truth may be cast to the ground. The Midrashic author *knows* that it is cast to the ground. He knows, too, that in the end Truth must rise again from the earth.

When dreams are shattered men are wont to seek refuge in wishful thinking. Our age is no exception. In a half-hearted version, collective make-believe is manifest in our current, self-enclosed, middle-class apotheosis of psychoanalysis. (Within its sober bounds, that discipline gives limited help to disturbed individuals, and quite possibly we are all disturbed. Expanded into systematic wishful thinking, it turns into a panacea for all the ills of our world.) In a radical version, collective make-believe is manifest in a self-enclosed ideologizing which would refashion all reality in its own image, while being itself out of touch with reality.

Being self-enclosed, collective make-believe can survive for a long period of time. Yet its nemesis is sure to come, and by dint of its greater honesty it is the radical version which is bound first to experience it. To be sure, ideology seeks to refashion reality. Being divorced from reality, however, it in fact refashions only ideology, and the conflict between ideality and reality in the end becomes so total as to result—when Truth springs from the earth—in despair.

Is despair, then, the only *truthful* outcome? Richard Rubenstein does not lack the courage of radically opposing the entire Jewish tradi-

tion with his affirmation that the only Messiah is death. Long before him
Arthur Schopenhauer wrote as follows:

> Death is the great reprimand which the will to life, or more especially
> the egoism which is essential to it, receives through the course of na-
> ture; and it may be considered as a punishment for our existence.
> Death says: thou are the product of an act which should not have
> been; therefore to expiate it thou must die.[16]

Once the sentiment expressed in this passage was attractive only to idle
drawing room speculation. Today one can detect on every side a veri-
table fascination with every kind of negation and death itself. Once the
denial of the will to live could seem to be a noble rejection of "egoism."
Today it stands revealed as the foe, nothing short of obscene, of a will to
live which, far from "egoistic," is a heroic act of defiance. And the
revelation is nowhere as manifest as in the survivor of the Nazi custom
of the two work permits. He is not blind to the shadows of death but has
walked through its valley. He does not cling to life but rather affirms it
by an act of faith which defies comprehension. He relives, in a form
without precedent anywhere, that great "nevertheless" which has always
been the secret of the enigmatic optimism of Judaism. His testimony is a
warning to men everywhere not to yield to death when Truth springs
from the earth. It is an admonition to endure Truth and to choose life.
It is a plea, anguished and joyous, to share in a defiant endurance which
alone reveals that Truth, despite all, remains the seal of God.

X

Twenty five years after, the present writer and his wife had the unique
privilege of participating in a pilgrimage of survivors which took us first
to Bergen-Belsen and then to Jerusalem.

When we arrived at Hannover, the city nearest to the murder camp,
it rained. Our leader said: "We have returned to this place of our suffering many times. It always rains when we come. God weeps. He weeps
for the sins He has committed against His people Israel."

And then we went to Jerusalem, once light years away, and now a
mere few hours. There a friend told us how once at six A.M. he went to
the Wall. There he was met by an old man with a bag of cookies and a
bottle of liquor who greeted him: "My friend, I have a *Simchah,* a cele-

bration! Share it with me!" Having partaken of food and drink, our friend returned some days later at the same time of day, only to be met by the same old man with the same greeting. And so it went three or four times. Finally, unable to restrain his curiosity, our friend asked: "What sort of celebration can last so long? Surely not a wedding! Surely not a Bar Mitzvah!" The old man replied: "I am a survivor of Auschwitz. Also, I am a *Cohen*, a priest, and, as you may know, a priest may bless the people everywhere in the world only a few times during the year; in Jerusalem, however, every single day. And since I must be at work in my kibbutz at 8 A.M., I come here every single day, the Sabbath only excepted, to observe my duty and my privilege. This is my *Simchah*. It will last as long as I live."

All sorts of men come to the Wall. The old man did not inquire into their credentials. He invited the devout and the not so devout. He invited Jews, Christians, Muslims—the world. He said to everyone: "Share my *Simchah*, my celebration! And may it last as long as life itself!"

(1971)

NOTES

1. *Midrash Genesis Rabbah,* VIII 5.

2. Truth is the seal of God.

3. *Works,* trans. R. B. Haldane and J. Kemp (London: Kegan Paul, Trench, Trübner & Co. 1909), vol. III, pp. 305ff., 446ff.

4. *The Secular City: A Celebration of its Liberties and an Invitation to its Discipline* (New York: Macmillan 1965).

5. See T. J. J. Altizer, *The Gospel of Christian Atheism* (Philadelphia: Westminster 1966); *The Descent into Hell* (Philadelphia: Lippincott 1970).

6. See, *e.g.,* J. Moltmann, *The Theology of Hope* (New York: Harper & Row 1967).

7. Alexander Donat, *The Holocaust Kingdom* (New York: Holt, Rinehart & Winston 1963).

8. Mumford writes: "Well before the first atom bomb was tested, the American Air Force had adopted the hitherto "unthinkable" practice of the wholesale, indiscriminate bombing of concentrated civilian populations: this paralleled, except for the distance of the victims, the practice employed by Hit-

ler's sub-men in extermination camps like Buchenwald and Auschwitz" (*The Myth of the Machine* [New York: Harcourt Brace 1970], p. 256). In the following it will emerge that, despite admittedly terrifying similarities, this "parallel" is totally false. Mumford's (unexplained) use of the word "sub-men" in the above passage already suggests that, rather than *argue* for a parallel, he simply begs the question. Elsewhere he even lapses into self-contradiction. His case for Nazism as *nothing but* a megamachine requires that (following Hannah Arendt) he must view Eichmann as a "banal" bureaucrat (p. 279), while at the same time murder-camps serving no end except murder itself require an (unexplained) "pathological hatred" in the Nazi leaders. (p. 250) If even Eichmann was a mere banal bureaucrat who were the "pathological" leaders? How many? In the end, perhaps just one? And what made all those "merely following orders" follow orders *such as these*—with a "faith" not shrinking from total self-sacrifice? Nazism was a demonic compact between *Volk* and *Führer* in which each exalted the other in an orgy of death and destruction—with the consequence that the view of Nazism as *simply* the extreme megamachine lies in shambles.

9. Mumford, p. 279.

10. "Überwindung der Metaphysik," *Vorträge und Aufsätze* (Pfullingen: Neske 1967), pp. 84–85. (The translation is mine.) I deal more fully with these and related Heideggerian views in Chapter Five of my *Encounters Between Judaism and Modern Philosophy*.

11. Except only for "non-Gipsy." The fate of the Gipsies in Nazi Germany is at least in one respect more tragic than that of the Jews—no one seems to bother with remembering it.

12. "Antisemitism" itself is nothing but a synonym for "Jew-hatred," concocted in the nineteenth century when hatred of Jews was fanned without explicit recourse to its ancient theological rationalizations. A secret Nazi order, dated May 17, 1943, reads as follows: "When the Grand Mufti visited Reichsleiter Rosenberg, the Reichsleiter promised to instruct the press that the word *antisemitism* was henceforth to be abandoned. This term seemed to include the Arab world which, according to the Grand Mufti, was overwhelmingly pro-German. The Allies utilize our use of that term in order to argue falsely that it is the national socialist intention to view Jews and Arabs in the same light." Poliakov-Wulf, *Das Dritte Reich und die Juden* (Berlin: Arami 1955) p. 369 (the translation is mine). This secret Nazi order might be pondered by those who believe (or pretend to believe) that "anti-Zionism" by definition cannot be antisemitic, on the grounds that Arabs as well as Jews are "Semites."

13. In the following I find myself compelled to return to a manifestation of the Nazi system which I first turned to in my "The People Israel Lives," *The Christian Century*, May 6, 1970.

14. See Hans Jonas, "Heidegger and Theology," *The Phenomenon of Life* (New York: Harper & Row, 1966), pp. 235–61.

15. For an attempt to bring rabbinic wisdom concerning idolatry to bear on Nazism, see Chapter Four of the work cited in note 10.

16. *Works*, vol. III, p. 306.

13

JEWISH PERCEPTIONS OF AMERICA
From Melting Pot to Mosaic

ABRAHAM J. KARP

O N AUGUST 17, 1790, the newly elected George Washington honored Newport, Rhode Island, with a visit. The following morning prior to his departure, deputations called upon the President to present to him expressions of affection and devotion. Moses Seixas, Warden of Kaal Kadosh Yeshuat Israel, the Hebrew congregation of Newport, presented to him a letter which begins:

> Permit the children of the stock of Abraham to approach you with the most cordial affection and esteem for your person and merits, and to join with our fellow citizens in welcoming you to Newport.

The letter contains an invocation to the God of Israel "beseeching Him that the Angel who conducted our forefathers through the wilderness into the promised land, may graciously conduct you through all the difficulties and dangers of this mortal life." Seixas no doubt felt that it was wisdom to sieze the opportunity to remind the Chief Magistrate of the American Jews' association with the biblical drama of liberation from foreign bondage and new nationhood, and their being descendents of David, Daniel, and Joshua, whose names he invokes. And more. Wouldn't it be all prudence to suggest to the head of government that no people has greater cause for loyalty to the new nation than the Jews, "Deprived as we heretofore have been of the invaluable rights of free citizens . . . we now behold a Government erected by the majesty of the people . . . a Federal Union whose basis is philanthropy, mutual confidence, and public virtue . . ."? And Seixas adds his perception of what makes this Government unique and distinguished, meriting God's approval and His people's blessing; "a Government which gives to bigotry no sanction, to persecution no assistance." What we have here is a perception of America by a leader of American Jewry at the birth of the nation. Seixas no doubt meant it to be more than a perception. In the context of the event and as it is phrased, it is an expression of expectation as well. The heirs of a people which has suffered persecution in the Old World now look to the New World, the new nation, and its newly elected Chief Magistrate to afford this new community of Jews the freedom and equality so long denied them. And he places this graciously worded expectation on public record.

Seixas was rewarded beyond his expectations. In the reply of George Washington "To the Hebrew Congregation in Newport, Rhode Island," he uses the felicitous phrase of Seixas, as *his* characterization:

For happily the Government of the United States, which gives to bigotry no sanction, to persecution no assistance, requires only that they who live under its protection, should demean themselves as good citizens, in giving it on all occasions their effectual support.

What began as a statement of a Jewish perception of what America was became a formal and oft quoted pronouncement by the Founding Father of what America was and ought to remain.

The perception of Seixas became a pronouncement of Washington. Though he was revered as the Father of his Country, his pronouncement was not Law. Bigotry was not sanctioned by the Government, but neither was it totally erased. In the same year that the Declaration of Independence proclaimed that "all men are created equal," the state of Maryland adopted a constitution guaranteeing religious liberty to "all persons professing the Christian religion," and requiring on assuming office an "oath of support and fidelity to the State . . . and a declaration of belief in the Christian religion."

In 1797, following the establishment of the nation, the adoption of the Federal Constitution, and the enactment of the Bill of Rights, "Solomon Etting and others," petitioned the Maryland Assembly for: "A sect of people called Jews . . . to be placed on the same footing as other good citizens."

The petition was termed "reasonable," but was not acted upon, a fate also suffered by subsequent submissions. In 1804, the struggle was suspended, not to be pressed again for fourteen years.

In 1818 men of good will, marshalled by the Jewish community of Baltimore and led by Thomas Kennedy, began the struggle anew. In the custom of the time pamphleteering was employed, none more effective than *Governor Worthington's Speech on the Maryland Test Act, 1824.* In it he argued that; "This disqualification is against the spirit of our constitution, and the letter of that of the United States," and "it is against the policy of this country." He crowns his argument with: "It is fortunate that I have in my hands, proofs that the Father of his country was in favor of political equality of the Israelites in particular." He quotes Washington's letters to Hebrew congregations in the cities of Savannah, Philadelphia, New York, Charleston, and Richmond, most tellingly the one to the Jews of Newport, Rhode Island. Worthington remarks, "the address of the Hebrew Congregation in Newport, Rhode Island, . . . is so handsomely written, that I must take leave to read it entire."

The *Maryland Jew Bill* was passed in 1825 and confirmed a year later. The stated perception of America presented by Seixas to Washington played its role in granting to the Jews of Maryland full equality, and removing from the American scene a blight on freedom and democracy.

A year or two after Washington's visit to Newport, a Jewish young woman, Rebecca Samuel of Petersburg, Virginia, wrote a letter to her parents in Hamburg, Germany. She writes:

> You cannot know what a wonderful country this is for the common man . . . One can live here peacefully . . . Ever since Hyman has grown up, he has not had it so good.

America she perceives to be a land of opportunity and prosperity, but a land of problems, as well. She writes:

> Dear parents,
>   I know quite well you will not want me to bring up my children like Gentiles. Here (in Petersburg) they cannot become anything else. Jewishness is pushed aside here. There are here ten or twelve Jews, and they are not worthy of being called Jews . . . The way we live is no life at all. We do not know what the Sabbath and holidays are. On the Sabbath all the Jewish shops are open . . . In our house we all live as Jews as much as we can . . . My Schoene is three years old . . . and my Sammy, God bless him, is already beginning to talk . . . It is sinful that such blessed children should be brought up here.

Spiritual peril there is, but there is a solution. Just as we left Hamburg in search of economic opportunity, now we had to leave Petersburg for spiritual sustenance. America was the goal for the former quest, Charleston, S.C. for the latter. "In that place," she informs her parents, "there is a blessed community of three hundred Jews."

Rebecca Samuel's perception of America in the 1790s is that of a land of economic opportunity but spiritual peril. What she perceives

America to be directs her course of action as she plans and arranges her life and that of her family.

More than a century later, the greatest Talmudic scholar to come to America, Rabbi Jacob Wilawsky, or as he was called, *The Ridvas,* had the same perception of America. After a brief visit in 1901, he returned in 1903, and made his home in Chicago, where he was installed as Chief Rabbi. In recognition of his scholarly pre-eminence his Orthodox colleagues in America conferred upon him the title of *Z'kan Harabonim,* Eldest of the Rabbis. A year later he published a biblical commentary, *Nimukei Ridvas.* In the Introduction, he writes of the America he knows:

> The Jews came to the United States, a land blessed with prosperity. Here they prospered and are honored among peoples. But the ways and customs of this land militate against the observance of the laws of the Torah and the Jewish way of life.

A long description of religious chaos follows. It pains him deeply. He inveighs against:

> those who have strayed from their faith, estranged themselves from truth, piety and Jewish observance, who enjoy with fulness of heart this country's pleasures—such are mostly to descend to the Gehenna.

He himself cannot remain in such a land, he is making ready to go the Holy Land. But for those who remain he has advice and admonition of how to defeat the spiritual perils which abound:

> Even though the laws of this land make it obligatory for the father to send his son to school, permission is granted to a Jewish community or a congregation to establish its own school, where the boys can study Torah as well as those subjects which are taught by 'teachers.' The Poles who have come to this country have done so. They have established schools in their churches, to preserve and foster their faith. Why should we not do the same for our children?
>
> My brethren, I see no other solution to the problem facing us . . . If we do not bestir ourselves now, I am sore afraid that there will be no Jew left in the next generation.
>
> Arise! Rouse yourselves to do valiantly for your children. Do at least that which our gentile neighbors do for theirs. Then you will be

worthy to see an upright generation, a worthy generation, a blessed generation.

Economic well-being and spiritual peril. As in the case of the wife and mother a century earlier, the perception is more than an observation, it is a call to action.

Even when the Rev. Gustav Poznanski cried out at the dedication of the new building of the Beth Elohim Congregation of Charleston, South Carolina, in 1841, "This synagogue is our *temple,* this city our *Jerusalem,* this happy land our *Palestine,*" it was more emotive than descriptive, for he continued, "and as our fathers defended with their lives *that* temple, *that* city and *that* land, so will their sons defend *this* temple, *this* city, and *this* land." Or when Isaac M. Wise asserted, "There in America the Salvation of mankind must originate," it was challenge, not an assertion, a challenge to the Jew to lead America in its spiritual manifest destiny. He re-echoed the constant claim of Reform Judaism in America, that this land was the most fitting setting for the acting out of Israel's mission to the nations. The preamble to the *Fundamental Principles of the Jewish Reform Society in Chicago,* adopted in 1858, stated it succinctly:

> We are deeply convinced that Israel has been called by God to be the Messiah of the nations and to spread truth and virtue on earth . . . This object will be best accomplished in a free and blessed America.

America, a land of freedom and blessing, is a perception, and more—it is an opportunity which becomes a mandate. There the noble calling can be accomplished, here then it *must* be accomplished.

What we have seen then is that the Jew perceived America in terms of the opportunities it presented for his own needs—personal or communal. Indeed he fashioned imagings of America which would best serve him in his legitimate self interests, be they political rights or spiritual well-being. It must be noted, however, that from the beginning there was the conviction that Jewish interests coincided with American well-being. At first this was implied, later explicitly argued.

So far, we have only touched upon what might be called *reactive* perceptions—responses to experiences in and fears and hopes about America. These were necessarily tentative and limited, as reactions tend to be. As the Jew became more and more integrated into American society, his perceptions of America broadened and became *conceptual.*

An image of America was projected—an image of an integrated society which made demands upon and offered accommodation to the corporate groups which comprise the nation. Jewish life, personal and communal, was to be conceived and organized in conformity with the image of the America delineated.

As we shall see, the early conceptual perceptions come from without, but increasingly they were drawn from the inner needs of the group. The ideologists of the 20th century, more at home in America than the generations which preceded them, took more seriously the words of the Declaration of Independence that the revolutionary premise and promise of America is that "pursuit of happiness" is an "unalienable right" and that to secure it "governments are instituted among men." The emphasis was shifted from demands made *by* America to demands made *of* America. The rhetoric of argument did not change: the larger interests of the nation run parallel to the self interest of its component subgroups, but one senses that the thrust was from groups in service of America to America accommodating itself to the legitimate needs of the groups which comprised it. In *their* strength and well-being are *its* strength and well-being.

It was argued, in both assertion and implication, that the promise of America was for a pluralistic society. Only such a society would preserve the freedom and democracy which justified the endeavor of the Founding Fathers and vindicated their faith that those who would come after them would share their vision and commitment.

We turn now to the conceptual perceptions of America and the role they played in the onfolding of the American drama; first, to fear and faith about America expressed by the one who knew it best.

In 1831, a young French nobleman, Alexis de Tocqueville was sent by his government to study the penal system of the United States. He spent two years here, and in 1835 he published *Democracy in America,* still an indispensable book for understanding America. He observes:

> Small nations have . . . ever been the cradle of political liberty . . .
> The history of the world affords no instance of a great nation retaining the form of a republican government for a long series of years.

He therefore concludes:

> (although) it is important to acknowledge the peculiar advantages of great states . . . as a general proposition . . . nothing is more opposed to the well-being of freedom of man than vast empires.

He finds, however, that the genius of the Founding Fathers had built into the American system a powerful corrective: the Federal System, which provides a division of sovereignty between the national government and the individual states.

> As the sovereignty of the Union is limited and incomplete, its exercise is not incompatible with liberty.

So he hails Federalism which makes

> The Union as happy and as free as a small people, and as glorious and as strong as a great nation.

Political Federalism, which provides for dual sovereignty, declares proper and legitimate multiple loyalties, and thus prevents a totalitarian system which insists on *one* and exclusive loyalty.

But by the end of the 19th century, Lord Bryce in his *The American Commonwealth* saw a "growing strength of the national government" which was putting an end to Federalism. Industrialization and international involvement made for an all-powerful central government. In 1930 when Harold Laski wrote *The Obsolescence of Federalism,* he meant it as a plea but it was really an observation.

Political Federalism came to an end, the corrective fashioned by the Founding Fathers faltered and failed, yet essential democracy has been retained!

What preserved in America the idea that it is acceptable, even right and desirable for a man to have more than one loyalty and allegiance, was a new federalism which came into being as political federalism waned. I call it a religio-ethnic federalism. It proclaims a new division of loyalty and allegiance: between the national state and one's religious, cultural or ethnic group. It maintains that a person can be and is at one and the same time a loyal citizen of the republic and a loyal member of this ethnic, religious or cultural group. The role of political Federalism as the guarantor of freedom was taken over by a religio-ethnic-cultural federalism.

It is the unique character of the Jew in America that he alone is a member of a group which is at one and the same time religious, ethnic and cultural.

Far beyond his numbers, the American Jew has played a central

role in fashioning this new federalism, a pluralistic society which preserves democracy. In his stubborn maintaining of his distinctive identity
—emphasizing now the religious, now the ethnic, now the cultural, but
always an amalgram of all three—the American Jew has made a signal
contribution to the retention of the central feature of democracy: the
right to be different, while living in unity. His story is a study of how a
nation "grown great" has preserved its democracy and retained its
freedom.

A leading historian of religion in America, Winthrop S. Hudson,
notes this. In his *Religion in America* (2nd ed., N.Y., 1973) he states:

> Perhaps one of the greatest contributions of Judaism to the United
> States will be to help other Americans understand how the United
> States can be a truly pluralistic society in which pluralism is maintained
> in away that is enriching rather than impoverishing, a society in which
> the integrity of different faiths is preserved . . . A pluralistic society
> is a society of dual commitments which need not be in conflict but
> can be complementary. But whether conflicting or complementary the
> citizens of a pluralistic society must bear the burden of both commit-
> ments. From the long experience of Judaism, Americans of other
> faiths can learn how this may be done with both grace and integrity.
> (pp. 440–41)

This perceptive historian issues this invitation and challenge to American
Jewry to demonstrate to others a life of dual commitment, to America
and to its own historic faith. This, he suggests, will be its greatest contribution to the unfolding of the promise which is America—the land of
the pluralistic society.

Because he is so gifted an historian, he recognizes that the Jew,
more than anyone else, has struggled with the challenge of how to live
creatively in such a society, how to partake most fully of the political,
social and cultural life of America while at the same time fashioning a
creative communal, cultural, and religious life of his own. To do so the
American Jew had to work out a conception of America and his own
identity within it.

From the first century of this Republic to the beginning of this
century, the Jew conceived of America as everyone else conceived of it. At
the birth of this nation, Michel-Guillaume de Crévecoeur in his *Letters
from An American Farmer* (1782) proclaimed America to be that place
and nation where "individuals of all nations are melted into a new race
of men."

In the middle of the last century, Ralph Waldo Emerson wrote in his *Journal* (1845) " . . . in this continent—asylum of all nations—the energy of Irish, Germans, Swedes, Poles and Cossacks, and all European tribes . . . will construct a new race, a new religion, a new state, a new literature, which will be as vigorous as the new Europe which came out of the smelting-pot of the Dark Ages." Its most popular expression was in a play by Israel Zangwill, *The Melting Pot* (1908). A Jewish immigrant composer, David Quixano, is writing the "American" symphony. He is in love with a cultured Gentile girl, Vera. The symphony finished and performed, the composer speaks to his love of this new nation.

> There she lies, the great Melting Pot. Celt and Latin, Slav and Teuton, Greek and Syrian, black and yellow, Jew and Gentile . . . how the great Alchemist melts and fuses them with his purging flame! Here shall they all unite to build the Republic of Man and the Kingdom of God. Ah, Vera, what is the glory of Rome and Jerusalem where all nations come to worship and look back, compared to the glory of America, where all races and nature come to labour and look forward!
>
> Peace, peace unto ye unborn millions, fated to fill this giant continent—the God of our children give you Peace.

This was America to the immigrant Jew. To the immigrant this view of America proclaimed: You are welcome to these shores and into this nation. But here is a price you must pay! Divest yourself of your traditions and culture. Purge from your being whatever made you distinct and distinguished. You may no longer be what you have been. Here you must become an "Anglo-Saxon" (an ersatz Anglo-Saxon, to be sure), for *this* is the *American* culture and civilization. Most immigrants were ready to pay the price, if this was the price that America demanded.

This conception of America resulted in such reactions as:

W. M. Rosenblatt in the *Galaxie* (January 1872), "The Jews, What They Are Coming To," wrote:

> Within fifty years . . . the grandchildren at the latest will be indistinguishable from the mass of humanity which surrounds them . . . Of that ancient people only the history of their perils and suffering will remain, and the story of the change which came over them in an enlightened age.

In 1898 the Hebrew writer Schwartzberg titled a Hebrew pamphlet *Tikatev Zot L'Dor Aharon, Let This Be Written for the Last Generation,* convinced that he was a member of the last generation in America which would be able to read Hebrew.

Rosenblatt, an assimilationist, hailed the Melting Pot and the disappearance of the Jew. Schwartzberg, a survivalist, wept over it. But both were convinced that the trend was irreversible. How conclude otherwise when Rabbi Charles Fleisher of Boston's Temple Israel urged Jews to intermarry to build "a new nation to emerge from the Melting Pot"?

But there were leaders of the Jewish community who raised the alarm. A Melting Pot America would destroy Jewish life. So Reform Rabbi Bernhard Felsenthal of Chicago and Professor Israel Friedlaender of the Conservative Jewish Theological Seminary, Socialist Yiddishist Dr. Haim Zhitlowski, and nascent Zionist Henrietta Szold inveighed against it.

And there were those in the Jewish community who saw the Melting Pot not so much as destructive of Jewish life as of American democracy. For it would produce a monolithic culture which would be the setting for an atmosphere of totalitarian sameness which would doom true democracy.

Horace Kallen, Harvard-trained son of an immigrant rabbi, published his seminal essay in *The Nation* in 1915, which he titled "Democracy vs. The Melting Pot," in which he presented a new image of America:

> As in an orchestra, every type of instrument has its specific timbre and tonality . . . so in society each ethnic group is the natural instrument, its spirit and culture are its theme and melody, and the harmony and dissonances and discords of them all make the symphony of civilization.

In the same year, in the Fourth of July Oration at Boston's Faneuil Hall, another son of a Jewish immigrant, Louis D. Brandeis, described what he called *True Americanism:*

> The new nationalism adopted by America proclaims that each race or people, like each individual, has the right and duty to develop, and only through such differentiated development will high civilization be attained.

They proclaimed, and gave ideological justification to *Cultural Pluralism:*

> Each American lives in two civilizations, that of America and that of his own ethnic group. In preserving and developing his own group culture, he contributes to American civilization by giving it the excitement and creativity that variety and diversity fashion. He helps preserve democracy in America by aiding the retention of the pluralistic character of American society.

No group in America reacted more vigorously or took more seriously the concept of *Cultural Pluralism* than did the Jewish. It not only provided ideologists for the concept, but it also refashioned its own communal and cultural life in response to it. Settlement houses became Jewish community centers. Church-like temples and insulated synagogues became congregations with rich cultural and social programs. Mordecai H. Kaplan of the Jewish Theological Seminary provided the ideology and example, and his student-disciples transformed the Jewish religious scene. Jewish community councils came into being. Hebrew and Yiddish literature, art, civilization received expression and emphasis.

And this was done 1) in response to Jewish needs, 2) as participation in American cultural life, and 3) as a contribution to the retention of essential democracy in America.

The post-World War II America saw a new imaging and a new emphasis. Ethnic identity waned and was replaced by a new religious imaging and identity. Will Herberg spoke of a triple melting pot, in which ethnic identities are fused, and religious identities are retained. Herberg gave this imaging its name and formulation: "America the Land of the Three Great Faiths: Protestant-Catholic-Jewish."

The World War brought an unprecedented unity to the American people. The nation needed unity; but democracy needed diversity. Once again the American Jew played a central role in providing both ideological formulation and practical application for the new imaging of America, *a land of ethnic assimilation and religious differentiation.* The Herbergs wrote the books, and the Jewish community undertook a restructuring of its institutions. Congregations became miniature communities, part of America, a component of its religious life; but also *apart,* retaining and maintaining a distinctiveness which served to preserve and strengthen the pluralistic character of the society.

The Jew seized upon this new image of America as the Land of the

Three Great Faiths, and his own identity as a member of a religious community. As an ethnic he was a member of a small minority group; as a member of one of the Three Faiths, he became one-third of America. And when the term Judeo-Christian tradition was used, as it was, he became one-half of America—and the "senior partner," to boot.

There is a new mood and spirit in America today. It may be characterized as the turning from sociology to psychology, from the concerns of the group to the existential needs of the individual. Formerly, a group, be it religious or ethnic, would justify its continued existence and demonstrate its worth through its contribution to America as a whole—its civilization and culture, its institutions, political and social; *today* its status and esteem would be merited by the degree to which it enhances the life of its individual members. There is abroad an as yet unarticulated but very real sentiment, that America's real strength and security are rooted in the well-being, psychological as well as physical, of its individual citizens. Rabbi Milton Steinberg was prophetic in this assertion made in 1941 in his *To Be or Not To Be a Jew*:

> If the only effects (of Jewish cultural life and creativity) were to bolster the shaken morale of the Jews to enrich their personalities with the treasures of a second heritage, the whole effort would have justified itself from the point of view of American interests. Quite obviously America will be benefited if its Jews, who constitute one segment of its citizenry, respect themselves, if they are psychologically adjusted rather than disaffected, if they are richer rather than poorer in spirit.

The pledge and promise of America was threefold: *life, liberty and the pursuit of happiness*. The first was secured by economic expansion and opportunity; the second was assured by democratic institutions; the third, the pursuit of happiness, is now the challenge facing America. There is growing feeling that in this enterprise, touching as it does on the person's perception of self and his place in the cosmos, dealing as it does with purpose in life and fulfillment, and the need for security and sense of worth that only a true community can provide, that these components of America's third pledge can best be provided by religio-ethnic groups. This then is a new perception of America, for which I still lack adequate tools of expression, but for which I would propose the image: America, A Mosaic.

The observer perceives a multifaceted and multicolored landscape.

Its components are different from one another in color and texture, yet blend together to form a unified whole. The whole is the sum of its parts, but as *gestalt* psychology has demonstrated, the whole is also different from the sum of its parts. It has its own character and individuality. In such an America each group states its own identity—religious, cultural and ethnic—and determines the components and content of that identity. It stands in relationship to the whole of which it is part and looks to the needs of those who give it substance and vitality. It serves America through its service to its individual members. It provides for the nation the solid strength and the energizing variety that characterize a mosaic.

The Jewish communal enterprise will need to provide for its members those components of religious vision, cultural expressions, and communal living which arm and strengthen one in his pursuit of happiness. To the extent, then, that the Jewish community, the Jewish enterprise in America, will help build Jews possessed of a sense of well-being, to that extent will it be respected and esteemed by America.

In doing so the Jewish community would make of Professor Hudson's challenge an opportunity for high and signal service:

> Perhaps one of the greatest contributions of Judaism to the United States will be to help other Americans understand how the United States can be a truly pluralistic society in which pluralism is maintained in a way that is enriching . . . From the long experience of Judaism, Americans of other faiths can learn how this may be done with both grace and integrity.

(1976)

14

AT THE THRESHOLD
OF THE THIRD CENTURY

ABRAM L. SACHAR

I

IN THE CLIMATE of the Bicentennial celebrations virtually every group
—ethnic, religious, social—has been concentrating on its contributions
to the enduring achievements of American life. The more thoughtful,
not content with self-congratulation, have gone deeper into the theme,—
evaluating the past two centuries, pondering whether the traditional roles
are still relevant, posing new challenges and revised techniques that may
be necessary to fulfill them.

In the case of the Jews, it must be recognized at the outset that, up
to the last century, they were only a minute part of the pioneering groups
who came to these shores, opened out the land, and made it a sought
after homeland for the millions who came later. To be sure, there were
isolated individuals who were part of the saga of discovery, colonization,
and the struggle for independence. The research of Jewish geographers
and astronomers, notably Abraham Zacuto, rendered invaluable service
to Columbus and, on one occasion, saved his crew. The financing of the
voyage was accomplished, not as the romantic story has it, by the
pawning of Queen Isabella's crown jewels, but by treasures derived from
confiscated Jewish property. It is said that the first Spaniard to land on
American soil was the Marrano interpreter, Luis de Torres. There are
other Jewish names that appear in the earliest periods, the most often
noted, Haym Salomon, long identified as one of the financiers of the
American Revolution, complimented by James Madison who acknowledged many personal kindnesses "to our little friend on Front Street,
near the coffee house."

Yet all such references and studies represent only peripheral relationships of Jews in early American history. They are fascinating as
scholarly monographs or as sentimental table conversation. But there is
no dispute that Jews, as a corporate entity, were too few in number to
play an important role in the first centuries after discovery and in the

257

American Revolution. Up to that period there were scarcely 2,500 geographically scattered Jews in the whole country. Lucy Dawidowicz notes that Jews identified with the early history of the Republic primarily through books, and not through family tradition. The foundations of American life were laid by the peoples of Western Europe, mainly the English, the Dutch, and the French Huguenots. It was their courage, and, it should be added, their ruthlessness, that established the settlements of New England and the Atlantic seaboard; they peopled the South and the Middle West; and they carried the doctrine of Manifest Destiny to the Pacific shores. It was they who set the pattern of the American way of life, the ethic of hard work and thrift, leading to the goal of material success. The classic historian, Charles Beard, based his interpretation of early American history on the property-oriented objectives of the founding fathers. Their national ideal, rarely questioned, was to be emulated by the ethnic groups who came pouring into the thinly populated country in the nineteenth and early twentieth centuries.

A somewhat more tangible Jewish identification with American life began after the collapse of the Central European revolutions of 1848, when leading German and Austrian liberals, many of them Jews, fled. Thousands of Jewish families sought refuge in America, fanning out from the East to many parts of the country. They began their new lives humbly, often as itinerant peddlers, but their acumen and determination kept cutting through inevitable immigrant obstacles. They excelled as merchants, and many of the department store and soft-goods manufacturing enterprises were the product of the commercial genius of Jewish families who tried their fortune in Savannah, Baltimore, New Orleans, Cleveland, Cincinnati, St. Louis, and other southern and midwestern communities. There was a *minyan* in San Francisco for intrepid souls who were attracted there in the gold rush of 1849. Another small strain of immigration was added after the revolution of 1863 was crushed in Poland, and the defeat of liberal hopes sent thousands of Jewish families to start anew in the land of promise.

II

The basic saga of Jewish life in America begins with the massive pogroms in 1881 that were launched in Russia in the benighted reigns of Alexander III and his hapless successor, Nicholas. Even without the pogroms there was incentive enough for families, then whole communities, bogged down by medieval restriction and repression, to seek means of escape.

Living conditions in Eastern Europe were deplorable for all peasant and proletarian groups, but for Jews they had become intolerable. The United States became the great objective and, from 1881 to approximately 1924, the flood never stopped, first in the thousands, then in the tens of thousands, finally in the hundreds of thousands. By 1924, in one of the great transplantations of history, nearly three million Jews had made their way to America, settling mainly in the huge ghettos of New York, Philadelphia, Baltimore, Chicago, and other large cities of the East and Middle West. The pioneering head of the family would come over first, leaving his wife and children behind until, by disciplined privation, he could save enough to bring them over, then other relatives too. Whole communities grew up that were virtually the transplantation from an Eastern European village, the *shtetl,* to the refuge of a big city American ghetto. The synagogues were often organized on a European community basis, and the *Landsmannschaften,* the base for social life, were the means by which those who came over first could offer help to those who followed.

These new immigrants, unlike those who came earlier, who were mainly middlemen, now included manual workers who joined the vast army of industrial laborers of other ethnic groups, toiling long hours, in primitive surroundings, as tailors, garment workers, carpenters, tinners, and in scores of other humble occupations. They endured the wretchedness of crowded factories that earned the name of sweatshops, or, if self-employed, lived in the back part of their pathetic little stores, driven on to any sacrifice either to resettle their families or to educate their children to make sure that they would be enabled to fit more easily into the American scene. This was the period of the nostalgic immigration literature that told the story, in a hundred different ways, of the primary hardships, invariably illumined by the hope that the rewards of a more secure economic future would vindicate the exhausting efforts of the past. During the transition, there was consolation that the struggle, however onerous, was at least not demeaning. "My cap is not worn out," one immigrant wrote, "from lifting it in the presence of gentlemen."

The obsessive drive for material success was accompanied by the quest for integration into the fabric of American life. The attainment of this objective was much more difficult, for the onus of alienism clung ineluctably to the Jewish immigrant and even to his more Americanized offspring. How could any later immigrants match the supercilious smugness described by Mark Twain as the "calm confidence of a Christian with four aces." It was not overt anti-Semitism that kept the Jew apart. It was a confusion of inherited folk memories, religious, economic, social, behavioral, that automatically identified the Jew as "alien corn," the stranger within the gate, not farmer, not proletarian, but, in the words of Eric Fromm, "market-oriented."

This is why virtually all the institutions built by the nineteenth century Jewish settlers were a substitute for those that were restricted to the host groups. When Jews could not become Masons, they organized B'nai B'rith; when they could not fit into the YMCA, they built the YMHA and the Jewish Community Center. Only rarely could they break through the admissions obstacles of the medical schools, and when they did, they were almost always excluded from the staff of the Christian-founded hospitals, nor could they gain internships there. Hence Jewish hospitals were established in nearly every large community, not only to serve patients, but to offer professional opportunities to Jewish interns and physicians. When Greek letter fraternities and sororities on college campuses were the monopolies of white Christian students, Jewish fraternities and sororities began their reponsive proliferation up to the time of World War II.

Communal organizations and institutions were thus reflexive, imitative, and a response to the restrictions of the outside world. In this period the older generation did not worry about such snubs and rebuffs, but they were a prod to the younger group to intensify their efforts for quicker immersion into the mores that were dictated by the host culture. Karen Horney's volume, *The Neurotic Personality of Our Time,* is a perceptive analysis of the compulsive drive for acceptance by the Jewish *arrivistes*. It should be added that when the achievement of integration seemed to require the shedding of ancestral religious loyalties, there were intense emotional conflicts that shattered Jewish family life. The recent immigrants tried ever more desperately to command the loyalty of their children to sanctions that were being cast aside. When the sons and daughters, swept up by the currents of their new world, defied their elders and went their own way, the interregnum was a purgatory of generational confrontation.

III

Then came a historic turning point, the silent but decisive revolution wrought by the passage of the Johnson Bill of 1924 that ended unrestricted immigration. Many attempts of earlier years to stop the flow into the United States had been thwarted by the vetoes of successive Presidents: Cleveland, Taft, and Wilson. But those who were concerned about flooding the country with impecunious and often "politically radical immigrants" finally won out in 1924, and their victory changed the course not only of American but of world history. For the immigration act dammed up millions in European lands who could no longer escape from poverty or repression by flight to America. There was now a firm plug on the liberation spout, and when frustration reached the boiling point, the kettle exploded in the revolts and counterrevolutions that shattered the European world in the generation that followed.

As for the Jews, when only a thin driblet of immigration was permitted after 1924, the already settled American Jewish community, no longer continuously reinforced by immigration from abroad, gradually nativized. They became nearly six million strong, the great majority far removed from kinship with the homelands of their forebears.

In the thirty years since the end of World War II the full import of the changes wrought by such nativization has become manifest. Jews, born and bred in this country, taking full advantage of ever more liberal interpretations of the law which consistently banned any form of restriction, have moved into every avenue of American life. The most respected educational institutions have opened to them. Jews are abundantly represented in medicine, science, research, the creative arts, teaching, government service, and in other professions long hedged in by restrictive practice. When I became president of Brandeis in 1948 I was the only Jewish college president in a privately endowed university, and I was named to that post only because the university itself was Jewish sponsored. Recently, many elite universities have been headed by Jewish presidents: Chicago, MIT, Dartmouth, Pennsylvania, and scores of others.

The sociologist Nathan Glazer reported a survey in California where, in the period between World War I and World War II, there was an increase of 25% in the entry into the professions by the children of non-Jewish immigrants, while similar entry by the children of Jewish immigrants increased by 400%. Economically, they have attained living standards that would have astonished their grandfathers, even their fathers. A few months ago published statistics indicated that Jews, in their income level, had moved into first place, forging ahead of the Episcopalians who had been the leaders for generations. Who would have dreamed a generation ago that there would be two Cabinet members, occupying key posts in the government, Henry Kissinger as Secretary of State, and Edward Levi as Attorney General. To be Jewish, in some areas, has become almost a status symbol! Earl Warren, when Chief Justice of the United States, spoke with pride of his Jewish son-in-law as did Tom Cabot, a New England Brahmin with roots that were deep in the American Revolutionary period.

All these changes did not mean that the Utopia of integration had arrived. Pockets of social prejudice remained. Many communities have developed country clubs with ingenious strategems to deny the entrance of Jewish families, and the restriction has compelled the multiplication of Jewish country clubs for the social and recreational outlet of even the wealthiest.

In truth, the visceral reaction to a clinging alienism is never really eliminated, long after Jews have been admitted to areas that had been rigorously reserved in the past. It did not disappear in European countries at the apogee of liberalism: why should it disappear here? I remember the poignant story told to me by Pierre Mendes-France, after he had served brilliantly as Prime Minister in one of the most crucial periods in postwar France. His family had lived in France for 400 years, ever since the Inquisition had driven them from Spain in the fifteenth century. He had ended the hemorrhage of the Vietnam war; he had withdrawn the French who were dying for a vain cause in Morocco and Tunis. He would have settled Algiers with honor as well, but General de Gaulle intervened and then, later, France had to yield to terms that conceded much more than Mendes-France had proposed. After this demonstration of statesmanship one of the Mendes-France's oldest friends said to him, "Pierre, it is fortunate that you were Prime Minister when such valuable French-held territory had to be amputated. A *real* Frenchman could never have done it." Mendes-France was not Catholic, nor peasant, nor Gallic. How could he be a *real* Frenchman?

This instinctive reaction can be retold endlessly in this country too, and it bothered those who craved acceptance. Fortunately, mature Jewish families have dismissed as inconsequential such vestigial "spirits from the vasty deep." What counted was that they had broken through the barriers of prejudice and discrimination that restricted opportunity. They could live full, creative lives, taking advantage of every opportunity that the democratic system of the country offered. At the threshold of the third century they could be proud of what they had achieved for themselves, and of what they were contributing to America.

IV

But the achievement exacted a price, a heavy price. The demolition of restrictive barriers brought with it freedom to opt for or against identification with the Jewish community and its interest. Responding to the blandishments of assimilation, group cohesiveness began to weaken. Synagogue attendance, especially among the young, declined radically. Intermarriage rates rose dramatically, and gone were the days when a Jewish family sat *shiva* if a son or daughter intermarried. There were none of the social punishments such as followed in the Weimar period when newspapers would publish the announcement of what was regarded as desertion: *Austritte aus dem Judentum*. Jewish leaders spoke in sorrow of the disastrous effects of affluence on the continuity of the Jewish heritage. The question was posed with growing concern: "While Jewish life can survive adversity, can it also resist the gravitational pull of prosperity and freedom?"

The anxiety was compounded when some of the most respected Israeli leaders went quite far in postulating that there could be no genuine Jewish life, except in Israel. When David Ben-Gurion came for a Convocation at Brandeis, he made an outright appeal for the young people to migrate and to join in the adventure that a resurgent Israel represented. His view of Jewish history was simple. "Nearly two thousand years ago," he said, "the free life of Israel was 'interrupted' by the Romans; it was resumed in Israel after the Wars of Liberation." He took a quantum leap across the flux of generations, treating all the intervening period from Roman days to the present as sterile chronology. He chided Jews who thought they were discharging their folk responsibility by monetary contributions to Israel. I cannot forget his contemptuous phrase, "These are alimony Jews!" Nahum Goldmann told the leaders of the World Zionist Organization that "assimilation has become the basic danger since we left the ghettos and the *mellahs*." He offered a macabre interpretation of Diaspora life, almost as if he believed that Jewish survival required regular injections of anti-Semitic excesses. Then he added a warning of doom for Jewish life outside of Israel. To him, there was no ultimate safety anywhere else. Jews lived for six hundred years in Spain, but they ended in the tragedy of the Inquisition and expulsion. The same fate came to the historic Jewish communities of medieval France and England and Germany. And now there were ominous signs in South Africa and Rhodesia, in the Argentine and Mexico and Chile. He added that if there should be a deep economic crisis, even in the friendliest nations, the tragic experience might well be duplicated. It could not be otherwise, he argued. How was it possible to overcome nineteen centuries of church teaching, of what Jules Isaac called "education by contempt."

Of course when these men painted a foreboding fate for Jewish life even in America, they were speaking not from historic conviction, but from "necessity's sharp pinch." They were confronted with the desperate need in Israel for emigration from the West, emigration with the know-how and skills that Israel needed to cope with a precarious future. But undoubtedly they were voicing their conviction when they forecast that easy assimilation in the countries of the West was loosening the ties of Jewish life. True Jewishness, they were saying, could not survive in a creative affirmative way in America since the eroding forces of the host culture were too powerful to resist.

With all respect to those eminent leaders of contemporary Jewish life, I submit that they were permitting their anxieties to becloud their judgment. Of course, it cannot be gainsaid that there are losses, prodigious losses, through assimilation and intermarriage, when there is complete freedom to make choices in identity. Often the losses represent remarkably creative spirits. I am saddened by the attrition that Jewish life suffers in the faculty world with so many gifted men and women in flight. But there is always the strong, tenacious nucleus, the core whom the prophets called "the saving remnant" who remain untempted and who provide a sustaining leadership. In truth, assimilation can never eradicate a people as tenacious as the Jews. However serious the losses, those who remain safeguard their legacy, nourish and strengthen it, supplement and transmit it to those who are proud to receive it.

Indeed, this saving remnant may actually have been as tough and steadfast through the centuries because the weaker elements have been eliminated by the seductions that they could not or would not resist. Several degrading examples come to mind. Early in the century, one of our most brilliant scientists, Dr. Karl Landsteiner, earned great prestige in the scientific world for his imaginative experiments in the problems of blood transfusion. The editors of the Jewish *Who's Who* were proud to include him in their biographical lists. He sued for libel (vainly) on the ground that he had kept his Jewish ancestry from his children so that they would not have to wrestle with the adversity of their Jewish origins. There was the self-contempt of Karl Marx who hated his Jewish origins and outdid many notorious Jew-haters in his own anti-Semitism. Albert Einstein's reaction to such self-debasement was that perhaps the Jewish group has had the strength and stamina to persist because the weaklings and trimmers have been screened out by the tests of time.

Following Einstein's logic, I would comment only that we need not be alarmed by natural or unnatural assimilation. There are six million Jews in America. Suppose, because of assimilation, we are left with only three million genuinely committed souls. Isn't it healthier to have the residue who are happy with their heritage than twice as many, large numbers of whom writhe in the agonies of unwanted descent? For that matter, where is the magic in numbers? Creative achievement that is enduring does not depend on size. Few realize what a tiny group Jews have been to become such a leaven in civilization. From us have sprung, in modern history, Spinoza and Bergson, Brandeis, Freud and Einstein, and thousands of other titans. Our Nobel Prize winners dominate the awards in virtually every field. Yet in 1648, Jews were 2/10 of 1% of the world's population, in 1848, 6/10, in 1936, 8/10. What amazing creativity from a people always less than 1% of total humankind! The irony of all this, I should add, is that the assimilator does not usually escape the fate he hopes to shake off. There is more realism than jest in the definition of an assimilationist as a Jew who associates only with Jews who don't associate with Jews.

V

Yet, it must be realized, continuity in Jewish life, even by the most loyal, cannot be assured simply by will, or by fiat. With so many options that are open to encourage flight, commitment must be won with effort. Filial respect as a binding force is not enough, nor is philanthropic compassion. Identification with faith and fate is not assured by repeating to ourselves that we are a very old people, relying on the pride of ancestry as a powerful catalyst. The gypsies are an old people too, probably older than the Jews. But they are without a historic tradition: they have lost their memory. When a people suffers from national amnesia it may survive, but simply as an atavism, just existing, without any substantive contribution. Continuity that is worth all the sacrificial devotion of a long and illustrious history must come through pride, and there is no pride without understanding, without respect for the treasures that have been the creation of past generations.

VI

I have spoken of our perilous losses through the attrition of assimilation. But is it not true that our losses are even greater by the disintegration of ignorance, the *am ha᾽aratzes* that plagues every community? Bernard

Shaw once observed that every man is an omnibus in which all of his ancestors travel. There is nothing more self-defeating and pathetic than to throw these ancestors off the bus because we know nothing about them.

The indissoluble bond between national resurrection and pride of heritage was fully realized in their survivalist ideologies by the imaginative leaders who relied upon understanding to rescue their people from debasement and indignity. Italians had once been a highminded and creative people. But by the nineteenth century they had lost nearly all relationship with their past. They were provincial Romans and Florentines, Neapolitans, Venetians, and Milanese; they remembered little to excite them as Italians. Their regeneration was not accomplished by the genius of Cavour and his needle-witted diplomacy, nor even by the buccaneering courage of Garibaldi and his Redshirts. It was accomplished by the gentle teacher, Mazzini, who organized *La Giovene Italia*, Young Italy, who taught the legions of his proteges the glories of their past. He created a contagious national spirit when he brought back to them the genius of Dante and Raphael, Michelangelo, Da Vinci and Donatello, and the glories of the Italian Renaissance.

Ireland, up to the end of the nineteenth century, was a shambles, nursing its shame and humiliation as a subject people, ridden with self-contempt. Frances Hackett wrote: "And its radiance dies, leaving Ireland cowering in the corner, horror in her eyes, the sickly moonlight on the wreckage of her feast." Her sons and daughters migrated in millions to become leaders in all the countries to which they fled. But in their own homeland they remained "shanty," for they had lost virtually all links with their past except their hatred of the English. Their pride was not revived by Charles Parnell, though his statesmanship was unsurpassed. It was revived by O'Brien and the pioneers of Young Ireland, by the founders of the Gaelic League, the fathers of Sinn Fein, by Yeats and Hyde and Synge and the lovely Lady Gregory, the rare spirits who went back into the mists of history to the glories of St. Patrick when all Europe was beholden to Ireland as the lonely beacon for civilized life.

Germany was long merely a geographical expression, more than 350 fragmented provinces, dominated by Prussia, sunk in the apathy that followed the Thirty Years' War. It was not transformed by Bismarck, the Iron Chancellor, with all his bellicose emphasis on the *Macht Mensch*, the Man of Power, *Blut mit Eisen*, blood and iron. It was transformed by Heinrich Heine who disinterred the soul of Allemania, the real Allemania. He created the *Burschenshaften*, the young peoples' groups who were reintroduced to an almost forgotten Germany, the

Germany of Lessing and Schiller, and the Grimm brothers and Beethoven and Brahms, the Germany that led the world in the arts of civilized life. He countered the *Macht Mensch* with the *Kunst Mensch,* the man of perception and sagacity.

In our own era I think of the passion with which Nikos Kazantzakis went back to the roots of Hellenic genius for his novels and epic poems of 19th century Greek life and brought inspiration and hope to a sunken and discouraged people. And of Germany's greatest novelist, Thomas Mann, the humanist who sought to save the German soul from Nazi decadence, who minted literary currency from the Faust legend and from our Bible, in his immortal Joseph stories.

We can draw lessons from such men of rare insight who knew that the integrating force for peoples comes from the mother lode of understanding. It is not a response to pain or sorrow, to danger or abuse. It emerges from authentic pride, deeply based, not dull or lackluster, not adhered to out of a sense of duty. It is stimulating, inspiring, above all, self-regenerative.

Fortunately there are signs all about us that indicate that this lesson is fully understood by prescient leaders among our people. Counterbalancing the anxieties over a trend to assimilation and flight is the realization that schools for Jewish studies are growing in number and influence; synagogues and temples and Jewish Centers are steadily expanding their cultural activities; more ample provision is being made in the budgets of welfare funds and federations for the promotion of such activities; trips to Israel are becoming integral parts of institutional planning; books of Jewish interest, once regarded as taboo by publishing houses as certain failures in the market place, are confidently promoted and find their way to best-seller lists; chairs of Judaic Studies are multiplying in leading universities at such a pace that there is now a shortage of qualified faculty people to fill the posts. When I address forum groups (and this is validated by my colleagues on the platform), the invariable questions from young people are no longer "Why should I be a Jew?" More often they ask, "How can I better express my Jewishness?" The sociologist, Hansen, observing the phenomenon of the turnabout from flight, noted, "The third generation wants to remember what the second generation was eager to forget." This is why I am not on the mourner's bench as I watch the many centrifugal forces in American Jewish life. I do not underestimate the toll as the fibre of loyalty weakens in all too many families. But it is being steadily balanced by a resolute spirit that eschews the defensiveness and the obsequious *mah yofis* of the past.

VII

It should be noted that there were special influences at work in this period that contributed to the greater emphasis on an affirmative Jewish identity, and counteracted the forces of assimilation. One was traumatic, the product of horror and sorrow: the Holocaust and its incredible human toll. The indifference, often bordering on callousness, with which the tragedy was received by the spokesmen for Christianity and by statesmen of the Western democratic bloc, left deep scars on the Jewish psyche. The Vatican, the most influential international Protestant bodies, labour leaders of Britain, such American patriotic bodies as the Daughters of the American Revolution and the American Legion, Franklin Roosevelt himself, long the trusted idol of the Jewish communities, all substituted sonorous platitudes for humanitarian action that might have salvaged some minimum remnant of the doomed victims. After the Holocaust, hundreds of thousands of emaciated survivors remained in displaced persons camps. When some of the most desperate escaped and boarded ships that sought refuge points for them, even temporarily, they were shunted from port to port, and thousands died when the unbearably overcrowded leaking tubs in which they were packed sank. The terror of those days made little impact on the Christian conscience to whom the Jews were an increasing nuisance. Christianity seemed to mean, as Emil Fackenheim suggested, that it is the Jew who must always turn the other cheek. The disenchantment multiplied through the years, climaxed when the ominous votes were recorded in the United Nations bringing the conclusion that, though Hitler is dead, the bitch that bore him is in heat again. It was understandable then that when eloquently phrased sympathy turned out to be a clucking piety, it bred the conviction that Jews must look to themselves, and to themselves alone, when there was a crisis to be faced. Jews concluded that while liberal Christian friendship was to be welcomed, there must be no reliance upon it, especially if it called for even moderate cost or sacrifice. The disenchantment with Christian concern thrust many families that had been in flight back to the sanctuary of renewed Jewish identification.

But this was a negative impetus. The positive force, beyond all parallel, was, of course, the emergence of Israel as a sovereign state, the fulfillment of the dreams and hopes of twenty centuries. The very fact that it was born in travail, that its independence had to be won with courage and will, at fearful cost, sent a surge of pride through Jewish life and even the most assimilated found reason for standing taller. There is a revealing paragraph in the last volume of memoirs of Harold Macmillan, the former prime minister of Great Britain, who had been asked what he envisaged for the future of the declining British Commonwealth. He discounted ancient Greece as a model for it had been built on slavery; he similarly discounted modern Sweden that opted for neutrality in World War II, building its prosperity by conducting profitable trade relations with both sides. Then Macmillan added, "The future I hope for Britain is more like that of Israel. In the time of Elizabeth we were only two million people; in the time of Marlborough, only five or six million; in the time of Napoleon, only ten million. The other day, while the world debated, Israel's three million imposed their will on their enemies. They had what any great people need; resolution, courage, determination, pride. These are what really count in men and nations." This inspirational tribute came from a prime minister of Great Britain who had served longer than any since the days of Gladstone. If the Israeli experience had this impact on a leader so proud of the heritage of his own people, one can better understand the impact on Jews as their image was transformed from the helpless victims of the Holocaust to the valiant heroes of the wars of liberation. When the beleaguered little land was in mortal danger in 1947, in 1956, in 1967, and in 1973, the response in immediate help came not only from deeply committed Jews, but from those who had assumed that they had long before shaken off vestigial ties with a forgotten and to-be-forgotten tradition.

Unfortunately, along with the tightening of loyalty that the emergence of Israel brought, there are serious problems that had not been foreseen. The Arab states had turned to the Soviet Union not only for economic underwriting that would bring them into the modern world, but for military aid with which to carry out their threats against continued Israeli existence. The United States, locked in the Cold War with the Soviets, offered matching aid to Israel, and for two generations there was a proxy contention, the conflicts carried by the Arabs and Israelis, the Soviet Union and the United States promoting their rivalry from the sidelines. The dangerous diplomatic embroilment was contained until the Arabs were suddenly enriched by billions in oil reserves, with the power to sell the indispensable energy resources or to shut them off, and they used this new-found weapon with commanding blackmail effect.

Out of this unforeseen development has risen a major threat to American Jewish life. More and more Americans, as recession deepened their own concerns, have begun to ask whether it is wise to continue with massive Israeli assistance. Would it not better serve the American interest if aid to Israel were modified or even suspended? As the argument gathers momentum, the old canard of dual loyalty has emerged. The question occasionally, but ominously, is raised, "If the crunch comes and hard decisions have to be reached, would American Jews opt for what is best for Israel, or what is best for America?" As yet such questions have appeared sporadically and have been attributed to more sophisticated Arab propaganda. But when they are asked by several liberal Senators, it is time for serious alarm.

Oil billions have apparently made possible Arab access to the best public relations resourcefulness of Madison Avenue and the accusation of dual loyalty is being brilliantly and effectively exploited. The Jewish response of course, must not rest on sentimentality, on the fact that little Israel is a democracy, indeed the only democratic oasis in a vast feudal desert, or that every American president since Wilson has validated an enduring friendship for Israel, or that after the horror of the Holocaust, the refuge that the survivors have created in Israel deserves the support of a contrite world. These reminders are all true, but great nations are not, and should not be, swayed by sentiment. Lord Palmerston spoke with sober realism last century when he said that nations cannot have permanent friendships, nor permanent enmities. They must be guided by permanent interests.

The only convincing argument that is relevant is that aid to Israel is a basic part of America's global defense pattern. Ever since World War II it has spent hundreds of billions of dollars around the world in grants to scores of nations to prevent them from falling under Soviet dominance. Through the Marshall Plan, launched in 1947, billions were allocated to 16 European countries to shore up their tottering economies so that they would not collapse and succumb to Communism. And, in every year since, billions more have been spent for the same purpose, sometimes unwisely as in Vietnam or, for a while, in Angola, but always for the purpose of resisting Communist absorption. The United States has a compelling stake in preventing the Mediterranean from becoming a Soviet lake. It has few dependable allies there. Greece is no longer reliable, nor is Turkey or Cyprus or Portugal—all NATO countries. Israel represents an inexpensive and prudent investment in a world of such shifting loyalties. Their people will never yield to the Arabs or their Russian manipulators. They will never threaten to change sides, or use blackmail by pitting the antagonists against each other, nor become disheartened by the ingratitude of nations such as the Africans whose economies they helped to transform.

For they did not come to Israel as the English came to India to live as colonials, to make their fortunes, and to retire to their homeland.

They did not come as the French came to Indochina or to the protectorates in Northern Africa to exploit their possessions and then to spend their sunset years in aristocratic leisure in their native France. They did not come as the Belgians to the Congo to wrest riches from the hides of the natives and then to return for opulent years in their motherland. The Israelis came to settle, to renew their ties with their ancient past; they came in an *Aliyah,* and they intend to remain no matter what Fate holds in store. They ask for no other people to fight for them. If there are sacrifices, they will be Israeli sacrifices. If there are casualties, they will be Israeli casualties. They ask only for the tools to protect themselves, and when they ask this of the United States, their request, by providential coincidence, is in the best interests of our country which gains a reliable ally at very little cost, to strengthen its defense in a highly vulnerable part of the world.

These then were developments that contributed to the renaissance of Jewish self-identity, the disenchantment with liberal, Christian protestations which proved to be empty verbiage when the time came to validate them, and the reawakened pride that Israeli courage and self respect brought to Jews everywhere. Even the left-wing Jewish radicals who decried nationalism and ethnic loyalty were now chastened.

VIII

And now, as we enter the third century, the time is indeed overdue for a re-evaluation of the meaning of Americanism. For two centuries it has aimed at absorption, the merging of all groups into a synthetic homogeneity. The "melting pot", the expression coined by Israel Zangwill early in the century, has been its most tangible symbol. It has now outlived its usefulness. Not only Jewish leadership but the interpreters of the cultures of other ethnic groups, equally proud of their antecedents and eager to integrate them into a new America, have begun to think in other terms. They too have returned to the concept offered several decades ago by the philosopher Horace Kallen. The flight from one's origins, Kallen reasoned, weakened America and thinned out its vitality. He paid tribute to the genius of the Puritan heritage, but he argued that the pioneering New England fathers themselves never expected that their outlook on life would swallow all others. He appealed to each group to hold fast to ancestral treasures so that they could become part of a many-hued mosaic that would represent the best and noblest traditions that the varieties of immigration had to offer.

Kallen used the phrase "cultural pluralism" to summarize his view of America. A contemporary, Waldo Frank, to whom America also no longer was a "melting pot," used the symbol of a symphony. Each ethnic group, he argued, had developed a special talent in the orchestration of its differences. It was necessary that each group play in harmony, else the result would be a dreadful cacophony. But when the harmony of the overall theme was protected, the very diversification of instrumentation added beauty and depth to the symphonic effect.

As we cross the threshold of the third century, it would be well for us to think more positively of this concept, not just for ourselves but for all groups. America is now strong enough and well enough integrated no longer to be fearful that freedom for each group to bring its singularities into the whole would create chaotic fragmentation. The overall concept of America, its respect for law, its promise of opportunity for the ful-fillment of capacity, its dedication to an orderly heterogeneity, can serve as the framework within which the uniqueness of each contributing group may develop.

In describing such a spiritual osmosis, I do not mean to imply that we shall escape threatening problems and frustrating grief. Life in tumultuous times can never be serene. We must accept what comes in the spirit of Hemingway's phrase, later used with effect by President Kennedy. "Learn to live with grace under pressure." If such tension is to be the continued fate of our generation, it will at least be creative tension. And as we develop our unique heritage within the orchestration of all other enriching diversities, the opportunity is opened to fulfill a destiny as rich and as significant as those which emerged from the most glorious epochs of our history.

                                                              (1977)